PREFACE

This exposition of utilitarian ethics, like comparable monographs in this series, is set out in a historical way. I have taken the paradigm of utilitarianism to be the ethical doctrines of Bentham and John Stuart Mill and, more specifically, I have treated as a utilitarian anyone who agrees with them that the rightness of actions is determined by the value of their consequences and that what determines the value of these consequences is the pleasure or pain that they include.

I argue, by reference to this standard, that Hume is more of a utilitarian than he is nowadays often made out to be. The same standard implies that 'ideal utilitarians' like Moore and Rashdall, who, although consequentialists, do not take pleasure or happiness as the criterion of value, are not really utilitarians at all.

The examination, criticism and, where appropriate, defence from criticism of the arguments and conclusions of Bentham and Mill has left space for no more than the barest survey of those aspects of utilitarian reasoning which most preoccupy ethical theorists at the present time, namely the structure and adequacy of consequentialist arguments in moral thinking. This is intentional and reflects my belief that the hedonistic aspect of traditional utilitarianism, its most widely repudiated ingredient, is equally deserving of consideration.

New Studies in Ethics

Volume Two
MODERN THEORIES

ST. MARTIN'S PRESS NEW YORK

All rights reserved. For information, write:
St. Martin's Press, Inc., 175 Fifth Avenue, New York, N.Y. 10010
Printed in Great Britain
Library of Congress Catalog Card Number: 74-76687
First published in the United States of America in
1970, 1967, 1969, 1973, 1967 and 1967 respectively

AFFILIATED PUBLISHERS: Macmillan Limited, London –
also at Bombay, Calcutta, Madras and Melbourne

CONTENTS

Editor's Foreword to Volume II   vii

1 UTILITARIAN ETHICS   *Anthony Quinton*   1

Preface   2
Introduction   3

   I. The Precursors of Utilitarianism   13
   II. Jeremy Bentham   29
   III. John Stuart Mill   40
   IV. Four Critics   84
   V. Epilogue: Contemporary Utilitarianism   108

Notes   113
Bibliography   116

2 AXIOLOGICAL ETHICS   *J. N. Findlay*   119

   I. Introduction   121
   II. Brentano and Meinong   136
   III. Moore, Rashdall and Ross   157
   IV. Scheler and Hartmann   177
   V. Final Suggestions   198

Bibliography   212

3 EVOLUTIONARY ETHICS   *Antony Flew*   217

   I. Introduction   217
   II. Darwin's Theory   223
   III. A Law of Progress?   229
   IV. From *Is* to *Ought*   247
   V. Seeing in an Evolutionary Perspective   268

Notes   277
Select Bibliography   281
General Bibliography   282

4 MARXISM AND ETHICS *Eugene Kamenka* 287

Acknowledgements 288
   I. Introduction 289
  II. The Ethical Impulse in the Work of Karl Marx 292
 III. Ethics and Alienation 303
 IV. Ethics and the Materialist Interpretation of
     History 319
   V. Human Welfare and Human Needs 332
  VI. Ethics in Soviet Philosophy 340
 VII. Conclusion 353

Notes 356
Bibliography 359

5 EXISTENTIALIST ETHICS *Mary Warnock* 361

   I. Introduction 363
  II. Kierkegaard 366
 III. Heidegger 374
 IV. J.-P. Sartre 380
  V. Conclusion 415

Notes 419
Bibliography 420

6 CONTEMPORARY MORAL PHILOSOPHY
  G. J. Warnock 421

   I. Introduction 423
  II. Intuitionism 426
 III. Emotivism 440
 IV. Prescriptivism 452
  V. The Content of Morals 470
 VI. Naturalism 484
 VII. Prospect 495

Notes 500
Bibliography 502
Notes on Contributors 504

The studies presented here were all published originally as separate booklets in a series entitled 'New Studies in Ethics'. The aim of that series was to provide a comprehensive survey of the main types of theory which have arisen in the history of moral philosophy. Each monograph was written by a professional philosopher, who had been invited to contribute a clear exposition and critical assessment of a type of ethical theory on which he was an expert. The series was well-received and the suggestion frequently made that the monographs should be bound up together and published in a composite work. This suggestion has now been implemented, in the form of the present two-volume edition. The text of each study remains as in the original publication, but errata have been corrected and, where appropriate, new material has been added to the bibliographies.

Volume One contains studies of six classical types of theory, viz. Greek Ethics, Aquinas and Natural Law, Ethical Naturalism, Ethical Intuitionism, the Moral Philosophy of Kant, and Hegelian Ethics.

In this, the second volume, some more modern theories are examined.

Utilitarianism is probably the most widely held point of view concerning morality at the present time. On this view, men ought to maximise happiness for themselves and others. Any version of this theory which is practically useful rests on certain presuppositions as to what constitutes human happiness and the ways in which men are capable of achieving it. Should men think first of themselves, or of others? Do they need general rules of conduct, which may in particular applications produce misery for some, or should each individual act be assessed in terms of the pleasure it gives to those immediately concerned? And so on. Anthony Quinton's study explains the thought of the classical Utilitarians, Bentham, Mill, Sidgwick and others, with due recognition of more recent discussions of the General Happiness Principle.

Axiological Ethics is a type of ethical theory which, amongst English-speaking students at any rate, does not have the vogue enjoyed by the other types of theory discussed in this volume. J. N. Findlay's conviction that this is a sorry state of affairs is reflected throughout his contribution. He maintains that there is 'an organised framework of values and disvalues within which our practical decisions must be made' and that the authors whom he discusses have done most to make this clear. Values and dis-values must not be conceived as creations of single individuals or societies. There is a 'value-firmament', just as there is a physical world, and only by discovering what the structure of this value-firmament is can we act with ethical wisdom, just as we can only walk with assurance in the physical world when we see how the land lies.

The theory of Evolution not only revolutionised natural science: it also had a profound effect on ethical thought. Processes of natural selection have undoubtedly resulted in the survival of species best suited to cope with their environments, but have they also led to the emergence of morally better kinds of behaviour? Must we say that the direction of evolution is necessarily good according to any realistic definition of 'good'? Antony Flew investigates these and related questions.

Marx's influence on economic and political thinking in our day has been epoch-making; but has he moral insights worthy of anything approaching the respect which his social philosophy has deservedly earned? Eugene Kamenka analyses Marx's well-known views about individual alienation and social progress with this question in mind.

Philosophical Existentialism has had – and still does have – a powerful influence in two spheres where human conduct is much discussed, namely literature and theology. Some of its foremost exponents have been novelists and playwrights such as Sartre and Camus, or religious thinkers such as Buber and Berdyaev. The essence of morality, Existentionalists hold, is that men should live freely as individuals and not inauthentically as types or conformists. But what is it to be free? And how is man's individuality related to his essential sociality? Mary Warnock's study introduces the reader to those Existentialists whose answers to such questions have been most influential.

Since G. E. Moore published his *Principia Ethica* in 1903 analytical moral philosophers have been mainly concerned with the language in which moral judgments are expressed. How is the meaning of such language like, and how unlike, the meaning of the language in which, say, scientific hypotheses, military orders, cries of emotion, or religious beliefs are expressed? G. J. Warnock's study of the main points of view which have emerged in this discussion brings the story of moral philosophy right up to date. The debate between Prescriptivists and Descriptivists, whose opinions he explains and criticises, continues.

University of Exeter   W. D. HUDSON

1

UTILITARIAN ETHICS

ANTHONY QUINTON

The monographs reproduced in this collection have been published separately in booklet form as part of the paperback series 'New Studies in Ethics'

INTRODUCTION

(i) DEFINITION OF UTILITARIANISM

Utilitarianism can be understood as a movement for legal, political and social reform that flourished in the first half of the nineteenth century, or, again, as the ideology of that movement. But it is also, and more persistently, a general ethical theory and it is almost exclusively in this sense that I shall be concerned with it. As a theory of ethics it provides a criterion for distinguishing between right and wrong action and, by implication, an account of the nature of the moral judgements that characterise action as right or wrong.

In its standard form it can be expressed as the combination of two principles: (1) *the consequentialist principle* that the rightness, or wrongness, of an action is determined by the goodness, or badness, of the results that flow from it and (2) *the hedonist principle* that the only thing that is good in itself is pleasure and the only thing bad in itself is pain. Utilitarians have generally taken it for granted, and have made trouble for themselves by doing so, that happiness is a sum of pleasures. Given this assumption, the doctrine can be expressed in the form of a single principle, the greatest happiness principle: *the rightness of an action is determined by its contribution to the happiness of everyone affected by it.*

This formula is, I think, a fair account of what Bentham and John Stuart Mill held to be their fundamental doctrine. Bentham says, 'By the principle of utility is meant that principle which approves or disapproves of every action whatsoever, according to the tendency which it appears to have to augment or diminish the happiness of the party whose interest is in question.'[1] The 'party in question' need not, and commonly will not, be a single person. Bentham goes on, 'An action then may be said to be conformable to the principle of utility . . . when the tendency it has to augment the happiness of the community is greater than any it has to diminish it'.[2] 'The interest of the community then is what? – the sum of the interests of the several members who compose it.'[3] There is a difference that is worth noticing between the first quotation, which speaks of what appears to contribute to the general happiness, and the second, which speaks of what actually augments or diminishes it. We shall have to inquire later which consequences of an action are relevant to its moral quality; its actual consequences, its intended consequences or the consequences it would be rational to expect from it.

John Stuart Mill says, 'The creed which accepts as the foundation of morals, Utility, or the Greatest Happiness Principle, holds that actions are right in proportion as they tend to promote happiness, wrong as they tend to produce the reverse of happiness. By happiness is intended pleasure, and the absence of pain; by unhappiness, pain, and the privation of pleasure.'[4]

There is an important moral distinction that is not explicitly provided for by the greatest happiness principle as I have formulated it, following Bentham and Mill. This is the distinction between a morally obligatory action and a morally permissible one. An obligatory action is *the* right thing to do in the circumstances, the one thing one ought to do, anything other than which it would be wrong to do. A permissible action on the other hand, is one it is quite all right to do but which is not required. An obligatory action is something it would be *wrong not* to do; a permissible action is one it would be *not wrong* to do.

Bentham is aware of this distinction but seems to think that it is of no importance. He says, 'Of an action that is conformable to the principle of utility one may always say either that it is one that ought to be done, or at least that it is not one that ought not to be done. One may say also, that it is right it should be done; at least that it is not wrong it should be done; that it is a right action; at least that it is not a wrong action.'[5]

What Bentham seems to be suggesting is that any action that detracts from the general happiness is wrong, it ought not to be done; while any action that adds to it is all right or permissible, but is not something that ought to be done, is not something obligatory. On this interpretation is any account possible of what positively ought to be done? The crucial point is that action is always the outcome of a selection between possible alternatives, at least if it is the kind of action to which moral judgement is appropriate. Now any possible action which would detract from the general happiness is wrong and therefore ought not to be done; it is obligatory to abstain from it, to do something else. If there are several other possibilities, all of them happiness-augmenting, it is obligatory to do one of them, but not any particular one of them rather than any other. Only if there is just one alternative possibility that augments happiness will it be obligatory.

But this produces certain problems. First, it is possible that all the available alternatives would detract from the general happiness to some extent. It would seem congruous with the spirit of the general happiness principle to choose that action which detracts least from it. But this yields a paradox: as detracting from the general happiness it ought not to be done, as detracting less than any other possibility it ought to be done. A way out of this difficulty, expounded, for example, with great laboriousness in G. E. Moore's *Ethics*, is to say that one ought in any situation to choose that alternative which contributes most or, if that is the way things are, detracts least from the general happiness. But this has the disconcerting consequence that in every situation there is one thing which it is obligatory to do and all other alternatives are wrong. Furthermore it is probably very rare for people's actions to be the *best possible* thing to do in the circumstances. So people nearly always act wrongly. I shall return to this later.

A second difficulty arises from inaction. Doing nothing at all is generally one of the possibilities open to an agent. But one who does nothing does not positively detract from the general happiness. Does it follow that inaction is never wrong? Often it is an alternative to a possible action which would greatly increase the general happiness or, an even more important case, which would greatly diminish general suffering. This again suggests that actions are not right or wrong absolutely, that is considered only with respect to their own consequences alone, but that their moral quality is a comparative matter, determined by the difference between their consequences, good or bad, and the consequences of the available alternatives. Most contemporary utilitarians, in the light of these difficulties, follow Moore in formulating the first principle of the doctrine in a comparative, rather than an absolute way.

There is a terminological point that needs to be made. There are many ethical theorists who accept the consequentialist theory of obligation advanced by standard utilitarianism but reject its hedonist theory of value. Either, like Moore, they think that the principal possessors of intrinsic value are quite distinct from pleasure (in Moore's case pre-eminent intrinsic value is ascribed to affectionate personal relations and the contemplation of beauty) or, like Rashdall, they take pleasure to be one intrinsically valuable thing amongst others, for example, virtue, knowledge, beauty. This type of view is often called *ideal* utilitarianism, in contrast to the *hedonistic* utilitarianism of Bentham and, with qualifications, of John Stuart Mill. When I refer to utilitarianism without explicit qualification it will always be to its standard hedonistic form.

Before leaving this matter of definition it may be useful to summarise three respects in which the classic formulations of utilitarianism are in need of clarification. First, there is the problem of deciding which consequences are relevant: *actual*, *intended* or *rationally expectable*. Secondly, there is the problem of deciding whether the consequences of an action should be assessed *absolutely* or *by comparison* with the consequence of available alternatives. Thirdly, there is the problem of deciding whether obligation should be defined *positively*, in terms of the maximisation of happiness, or *negatively*, in terms of the minimisation of suffering. These issues will be discussed further as will the problems arising about the precise interpretation of the hedonist principle, in particular that of the supposed identity of happiness (or welfare) with a sum of pleasures.

The classic utilitarians, like most ethical theorists before the twentieth century, took it for granted that moral judgements are genuine statements, true or false. Furthermore they took them to be statements of ordinary natural fact. The primary judgements of value they saw as introspective reports of experienced pleasure or pain. From these could be derived the judgements about the happiness or suffering of people in general on which judgements of obligation should be based, these judgements of obligation being themselves causal propositions of a rather complicated kind.

A leading theme of moral philosophy in this century has been that any such naturalistic account of moral convictions and affirmations, which treats them as statements of empirical fact, must be mistaken. In its developed form this doctrine of anti-naturalism argues from the fact that moral judgements are practical in a certain way, that they constitute sufficient reasons for action without additional assumptions, for example about the agent's wants or tastes or purposes, that they cannot be statements but must be imperatives or proposals or the announcements of decisions. However, there are convinced anti-naturalists who would still describe themselves as utilitarians but, as it might be put, of a *normative* kind. For them the utilitarian principle is not a fundamental moral truth, or truth about morality, but rather a basic moral choice or commitment which they are prepared to make and which they recommend to others. J. J. C. Smart's version of this procedure will be examined later.

(ii) EGOISM, MOTIVATION AND THE HARMONY OF INTERESTS

The famous first three sentences of Bentham's *Principles of Morals and Legislation* join together two things whose intimate involvement with each other has been at once a central feature of utilitarianism and a source of much confusion. 'Nature', Bentham says, 'has placed mankind under the governance of two sovereign masters, *pain* and *pleasure*. It is for them alone to point out what we ought to do, as well as to determine what we shall do. On the one hand the standard of right and wrong, on the other the chain of causes and effects, are fastened to their throne.'[6] Bentham, in effect, asserts both utilitarianism, which states that men ought to aim at the general happiness, and egoism, which states that in actual fact men always aim at their own happiness. His utilitarianism is an ethical theory; his egoism a psychological one.

What is more, the closely intertwined way in which he presents the two doctrines implies that there is some connection between them. This implication is drawn out in Mill's notorious proof, or 'proof', of the utilitarian principle, one of whose premises is 'that there is in reality nothing desired except happiness'[7] or that 'happiness is the sole end of human action'.[8]

Critics have often argued that these two doctrines are in some way inconsistent. It is obvious enough that they are not directly incompatible, since one of them says how men in fact behave, the other how they should. But it is commonly supposed that it cannot be the case that a man ought to do something unless he can do it. Thus if he can aim only at his own happiness it cannot be the case that he ought to aim at the general happiness.

This argument would be valid if it could be assumed that the general happiness and the agent's own happiness are distinct. But can this assumption be made? There is an *ad hominem* argument that might be used to justify it. Utilitarians have often said that each man is the best judge of what his own happiness consists in. But it seems manifest that men often act in ways that do not promote the general happiness, or do not promote it as much as some possible alternative action they might have done. But, if psychological egoism is true, the way in which they act shows what they take their happiness to consist in and this is often in conflict with the promotion of the general happiness.

To be consistent, then, the utilitarian who is also a psychological egoist must say that the set of alternative actions open to an agent in given circumstances is not limited, by the egoist principle, to that single action which he believes will contribute most to his own happiness. And this, in fact, they usually do. For them what an agent *can* do, in the sense required for it to be the case that he ought to do it, is what he could be induced to do by sanctions. These sanctions should ideally conform to the principle of utility by contributing more to the general happiness than they detract from it. The sanctions in question must be efficient, in that they really would induce the agent to act in the required way, and economical, in that the contribution to the general happiness made by the action they produce outweighs the suffering endured by the agent from the sanctions or the threat of them. There are many things, other than what an agent in fact does, that he could do, on the principle that one can do what one can be got to do. But this ideal alternative is the morally relevant one.

In general, utilitarians claim that there is a *natural harmony of interests*. By this they mean that action aimed at the general happiness will in fact most fully realise the agent's own happiness. To the extent that this is true, or more precisely that there is good reason to believe it, a rational agent will, in pursuing the general happiness, follow the most rational policy for the achievement of his own greatest happiness. But this natural harmony of interests is not something that will be consummated if men are left to act as they choose, without guidance or interference from outside, because men are not all rational and perhaps none are wholly rational. A system of sanctions needs to be instituted which, by making action that is unpropitious for the general happiness obviously damaging to the agent's own happiness, brings about an *artificial harmony of interests*.

Bentham, indeed, enumerated three sanctions over and above ne 'physical sanction' which is the pain or pleasure resulting from an action by purely natural causes and independent of any exercise of the human, or divine, will. There is the political sanction, applied by the state under its laws; the moral sanction, applied informally by the community in accordance with its moral convictions; and the religious sanction, applied by God in the form of eternal rewards and punishments. But law was the device for bringing about an artificial harmony of interests with which he was most concerned. J. S. Mill added to these the 'internal' sanction of conscience.

The idea of a natural harmony of interests was inspired by the classical economic theory of Adam Smith which argued that the greatest economic advantage to all would accrue from the unremitting and wholly rational pursuit by each of his own economic advantage. (A remoter source is Mandeville's affectedly 'wicked' thesis that private vices yield public benefits.) But even this natural harmony of economic interests presupposes the complete rationality of men's economic behaviour. Although not true it is less obviously false than the wider assumption that men's behaviour in general is completely rational.

There is, it is held, then, an ultimate natural harmony of interests. The pursuit of the general happiness is what would in fact most promote the happiness of individual men and, if they were wholly rational, that is what they would pursue. But they are not. They aim at what they mistakenly think will yield their own greatest happiness. It is easier to get them to act rightly by altering the probable short-run consequences of their actions, by attaching legal and other sanctions to the undesirable actions they are prone to do, than to get them to realise their mistakes about the long-run consequences of their actions for their own happiness.

Is there any such ultimate natural harmony of interests? It seems unlikely. Of course the happiness of some people, those I love, is a constitutive part of my own happiness. If everybody loved his neighbour as himself, general and particular happiness would coincide. Furthermore, the happiness of some people is a causally necessary condition of my own happiness in various ways. I am unlikely to be happy in a society of miserable and desperate people and I am certainly going to be unhappy in a society whose members have identified me as the cause of their unhappiness. 'Revenge', as Hobbes remarked, 'is a kind of wild justice', a human, but nonetheless natural device for bringing about a harmony of interests.

What this shows is that I have a direct interest in the happiness of the people I love (who are likely to be a rather small part of the human race as a whole), a moderate indirect interest in the non-misery of people whose misery might have a bad effect on my own happiness (which nowadays, at any rate, covers the entire human race) and a rather stronger interest in not causing misery to people who might take revenge on me. In fact every sane, morally adult person has other motives than these for avoiding action, however attractive in other respects, that would cause suffering to others and again for performing actions, otherwise unattractive, that would contribute to the general happiness. For one thing, our moral education makes us capable of being disgusted with ourselves.

These considerations clearly show that there is no direct conflict between a man's own happiness and the general happiness, no necessary opposition between them. It shows, indeed, that some concern for the general happiness is essential to the pursuit of one's own happiness, either as a constitutive part of it or as its causal condition. But they fall well short of showing that the pursuit of the general happiness and the fully rational pursuit of one's own happiness are identical. At most, given one man's dependence on and vulnerability to other men, it is a necessary condition of the achievement of his own happiness and the avoidance of suffering that he should not cause gross suffering in others and that he should do something to relieve suffering that is not of his making. This provides some sort of answer to the question 'why should I be moral?' but not, perhaps, to the question 'why should I be as enthusiastically moral and self-sacrificing as classical utilitarianism enjoins me to be?'

Now it could be argued that no ethical theory is complete until it does answer this question, in the sense of 'moral' appropriate to it. But if the utilitarian answer is less than fully convincing this is not a weakness peculiar to it. The main point of this section has been to show that there is at any rate no inconsistency between utilitarianism and the psychological egoism with which it has usually been associated. If men do always aim at their own happiness it does not follow that they cannot aim at the general happiness. Men can act otherwise than they do, in the utilitarian view, because they can be induced to act differently in an acceptable way. Furthermore, even if not clearly identical with the greatest happiness of each individual, the general happiness is to some extent a constituent and to some extent a causally necessary condition of individual happiness.

I. THE PRECURSORS OF UTILITARIANISM

(i) ETHICS BEFORE UTILITARIANISM

Both of the essential constituents of utilitarianism, as I have defined it, hedonism and consequentialism, are present in Greek ethics. But there is still something crucial missing. This is the element of universality, the insistence of standard utilitarianism that it is the *general* happiness that is the criterion of right conduct. The reason for this omission is the way in which the philosophers of ancient Greece conceived the central ethical problem. For them the question 'how should I live?' took what to us seems a fundamentally prudential or self-regarding form. It amounted for them to an inquiry as to how a man could secure *his own* happiness, fulfilment or perfection. Benevolence, altruism, philanthropy, a concern for the happiness of others occupied a secondary, and even marginal, position in their ethical recommendations. It was not conceived as an end in itself but rather as a means to, or a condition of, the self-realisation of the individual. Greek philosophers in general, and Plato and Aristotle in particular, found a place for restricted benevolence by emphasising the role of friendship in a fully satisfying life and Aristotle made a somewhat disdainful 'liberality' part of his conception of the ethically ideal or 'magnanimous' man. But it was Christianity that first established an essential connection between morality and the happiness or well-being of humanity at large.

In developing their more or less prudential life-styles the Greek moralists unreflectively assumed a consequentialist position. The only way in which they conceived it to be possible to justify a type of conduct was by reference to the results to which it gave rise, for the agent, of course. Many of them were hedonists. Aristippus of Cyrene, indeed, was a hedonist in the colloquial sense, urging the pre-eminent claims of bodily pleasure as an end, in view of its greater intensity. But more commonly, as with Democritus, it would appear, and above all Epicurus, a distinction was drawn between the more intense but also more turbulent pleasures of the body and the calmer but ultimately more satisfying pleasures of the mind. This distinction between lower and higher pleasures was to be revived by John Stuart Mill as one of the most disputed elements in his exposition of utilitarianism.

Others, the Cynics and Stoics, in effect denied the utilitarian identification of happiness with a sum of pleasures. Taking the achievement of happiness as the ultimate justifying end of conduct, they believed the surest way to it to be the suppression of desire and, as a result, indifference to the ordinary sources of pleasure. Plato shared this asceticism but his point of view was less negative. The point of freeing oneself from the solicitations of ordinary desire was not, for him, the attainment of a merely passive condition of peace of mind but rather to clear the ground for the highest satisfaction possible to men, the rational contemplation which is fulfilled by the achievement of wisdom, the most elevated of the virtues.

With Christianity morality came to be endowed with what for us is its essential content, a concern for others. But in two absolutely fundamental respects this altruism was unutilitarian. In the first place, its conception of the happiness or well-being of mankind was ascetical and non-hedonistic. Men are morally required not to injure others, but this is to be achieved at least as much by denying them pleasures in the ordinary sense as it is by supplying them with them. Man's greatest felicity is the beatific vision of God that is to be enjoyed after bodily death by those who have been saved. It follows that the greatest kindness one man can do to another is to work for his salvation and that will generally mean to detach him from the natural earthly satisfactions. In the extreme case of the obstinately heretical the achievement of salvation may require the ultimate bodily suffering of being burnt at the stake. Nevertheless the Christian obligation of charity was not as indifferent to natural, bodily wants and needs as this might suggest. It called for the relief of those afflicted by hunger and sickness. But if the diminution of pain and the provision of pleasure, in a fairly elevated sense, are not altogether ignored by Christian morality, it conceives them as secondary, and, indeed, comparatively trivial, ends of conduct.

The second highly unutilitarian feature of Christian ethics is the account it gives of moral knowledge, of the way in which the principles of right conduct are discovered. In its simplest and most rudimentary form it bases the validity of the moral principles it enjoins on the fact that they are the commands of God. That God will reward or punish me eternally for complying with or disobeying his commands is an adequate, though not ideally estimable, motive for obeying them. But it is not this consequential property that makes them obligatory.

Some Christian theologians, conspicuously Aquinas, mitigated the irrational authoritarianism of this doctrine by maintaining that at least the demands of morality that were not specifically religious were discoverable by the natural reason of man. Several considerations lay behind this. It seemed intolerable to suppose that everyone who was ignorant, because of the time or place at which he lived, of the Christian revelation, its scriptural record and its authoritative interpreter, the Church, must on that account be altogether without knowledge of morality. Secondly, the external means by which God's commands are communicated to men are liable to various kinds of failure and even corruption. The moral content of the Bible requires interpretation and its official interpreters may be misguided or even morally deficient.

Although some, like Duns Scotus and William of Ockham, held that right actions are right because God commands them and that if his commands had been quite different from what they are they would still have been right, the more usual view was that God, being by definition good, is logically constrained to will what is right. An essential aspect of God's goodness indeed, is his benevolence, his desire for the happiness of his creatures. But this does not imply a utilitarian morality since God's conception of what the true happiness of his creatures consists in is more authoritative than their own, and differs from what they are naturally inclined to suppose.

The prevailing account of moral knowledge that emerged from the developed Christian theology of the late middle ages was rationalistic. It maintained that the basic principles of right conduct owe their authority to the fact that they are divine commands. God has provided two ways in which they can be discovered: externally in scripture, whether interpreted by the church or the individual believer, and internally, by an innate capacity for apprehending the self-evident truth of the principles in question, a moral reason analogous to the reason by which men apprehend the fundamental truths of mathematics. Aquinas's doctrine of natural law was conveyed by way of Hooker to Locke, who explicitly associates morality with mathematics and the existence of God as items of demonstrative knowledge. In the ethics of Samuel Clarke and Richard Price this ethical rationalism, which understands the moral quality of a kind of action as intrinsic to it, as being logically essential to it in the way that three-sidedness is to a triangle, is altogether detached from revelation and advanced as an autonomous and sufficient explanation of our knowledge of morality. Clarke elaborates the comparison of moral with mathematical knowledge (which Locke had only outlined in general terms, and very unconvincingly illustrated) speaking of the obligatoriness of an action as an abstract relation of fittingness between it and its circumstances, in precise analogy with the abstract relations studied by the geometer.

Christian ethics, then, and the kind of ethical rationalism that emerged from it to become the prevailing theory of moral knowledge in the seventeenth and eighteenth centuries, fostered an account of the *content* of morality as altruistic and benevolent which was to be central to utilitarianism. But their account of the nature of the general well-being at which right conduct should aim was non-hedonistic. Furthermore the rightness of a type of conduct was not to be inferred from the generally beneficial consequences to which it would give rise. Rather, true benevolence was defined in terms of the intrinsic and rationally self-evident rightness of actions.

(ii) UTILITARIANISM EMERGES

Classical utilitarianism is a secular and naturalistic doctrine. It conceives morality as an institution designed to harmonise the conduct and satisfactions of men on earth and takes the correct method of acquiring moral knowledge to be empirical. It might, then, seem reasonable to expect that an explicitly utilitarian ethical theory would emerge with the development of a systematic secular naturalism in philosophy in general. The philosophy of Hobbes was such a system, the first and most closely-knit of the modern age, yet Hobbes was not a utilitarian, indeed he was not, except in a very marginal sense, a hedonist. The starting-point of his ethics is a firmly, even brutally, egoistic theory of human motivation. The universal end of men's actions is the satisfaction of their desires. But there is one object of desire to which men will, if rational, give an absolute pre-eminence, self-preservation, or more precisely, the avoidance of violent death at the hands of other men. No very clear reason is given for according this primacy to self-preservation. Hobbes holds that pleasure is the natural accompaniment of those impacts of the external world on the human organism which are propitious to its continued vitality and that pleasure is a determinant of desire. This might seem to suggest that the real point or purpose of the appetitive side of human nature is self-preservation. Again the satisfaction of the desire for continued life is a condition of the satisfaction of any other desire. (But that form of reasoning would prove that salt, since it is indispensable to our diet, is an ideal diet on its own.)

Rational reflection shows that, since every man is vulnerable to every other, security from violent death can be established only by the acceptance and enforcement of a system of rules that require men to abstain from injuring each other. All have an equal interest in the operation of such a system of rules. It is rational to comply with such rules only if they are generally enforced and they can be enforced only if they are generally accepted. In this theory morality dissolves into law and the obligation to obey the law is strictly self-regarding and prudential.

Hobbes is often described as a subjectivist and he does say that men *call* good whatever is the object of their desire.[9] But what he believes really is good is self-preservation and, although one man's preservation is distinct from another's, the rationally discoverable condition of these various singular self-preservations is general: an effectively enforced system of laws requiring abstention from mutual injury. The ultimate justifying end of obligation then is egoistic; only its indispensable condition is general and this derivative end is a means not to happiness but to survival.

But although Hobbes was not a utilitarian his ethical views did evoke the first clearly utilitarian account of morality, that of Richard Cumberland, whose *De Legibus Naturae* was published in 1672. Although a bishop and primarily concerned to refute Hobbes, Cumberland, for sound polemical reasons, chose to argue his case as much as possible in Hobbes's grimly economical terms. He agrees with Hobbes that the laws of nature, in other words the general principles of morality, need explanation and are not adequately justified by the theories which see them as divine commands or self-evident truths. They are means to an end, in particular the 'joint felicity of all rationals', 'the aggregate or sum of all those good things which either we can contribute towards, or are necessary to, the happiness of all rational beings, considered as collected into one body'. Right action, he says, is 'the endeavour, to the utmost of our power, of promoting the common good of the whole system of rational agents' and it conduces 'to the good of every part, in which our own happiness, as that of a part, is contained'.[10]

Apart from making the general happiness, rather than the, inevitably general, preservation of life, the ultimate moral end, Cumberland's main difference from Hobbes lies in the account he gives of human motivation. Human nature is not

as destructively egoistic as Hobbes makes it out to be; benevolence is as much a part of it as naked self-interest. It was this
project of undermining Hobbes's egoistic theory of motivation
which was to dominate the ethical thinking of the subsequent
century. Hobbes's challenge to conventional morality did not
attack its content but the basis of its claim on us. It did not cast
doubt on the received ideas about what we ought to do but only
on the usual account of why we ought to do it. Thus, in the
moral sense theories of Shaftesbury and Hutcheson, the problem
of the criterion of right conduct occupies a small place. There is
a general assumption of the identity of virtue and benevolence
and Hutcheson actually uses the phrase 'the greatest happiness
of the greatest number'. But the main emphasis is laid on the
springs of benevolent action in the social nature of man. The
content of morality became problematic only with the decay of
Christian belief, which had hitherto ensured a fair measure of
moral uniformity, together with increasing knowledge of the
deviant moral convictions and practices of remote peoples.

(iii) HUME

By far the most important, elaborate and philosophically
penetrating anticipation of the utilitarianism of Bentham and
Mill is to be found in the ethical writings of David Hume; Book 3
of the *Treatise of Human Nature* (1740) and the *Enquiry Concerning
the Principles of Morals* (1751). Cumberland's purpose had been
polemical rather than constructive; he was an ungainly writer
and a very imperfect expositor. Something very like the greatest
happiness principle does indeed figure in his book as the ultimate
standard for the justification of specific moral principles. But it is
only one feature in a doctrine which embodies numerous non-
utilitarian elements; for example, a conception of the general
good in terms of perfection almost as much as in terms of happiness and the acceptance of a religious foundation for morality.
At all levels Hume's approximation to utilitarianism proper is
much closer: he conceives morality in a wholly secular way and,

more superficially, there is constant explicit mention of utility.

Nevertheless Hume is not quite a utilitarian. In the first place he does not conceive it to be his task as a moral philosopher to consider the way in which moral beliefs are to be justified so much as to explain causally how they come to be made and how they work. Morality for Hume is a phenomenon which is to be investigated in the spirit of the sub-title of his *Treatise*: 'An Attempt to Introduce the Experimental Method of Reasoning into Moral Subjects'. But here, as elsewhere in Hume's philosophy, what is presented as the outcome of a causal inquiry is readily available for reinterpretation as an analysis or a criterion of validity. Hume explains causal belief as the result of the workings of constant conjunction on the mind by way of the principle of the association of ideas. This is easily converted into the regularity theory, which analyses assertions to the effect that one event is the cause of another as implicitly general statements about the regularity with which events like the first are followed by neighbouring events like the second. (Indeed Hume himself at times defines causation in this way.) Again Hume explains our belief in the existence of material objects, which are continuous and distinct from us, in a way that our impressions of them are not, as the causal outcome of the characteristic constancy and coherence of the sequence of our impressions. It is a short step from that to the phenomenalism which *defines* a material object as a systematic, or 'constant and coherent', array of actual and possible impressions of the senses.

A second and, to many contemporary ethical theorists, more substantial deviation from utilitarianism in Hume is his uniquely serious realisation, as compared with all moral philosophers until very recent times, of the essentially practical nature of moral judgements. 'Morals', he insists at the beginning of his discussion, 'have an influence on the actions and affections', they 'excite passions, and produce or prevent actions'.[11] His position is expressed in a famous quotation that has served as the motto of much recent ethics: 'In every system of morality, which I have hitherto met with, I have always remarked, that the author proceeds for some time in the ordinary way of reasoning, and establishes the being of a God, or makes observations concerning human affairs; when of a sudden I am surprised to find, that instead of the usual copulations of propositions, *is,* and *is not,* I meet with no proposition that is not connected with an *ought,* or an *ought not.* This change is imperceptible; but is, however, of the last consequence. For as this *ought,* or *ought not,* expresses some new relation or affirmation, it is necessary that it should be observed and explained; and at the same time that a reason should be given, for what seems altogether inconceivable, how this new relation can be a deduction from others, which are entirely different from it.'[12]

This, in the view of many interpreters, seems to amount to the recently popular conviction that moral judgements are logically unique and autonomous. The interpretation is supported by Hume's denial that 'moral distinctions' are derived from either reason or the senses and by his insistence on the practical nature of moral judgements which is what is usually invoked to explain their logical uniqueness and autonomy.

Hume rejects ethical rationalism of the kind hinted at by Locke and developed by Clarke. Equally he maintains that the moral qualities of actions are no more matters of fact perceptible by the senses than they are abstract 'fitnesses' apprehensible by the understanding. 'Take any action allowed to be vicious: wilful murder, for instance. Examine it in all lights, and see if you can find that matter of fact, or real existence, which you call *vice.* In whichever way you take it, you find only certain passions, motives, volitions and thoughts. There is no other matter of fact in the case. The vice entirely escapes you, as long as you consider the object. You can never find it, till you turn your reflexion into your own breast, and find a sentiment of disapprobation, which arises in you, towards this action. Here is a matter of fact; but it is the object of feeling, not of reason. It lies in yourself, not in the object.'[13] But the moral judgement is not a report or description of this sentiment or emotion. 'To have the sense of virtue, is nothing but to *feel* a satisfaction of a particular kind from the contemplation of a character. The very *feeling* constitutes our praise or admiration. . . . We do not infer a character to be virtuous, because it pleases: but in feeling that it pleases after such a particular manner, we in effect feel that it is virtuous.'[14]

Moral judgements, then, are neither necessary truths, demonstrable by reason, nor descriptions of external matters of fact. They are the unreflective expressions of a particular kind of inward sentiment or emotion, that of approbation or its opposite. From this point on it is Hume's task to explain how and in what circumstances the characteristically moral emotion, the pleasure of approval or the pain of disapproval, is brought about. His answer is that approval is caused by our awareness that actions and characters are either agreeable or useful to ourselves or to others, in other words afford pleasure or the means to it to someone.

This conclusion poses the favourite ethical problem of the age, in the form in which Hume confronts it: that which concerns the appeal to an individual of what contributes to the happiness of others. Why should I be pleased by the disinterested contemplation of the happiness of another, especially to the extent of being led thereby, at some cost to myself, to promote it? Hume's answer is in three parts. First, men are all naturally benevolent, even if only to a mild extent and towards a restricted circle of people. 'There is no such passion in human minds, as the love of mankind, merely as such';[15] but equally there is no such thing as absolute, disinterested malevolence. Secondly, there is sympathy, the tendency, based associatively on the similarity of other men to ourselves, to feel pleased and pained when they do, even if less intensely. 'When I see the *effects* of passion in the voice and gesture of any person, my mind immediately passes from these effects to their causes, and forms such a lively idea of the passion, as is presently converted into the passion itself.'[16] Finally, Hume alleges, the limited, parochial tendency of benevolence and sympathy is corrected to provide for the necessities of communication. 'It is impossible that we could ever converse together on any reasonable terms, were each of us to consider characters and persons, only as they appear from his particular point of view.'[17]

For these three reasons, then, men are prone to submit the actions and characters of themselves and others to *disinterested* contemplation. If what they contemplate is agreeable or useful to anyone, is pleasant or a means to pleasure, it arouses in the contemplators sentiments of approval, which are verbally expressed in moral judgements and practically expressed in conduct. Hume presents this thesis as a causal law of human psychology. But it is easily converted into an ethical theory proper, into an account of the criteria of validity of moral judgements. If what we *believe* to be agreeable or useful is what we *judge* to be right, it is natural to conclude that what *really is* agreeable or useful really is right.

This closely related, and genuinely utilitarian, position, to which Hume approximates in his general observations about morality, is something to which he comes even closer in his account of the part of commonly accepted morality to which he devotes the most detailed attention: the requirements of justice. Justice, which Hume curiously identifies with respect for the rights of property, is described, together with promise-keeping and obedience to law and the state, as an artificial virtue, in contrast to the natural virtue of benevolence. What makes justice and the other virtues like it artificial is the fact that there is no instinctive impulse in men to act in accordance with its dictates, whereas there is such a natural impulse, even if not a very powerful one, to benevolence.

Hume's distinction between natural and artificial virtue is not very precise but it is essentially that while the utility of benevolence is obvious (it is in fact truistic), that of justice can be recognised only as the result of more or less complicated reasoning. Hume speaks of property, promises, and the state as conventions, and this suggests a possibly better way of drawing the distinction he has in mind, one that has affinities to Hobbes's account of the necessity for generally applicable rules of conduct. Benevolence,

provided it is not accompanied by gross misinformation about
the incidence of happiness and suffering, is guaranteed to promote
utility. But the artificial virtues promote utility only if they are
fairly generally followed. Property, promises, and the state are
institutions which it is useful to respect only if they are generally·
respected. It is the utility of the institution, of the general rules
that it embodies, that explains why it is right to act in accordance
with such institutional rules in particular cases where the immediate consequences of doing so are of negligible or even negative utility.

In general, Hume takes men's propensities towards approval
and disapproval as given. His aim is to explain them, not to
justify or criticise them. Yet his own rejection of religion has
·obvious critical implications for conventional morality. If there is
no God, and no life after death for him to reward or punish us in,
this must have a bearing on the utility of our actions. Bentham
acknowledged a great indebtedness to Hume but he put his
ethical inheritance to critical uses that formed no part of the
intentions of his benefactor. Where Hume sought to show that
ordinary, unreflective morality has a rational foundation of which
men are largely unaware, Bentham put this rational foundation
to work as an instrument for the radical criticism and reformation
of ordinary morality.

In this critical and reformist use of the principle of utility,
Bentham was anticipated and influenced by two European
students of Hume: Helvétius and Beccaria. The main topic of
Helvétius's *De L'Esprit* (1758), is an account of human nature
as an associatively developed system of sensations, including
pleasure and pain, from which he derived the conclusion that
men are unrestrictedly malleable by education and law. 'L'éduca-
tion peut tout.' Men can be made to do almost anything by
appropriate modification of their environment and experience.
The question arises: in what direction should they be influenced?
Helvétius took it as beyond question that this aim should be public
utility, the general interest, the general happiness.

Beccaria, in his highly influential essay *Dei Delitti e delle Pene*

(1764), applied the criterion of utility in an account of the nature of a rational system of judicial punishment which consciously deviates in numerous respects from the accepted judicial practices of his age. 'In order for punishment not to be, in every instance, an act of violence of one or of many against a private citizen, it must be essentially public, prompt, necessary, the least possible in the given circumstances, proportionate to the crimes, dictated by the laws.'[18] All the properties that the principle of utility recommends here for punishment were more or less conspicuously absent from the actual administration of the sanctions of the law.

Hume was by no means the only conservative utilitarian. Paley, for example, found utilitarian justifications for all the details of the established order. What is singular about Hume's position is that he is at once conservative and anti-religious. As a patriotic Scotsman Hume was inevitably hostile to the Whig oppressors of his country. A more direct and theoretical reason for his conservative point of view is his pervading scepticism and his associated respect for whatever is customary: 'Men generally fix their affections more on what they are possessed of, than on what they never enjoyed: for this reason, it would be greater cruelty to dispossess a man of any thing, than not to give it him.'[19] This absence of a critical impulse towards ideas and institutions, provided always that they are not religious, is congruous with his consistent preference for an explanatory over a justificatory approach to morality.

(iv) THEOLOGICAL UTILITARIANISM

In 1731 John Gay published, anonymously, his *Preliminary Dissertation* to a work by somebody else on the origin of evil. Despite the furtiveness of its presentation to the world, Gay's utilitarianism was much less entwined with extraneous matter than Cumberland's and much less complicated and idiosyncratic than Hume's. Gay defined virtue as 'conformity to a rule of life directing the action of all rational creatures with respect to each other's happiness'.[20] His starting-point was a straightforward acceptance of the essential benevolence of God. Since God, by his very nature, must will the happiness of his creatures, it follows that we must discover what his will is, and thus what is morally required of us, by determining what actions promote the happiness of mankind. The happiness of mankind, in other words, is the criterion of the will of God.

As well as validating or authorising the principle of utility, God, according to Gay, also provides us with a sufficient motive for conforming our actions to it. Gay defines obligation in a Hobbesian, seemingly non-moral and misleading way as 'the necessity of doing or omitting an action in order to be happy'.[21] This comes near to assimilating the sense of obligation relevant to morality to that in which we commonly speak of, for example, being obliged to let go of something that is too heavy to hold. What is misleading about this, in the particular context of Gay's theory, is that while an action is held to be *right* if it contributes to the happiness of all, it is obligatory only if it contributes to the happiness of the agent. Right and obligatory action, which for us are much the same thing, are thus conceived as logically distinct. They coincide in fact only by way of the benevolence of God, who adjusts the sanctions of conduct so as to make the pursuit of the general happiness by each agent the best, or only, way to secure his own happiness.

In the course of his discussion Gay anticipates Bentham's four sanctions of morality in precise detail. He distinguishes natural, virtuous, civil and religious sanctions; a classificatory scheme to which Bentham was to make only verbal alterations. Furthermore Gay anticipates Bentham's clear-cut and simplified view that happiness is a sum of pleasures, between which the only relevant distinctions are quantitative. This is the presupposition of Bentham's hedonic calculus which explains the respects in which pleasure is to be measured and how the results of these measurements are to be summed.

Abraham Tucker, in his *Light of Nature Pursued* (1768), a vast, diffuse work at the opposite literary extreme from Gay's brief, consecutive essay, presents essentially the same body of ideas.

He follows Hartley in pointing out that there are good utilitarian reasons for guiding action by general rules, rather than
working out the consequences of each proposed action. We often
need to make moral decisions quickly and adherence to general
rules worked out in an impersonal way is a safeguard against any
tendency to self-regarding miscalculation in cases where our own
interests are involved. He differs from Gay, and even more from
Bentham, in holding that the computation of the amount of
value to be realised by action must be impressionistic, not mechani-
cally arithmetical.

Tucker's manner of writing ensured that he would be read
very little. It was left to William Paley, a most lucid and elegant
expositor, to express his and Gay's ideas in a sufficiently attractive
way to make them really influential. For many years this influence
was institutionalised, so to speak, by the fact that Paley's
Principles of Moral and Political Philosophy (1785) was the official
medium of ethical instruction at Cambridge. He added little to
what he acquired from Gay and Tucker. With them he holds the
general happiness to be the *summum bonum*, he regards happiness
as a sum of pleasures that differ relevantly only in quantity, and
he maintains that God must, as it were by definition, desire the
happiness of mankind and takes the sanctions of eternal reward
and punishment through which God seeks to realise this end as
providing the only rational motive for morally correct conduct.
His main contribution to theological utilitarianism is a certain
ingenuous openness which often amounts to simple blatancy,
as in the famous definition of virtue as 'the doing good to mankind, in obedience to the will of God, for the sake of everlasting
happiness'.[22] Bentham had a substantial measure of Paley's self-
confident naïveté. He follows Paley in rejecting the moral sense
or intuitionist alternatives to utilitarianism as arbitrary and
irrational. The chief ethical difference between them is that
Bentham provides a very different account of moral motivation.
There is also a more practical or ideological difference. Paley
invoked the general happiness principle to endorse the practices
and institutions of the *status quo* while Bentham invoked it to

make something very like a clean sweep of them. This flat opposition suggests that agreement that the pleasure or happiness of all is the *summum bonum* is no guarantee of the settlement of disputes about specific moral and political issues. The conditions of the general happiness may seem to be as inscrutable as the will of God.

II. JEREMY BENTHAM

Within the vast, and still not completely published, body of Bentham's writings the strictly ethical element bulks very small. In effect this element consists of the first five chapters of his *Introduction to the Principles of Morals and Legislation* (1789). This book, which had been printed but not published, in a manner highly characteristic of Bentham's literary enterprises, in 1780, was the somewhat overgrown outcome of what had originally been intended as the introduction to a plan for a rational penal code. That intention was representative of Bentham's concern with the practical and minutely detailed work of carrying out a thorough reform, rationalisation and codification of the legal system, its laws, its procedure, its institutional arrangements and its system of punishments. This may explain an air of bluff impatience, an animated desire to get on with it, that surrounds Bentham's exposition and defence of his fundamental criterion against abstractly philosophical criticism. Indications that his primary interest was in the use of his principle to devise new schemes of legislation abound in the ethical part of the book. Indeed, as will be seen, his conviction of the obvious correctness of the principle of utility is too absolute to allow him to examine alternatives to it in more than a dismissive and perfunctory way.

He compares the ethical investigations of the *Principles* to pure mathematics, conceived in a very pragmatic spirit. 'One good at least', he writes in the preface, 'may result from the present publication; viz. that the more he [the author] has trespassed on the patience of the reader on this occasion, the less need he will have to do so on future ones: so that this may do to those, the office which is done, by books of pure mathematics, to books of mixed mathematics and natural philosophy.'[23] The future occasions he has in mind are enumerated on the next page:

no less than ten volumes setting forth articulated schemes of legislation of various kinds.

As we have seen, he begins with the misleadingly compact observation that pleasure and pain determine both what we shall do and what we ought to do. This formula obscures the fact that pleasure and pain must be conceived in one way in connection with what we in fact do and in another in connection with what we should do. But Bentham himself is fully aware of the difference between the agent's own happiness and the happiness of the community. 'The greatest happiness of all those whose interest is in question', he says, is 'the right and proper, and the only right and proper and universally desirable, end of human action.'[24] Utility is the production of benefit, advantage, pleasure, good or happiness; he sees no need to differentiate between the items in this list. The community whose happiness is the right and proper end of human action is a fictitious body and its interest is simply the sum of the interests of the individual men who compose it. As has been mentioned, an important issue is obscured by his failure to see the significance of the distinction between actions that conform to the principle of utility as being those that ought to be done and those of which it is at any rate not true that they ought not to be done. But towards the end of the book he draws a distinction between the spheres of law and 'private ethics' which throws some light on the question.[25] The principle of utility enjoins *probity*, which is 'forbearing to diminish' the happiness of others, and *beneficence*, which is 'studying to increase it'. Law and private ethics have the same ends, the general happiness. But not everything which is required by ethics should be made an object of legislation. Men should not be required by law to do those things they morally should do which it would be mistaken to punish them for failing to do. An offence is 'unmeet' for punishment where punishment would be groundless (because no mischief has been done), inefficacious (because it cannot prevent mischief of that kind), unprofitable (because the advantage to be gained by inflicting it is outweighed by its intrinsic evil) or needless (because the mischief can be prevented in some other and less painful way, by 'instruction', for example). Private ethics will not, of course, condemn acts for which punishment would be groundless, but it will operate where legal sanctions would be inefficacious, unprofitable or needless. Now Bentham believes that there is a rough coincidence between the sphere of probity, as he defines it, and the domain where punishment is appropriate. 'As to the rules of beneficence, these, as far as concerns matters of detail, must necessarily be abandoned in great measure to the jurisdiction of private ethics.'[26] In other words the law should be largely restricted to the prevention of harmful acts; the positive augmentation of happiness is a matter for private morality. But this coincidence between the proper sphere of law and the prevention of mischief is only approximate. 'In cases where the person is in danger, why should it not be made the duty' (Bentham means here the legal duty) 'of every man to save another from mischief, when it can be done without prejudicing himself, as well as to abstain from bringing it on him?' ('A woman's head-dress catches fire: water is at hand: a man instead of assisting to quench the fire, looks on, and laughs at it. . . . Who is there that . . . would think punishment misapplied?')[27] What all this implies is that for Bentham any opportunity to augment the general happiness presents a positive duty, and not just a possible action it would be wrong not to do.

Like Mill, Bentham maintains that a proof of the principle of utility is neither necessary nor possible. 'That which is used to prove everything else, cannot itself be proved.'[28] But it can be provided with indirect support in various ways. All men, on most occasions of their life, defer to it 'if not for the ordering of their own actions, yet for the trying of their own actions, as well as of those of other men'.[29] The trouble is that they do not follow it consistently. Bentham's main point is that 'when a man attempts to combat the principle of utility, it is with reasons drawn, without his being aware of it, from that very principle itself'.[30] There is, of course, something in this. If someone insists on reasons being provided for specific moral principles, such as those which enjoin the keeping of promises or telling the truth, there seems to be nothing left to appeal to but considerations of the general good. But the traditional opponents of utilitarianism, intuitionists or deontologists like Kant and Prichard, in holding principles like these to be self-evident are committed to the view that it is a mistake to ask for reasons for them. To suppose that reasons for them must be available is, on this view, to misunderstand their nature as *moral* principles and has the effect of transforming them into counsels of prudence, individual or collective. Such theorists agree with Bentham that nothing can be proved unless something is accepted without proof; they differ from him as to what these unprovables are. They can argue, with some plausibility, that the principles they take to be ultimate are regarded as more certain and authoritative by the 'common moral consciousness'.

Bentham's view is that opposition to the principle of utility is either the outcome of sinister interest or else confusion and prejudice. The task of its defender is to expose the former and dissipate the latter. Let anyone who doubts the principle of utility, Bentham says, ask himself if he would really wish to discard it altogether. Does he propose any other principle in its place: if so, is it really a distinct principle or is it just a policy of giving a respectable form to his private and capricious sentiments? If he takes his own emotions of approval to be the criterion of morality 'let him ask himself whether his sentiment is to be a standard of right and wrong, with respect to every other man, or whether every man's sentiment has the same privilege of being a standard to itself?'[31] In the former case he is setting himself up as a moral despot; in the latter he is endorsing moral anarchy.

This general programme of refutation is put into effect in the second chapter of the *Principles*, where Bentham considers 'principles adverse to that of utility'. In this rather knockabout discussion all alternative ethical theories are subsumed under two heads. First there is the principle of asceticism, a fairly satirical version of Christian morality, which is taken to enjoin the exact opposite of the end proposed by utilitarianism, favouring the diminution and disapproving the augmentation of happiness. It has a stronger, religious form in which, inspired by the fear of God, its adherents make the pursuit of pain a duty, and a weaker, philosophical form, in which, for the sake of reputation, the grosser pleasures are rejected and the other pleasures are called by any other name than 'pleasure'. The principle of asceticism has never been applied in the public business of legislation and cannot be consistently pursued. (Bentham says the attempt to pursue it would produce a hell on earth but his underlying and less question-begging reason for denying its possibility must be its manifest conflict with the basic motivation of human conduct.) It is the outcome, to the extent that it is rational at all, of a self-destructive extrapolation of the discovery that certain immediate pleasures turn out in the long run to produce a more than equivalent amount of pain.

Secondly, there is the principle of sympathy and antipathy, or principle of caprice, which takes the mere fact of approval or disapproval as the measure of right or wrong. Into this capacious container are swept the whole variety of more or less intuitionistic ethical theories: those that base morality on a moral sense, or common sense, or a moral understanding of the fitness of things, or the law of nature, and several others. In regarding all these as equivalent to each other and as amounting to no more than a mischievous disguise for unreasoned moral prejudice Bentham greatly simplifies his task of refutation at the cost of failing to address himself to the more serious alternatives to his own position. Even the kind of subjectivism that he does indentify as the common core of these alternatives is not very convincingly disposed of. His objections to it are mostly simple moral objections that presuppose the utilitarian principle he is supposed to be defending. The principle of caprice is despotic. Although, more often than not, the results of applying it coincide with those of the principle of utility it tends to err on the side of severity. Finally Bentham adverts to the theological principle that morally right action is that which accords with the will of God. This, he maintains, is not really a new and distinct principle. What God wills must always be a matter of presumption and is always in need of interpretation. In effect the view that God's will is the criterion of morality must be reducible to one of the three principles already considered: asceticism, caprice or utility.

The real objection that lies behind what Bentham has to say about the principle of caprice is that it fails to distinguish between what men as a matter of fact approve of and what they should, if rational, approve of. Most people at least pay lip-service to the existence of such a distinction; they believe that their unreflective approvals and disapprovals are susceptible of criticism and, perhaps, amendment, if only by being adjusted to a more correct conception of the actual facts of the case in hand. But Bentham's actual procedure is not well calculated to make this point. He insists that there is a difference between the motive of an action and the ground of approval for it. We unconsciously transfer, he suggests, our approval of the effects of a moral sentiment to that sentiment itself. But a moral sentiment, such as antipathy, can never be a right ground of action; only utility can be that. Moral sentiment 'requires always to be regulated, to prevent its doing mischief. . . . The principle of utility neither requires nor admits of any other regulator than itself.'[32]

From this point on in the *Principles* Bentham's lust for classification is given its head. Following Gay, he enumerates four sanctions, or sources of pleasure and pain, capable of influencing men's conduct. There is the physical sanction of pleasant or painful natural consequences of action which occur independently of the operation of any human will. There is the political sanction, which consists principally of punishment meted out by a judge, under a sovereign. There is the popular sanction, by which 'chance persons' influence the conduct of others through various 'mortifications and inconveniences'. And, finally, there is the religious sanction, the allocation of pleasures and pains, in this life or the next, by a 'superior being'. Bentham's ostensible reasons for neglecting the religious sanction in what follows is that it is difficult to tell which advantages and misfortunes in this life do display the hand of God and even more difficult to determine what will happen in the next.

In the fourth chapter Bentham presents, very briefly, what has come to be called his hedonic calculus. Here a sevenfold distinction is employed. In order to measure the magnitude of a pleasure or pain, or to compare one pleasure or pain with another, we need to consider, first, certain properties that the pleasure or pain has considered on its own. These are its *intensity*, its *duration*, its *certainty* of actually taking place and its *propinquity*, its distance in time from the calculation. It has often been pointed out that, if the · certainty of a future pleasure or pain is allowed for, its propinquity is irrelevant. Remoteness in time is fairly generally associated with uncertainty but it does not make any difference except as a reason for uncertainty. Secondly, there are two causal relationships in which pleasures and pains stand to other pleasures and pains: *fecundity*, 'the chance it has of being followed by sensations of the same kind' and *purity*, 'the chance it has of not being followed by sensations of the opposite kind.[33] Finally, in all cases where the interests of a number of people are in question, the *extent*, or number of people affected, needs to be taken into consideration.

These seven properties are described by Bentham as the *dimensions* of pleasure and pain and he says that in estimating the tendency of an action we must first take an account of the value of each pleasure and pain that it will produce, directly or indirectly, and then balance the sum of pleasures against the sum of pains. Arithmetical terminology abounds in his discussion. But it is not at all clear that it is meant to be taken with absolute literalness. The obvious objection to Bentham's use of the word 'dimension' for the various ways in which pleasures can be assessed is that it implies a comparison with measurement of volume in the three dimensions of space. But in the latter case there are units of measurement that are just the same when applied to height or depth or width: there are measuring-rods which can be aligned with what is to be measured in all dimensions. There is no such congruity between the items in Bentham's list, no common unit correlating a certain amount of intensity with a certain amount of duration. At most we can say that a comparison of pleasures which takes all of Bentham's dimensions into account is better, more rational, than one that does not. The use of the 'calculus' is to remind us of what we must take into consideration if our assessment of two alternative possibilities is to be complete. Bentham does say that such calculations should not be undertaken in the case of each particular act, and even, more surprisingly, in the case of èvery 'legislative operation'. The procedure should, however, be 'kept in view'. There are, of course, good utilitarian reasons for this economy of calculation; in particular, we often need to act quickly if any utility is to be realised at all.

In most of the rest of the *Principles* Bentham luxuriates in classificatory self-indulgence. One variety of simple pleasure, the pleasure of sense, has itself nine forms. Pleasure and pain are not directly proportional to the external factors that excite them. Human sensibility varies, for no less than thirty-two different kinds of reason. This taxonomical orgy is followed by a long discussion of the nature and mental causes of the antecedents of action: the intention behind it, the consciousness or beliefs that accompany it, its underlying motive and the disposition to which the presence of that motive testifies. The point of this discussion is to assemble the material for a rational theory of punishment. For, he says, 'the business of government is to promote the happiness of the society, by punishing and rewarding,'[34] a somewhat reductive point of view.

Only in the final chapter, on the limits of the penal branch of jurisprudence, does he return to anything of general ethical interest: the distinction between law and private ethics discussed earlier, and his somewhat parenthetical solution to the problem of moral motivation. 'What motives', he asks, '(independent of such as religion and legislation may chance to furnish) can one man have to consult the happiness of another?'[35] His reply is that on all occasions there is the social motive of sympathy and benevolence, and, in addition, there are the 'semi-social' motives of love and amity and reputation, a thesis further developed in J. S. Mill's account of the internal sanctions of morality.

Bentham's *Principles* is something of a mechanical contraption for much of its considerable length. But it would be wrong to leave it without giving an example of Bentham's lively and generous humanitarianism. This footnote on fanaticism shows that Bentham was no impersonal and desiccated moral calculator. 'If a man happens to take it into his head to assassinate with his own hands, or with the sword of justice, those whom he calls heretics, that is, people who think, or perhaps only speak, differently upon a subject which neither party understands, he will be as much inclined to do this at one time as at another. Fanaticism never sleeps: it is never glutted: it is never stopped by philanthropy; for it makes a merit of trampling on philanthropy: it is never stopped by conscience; for it has pressed conscience into its service. Avarice, lust and vengeance, have piety, benevolence and honour; fanaticism has nothing to oppose it.'[36]

There is no need to spend much time on James Mill. His ethical writings were the least significant of his many services to utilitarianism in general and to Bentham in particular. His main theoretical achievement was the systematic presentation of the associationist theory of the development of the mind, which the utilitarians derived, by way of Hartley and Priestley, from Hume, in his large *Analysis of the Phenomena of the Human Mind*. The chief relevance to ethics of this theory is the account it contains of the way in which the moral sentiment of benevolence, a steady regard for the general happiness, is derived from the initially self-regarding impulses of man. Mill insists that the fact that the social or other-regarding sentiments can be causally explained in self-regarding terms does not mean that they do not really exist. Mill's psychology provided utilitarianism with a theory of education, a thoroughly environmentalist one, on the same lines as that of Helvétius. It was put into fairly terrifying practice, as we learn from the *Autobiography* of John Stuart Mill. Perhaps James Mill's most significant influence was exercised through the political theory, presented in his *Essay on Government*, which converted Bentham to democracy from his earlier confidence in the enlightened despotism of a truly rational and philanthropic legislator, the *deus ex machina*, who, mysteriously exempt from ordinary human frailties, is to bring about an artificial harmony of interests by the introduction of a brand-new system of laws. Mill's point is very simple. The end of government is the general happiness; the only group of people who can be guaranteed to have a reliable interest in the pursuit of this end is the public at large. Democracy, by making the rulers' continuance in power dependent on their being seen to pursue the general happiness, provides them with an adequate self-regarding motive for legislating and governing in the way they should. Mill mitigated the democratic implications of this theory by maintaining that it is quite sufficient to restrict the vote to the fathers of families who, by reason of the ties of natural affection, can be counted on to represent the interests of their womenfolk and sons under forty.

James Mill's main purely ethical work is his last, the quaintly named *Fragment on Mackintosh* (1835). The strictly ethical interest of this substantial volume is almost negligible. For the most part it consists of the type of ponderous abuse that is often employed for the relief of self-righteous indignation. The abuse was not undeserved. Mackintosh's critique of utilitarianism was fatuous and superficial. Mill was right to take exception to the view that Bentham and his disciples 'clung to their opinions because they were obnoxious' or that they were concerned to wrong 'the most respectable feelings of mankind.' But Mill's controversial manner, with its futile hair-splitting and theatrical apostrophes, under-mines the case he wants to make. By any standards, the utilitarian included, the *Fragment* is an immoral volume. Mill was perhaps unfortunate in having such a very flimsy antagonist to refute.

There are a few points of interest. Against moral sense theories Mill argues that utilitarianism is more economical: no special faculty is needed to explain the perception of utility. Mackintosh had argued that by allowing exceptions to the established specific principles of morality utilitarianism was an encouragement to laxity. Mill strenuously retorts that the only exceptions allowed by utilitarians are those sanctioned by utility itself, by the general interest and not, as Mackintosh had implied, by private interest. A large issue is raised here but not very deeply explored.

Mackintosh holds that there are some, intrinsically base, things, which a truly moral man would never do, however they contributed to public utility. Mill replies, in effect, that this is frivolous if the public utility is really at stake. Bentham had committed himself to the view that the motives of action, being desires for what is itself good, are themselves always good. The morality of an action depends on its intention, defined as the whole of the expected consequences of the action. Mill loyally supports this account of motives and intentions. Like Bentham he makes no clear distinction between the *rightness* of an action, to be determined by its consequences, expected or expectable, and its *praiseworthiness* or virtue, a property of the agent rather than the deed, to be determined by the motive which led him to do what he did. Mill does suggest that the consequences that 'might have been foreseen' are more relevant than those that were actually expected, but does not develop the point. Like all hedonists Mill is compelled to protest that utilitarians are not, as Mackintosh alleges, indifferent to the 'pleasures of taste and imagination' and interested only in 'visible and tangible' pleasures. Finally, Mill takes a clear position about the logical status of the principle of utility. 'The theory of utility', he says, 'makes the utility of an act and the morality of an act two names for the same thing.' In other words for him the principle of utility is an analytic truth, true in virtue of the meanings of the words of which it is composed. But this is a somewhat parenthetical observation and Mill does not explore its implications. In particular, he does not ask how those who have denied it could have failed to be aware that they were guilty of self-contradiction.

III. JOHN STUART MILL

(i) INTRODUCTORY

James Mill's education of his son was in strict conformity with the recommendations of Helvétius. The instilling of Bentham's unqualified version of the greatest happiness principle was a central ingredient in it. That principle was used by Bentham in a radically critical way to undermine conventional assumptions. John Stuart Mill came to turn the kind of rationalism it exemplified against the principle itself.

We know, from his *Autobiography* and from the essays on Bentham and Coleridge which he wrote in his early thirties and published soon after the deaths of Bentham and his father, that Mill was deeply dissatisfied with the conception of human nature embodied in the teaching to which they had subjected him. In his early twenties he had lapsed into a state of emotional prostration as a result of his father's educational regime. He says that Wordsworth's poetry played a large part in his spiritual recovery. In the related ideas of Coleridge he found an intellectual equivalent, an altogether more perceptive account of human needs and powers than the one that he had been brought up to believe in.

Thus in *Utilitarianism*, published in 1863 when Mill was in his middle fifties, there are several heretical deviations from Benthamite orthodoxy. The most conspicuous of these is his distinction between higher and lower qualities of pleasure. Another is his emphasis on conscience as derived from the social instincts of man in contrast to the Hobbesian account of the essentially self-interested nature of human motivation given by Bentham and his father. The book begins with a survey of criticisms of utilitarian ethics which tends to meet them half way as much as to rebut them. As a result of these modifications Mill's utilitarianism is very much his own.

In his other writings in relevant fields, in particular on politics, he departs even further from the letter of his intellectual inheritance. *On Liberty*, for example, is only vestigially utilitarian. The ultimate value on which his defence of freedom, personal, intellectual and political, depends is the self-development and perfection of the individual. He relates this to the utilitarian end of the general happiness only in passing, by way of a reference to 'the permanent interests of man as a progressive being',[37] a more flexible and elusive notion than happiness as Bentham conceived it.

All the same, in spite of the insecure and marginal character of his commitment to it, Mill's essay has always been and is likely to remain the authoritative exposition of utilitarian ethics. There are several reasons for this. In the first place his book is short, lucid and eloquent. Secondly it is exclusively concerned with utilitarian *ethics*, a topic which Bentham hurried past on his way to the more engrossing subject of public legislation. Finally it is more philosophically satisfying than Bentham's breezy dogmatism. Mill offers his famous 'proof' of the principle of utility and develops its consequences with sensitive attention to difficulties that Bentham would have brushed aside. Mill admirably combines candour with perceptiveness.

(ii) THE REMOVAL OF MISUNDERSTANDINGS

The second chapter of the book, 'What Utilitarianism Is', after setting out Mill's well-known definition of 'the creed which accepts as the foundation of morals, Utility or the Greatest Happiness Principle', is mainly concerned to remove misunderstandings. Three at least of these are verbal, turning on the words *utility*, *expediency* and *pleasure*. To regard utility as the foundation of morals is not, he points out, to deny the value of pleasure, but is emphatically to affirm it. To possess utility is to be valuable derivatively, by reason of consequences that are valuable in themselves and the only intrinsic, or non-consequential, value is pleasure and the absence of pain. Again when utilitarians ascribe the rightness of actions to their expediency they are not using this word in the colloquial sense in which it is contrasted with principle. The expediency they have in mind is general or public expediency which, in their view, is what principle in fact amounts to, as opposed to the private expediency of self-interest.

These are minor points that need only to be made in order to forestall the tactics of unscrupulous debaters. The interpretation of pleasure as it figures in the utilitarian principle is a more serious matter. Mill was very sensitive to the accusation that utilitarianism was a pig-philosophy, a Cyrenaic endorsement of voluptuousness. It is hard to doubt that Bentham's emphasis on the word, and his connected view that happiness is no more than a sum or aggregation of pleasures, was deliberately provocative. Mill, at any rate, found it an embarrassing inheritance.

It is clear that the first thing that the word *pleasure* puts us in mind of is what may be called bodily or animal pleasures, what Mill was to call the lower pleasures, whose full achievement would still leave Socrates dissatisfied. It is with this application that the word appears in such phrases as 'the pursuit of pleasure' or 'man of pleasure' or 'pleasure-lover'. As the word is ordinarily employed these phrases serve to distinguish some lines of conduct and some types of human being from others. But in Bentham's extended sense they must apply to all intended acts and to all men.

The elementary pleasures of eating, drinking, sexuality, resting and so forth have a number of properties that are broadly common and peculiar to them. First of all, they essentially involve bodily sensation. Secondly, they are almost universally enjoyed, at least to the extent that failure to enjoy them is ordinarily conceived as a basic constitutional abnormality and as in need of explanation. A third feature, connected with their universality, is the fact that they can be profoundly enjoyable although no effort has been involved in experiencing them, in particular that of training for them or acquiring a taste for them. Of course effort is usually necessary to secure the external means to these satisfactions, the meals, drinks or sexual partners required for them. If not too laborious these efforts may augment the satisfactions that reward them. But the satisfaction is not much diminished if it is achieved without effort. Again training in cookery, the choice of wine and amatory technique may intensify the pleasures with which they are connected but they are only indispensable in special and unusual circumstances of jadedness through indulgence.

Finally it is characteristic of pleasures in the colloquial, bodily sense to be much more intensely gratifying than more elevated or spiritual satisfactions. The pains of deprivation are also correspondingly more intense in these cases. But this intensity is very closely linked to short duration. Bodily pleasures tend to preoccupy the consciousness of those who enjoy them while they last but they do not last for very long. This defect of fleetingness does not seem to be compensated for by a correspondingly limited endurance of the pains of being deprived of these sources of pleasure. Hunger, thirst and, perhaps to a lesser extent, sexual frustration show considerable staying power.

Elementary animal pleasures, then, are bodily, universal, need neither effort nor skill for their enjoyment and are characteristically intense although short-lived. If they are what is first brought to mind by the word *pleasure* they do not wholly appropriate it in its colloquial use. Stamp-collecting, deep-sea fishing and playing the cello can be described as pleasures without any trace of metaphor or figurativeness, and so can professional achievement, friendship or being the parent of happy, healthy and successful children. Recreations involve specific bodily activities but of a kind which are negligibly gratifying in themselves; achievements have no definite bodily aspect. Recreations are far from universally pleasing although most achievements, if conceived in a fairly generic way, would seem to be. Both require effort and skill. The pleasure of a recreation cannot be enjoyed at all unless it is engaged in for a period much longer than the ordinary duration of a direct bodily· delight. The pleasure of an achievement is necessarily protracted; it is a continuously satisfying background to the detailed activities and incidents of life.

The cluster of rather significant structural properties that are characteristic of the elementary pleasures provides a good reason for distinguishing among the extremely heterogeneous array of things to which the word *pleasure* can be properly applied or, as Mill puts it, for distinguishing qualities of pleasure. What is questionable about Mill's position on this topic is that he takes this distinction of quality in an evaluative way. To dispel the accusation that the utilitarian advocates the supreme value of bodily gratification he seems to say that a non-bodily pleasure is more valuable than a bodily pleasure that is its quantitative equal, or even superior, in pleasantness. This, at any rate, is what he has been generally taken to mean and with good cause.

To start with, he explicitly says, 'it would be absurd that . . . the estimation of pleasures should be supposed to depend on quantity alone'.[38] Secondly, he plainly rejects the argument a strict Benthamite would employ to demonstrate the superiority of mental to bodily pleasure from what he calls the 'circumstantial advantages' of the former: its greater 'permanency, safety, uncostliness'. The strict Benthamite, or consistent hedonist, would argue that the commonly high estimation, at least in practice, of the pleasures of the body is due to a misguided obsession with intensity at the expense of the other 'dimensions' in which quantitative differences between pleasures are to be found, according to the doctrine of the hedonic calculus. The pleasures of friendship or cello-playing are no doubt less intense than those of heavy eating or dedicated sexuality but they are more enduring, in that they can be practised for a much longer time before pleasure turns into its opposite, are more fecund, in that they can be more pleasurably repeated, and more pure, in that there is less likelihood with them of associated displeasure. Mill does not deny the validity of this line of reasoning as far as it goes but its adherents, he says, 'might have taken the other, and, as it may be called, higher ground, with entire consistency'.

But, as Mill's critics have generally agreed, such a view is *not* consistent with the hedonistic principle that pleasure alone is valuable in itself. If two situations are identical with regard to the amount of pleasure they contain, and, one should add, give rise to, then, if they differ in value, it must be on account of something other than pleasure. Mill's confusion on this point may have been assisted by the fact that *quality*, most notably in the language of advertisement, is itself often an evaluative word.

What has not been noticed is that the reason Mill gives for supposing that mental pleasures are more valuable than bodily ones can very naturally be interpreted as reinstating the identification of value with quantity of pleasure that he ostensibly rejects. His argument for the superiority is that of those who have had a wide experience of pleasures of both kinds all, or almost all, give a 'decided preference' to the former. But what can this decided preference be but the outward sign of a stronger desire for the kind of pleasure preferred? Mill's view is that to desire something is to think it pleasant. It would seem to follow that to desire one thing more than another is to think that it is the more pleasant of the two, to estimate it as quantitatively the greater pleasure.

It is a reasonable conclusion that the intensely respectable Mill was thrown off balance by the kind of moral objection to utilitarianism that Bentham's provocative emphasis on the word 'pleasure' invites. If pleasures are to be compared at all as greater and less it is irrational to concentrate on their intensity to the exclusion of all other respects in which they may relevantly differ. In fact, despite his lip-service to the validity of the circumstantial argument for the superiority of mental to bodily pleasures, Mill does not believe in the hedonic calculus with which it is associated. He insists that pleasures and pains are far too heterogeneous for any mechanical routine of computation to yield acceptable estimations of their quantity of the sort Bentham had in mind. But to deny that pleasure and pain can be appraised by a numerical calculus is not to deny that they can be compared in a more total and impressionistic way and any such comparison will be rational just to the extent that it takes relevant factors other than intensity into account.

None of the other objections that Mill considers in this chapter lead to such substantial amendments of the utilitarianism he derived from Bentham. Two of them are fairly trivial; three others are important in principle but in the form in which Mill confronts them their real point is not made. The two trivial objections are that utilitarianism is godless and that it 'renders men cold and unsympathetic' by fixing their attention on the consequences of actions rather than on the characters of their agents. The example of Paley was available to show that as long as God moves in an unmysterious way, as long as his benevolence consists in a desire for his creatures' happiness in a sense that they can recognise and understand, God's commands can be shown to coincide with the dictates of the principles of utility. On the other point Mill reasonably observes that utilitarian ethics is, in the first instance, a theory of the rightness of actions. Such a theory does not exclude a theory of the praiseworthiness of agents. If it should be completed with an account of virtue or moral goodness this need not differ in form from that with which any theory of right action, however unutilitarian, might be associated, namely that a morally good or virtuous agent is one whose dispositions are calculated to lead to right actions. Since, for utilitarianism, right action leads to general happiness it would seem that benevolence, a desire for the happiness of all, would be the supreme virtue, in his view. It is certainly hard for the utilitarian to detach benevolence from conscientiousness, the desire to act rightly, in the manner of sterner moralities like those of Butler and Kant. To desire the means, right conduct, is to desire its necessary and defining end, the general happiness.

The three more serious objections whose potential force, I have said, Mill does not appreciate, are that happiness is unattainable, that utilitarianism demands too much of men in the way of public spirit and self-effacement, and that it imposes requirements of calculation on moral agents which it is impossible to satisfy.

Mill is disposed to regard the objection that happiness is unattainable as largely a verbal quibble but with a significant point underlying it: that in an imperfect world some self-sacrifice must be required from us. It may well be true that men cannot be absolutely happy all the time, but they can still obtain some happiness. There is a certain lack of polemical energy about this reply. Two powerful considerations that he could have appealed to are, first, that the utilitarian end is not the achievement of total and unqualified happiness but its maximisation to the greatest possible extent together with the greatest possible minimisation of pain and, secondly, that an ideal of conduct does not have to be strictly attainable to be effective: doctors are right not to yield to any discouragement arising from the knowledge that all men are mortal.

The more serious point underlying the objection is that the Benthamite definition of happiness as a sum of pleasures is far too neat and simple to be adequate. Mill does not explicitly dissent from the orthodox formula but he comes near to undermining it when he says that for happiness men need both tranquillity, in which absence of pain is secured at the cost of a low level of pleasure, and excitement, in which intense pleasure is likely but with the added risk of much pain. However, utilitarianism can easily survive the rejection of Bentham's over-simplified additive reduction of happiness to pleasure. The inadequacy of this reduction does not mean that happiness has to be conceived as some mysterious and unanalysable state, logically unrelated to pleasure. A man is happy to the extent that his more persistent and deep-seated desires are either satisfied or are known by him to be readily satisfiable. No aggregation of intense bodily delights can compensate for the frustration of long-term and serious desires for more than a short time. Nevertheless pleasure, in the inclusive sense of the word, remains the essential ingredient of happiness.[39]

A more sophisticated version of this criticism is advanced in the chapter on 'pleasure for pleasure's sake' in Bradley's *Ethical Studies*. Bradley argues that since pleasure is something passing and evanescent, a 'perishing series' is the quaint phrase he uses for it, it is not a logically acceptable general end of conduct. I shall return to this later when I come to consider three classical criticisms of utilitarian ethics.

Mill's observation that self-sacrifice is morally inevitable in an imperfect world is introduced as an acceptable practical limitation to the complete achievement of the utilitarian end. The real difficulty this fact presents is not to his conception of the moral end. (That end is the *general* happiness and it is not surprising that it should require some foregoing of possible individual happiness.) What it does conflict with is the egoistic theory of motivation associated with utilitarian ethics. Mill's solution to that problem is, in the end, Hobbesian. Self-sacrifice is, he argues, despite appearances, a way of satisfying one's desires. By enabling us to rise above fate it contributes to happiness.

The second major objection he considers is that utilitarianism makes too heavy a demand on the moral virtue of the individual. Mill's initial answer, that an action can be right whatever the motive from which it is undertaken, does not really meet it. For the theory does entail that in every situation of choice the agent *ought* to choose that of the options available to him which will make the largest contribution to the general happiness. Mill's initial answer is that in many cases agents will straightforwardly want to choose the most publicly beneficial course anyway. Now this seems reasonable enough if the principle involved is not taken too strictly. It is very often true that agents in a situation of choice do not unreflectively want to do something that will significantly *detract* from the general happiness. Some such negative interpretation of the fundamental utilitarian principle of conduct seems to lie behind Mill's observation that most ordinary people are very seldom in a position to make any significant positive contribution to the general welfare, although they can often act so as to diminish it. But, unless an unplausibly fatalistic conception of what people could do for the general happiness is embraced, this objection can be met only by recasting the principle of utility, as a thesis about morals, in a negative way. In most situations of life people are not doing any positive harm but it is also true that they could be doing more positive good than they are doing, even when this good is not merely that of others but is taken to include their own happiness.

The essential point is that the principle of utility divides all possible choices into two classes: that of what definitely ought to be done, which in every situation, except those in which two or more choices are both equally beneficial and more beneficial than any other alternative, will be unique, and that of what definitely ought not to be done. Thus every choice that is not morally compulsory is morally forbidden. The only morally indifferent choices the principle can countenance are those between alternatives that are at once equally and supremely beneficial.

Even a negative formulation of the principle of utility will not avoid this kind of moral totalitarianism if it requires action to minimise suffering. In most ordinary situations of morally acceptable conduct there is probably something more that the agent could have done to achieve this end than he did. What is needed is a *limited* negative formulation of the principle which lays down that every action that reduces the general happiness should be avoided, unless every possible alternative would reduce it still more. Mill's remarks about the capacity of ordinary agents to augment or diminish the general happiness have the effect of so circumscribing that capacity that the usual unrestricted principle amounts to no more in practical application than its limited, negative version. But the limits he sets to human moral capacity are unrealistically narrow. It may be that men cannot be reasonably expected or enjoined to act in a very much more public-spirited way than they usually do but it seems clear that they could do so all the same.

The third and last of these more serious objections is that utilitarian ethics lays an impossible burden of calculation on the moral agent. In every situation it requires him to determine all the possible lines of action he could adopt, including inaction, and then to calculate what the total consequences for the general happiness of each of these alternatives would be. Mill presents the difficulty in concretely practical terms, as arising from the time the required deliberation would take. His indirect, and rhetorically expressed, answer is that the time available is that of the elapsed and recorded moral experience of the human race. That accumulated experience provides us with knowledge of the moral *tendency* of actions of particular kinds, embodied in rules or principles that are subordinate to the principle of utility itself. This is one of two clear pieces of evidence that Mill was a rule-utilitarian and not an act-utilitarian. In other words his position was not that an act is right because it has good consequences but because it is an act of a kind which generally has good consequences. The other place where he appears to subscribe to the rule-utilitarian doctrine is in his main formulation of the principle of utility, where he says that an act is right if it *tends* to promote happiness. An individual action cannot have a tendency. Producing certain effects more often than not cannot be a characteristic of an individual action which occurs once and once only and has one and only one set of effects. Only a kind or class of actions can have a tendency to promote happiness or anything else.

The necessity of rules, or subordinate principles, as yielding economies of calculation, has been argued for on utilitarian grounds. Effective, value-realising action very often needs to be swift; opportunities pass. Furthermore time should not be wasted. The more of it that is taken up in deliberation the less there will be for effective action. Any greater refinement in evaluation that might be secured by carefully thinking out alternative possible outcomes in a situation of choice is very unlikely to outweigh the benefits of rapidity conferred by reliance on rules. This argument applies the principle of the division of labour to the domain of moral activity. It holds that the reflective task of elaborating general rules of beneficial conduct should be undertaken on the one hand *by* specially qualified people, that is to say moralists, or, on the other, *during* periods of time that are free from exigencies of action. In this way a stock of ready-made rules will be made available for moral agents confronted with the need for choice.

I do not think that this style of argument for rule-utilitarianism gets to the root of the matter. I believe it can be shown that something like rule-utilitarianism must be accepted by any theory which evaluates actions in the light of their consequences. One argument for this conclusion turns on the reasonable, but disputable, view that the consequences of an action that are relevant to its moral quality are not those which it actually has but those which it would be reasonable for an agent to expect it to have.

Another, perhaps more securely based, is derived from the widely held assumption that regularity is an essential element in the concept of causality which must be used in the calculation of consequences.

The first of these arguments may be introduced by reference to a threefold distinction drawn by C. I. Lewis.[40] An action, he says, is *absolutely* right if it has the best actual consequences, *objectively* right if it is reasonable to expect that it will have the best consequences and *subjectively* right if its agent expects it to have the best consequences. Which of these is the central concept? Clearly not that of subjective rightness, for we should naturally say of someone who did an act that was subjectively but not objectively right that he thought that what he was doing was right but that in fact it was not. A reason for taking the objective concept rather than the absolute one as central is that the person to whom the notion of rightness is of primary importance is the agent, who has to decide about its application before the possible action to which it is applied has actually taken place, and therefore before any of its consequences have come about. Only the subsequent critic of action is in a position to determine what is absolutely right. The most the agent can know and act on is the objective rightness of actions. An objectively right act could be described as right *simpliciter* and one which is absolutely but not objectively right, which has unpredictably good consequences, as a merely fortunate act.

If we make this assumption, that a right act is one which it is rational to expect will have the best consequences, something like rule-utilitarianism inevitably follows. For the possible act that is judged right can be expected to have good consequences only by way of the generally beneficial tendency of the set of properties by which it is defined. It is possible for me to do A or B. A is right as against B since its rationally expectable consequences X are better than B's rationally expectable consequences Y. But for A to have the consequences X is only a rational expectation if it is generally the case that acts of *kind* A have consequences of *kind* X. The reasoning required for a rational expectation that a particular act of kind A will have good consequences is inevitably sufficient to establish the rule that acts of kind A are right or, in a comparative case of the sort I started from, that an act of kind A is right as against an act of kind B.

It is now easy to see that it is not essential to the argument that the rightness of an action should be defined in terms of its rationally expectable consequences. Suppose, instead, that rightness is taken in what Lewis calls its absolute sense. In that case the most authoritative and least conjectural judgement about the rightness of an action will have to be made after the event. Now one form such a judgement could take is comparative. We have to compare the consequences of the action actually performed with those of the possible alternatives to it. But, since these, *ex hypothesi*, have not been performed, all that can be done is to work out what consequences it would be rational to expect that they would have had if they had been performed, that is what the general tendency is of actions of those possible, but in this case unperformed, kinds.

If the judgement is comparative, then, at least the consequences of the unperformed alternatives have to be worked out in general terms. But this appeal to general regularities must also be present in establishing the consequences of the act that actually was performed. This is somewhat concealed by the fact that its consequences, unlike those of its alternatives, really occur, but they still have to be selected from the broad array of states of affairs which temporally follow it, to the vast majority of which it will be causally irrelevant. Its consequences proper have to be picked out from the mass of its mere successors, and this can be done only by reference to the known general tendencies of acts of its kind. From this it also follows that, even if judgements of rightness are non-comparative, they have to be based on general truths about the kinds of actions in which the action in question is included. In other words, even if all that has to be considered in deciding whether a particular action is right is its actual consequences these still have to be discriminated, within the large class of events and states which temporally succeed it, by reference to knowledge about the kind of events and states which regularly follow actions of that kind.

This is a very abstract argument and I have been careful to claim no more for it than that it establishes 'something like rule-utilitarianism'. For in the type of case which might seem least propitious for rule-utilitarianism, a non-comparative judgement of the absolute rightness of an action that has actually been performed, although some of the materials for a rule are present the reasoning may not be throughout of the generality required for a rule to be formulated.

Action a_1 of kind A has been performed. It is temporally followed by events and states of affairs $b, c, d \ldots h, i, j \ldots p, q, r$. To pick out c, i and q as its consequences I have to rely on the causal propositions A *causes* C, C *causes* I and I *causes* Q. I also have to rely on what may be called hedonic propositions to establish the goodness of these consequences. If these are of the form C *is pleasant*, then I am in a position to say that, provided the other consequences of A are not so bad as to outweigh this, A is right. But it is possible that c, i, and q, the particular consequences of a_1, are pleasant, although this is not true of $C, I,$ and Q generally. In that case the generality of the premises from which a *is right* is derived is not complete enough for the corresponding rule A *is right* to be established. So only if the hedonic quality of a particular state of affairs is regularly associated with its other properties, in particular those of its properties which would be mentioned in causal propositions about it, will the premises of a utilitarian judgement of rightness contain the materials for a rule. But it seems reasonable to suppose that these hedonic qualities are regularly associated with the other properties of the states of affairs that they characterise. For unless this were the case the pursuit of pleasure and the avoidance of pain would be a much more random and chancy affair than it is. Finally, the fact that the materials for establishing a rule are present in the reasoning that underlies a judgement of rightness does not entail that any such rule is actually formulated. It may facilitate a much greater flexibility in judging the rightness of acts to assemble causal and hedonic knowledge separately. A reason for this is that a great many different pieces of causal and hedonic knowledge may be relevant to a particular judgement of rightness which may be needed in quite different combinations on other occasions.

In the form in which Mill confronts it, the objection that utilitarianism demands too much in the way of calculation is practical. But there is a logical objection to its requirements of calculation which he does not raise. This is that the consequences of an action extend indefinitely into its future and, therefore, that an evaluation of its total consequences is logically impossible. The legendary horse-shoe nail whose loss led to that of a horse, a rider, a charge, a battle, a war and a kingdom is a favourite instance of the incompletable openness of an action's consequences.

It is a virtue of the objective conception of rightness, as Lewis defines it, that it is not exposed to this objection. What is rationally predictable at any given time, in the light of the necessarily finite body of knowledge available at that time, must itself be limited. But this advantage draws attention to a countervailingly unattractive implication of the objective concept. This is that the rightness of an action is relative to the time, more specifically to the state of knowledge prevailing at the time, at which it was decided upon. A type of conduct that was right a hundred years ago may no longer be right, now that we know that its probable consequences are not what it was then rational to expect they would be, even though there has been no change in the relevant external circumstances, in the consequences which actually follow actions of that type, and only a change in the knowledge that an agent can reasonably be expected to have of them. But perhaps the implication is not insupportably unattractive. For it does not follow that any particular action was right at the time it was performed, but subsequently became wrong. The rightness of any particular action is defined, according to the objective concept, in relation to the time it was decided upon, whatever may be the time at which its rightness is being considered.

Suppose that, shortly after his birth, Adolf Hitler was being carried by a decrepit great-aunt who slipped and was confronted with a choice between dropping the infant in a way that would inevitably prove fatal to it or suffering a heavy and painful fall herself. What should she have done? Nearly everyone would have been better off if she had made the former choice and, by dropping the baby, have prevented Nazism, the Second World War and the final solution of the Jewish problem. It would have been the absolutely right decision in Lewis's sense. Since she could not possibly have known the benefits that would accrue to mankind from making the first choice, her decision to take all the unpleasant immediate consequences of her slip on herself was plainly the objectively right thing to do. It is hardly open to doubt that this second choice, however unfortunate it turned out to be, was also the right one pure and simple.

But in fact, although the objective concept does escape the objection of indefinite consequences altogether, there is still an argument by means of which the absolute concept can avoid most of its impact. This argument draws on the plurality of causes to show that the share of the badness of some consequential state of affairs attributable to individual causal factors decreases as some multiple of their remoteness. In the Hitler example it is reasonable to suppose that his historically disastrous personality was fully formed in infancy. No doubt humiliations and disappointments in his early life contributed to it and must, therefore, share some of the causal responsibility for it. But even if his personality was innate, a vast array of contributory conditions had to obtain for it to be able to exercise its massively maleficent effect: the treaty of Versailles, the German inflation of the 1920s, Stalin's policy for the German Communist party and so on.

In general, the colloquial convenience of picking out some notably manageable or unusual factor as *the* cause of a given state of affairs should not be allowed to obscure the fact that a large number of conditions must obtain for any effect to be produced. Causes are always plural. It follows that the direct causal ancestry of an effect multiplies with each step backwards in the effect's causal hierarchy. Many of these causal progenitors of an event will either be human actions or events that human action could have prevented, and thus within the proper domain of moral judgement. Given that at each stage the plurality of causes involved is fairly numerous the proportion of responsibility for the effect that can be reasonably imputed to any single factor at any remote stage will be vanishingly small.

In the case of the lost horse-shoe the farrier cannot be given all the blame for the loss of the kingdom. The rider should have been adroit enough to survive the horse's fall; the troop commander should not have ordered a charge whose chances of success were so finely balanced; the army commander should have been able to overcome the misfortune of an unsuccessful charge; and so on. The final disaster, in other words, was the result of a collaborative effort, in which many besides the careless farrier participated.

(iii) THE SANCTIONS OF MORALITY

Having removed as misunderstandings what were offered as objections, and having, in the course of doing so, introduced his damaging and unnecessary qualification about qualities of pleasure, Mill turns to the question of explaining the motives men have for conforming their conduct to the principle of utility. It is not clear why Mill should have chosen to take up the topic of the motives of morality at this stage in his exposition. The principle of utility is the crucial element in an account of the meaning of moral judgements or, it might be less abrupt to say, an account of the rational method of arriving at moral judgements; it provides an ultimate criterion of truth for such judgements. The question which he now raises – why should anyone act on such judgements, how can their practical effect on conduct be psychologically explained – is apparently independent of the initial question of their validity.

For most of the last fifty years moral philosophers have been developing theories in which the practical, action-guiding force of moral judgements is taken to be an essential part of their meaning. An influential example of theories of this kind is that a moral principle is, and a moral judgement implies, a universal imperative, of the form: *let everyone do X in circumstances Y*. Such a theory gives an account of the meaning of moral affirmations which automatically settles the question about motives. No one will seriously call on everyone, including himself, to act in a certain way unless he wants himself and others to act in that way. The difficulty for theories of this kind is the subjectivisation of morality that it implies. Agreement in moral attitudes becomes accidental, or at least contingent. Again, while it is clear enough why one who makes a moral judgement should guide his own actions in accordance with it, it is not at all clear why his expression of it to anyone else should be supposed to be effective unless they happen to share his moral attitudes or fear him or aim to please him.

Mill's concern with motivation may be a sign that he does implicitly recognise that practical effectiveness is somehow intimately bound up with moral judgements. A more direct incentive to taking up the question is provided by one of the essential elements of his 'proof' of the principle of utility in the chapter following that in which he discusses the sanctions of morality. He argues there that the only thing that men desire for its own sake is pleasure. If the assumption, which he undoubtedly made, that all action is prompted by desire, is added to this thesis, the conclusion follows that all action is ultimately for the sake of the agent's own pleasure. In the light of this conclusion Mill, if he is to represent moral judgements, in their utilitarian interpretation, as practically effective, must show that the pursuit of the general happiness is or can be a source of pleasure to men, that it is an actual or rational object of desire, that it is pleasing in itself or is a means to pleasure.

But, placed as it is before the argument that the principle of utility depends on the hedonistic theory of motivation, Mill's consideration of the sanctions of morality is a little confusing. It is one thing to inquire how men are to find out what they morally ought to do, another to ask whether they can be expected, and how they can be got, to do it.

Bentham's account of the sanctions of morality is largely

Hobbesian and external. Our actions can be influenced by their
natural consequences, occurring independently of the human
will, by the state through its penal institutions, by the reactions of
our fellow-humans to what we do and by the reactions of God
in this life and the next. Mill begins by recognising that the principle of utility, because it is not the customary basis of morality,
is not an object of unreflective moral emotion. The idea of deviation from it does not immediately excite the same disapproval as a
familiar moral offence. He also recognises that there are external
sanctions: 'the hope of favour and the fear of displeasure, from
our fellow-creatures or from the Ruler of the Universe'.[41] But his
main emphasis is on the internal sanctions: 'the conscientious
feelings of mankind'.

There is a kind of natural basis for these conscientious feelings
in sympathy with and affection for our fellows; but conscience
itself is something more than these natural emotions. 'It is a pain,
more or less intense, attendant on violation of duty, which in
properly cultivated moral natures rises, in the more serious cases,
into shrinking from it as an impossibility.'[42] Even if it is acquired
rather than innate, as Mill's reference to 'properly cultivated
moral natures' seems to suggest, it is still natural, as much as it is
to speak or reason, or to live in societies, for whose secure continuance the existence of a measure of concern for the general
welfare among their members is an indispensable condition. 'The
moral faculty, if not a part of our nature, is a natural outgrowth
from it.'[43]

Mill allows that education can cause the moral faculty to develop
in any of a number of directions. He admits, too, that subsequent
'analysis' may undo the work of education and dissolve the
associations it has set up. But, he argues, utilitarian morality is
protected from this danger by being rooted in natural sentiment,
in 'the social feelings of mankind', 'the desire to be in unity with
our fellow-creatures'.

Throughout this chapter Mill reasonably insists that there is no
special problem for utilitarian morality, as compared with any
other system, in accounting for action in accordance with it.

His main contribution is his argument that there are internal as well as external sanctions for utilitarian morality. Action in accordance with the requirements of morality can be, in terms of a distinction he draws in the following chapter, a *part of* as well as a *means to* happiness. What begins as a more or less onerous means to some end that we desire may come to be desired for itself. Mill's illustration of this phenomenon is miserliness. A miser is one for whom money has ceased to be what it is for most men, an intrinsically uninteresting means to getting what they desire, and has become a thing desired for its own sake.

This is an unfortunate illustration since it is hard to conceive the miser's attitude to money as anything but a pathological aberration. The association of ideas often brings about the transference of an attitude, that is perfectly reasonable when adopted towards a certain thing, to something else associated with it in a striking way, which is not a reasonable object of the attitude in question. A person who has been very badly treated by a bearded man may come to fear and hate everyone who has a beard. But such associative transfers of emotion can be rational and life-enhancing, above all when they are connected with the discovery of new potentialities of satisfaction. An adolescent ploughs through D. H. Lawrence in pursuit of pornographic matter and comes to acquire a taste for writing that is more passionate, original and imaginative than the works of Ian Fleming. A man who settles down grimly to clearing a way from the front door of his house to the gate may come gradually to be entranced with horticulture. Liking what one gets can enlarge one's ability to get what one likes.

In fact it is unrealistic to suppose that the acquisition of a moral faculty, the development of conscientious feelings, is a kind of taste that is acquired by comparatively mature human beings. The foundations of the conscience, as Freud's theory of the super-ego contends, are laid very early in life. Approved conduct is chosen, against the pressure of instinctive impulses of selfishness and aggression, at an early stage of life as a means to the preservation of parental affection. The 'introjection' of parental commands that Freud speaks of is much the same thing as Mill's associative transfer of desire from end to means.

With maturity what Mill calls 'analysis' may tend to weaken the hold of this early conditioning. In effect, Mill's argument is that unreflective morality, authoritatively implanted in childhood, may be preserved in a new form when, with the achievement of reason, it is reconstructed on utilitarian foundations. The universal human need for a peaceable and co-operative society is better calculated to withstand the effects of rational criticism than the wishes of parents who no longer are so powerful and no longer seem so wise, or of a God whose existence may be doubtful.

(iv) THE PROOF OF THE PRINCIPLE OF UTILITY

Mill begins the handful of pages, as much discussed as any in moral philosophy, which he devotes to the proof of the principle of utility, by reiterating what he had said at the outset. 'Questions of ultimate ends are not amenable to direct proof,' but an 'equivalent to proof' is available. 'Considerations may be presented capable of determining the intellect either to give or to withhold its assent.'[44] Before we examine the considerations, supposedly equivalent to proof, that Mill presents there are two preliminary comments to be made.

The first is that Mill's thesis about the unprovable nature of ultimate ends is based on a very restricted conception of what could be admitted as a proof in this kind of case. 'Whatever can be proved to be good, must be so by being shown to be a means to something admitted to be good without proof.' If that is all that proof can be then it is a tautology that ultimate ends cannot be proved. That, whose goodness does not derive from the goodness of something else, cannot be shown to be good by deriving its goodness from that of something else.

To illustrate his point Mill says, 'the medical art is proved to be good by its conducing to health; but how is it possible to prove that health is good?'[45] One way in which the goodness of health could be proved is by showing that it is a necessary truth, arising from the fact that 'to be healthy' *means* 'to be in a good bodily condition'. First principles *can* be proved, by demonstration rather than by derivation from other truths of the same kind, provided that they are implicit definitions. The task of substantiating the underlying truths about meaning which render such first principles necessary is not likely to be simple. An appeal to intuition, or, less mysteriously, to the evident contradictoriness of the negation of the first principle in question, is almost bound to fail. If the necessity of the first principle had been obvious its truth would never have been put in question.

What has to be done is to develop the logical consequences of the assumption that the first principle under discussion is false until something whose contradictoriness is evident is reached. Alternatively, competing first principles have to be examined by applying them to circumstances in which acceptable consequences can be secured only if the original first principle is assumed. Mill is no doubt right in thinking that questions about ultimate ends are not amenable to *direct* proof. But that does not mean that they cannot be proved at all.

The second preliminary point is that the argument that Mill actually produces, with a view to 'determining the intellect either to give or to withhold its assent', is a proof, in a strict sense of the term, or, rather it is a deductive argument that would be a proof if its premises were true and the steps of reasoning it contains were valid. There is nothing at all roundabout or indirect about it, on the one hand, nor is it a matter of suggestion or persuasion, but has a strictly inferential form, on the other. Let us look at the argument itself.

Its first step is an affirmation of the principle of psychological hedonism: *pleasure, or happiness, is the only thing that men desire for its own sake*. The form in which this is put for the next stage of the argument is that each man (ultimately) desires nothing but his own pleasure. The second thesis may be called the principle of subjective ethical hedonism: *each man's pleasure is a good to him*. The connecting-link between this and the first principle is the claim that nothing can be desirable, or good, but what is actually desired. The final step in the argument is the derivation of the principle of objective ethical hedonism: *the general happiness is good for all*, which Mill sees as a direct consequence of the proposition that each man's happiness is a good, or the ultimate good, for him.

The third paragraph of Mill's fourth chapter suffices for the presentation of this argument. The remainder of the chapter is concerned to show that not only do men desire pleasure but that, in the end, they desire nothing else, that pleasure, or happiness, is the sole (ultimate) object of desire. His procedure here is to argue that all goods, or objects of desire, that appear to be distinct from pleasure or happiness are either means to it, and thus not ultimate objects of desire, or else are parts of happiness, in the sense discussed in the previous section. 'Whatever', he says, 'is desired otherwise than as a means to some end beyond itself, and ultimately to happiness, is desired as itself a part of happiness.'[46]

Mill's account of the status of his initial premise that pleasure alone is the ultimate object of desire is obscure. On the one hand he says that it is a fact of experience; on the other that 'desiring a thing and finding it pleasant . . . are phenomena entirely inseparable . . . two different modes of naming the same psychological fact'.[47] The first implies that it is a truth of empirical psychology, that could logically be false but in fact is not; the second that it is an analysis or conceptual truth, of the kind to which in his *System of Logic* he applied the phrase 'propositions merely verbal'. The same unresolved duality attaches to his concluding observation: 'to desire anything, except in proportion as the idea of it is pleasant, is a physical and metaphysical impossibility'.[48]

It will assist clarity at this point if two arguments that are commonly urged against Mill's first thesis are considered. Both rest on misunderstandings of his intent that are so unmitigatedly obvious that it is hard to credit the critics who exhibit them with both intellectual honesty and a minimum capacity for abstract reasoning. The first of them identifies pleasure with bodily pleasure, the lower quality of pleasure that Mill has laboured to distinguish from pleasure of a more elevated kind. On this interpretation Mill's thesis is a simple empirical falsehood. Bodily pleasure is, indeed, as nearly *universal* an object of desire as could be asked for. But it is quite obviously not the exclusive object of human desire. Men want power, status, achievement and a host of other things which have no essential bodily ingredient. This objection does not really deserve the name of criticism. It is a form of lazy abuse, no doubt expressive of thoughtless moral excitement, which merely discredits its proponents.

The second misunderstanding is rather more interesting. This maintains that it is not merely false that men desire only pleasure but that it is logically impossible that they should desire pleasure at all. What is desired is always some specific thing: a glass of wine, a good-looking woman, a peerage. The achievement of these objects is no doubt attended with pleasure, but it is the objects and not the pleasure that is desired. Why should it be supposed that the desire for some specific thing is not a desire for the pleasure that the thing can provide? After all what is desired is the thing in circumstances in which it will give pleasure. Suppose I have a desire for a glass of wine. More explicitly what I desire is to drink it. But that is not quite explicit enough. I shall not be satisfied if I am rendered unconscious and the wine is poured into my mouth and got down my throat while I am in that state.

It is true that all pleasure is pleasure from some fairly specific experience. There is no such thing as the enjoyment of pleasure by itself. A man who says 'Now I want some pleasure' but rejects every specific pleasant thing that is offered him – the coffee, the steak and kidney pudding, the swimming pool – not because he does not think that those particular things will please him, but because, he says, he wants pleasure in itself, uncontaminated by containment in any such concrete vehicle, is talking nonsense. Pleasure, one might say, is not a stuff but a relation. One can, of course, enjoy oneself and get pleasure without being able to say precisely what it is that is pleasing about one's situation. This will commonly happen when one is doing something so familiar as to seem intrinsically uninteresting, like combing one's hair or dressing, or something that is ordinarily taken to be more or less unpleasant, like washing up or shovelling manure. But even here one is not experiencing pleasure pure and simple, one is enjoying whatever the ordinarily uninteresting or disagreeable activity one is engaged upon is.

A man who seeks pleasure by itself and not the pleasure of something is like a business-man who seeks to reduce costs and yet who wants to do so without reducing the costs of any particular factor of production in his enterprise. But just as a business-man is efficient, in part, to the extent that he reduces costs, whatever they are the costs of, so an agent can desire pleasure, even if it is always the pleasure of some particular thing.

What perhaps lends some slight colour to this objection is Mill's tendency to say that men never desire anything but pleasure or that the ultimate object of desire is pleasure by itself. But these ways of speaking need not be taken in the absurd interpretation against which the objection is directed. If a specific pleasure-giving thing is logically implied by pleasure then to desire pleasure is necessarily also to desire some such thing. What Mill means by saying that nothing but pleasure is desired is that a thing cannot be desired unless it is conceived as pleasant. It is this that he holds to be a 'physical and metaphysical impossibility'.

Incidentally, at the point at which this phrase occurs, Mill identifies desiring a thing with the idea of it being pleasant. This is fairly clearly a slip. What a desire for something is, or at any rate necessarily implies, is the belief that the thing if obtained will be pleasing, is an idea of it, in other words, *as pleasant*. But that is very far from being the same thing as the thought or idea of the thing being itself pleasant. Whether or not the desire is itself pleasant will depend on the desirer's belief about the likelihood of its being satisfied. If his belief is that it is not in the least likely to be satisfied, then, the more pleasant he conceives the object of desire to be, the less pleasant, the more frustratedly painful, his desire for it will be.

This is a convenient point for a parenthetical comment on a related view which holds, not that the pursuit of pleasure is impossible, but that it is inevitably self-frustrating. Anyone, it has been said, who deliberately aims at pleasure is bound to be disappointed. Pleasure is, as a matter of psychological necessity, a by-product of the pursuit of other things for their own sakes. There is no doubt something to be said for this view, if pleasure is taken in its narrow, bodily sense. Intensely desired and intensely satisfying in the short run, bodily pleasures lack staying power. Few of those who can afford as much food and drink as they can physically contain accord them a very large place in their system of satisfactions. It is more common to make the pursuit of women a way of life but this would seem to owe its appeal to a great extent to its impurity from a bodily point of view. It is the pride of conquest, not sensuality, the power and the respect that he acquires, that keep Don Juan going. A harem would interest him no more than larders full of expensive food would gratify the person who likes to be seen at the best restaurants.

It is also true that many situations are pleasing only because they are spontaneous and unplanned. A car-trip designed like a major military operation may be oppressively dull. But there is no paradox in planning for unplanned pleasure. There are decisions, like where to stop for a picnic lunch, which can quite rationally be left to chance impulse. But, in general, it is rational to pursue pleasure and avoid its opposite deliberately. Provided that you can understand it, it is wiser to study the menu than to pick something at random.

There is a sense in which it is true that only pleasure is desired. To desire something is, in part, to conceive of it as something that will give pleasure. Expected pleasure is a logical shadow cast by desire. Or again, pleasure is the internal accusative of desire. It is important to see that the pleasure to which desire is logically or internally related is *expected* pleasure. Desired objects often turn out not to be pleasant when achieved, or not to be as pleasant as was expected. In such cases it is rational to look for some feature of the circumstances which can explain the failure. If none can be found the failure should be noted, to modify the desire for that kind of thing in the future.

The initial premise of Mill's proof is, then, a tautology, in the only sense, at any rate, in which it is true. Furthermore, the sense of pleasure involved is the most inclusive and attenuated sense of the word that is possible. It seems unlikely, to say the least, that anything as controversial as the utilitarian principle could follow deductively from such a proposition together with a handful of other comparably uncontroversial assumptions.

But, in fact, the assumption which Mill invokes to arrive at the next stage of his proof is very far from uncontroversial. Universal execration has justly fallen on his view that only what is actually desired is desirable. Mill's critics uniformly and correctly observe that *desirable* means *ought to be desired* and not *can be desired*. It could further be objected that although the fact that something *is* desired is good, and, indeed, logically conclusive, evidence that it *can* be desired, the two are not, as Mill seems to suggest, one and the same (unless, which is perhaps the case, everything that it is possible to conceive as the object of a desire has been desired by somebody, somewhere).

What Mill attempts to do with this assumption is to establish a connection between desire and value. The excessively simple connection he asserts between them is that of identity. But the blatant unacceptability of his account of the connection does not mean that there is no logical relationship between them at all. It is a verbal truism that the desirable is of value; it is another that the desirable is that which ought to be desired. Could this last notion not be interpreted as *that which it would be rational to desire?* Now, considered in itself and without relation to other desires, the only feature of a desire which would expose it to criticism as regards its rationality is the necessarily implied belief that its object will, when achieved, yield satisfaction. One case, at any rate, in which a desire can be condemned as irrational is that in which the implied belief about the satisfyingness of its object is false. The obvious, paradigm instance of an irrational desire is one the achievement of whose object will prove displeasing to the agent. In the nature of the case this must be a fact he does not realise, for if he did the desire would disappear.

It might be objected that this conception of the rationality of a desire is merely prudential, that it identifies the desirable with that which a man ought, in prudence and for the sake of his own advantage, to desire. A partial reply to this objection is that in many cases it is to just this property of a situation that the word *desirable* is used to refer. When a house-agent describes a house as desirable or a doctor says that it is desirable for someone to winter in a warmer climate it is just this property that he has in mind. But it is a natural extension of the concept of the desirable to convert the prudential formula – that which would satisfy *anyone* – into the moral formula of utilitarianism – that which would satisfy *everyone*.

I have called this generalised or socialised concept of the desirable a 'natural extension' of the self-regarding or prudential concept. But a 'natural extension' is not an argument. A doubter might well regard it as a verbal confusion of a familiar kind about the two ordinary-language quantifiers 'anyone' and 'everyone'. Sometimes these terms can be substituted for each other without change of meaning, but sometimes they cannot. To borrow Quine's example: the affirmative sentences 'John can outrun anyone' and 'John can outrun everyone' mean the same; but their negations 'John cannot outrun anyone' and 'John cannot outrun everyone' very definitely do not.

It remains true, however, as C. I. Lewis has often insisted, that there is nothing peculiar or figurative about the use of such evaluative terms as 'ought' and 'good' in prudential discourse about the advantage of particular agents.[49] In discourse of this kind judgements of the desirability or value of things undoubtedly rest on their satisfyingness to those agents. Where the satisfaction involved is one which is universally felt the judgement can be expressed impersonally. To judge that such-and-such is a good car or headache-reliever is to assert that it would prove satisfying to anyone who wanted to own a car or relieve a headache. But sometimes the conditions of individual satisfaction differ as between one person and another: a woman who would make Smith very happy might do the opposite for

Jones and so would be a good wife for one but not for the other.

The prudential consideration of actions is concerned only with the satisfyingness or otherwise of those consequences to a particular agent. There are many actions all of whose significant consequences of this kind relate only to the particular agent. But equally there are many actions which contribute to or detract from the satisfaction of many people. It is these actions pre-eminently which are the field of application of moral judgement.

Now the conclusion that Mill reaches at the second stage of his proof of the principle of utility is that each man's happiness is a good to him. Although he bases it on the unacceptable assumption that what is good or desirable for a given person is simply what he desires, the conclusion can be given a more compelling basis. A man's prudential good is not what he does desire, I have argued, but what it would be rational for him to desire. In the first instance, this is what would in fact satisfy him, whether he realises it or not. Less restrictedly, it is what, through the totality of its consequences, yields the greatest satisfaction to the whole system of his likes and dislikes, his appetites and aversions. So, if the reasoning behind the second stage of Mill's argument is revised, it can be claimed on Mill's behalf that something amounting to a proof of a hedonistic principle of prudence is possible. The problem that remains is to justify the utilitarian account of the morally desirable as that which would yield satisfaction to *everyone*, corresponding to the account of the prudentially desirable as that which would yield satisfaction to anyone. It needs to be shown that this natural extension, as I have called it, of the concept of the desirable is a legitimate manœuvre and not the result of a failure to distinguish between the distributive and the collective ways of referring to people in general.

In the third and final stage of his proof Mill attempts to do this by arguing that since, as he claims to have shown, each man's happiness is a good to him, the general happiness is a good to all, to 'the aggregate of all persons', and thus is good in itself and without qualification. Here again a conclusion that is not in itself unreasonable is prejudiced by being derived in a hopelessly defective way. Mill, as is universally agreed, has committed a gross fallacy of composition. From *each man's X is Y to him* it simply does not follow that *every man's X is Y to everyone*. It certainly does not follow from the fact that each man's dreams are fascinating to him that everyone's dreams are fascinating to everyone. It would, perhaps, be possible, with a little strain, to take the word 'everyone' in the sentence 'everyone's dreams are fascinating to everyone' in a distributive sense, in which case it would be no more than an ungainly restatement of the premise. But that would not suffice for Mill's purpose. His final conclusion is that the *happiness of everyone, taken as a whole*, is a good to everyone. All that follows from the fact that each man finds his own dreams fascinating is that each man finds some part of the totality of men's dreams fascinating and that every part of that totality is fascinating to someone. Likewise the fact that each man's happiness is good to him implies only that each man finds some part of the general happiness good to him and that every part of the general happiness is good to someone. But what Mill wants to prove is that the general happiness, taken as a whole, is good to everyone.

One way in which moral philosophers have tried to do this is by giving a prudential answer to the question: why should I be moral? Men are social beings, both practically and emotionally. It is a practical or external condition of their well-being that they should be members of a happy community and, more particularly, a community that does not blame them for any of the unhappiness it suffers. It is also emotionally necessary to the happiness of most men, of all but the small minority of psychopaths who have failed to respond to moral education in childhood, that they should not know or think themselves to be responsible for the sufferings of others.

In other words, the general happiness is a good, a rational object of desire, to everyone, in view of the practical and emotional dependence of everyone on others. Now this familiar line of reasoning is rather generally thought to be insufficient. It seems to degrade morality by reducing it to mere policy, an insurance against social disorder, revenge and guilt. To some extent this ignores the fact that the general happiness is an emotional as well as a practical condition of individual happiness or, in Mill's terms, that it is a part of individual happiness rather than a means to it, something internally as well as externally sanctioned. But even if this is borne in mind some further support seems necessary.

I think that there are three further considerations that can be adduced in support of the utilitarian principle that the general happiness, or something closely related to it, is the ultimate moral criterion. (1) The first of these arises from the problem of attempting to provide a criterion which will distinguish moral values and principles from values and principles of other kinds, such as prudential, technical, aesthetic or hygienic.[50] In recent times moral philosophers have followed Kant in offering formalistic solutions to this problem. The distinguishing feature of moral principles, it has been claimed, is that they are *universalisable*, in the sense that to apply them to anybody is implicitly to apply them to everybody, or *autonomous*, in that subscription to them must be freely chosen and not by submission to an external authority, or *overriding*, in that they are supreme in any case where they come into conflict with principles of other kinds.

I believe that all of these three formal criteria of morality are inadequate. Certainly all moral principles are universalisable, but then so are all other rational prescriptions for or recommendations of conduct. If I ought prudentially to save some of my income then so ought everyone else placed as I am. Universalisability is a necessary, but not a sufficient, condition of the moral status of a principle. Autonomy is an obscure requirement. If it means that a principle is not moral unless it is a creative innovation on the part of its exponent then it is not peculiar to morality, for there are technical innovations, nor is it a necessary condition of the morality of a principle of conduct, unless no docile conformist could be a moral agent. If it means the sincere endorsement of professed principles then it is just as applicable in the other, non-moral fields of conduct. There is also obscurity about the interpretation of overridingness. Does it mean that a principle is moral if and only if it *does in fact* prevail over principles with conflicting implications for conduct or if and only if it *should* do so. The first view leads to wildly counter-intuitive results, for example, that a man who prudently restrains his charitable impulses does not accept charity as a moral obligation. The second view involves a vicious circularity.[51]

In the face of these difficulties a material criterion of morality, in terms of its subject-matter, is plainly indicated. What material aspect of actions makes them liable to moral consideration? Generally, it would seem their bearing, favourable or unfavourable, on the interests, happiness or welfare of the people affected by the actions in question.

(2) This conclusion is supported by some rather obvious, if diffuse, empirical facts about what is ordinarily regarded as morality. Most codes of conduct that are unreflectively recognised as moral prohibit, with occasional exceptions, killing, injuring or inflicting physical pain on other people, taking their property, telling them lies, breaking promises made to them. Now all of these are actions which are calculated, if not by logic then by the most obvious and irresistible causality, to cause suffering. Most such codes also call for active benevolence, at least to the extent of alleviating suffering, if not of positively augmenting existing happiness.

Not only does a negatively utilitarian conception of the ultimate moral end, as the prevention of suffering, cover most of the broad principles which would commonsensically be held to be the foundation of a moral code. It also explains the exceptions that are customarily admitted to these broad principles. Killing is permitted for self-defence, in war or as legal execution. The property of others can be appropriated in an emergency. The duties of truth-telling and promise-keeping can be overridden if it is plain that much more suffering will ensue if they are kept than if they are broken.

(3) Essentially the same point is made by an inference it is natural to draw from the fact of the temporal and spatial variety of moral convictions. It is notorious that conflicting moral ideas

prevail in communities that are historically or geographically distinct from each other. Once madmen were beaten. The purpose was the utilitarian one of rendering them sane again. The means adopted were appropriate to the false belief that madmen were possessed by demons, who were expected to vacate a physical container that was being beaten. Those who come to think of this theory of demonic possession as false replace the flail as therapeutic instrument by the analyst's couch. In either case the underlying reasoning is utilitarian.

Eskimoes, we are told, endorse euthanasia of the unproductively aged. In a society living at the very margin of subsistence the survival of all has to be bought at the cost of the lives of some. Those who cannot now or in the future make any contribution to what is necessary for the society's survival are the natural candidates for sacrifice. Utility selects them as those whose going will bring about the smallest overall loss of welfare.

The hard core of morality, then, as it is ordinarily conceived, is utilitarian in character, at least negatively. Furthermore, the theory that the principle of utility is fundamental to morals affords, in conjunction with the manifest differences of belief that there are about the causes of happiness and suffering and of circumstances in which actions and their hedonic consequences are differently related, a coherent explanation of many of the differences of moral opinion as between differently informed or circumstanced societies. It is also a considerably more plausible reaction to the fact of large-scale moral disagreement than the subjectivist conclusion that ultimate moral convictions are simply a matter of brute, unarguable preference.

Mill's 'proof' of the principle of utility is by no means the tissue of errors most of its critics have supposed. Much of it is defensible as it stands: that the object of desire, and thus of action, is expected pleasure and that there is an intimate connection between value and desire, in that what is good for a person is what he would desire if he were rational, namely that which being really pleasant, would fulfil the expectations of pleasure which, in desiring it, he ascribes to it. The weakest point is the transition from this latter conclusion to the utilitarian principle itself, that the good of all is really identical with the good of each. The argument from the external sanctions of morality shows that the good of all is a *causal condition* of the good of each. It is hard to be happy in a generally miserable society and individual happiness in such circumstances is likely to be very insecure, especially if the individual in question comes to be seen by his fellows as responsible for some of their misery. The argument from internal sanctions shows that the good of all is *part* of the good of each. We have an intense interest in the welfare of some other people and some direct interest in the welfare of nearly everyone. What has not been shown is that the good of all is the total, ultimate and overriding good of each. But this, for all the lip-service that is paid to it, is a very extreme and millennial belief. Its truth is not necessary to substantiate the hard, common-sensical core of morality, for this does not require that we should devote ourselves in a totally disinterested way to the general welfare but, more modestly, that we should abstain from positive injury to others and, perhaps, alleviate their sufferings where it is not too prejudicial to our own welfare to do so. For this more restricted policy each of us has good and sufficient reasons of interest, externally sanctioned. The morally heroic or supererogatory conduct of the saint is rational only for those whose direct concern for the welfare of others is of a scope and intensity which are not to be found in the structure of interests derived from the innate constitution and moral education of most of us.

(v) JUSTICE AND UTILITY

The most persistent objection to the claim of utilitarianism to impart rationality and coherence to ordinary moral beliefs is that it fails to substantiate our unreflective convictions about justice. The point can be made more forcefully. There are principles of justice, it may be held, which are at once more certain or self-evident than the principle of utility and yet which are not compatible with it. Mill addresses himself to this problem in the fifth and concluding chapter of *Utilitarianism*. His discussion has many merits. It covers a great deal of ground, especially in elaborating the various more or less distinct ideas which the word 'justice' has been used to convey. But he does not really engage himself fully and satisfactorily with the main difficulties that common convictions about justice put in the way of the position he is defending.

These difficulties are two in number. The first concerns distribution. The principle of utility, it is objected, evaluates actions only by reference to the total amount of good or evil, pleasure or pain, that they produce. But, the objection continues, it is intuitively obvious that two actions which bring about resulting situations that are identical in the overall balance of good and evil they contain will differ very markedly in value if, for example, the good and evil involved are equally distributed in one case but very unequally distributed in the other.

The second difficulty concerns rules. It is objected that two actions that produce identical overall amounts of good and evil will differ in value if one involves the breach of a rule, such as that of promise-keeping or truth-telling, but the other does not.

In his discussion of justice Mill does have a little to say about the problem of distribution, making the rather perfunctory claim that it is catered for by Bentham's formulation of the greatest happiness principle. The reference to the happiness of the greatest number in that formulation, Mill contends, secures the equality of treatment on which the exponents of justice insist. But he does not have anything to say here about the problem of rules and it may be reasonably complained that, for all its merits, his chapter on the subject never really takes the measure of the difficulties which the notion of justice presents to the utilitarian.

The issues Mill does concern himself with are somewhat tangential to the more serious difficulties. First, he considers the objection that there is a direct conflict between justice and the utilitarians' *summum bonum*: expediency. At this level of generality it is easy enough for him to dismiss the conflict as merely verbal.

He can freely admit that there are frequent divergences between the claims of justice and personal or individual expediency, which is what we usually have in mind when we use the word. But the expediency which the utilitarian regards as the ultimate moral criterion is not personal but public; it is the general happiness and not individual advantage. This fails to meet the point that there are apparent conflicts between justice and what is *socially* expedient, to take a familiar example, the exemplary punishment of an innocent man.

His second, and principal, concern is the claim that there is a natural or instinctive sense of justice which yields injunctions incompatible with those implied by the principle of utility. Since he admits that even if it were natural and instinctive that would not imply the validity of its pronouncements, his attempt to show that it is nevertheless explainable in terms of self-preservative and sympathetic impulses, which are acknowledged by the utilitarian theory of human nature and which constitute the psychological foundation of the principle of utility itself, is lacking in theoretical interest.

Mill discerns five different notions of justice: (1) respect for legal rights, (2) respect for moral rights, the rights accorded by an ideal system of law, (3) distribution in accordance with desert, (4) keeping faith or fulfilling reasonable and justified expectations and (5) impartiality. He sees that the idea of equality is intimately associated with that of justice and suggests, on etymological grounds, that the basic notion of justice, underlying its varied specific senses, is that of conformity to law, actual or ideal.

He then goes on to argue that the distinction between the obligations of justice and the other obligations of morality more or less coincides with that traditionally drawn by moralists between perfect duties, which are correlative to a right possessed by a particular individual, and imperfect duties, such as that of charity, which are not. The perfect obligations of justice, he goes on, are the most important part of justice. What they are chiefly concerned with is abstention from doing harm to others, either by aggression against the persons or property of other people or by failure to comply with their justified expectations about one's conduct in relation to them, as in breaking promises and telling lies. What makes these obligations the most important that there are is that the ordinary person's power to affect the welfare of his own fellow-men is largely confined to the field that they cover.

Although there is much to be said for Mill's view that abstention from acts that would harm others is the most important part of morality, the point has nothing very much to do with justice. Murder, assault, theft, lying and promise-breaking are ordinarily (or, in the case of murder and theft, necessarily) wrong. They are, indeed, invasions or floutings of the rights of their victims, but they are not exactly unjust, at any rate in the current sense of that word, any more than incest, the favourite example of an act, which though morally wrong, is not unjust. What is primarily wrong with murder is that a man is *killed*, not that *he*, rather than somebody else, is.

Justice, as we understand it and in the sense in which it is commonly alleged to be unprovided for by utilitarianism, is first and foremost a distributive notion. It applies primarily to the comparative allocation of benefits and burdens as between different people. The simplest criterion of justice is equality. But its simplicity is somewhat spurious: different concrete modes of treating people can each make a claim to being truly equal treatment. As Mill himself observes, communists, who agree that there ought to be equality of incomes, disagree as to what precisely this equality consists in. Is it a matter of strictly identical income for each person or of proportioning income to needs or of proportioning income to the individual's productive contribution to the pool from which income is distributed? More generally, Mill makes the point that the requirements of justice are no less controversial than those of utility. He cites income-distribution, taxation and punishment as practices or institutions whose just administration is a matter of persistent dispute. Should taxation, for example, be a fixed proportion of income or should it be graduated so that the rich pay a higher rate of tax or should it be the same for all, the services of government being conceived like any other marketable good?[52]

Mill's claim that the intuitive demand for equality of treatment is sufficiently catered for by Bentham's reference to 'the greatest number' in his formulation of the principle of utility is unconvincing. If anything it draws attention to a defect in that formulation. Suppose that one of two alternative actions causes a large amount of happiness to a small number of people while the other produces a smaller aggregate of happiness but distributes it more widely. Bentham's formula suggests at least that the aggregate happiness involved in the two outcomes is not decisive, that it has to be balanced against width of distribution for a final evaluation. In fact what Bentham seems to have intended is that the criterion of value is the happiness of everyone affected. This does provide a minimal equality of treatment: an adequate evaluation of an action must take into account the happiness or suffering of all who are affected by it. Does the utilitarian principle, thus interpreted, have any further implications about the proper distribution of good and evil?

I believe it has. This can best be shown by considering the most naïve way in which the supposed indifference of utilitarianism to the distribution of good and evil is argued for. Suppose, the objection runs, that there are a hundred people and a hundred units of utility or value to distribute. The principle of utility supplies no ground for preferring an allocation of one unit to each person over an allocation of the hundred units to one lucky man and of nothing at all to the other ninety-nine. The mistake in this argument is its assumption that the utility accruing from the distribution of some good is independent of the manner of its distribution. But this is obviously false. We do not distribute utilities of fixed value, in fact, but concrete things such as oranges, medals and so forth which will have different utilities depending on the way in which they are distributed.

In most imaginable circumstances the distribution of a hundred oranges among a hundred people that will bring about the largest

total utility is that in which each person gets only one. Like most
objects of desire oranges are subject to the law of diminishing
marginal utility. The second orange that a man eats at a particular
time is ordinarily going to satisfy him less than the first did.
This is, broadly speaking, a consequence of the finite satisfiability
of desire. If the desire for a given kind of thing within a given
period is finitely satisfiable there must be a finite amount of that
thing which will wholly extinguish the desire for it and whose
final or marginal portion will yield no satisfaction at all. Provided
that the curve which describes the satisfactions yielded by
successive increments of the good in question, from the first, and
positively satisfying, one to the last and neutral one is regular
and without major changes of direction there will be a continuous
decrease of satisfaction accruing from one point on the curve to
the next.

It follows that if two men get much the same satisfaction from
the first orange they are given and that for both the marginal
utility of oranges steadily diminishes at much the same rate the
greatest total utility will be achieved by giving them one orange
each rather than by giving two oranges to either of them. Only
if giving a second orange to either yields more satisfaction
than giving a first orange to the other will equal distribution produce less overall satisfaction than one of the other, partial,
possibilities. That would be the case only if there was a very
considerable difference between the utilities of a first orange to the
two men or if there was some difference of this kind and also a
much smaller diminution of utility in the case of the man whose
first orange had the higher utility.

Under this abstract, but not unnatural, assumption, then, the
principle of utility strictly implies arithmetical or external
equality of distribution as the necessary means for the maximisation of overall satisfaction. If that sort of equality is what is
required by men's intuitions about justice then utilitarianism,
within the limits set by the assumption about the conditions of
satisfaction, endorses it. But although arithmetical equality of
distribution is the criterion of justice that recommends itself to

the first unreflective glance of moral intuition, qualifications suggest themselves on second thoughts. The first of these is the principle that men's differing *needs* must be taken into account if just distribution is to be assured. There is, it could be argued, no injustice in giving both of two oranges to a man who is starving, even when there is another man about who is mildly interested in having an orange although he has just had a substantial meal. A second widely supported departure from raw equality takes account of men's differing *deserts*. If a man has laboriously tended a small orange tree on which two oranges have finally come to fruition it would be no injustice if he were to eat both of them and not give half his crop to another man who happens to be passing by at the time when it becomes ripe.

Now both of these departures from bare, external equality are implied by the principle of utility since in each case the assumptions about the satisfaction-patterns or utility-schedules of the men involved, which must be correct if the principle is to entail external equality of distribution, are not correct. In the case of differing needs the utility to the starving man of a second orange will be much greater than that of a first orange to the man who has just eaten. In the case of differing deserts a larger set of utilities is relevant. The laborious cultivator has incurred a good deal of disutility through his labour which the passer-by has not had to undergo. To bring him up to the normal level of satisfaction, which the passer-by may be presumed to enjoy, he needs both oranges. Or, less figuratively, the generally lower level of satisfaction of the orange-tender implies that a second orange will provide him with more utility than a first orange would provide for the passer-by.

In these two cases, then, there are differences between the satisfaction-patterns of the individuals involved which, if the principle of utility is accepted, imply precisely the departures from strict, external equality that reflective moral intuition requires if just distribution is to be assured. Utilitarianism provides here a connected and systematic derivation of widely-recognised principles of justice that the intuitionist must, it seems, lay down as an unrelated set of axioms, or dogmas, of just distribution. The situation looks much like that which prevails with regard to right action in general. Utilitarianism presents generally acknowledged principles of right action in a systematic way, although it deprives them of their supposedly absolute and exceptionless character; intuitionism can only assert the principles singly and without connection to each other, a fact which gives rise to the problem of the conflict of duties.

However, in the case of justice, the intuitionist can argue that the three principles of external equality, needs and deserts are not as disconnected as they may seem. For the two departures from *external* equality, that is equality in respect of the objective, physical amount of the good distributed, are both justifiable on egalitarian grounds. Each of them is invoked in circumstances where some peculiarity in the satisfaction-patterns of the beneficiaries (or, of course, burden-bearers, where something of negative utility is being distributed) causes there to be an incongruity between the objective amount distributed and the satisfaction experienced as a result of the distribution. Where men's satisfaction-patterns are much the same, in both level and shape, so to speak, external equality will produce equal satisfaction. Where they are not, equality of satisfaction can be secured only if there is some inequality of external distribution. So the intuitive egalitarian can claim that his fundamental criterion of justice, now restated as that of equality of experienced satisfaction, connects and systematises the three specific principles of justice as well as utilitarianism does, even if it takes equality to be axiomatically just and does not derive it from a further principle. Such an egalitarianism of satisfaction is, indeed, hedonistic in what it regards as the value to be equally distributed. But by detaching equality from maximisation it is not utilitarian.

The egalitarian can argue further that utilitarianism has additional implications about right distribution which are directly incompatible with intuitive notions of justice. In a perfectly competitive economic system people are rewarded in accordance with their achievements; the more they contribute to the total output of utility the larger their income. Such a system is rational from a utility-maximising point of view because it provides inducements to ensure that those with special productive capacities go into the type of employment in which their largest possible contribution to the total stock of utility is realised. This method of income-distribution must be the best one to the strict utilitarian: any departure from it will reduce the total amount of utility made available by the system.

The practice of rewarding people in proportion to the services they actually render in augmenting utility is often described as one of treating them in accordance with their deserts. But what people deserve in the light of the results they achieve is not generally the same as what they deserve in the light of their efforts. A popular singer may intensely gratify a vast number of people at the cost of no disutility to himself at all, if, as may well be the case, he would prefer to be singing to a crowd of enraptured devotees than to be doing anything else. An unpopular epic poet, on the other hand, may toil in the most painful and arduous fashion to produce a huge, unreadable work which pleases neither him nor anyone else.

A system of rewarding people in accordance with their differing natural endowments in the way of utility-producing capacity seems unjust since it simply reflects the 'natural injustice' with which the innate power to be socially useful is distributed. It may often be true that under such a system even the worst off will be absolutely better off than they would be under a system in which everyone was allotted an equal share of the total stock of utility produced, but in which, because of the 'irrational' allocation of people to particular jobs, the total stock in question would be a small one. But the latter is a very extreme alternative to a perfectly competitive system. There are many intermediate possibilities in which an incomplete approach to equality of income could be achieved without much diminution of the total output of utility. It is these intermediate possibilities that the technique of redistributive taxation seeks to exploit.

It should be stressed that although utilitarianism endorses maximisation it is maximisation of utility that it is concerned with and not maximisation of output of typically utility-bearing things. It does not, therefore, endorse unqualified enlargement of the Gross National Product, although the G.N.P. is, no doubt, the most accessible measure of the total stock of utility produced by a social-economic system. Nevertheless it does seem to imply that unequal natural gifts should be unequally rewarded for the sake of maximisation and thus that the best method of distribution is not necessarily that which is intuitively the justest.

There is a possible defence to which the utilitarian could appeal at this point which develops the analogy that has already been mentioned, and shown to be imperfect, between the principles of justice and the principles of right conduct generally. On the whole utilitarianism is in favour of honesty. By and large the fact that an action is honest is a sufficient reason for thinking that it is right. But, for the utilitarian, the rightness of honesty is not absolute and unconditional. He recognises that there are circumstances in which the honest thing to do is not the right thing to do, because, for example, it would cause pain or endanger the state. Similarly, he could argue, the fact that an action or practice is just, in the intuitive sense that has been examined, is generally a sufficient reason for taking it to be right. But its rightness may be no more absolute and unconditional than that of honesty. Let justice be done, he says, as long as it does not make the heavens fall.

There are good utilitarian grounds for thinking that a method of distribution which aims to bring about equality of satisfaction will generally secure the maximisation of utility, the grounds provided by the utilitarian defence of the principles of external equality, needs and deserts, in the sense of compensation for disutility incurred. But it also allows that there can be good reason for departures from just distribution so defined. The recognition of desert in the sense of reward for services actually rendered may be required for the overall maximisation of utility, even if the worst-off are not absolutely better-off in the service-rewarding system.

In fact, of course, nearly everywhere men live under systems in which income and property are very unequally distributed and also, presumably, satisfaction, though, to a lesser extent, no doubt. In assessing the effects of any move towards equality in such a system we need to consider not merely the pattern of satisfactions that would prevail once the new system was established but also the effects of the transition itself. To this Hume's point about fixed expectations is relevant: 'It would be greater cruelty to dispossess a man of any thing, than not to give it to him'.[53] This does not mean that utilitarianism excludes social-economic reforms of an equalising tendency but it does imply that they should be gradual and achieved by redistributive taxation rather than outright expropriation.

At the present time the alleged inadequacies of the utilitarian theory of justice is the main theme of the destructive criticism that is brought to bear on the doctrine. It replaces in this role the objection that utilitarianism commits the 'naturalistic fallacy' which was itself the successor to the criticism that its hedonist criterion of value was immorally degraded. This discussion has done no more than outline some of the main points at issue in the controversy and certainly does not pretend to have resolved it. What does seem clear is that justice is less easily accounted for by utilitarianism than Mill supposed.

IV. FOUR CRITICS

Mill's *Utilitarianism* first appeared as a series of articles in *Fraser's Magazine* in the latter part of 1861. Two years later these were republished as a book. For the next forty years, until the publication in 1903 of G. E. Moore's *Principia Ethica*, they remained the authoritative exposition of a major option in ethical theory and attracted serious criticism as such. Moore's examination of Mill's doctrine had the effect, for reasons it is now not easy to discern, of converting utilitarianism, in the view of prevailing philosophical opinion, into an exemplary tissue of error. It was not until the widespread rejection of Moore's antinaturalism in the last couple of decades that Mill's doctrine recovered its status as a genuine theoretical possibility and, with this, came to receive once again the kind of criticism that does not presuppose, from the outset, that it is fundamentally misguided.

Four critics stand out in the period 1863 to 1903 by reason of the intrinsic interest or actual influence of their objections to utilitarianism. The first of these is John Grote, Whewell's successor in the Knightbridge chair at Cambridge and younger brother of the historian of Greece. His *Examination of the Utilitarian Philosophy* was written as Mill's articles first appeared and was published in 1870, four years after its author's death. Grote's pupil, Henry Sidgwick, was much more sympathetic to Mill. His massively thorough and scrupulous *Methods of Ethics* was first published in 1874. Although more utilitarian than anything else, the book is wholly explicit about its departures from Benthamite orthodoxy in contrast to the defensive and unacknowledged character of Mill's own revisions to his ethical inheritance. Two years later in 1876 F. H. Bradley published his *Ethical Studies,* the long third chapter of which, 'Pleasure for Pleasure's Sake', is a violently polemical assault on Mill's position.

Finally, and most lethally for utilitarianism, Moore's *Principia Ethica* in 1903, despite its heavy dependence on Sidgwick and its unreflective confidence that the rightness of actions is self-evidently determined by the goodness of their consequences, provided, in its critique of naturalism and in its detailed objections to Mill's views in its third chapter, the means with which utilitarianism was largely deprived of serious discussion, let alone positive development, for half a century.

(i) JOHN GROTE

Grote's *Examination of the Utilitarian Philosophy* was not, according to his editor, originally intended for publication but rather for the purpose of clarifying his ideas on the subject for himself. The fact may explain the somewhat desultory and repetitive nature of the book. It also renders all the more creditable its consistently gracious tone which is in the greatest possible contrast to the abusiveness of most of Mill's critics, a feature which attains its most extreme development in Bradley.

A persistent theme in Grote's criticism of Mill is his dissatisfaction with the claim of utilitarianism to be a pre-eminently *scientific* ethical theory. An adequate moral philosophy must, as he puts it, be idealist and not positivist. There is an essential imperativeness about virtue. There would seem to be a number of distinct points in a state of unresolved confusion here. In the first place he seems to be saying that conclusions about what is morally imperative cannot be validly derived from empirical facts about human nature and conduct, that there is no logical connection between what ought to be and what is. To the extent that utilitarians try to deduce the greatest happiness principle, as Mill does in his 'proof', from psychological hedonism they are exposed to this criticism, at least in so far as their psychological premise is, or is taken by them to be, an empirical generalisation. But, secondly, Grote denies that there can be a science of the kind of free action that must occur if morality is to have any application. A third point is that Grote is dissatisfied with the kind of ideal that utilitarianism, for all its empirical pretensions, has to assume. Happiness is too passive an end. The positive improvement of human character, through, for example, self-control, is an essential ingredient in an adequate morality. The facts, then, to which utilitarianism appeals in support of the greatest happiness principle do not have the logical capacity to establish it. That principle, as Grote puts it, is not empirical and inductive; it is *a priori*. What is more, the facts in question are not available; there are no laws of free action. Finally, the ideal that utilitarianism inevitably does adopt fails to recognise the true nature of virtue by defining it in terms of happiness.

Grote's well-taken point that the utilitarian principle is *a priori* does not undermine the claim of utilitarianism to be empirical and inductive as radically as he supposes. Where the intuitionist has to invoke a multitude of non-empirical intuitions of rightness, the utilitarian derives all his specific, detailed moral principles, with the aid of the greatest happiness principle, from empirical generalisations about the consequences of action. There is a parallel with natural science here. Science is not rendered un-empirical by the conception that singular observations yield theories only with the aid of a non-empirical inductive principle, neither need morality be if it is taken to involve an analogous dependence on the non-empirical principle that right actions augment the general happiness. If Mill wrongly supposed that the utilitarian principle is an empirical generalisation, he was equally wrong about the law of universal causation, which he took to be the indispensable foundation of scientific, eliminative induction.

Moving on from this more or less methodological issue, Grote says that there are two main deficiencies in utilitarianism. The first is its account of the right distribution of happiness, of who it is that actions, if they are to be right, are to be useful to. The second is its account of happiness itself. On the matter of distribution Grote's position is the conservative opposite of the type of egalitarian criticism of the utilitarian theory of justice considered in the last section of the chapter on Mill. Grote takes utilitarianism to entail the strictly equal distribution of happiness, a very questionable assumption, as I have shown, and objects that this is altogether too abstract, mechanical and unfeeling. It ignores, in his view, the special moral claims of those to whom the moral agent is specially related, a point of view dramatically represented in Godwin's hypothetical decision, on grounds of public utility, to rescue Archbishop Fenelon rather than his grandmother from a burning building. Duty, Grote maintains, is particular before it is general. He dismisses Mill's utilitarian justification of the priority of the moral claims of those to whom agents are specially related, in terms of the painful disappointment of expectations the neglect of those claims would involve, as being 'not really utilitarian'. As it stands this a very weak objection. In such cases the expectations really exist and must be taken into account in the evaluation of consequences. If Grote had argued that, in a world of utilitarians, such expectations ought not to exist, he could have gone on to argue that, with the dissemination of utilitarianism, special, relative duties might evaporate. But, first, that is not the situation that we are actually in, as far as actual expectations are concerned, and, secondly, even in a world of utilitarians there would be good arguments of effectiveness for the position that charity begins at home.

On the question of the kind of happiness which utilitarianism takes as its ideal Grote is too honourable a controversialist to indulge in comminations of animal sensuality. He objects that Mill hovers between idealist and positivist conceptions of happiness, between defining it as what men should desire and as what men do desire. In fact, I think it is fairly clear that Mill takes happiness to be the former: *actual* or realised happiness, in other words, as against (perhaps mistakenly) *expected* happiness. In this connection, discussing Mill's unfortunate distinction between different qualities of pleasure, Grote neatly argues that Mill's criterion in terms of the preference of qualified judges is in fact quantitative, since in simply preferring 'higher' to 'lower' pleasures the judges are simply asserting the former to be *more* pleasurable.

Discussing Mill's proof Grote sees that, in Mill's interpretation of the words involved, the proposition that men desire only pleasure is trivially true. He thus rightly concentrates his criticism on Mill's naïvely invalid deduction from this truth of the conclusion that pleasure is ideally desirable, and on the fallacious generalisation by which he moves from the premise that each man desires his own happiness to the conclusion that everyone desires the happiness of all.

His fundamental difference with Mill here concerns the utilitarian subordination of virtue to happiness. On the one hand he has an unarguable primary conviction that virtue has an intrinsic value of its own and not merely as a human disposition contributory to the general happiness. On the other he is dissatisfied with Mill's theory of moral motivation, of his account of how the general happiness can become an operative end for the individual.

On the first point Grote himself denies the value of asceticism or self-sacrifice for its own sake, that is to say, of pointless asceticism, which makes no contribution to happiness. It is thus a little hard to see what, apart from a certain instinctive moral decorum, prevents him from agreeing that virtue derives its value from the contribution to happiness which it is, of all things, the most calculated to make. In this connection it is worth noticing a distinction he draws between duty, which he sees as, so to speak, negatively prompted by conscience, by fear of guilt, and virtue, which he regards as altogether more spontaneous, a finite analogue of the overflowing of divine grace, expressive of a constitutional benevolence, the genial, rather than the stern, daughter of the voice of God. His difference from Mill here is very elusive, almost a matter of tone.

As for Mill's account of the motives of morality, of how it is that men come to find pleasure in the pursuit of the general happiness and make it a direct end of conduct, Grote holds that this is one of the two respects, along with his misguided distinction between different qualities of pleasure, in which Mill represents a radical departure from orthodox utilitarianism as no more than the removal of a prevalent misunderstanding of it. Certainly Mill does emphasise the internal sanction of morality, founded on sympathy and 'social feeling', as well as the external sanctions enumerated by Bentham: physical, political, 'moral or popular' and religious. But what Mill identifies as an internal sanction Bentham acknowledges in a different way, as one of the simple pleasures (number eight in fact), the pleasure of benevolence and good-will. Grote agrees with what is implicit in Bentham's practice here, the view that sanctions must be external to the agent, and then, insisting that morality is an internal phenomenon, concludes that Mill should not have treated sympathy as a sanction and that sanctions cannot account for morally right conduct. This is at best a verbal point. Bentham and Mill both recognise sympathy or natural benevolence as an explanation of right conduct. Mill, perhaps figuratively, calls it a sanction and Bentham does not. Grote prefers Bentham's terminology but fails to see that Bentham, as much as Mill, if with less ceremony, provides an internal determinant of moral action.

(ii) HENRY SIDGWICK

It may seem odd to treat Sidgwick as a critic of utilitarianism, rather than as a continuator of it. As was said earlier, his *Methods of Ethics* is more utilitarian than anything else, for all its large admixture of intuitionism, and, if he has to be categorised definitely under one head, it must be as a utilitarian. For all his qualifications he does remain an unwavering ethical hedonist. The ultimate good is, in his view, 'desirable consciousness' and this, he argues, cannot be anything but happiness, conceived in the traditional utilitarian way, as a sum of pleasures. The repugnance this conclusion tends to excite at a first glance he explains away as the result of a set of mutually reinforcing misunderstandings. Pleasure gets confused with animal pleasure; much pleasure occurs only because it has not been consciously sought; the pleasure in question is thought to be that of the agent and not that of all.

But Sidgwick differs from the classical utilitarianism on four major points. In the first place, he is not a psychological hedonist. Pleasure, conceived as 'agreeable feeling', is not, experience shows, the sole object of desire. He lays stress here on the point just mentioned, that much pleasure can be attained only if it is not consciously pursued. Even if psychological hedonism were true it would not imply the greatest happiness principle. Sidgwick firmly rejects Mill's proof.

Secondly, benevolence, the pursuit of happiness in general, is not enough. To start with, the happiness that is relevant to morality is not just that of human beings, but that of the whole sentient creation, of every being that is capable of happiness or its opposite. Sidgwick raises the question, which has become much more pressing with the advances in reproductive technology since his time, of whether we should aim at the greatest *total* happiness or the greatest *average* happiness, given that the actual number of sentient beings is something that is to some extent dependent on our voluntary decisions. Should one have four children who attain six units of happiness each or five children who attain five? But his main point here is that not only must we increase the happiness of others, we must ensure that happiness is rightly distributed. He concludes that equal distribution is the principle of just distribution that recommends itself to reason but that it is not a consequence of the, equally rational, principle of benevolence itself.

Sidgwick's third main departure from standard utilitarianism arises from his belief that prudence, the maximisation by the individual agent of his own happiness in the long run, is as intuitively evident as benevolence, but that there is no guarantee that the dictates of these two principles will coincide. Benevolence calls for acts of self-sacrifice for which there is no earthly recompense in prudential terms. The only way in which duty and interest can be reconciled is by the activities of a divine governor of the universe, distributing rewards and punishments, an echo of one of Kant's postulates of practical reason. Sidgwick's religious doubts led him to resign his Cambridge fellowship early in his career. Even if they concerned the Thirty-nine Articles, rather than the existence of God, and although he thought belief in God natural to men, he did not think that belief provable. This disquiet about the availability of that without which the equally imperative claims of prudence and rational benevolence could not be harmonised may be thought to underlie his long and intense interest in psychical research.

Finally, Sidgwick departs most radically from standard utilitarianism in his theory of moral knowledge. On the one hand, for reasons that were later to be less cogently but more influentially stated by Moore, he was convinced that the first principle or principles of morality could not be true by definition or analytic.[54] On the other hand they seemed to possess a degree of certitude which they could not have if merely empirical, since, as highly general, they would then have to be inductions. They are, then, substantive or synthetic, but at the same time a priori. The only way in which they could be known is by intuition, which, in view of the generality of its deliverances, is better described as reason than as sense.

Sidgwick lays down four criteria for the validity of moral, or other, intuition.[55] It must be expressed in clear and precise terms; it must be self-evident to reflective attention; it must be consistent with other deliverances of intuition; it must be endorsed by the general agreement of experts about it. By these criteria, Sidgwick argues, the moral first principles of common-sense intuitionism are a failure. Exceptions can always be found to absolute specific principles of duty such as those that enjoin truth-telling and promise-keeping. Such principles typically can conflict. If amended and qualified to cover such exceptions and conflicts they become too complex to be intuited and the work of amendment is not completable anyway.

There are principles, however, which, according to Sidgwick, do pass his four tests.[56] The most important of these are, first, two somewhat tautologous-looking formal principles: that what is right for one person is also right for others similarly circumstanced and that general rules should be applied impartially.

Rather more substantial is the principle, integral to prudence, that there should be an equal concern for all the temporal parts of conscious life, in other words that future goods should be treated as on a level with present good, with due allowance for the lesser certainty of the former. Then there is the principle that the good of one individual is 'no better from the point of view of the Universe', and, therefore, to the eye of reason, than that of any other. Finally, there is the principle that makes goodness effective for conduct, that a rational being ought to aim at realising good. The last two put together amount to what Sidgwick calls the principle of rational benevolence and, if good is interpreted in his way as happiness, an improved, rationalised, version of the fundamental principle of utilitarianism is achieved. Sidgwick adds in confirmation of the intuitive and self-evident status of this principle that it is, empirically, the touchstone by reference to which conflicts between the more specific principles of common-sense morality are adjudicated. Furthermore, to the extent to which they are deserving of acceptance, these common-sense principles are themselves implications, in the light of empirical knowledge about the consequences of action, of the principle of rational benevolence. It follows that an amended utilitarianism coincides with the findings of intuitionism, at least to the extent that it is rationally to be expected that it should.

Two specific points remain to be mentioned. Sidgwick is much more of a moral conservative than Bentham or Mill. He does not believe that the principle of rational benevolence dictates its own systematic application *de novo* in the project of a clean sweep of existing moral convictions. It should rather be used to support common-sense or intuitionist morality in general and to rectify it in detail. Moral reform should be 'positive and supplementary', not 'negative and destructive'.[57]

Also of interest is Sidgwick's anticipation of Moore, in his thesis that moral terms are indefinable. On this matter, unlike Moore, it is 'ought' and not 'good' whose indefinability he stresses. (Moore was prepared to define 'ought' in terms of 'good', in a way that makes Sidgwick's principle that a rational being ought to aim at good analytic, as 'more productive of good than any other possible action'.) From this it follows that even if, as Sidgwick believes, happiness, or 'desirable consciousness', is good 'it does not involve in its analysis any obligation to seek it.'[58]

It may be that part of Sidgwick's reason for thinking this is that, as he puts it, the judgement that something ought to be done, at least where the 'ought' in question is moral and categorical, carries with it 'an impulse or motive to action'.[59] But if, as most contemporary moral philosophers would maintain, the same practical implication is carried by the judgement that something is good (namely, that of bringing it into existence if it does not exist and of preserving it in existence if it does) there is no objection to a Moorean definition of 'ought' in terms of 'good', and Sidgwick's principle that one ought to aim at good is the tautology it surely appears to be.

Of Sidgwick's three main departures from classical utilitarianism, the first, that the principle that the happiness of all should be pursued needs to be supplemented with principles of distribution, is a reasonable enough criticism of Bentham and Mill. As was argued in the last section of the previous chapter, the treatment of the question at the end of Mill's book does not really take the measure of the problem. On the other hand, as it was further argued above, there are available to utilitarians arguments which seek to derive the intuitively acceptable principles of just distribution from the greatest happiness principle together with the law of diminishing marginal utility and other, more obviously factual, considerations about the inequality with which disutilities are distributed between men, by the circumstances in which they are placed or through the services they perform.

Secondly, the basic conflict that runs through Sidgwick's ethical reflections is an idiosyncratic version of an ancient preoccupation of moral philosophers with the reconciliation of egoism and altruism. Where it has ordinarily been found difficult to explain how it is that men ought to pursue the good of all when they are psychologically so constituted so as to pursue only their own good, Sidgwick, denying that men always pursue their own good, if this is conceived as pleasure, as he thinks it should be, holds that it is self-evident that they *ought* to pursue both their own good and the good of all and that, despite a wide measure of coincidence, these two principles do at times have inconsistent implications. There must, surely, be something wrong here which is of a logical character and not merely an emotionally dissatisfying lack of harmony between our aspirations and the nature of things. Either the two principles are consistent (in accordance with the third of Sidgwick's criteria for axiomatic status) or one of them, at least, must be false. To those who believe in the overridingness of the moral 'ought' it will be the egoistic principle that one ought to aim at one's own good. Sidgwick's more elevated and dignified version of the clash between egoism and altruism, which represents it as a conflict between two equally rational convictions and not as one between selfish desire and impersonal reason, seems more readily resoluble than its more familiar analogue.

Sidgwick's theory of moral knowledge, finally, has little positive to commend it. Negatively, it has the merit of drawing attention to the indefiniteness of the classical utilitarians' account of the logical status of their fundamental principle. Is it analytic and true by definition or synthetic and substantive? If the latter, and thus, by reason of its generality, inductive could it possibly be strong enough to sustain the weight of the specific moral principles it is supposed to validate? It should be mentioned that many present-day critics of utilitarianism, particularly those who regard it as unable to accommodate our intuitive convictions about justice, distributive and retributive, appeal as he does to the self-evidence of the additional, independent principles they believe in. But for the most part they fail, as he with typical scrupulousness does not, to explain what sort of truth and justification such principles can aspire to.

(iii) F. H. BRADLEY

Bradley was, in his time, the most admired of the British idealists of the late nineteenth century. He was more imaginative and much more of a literary artist than T. H. Green, the founder of the school. Green had called on the philosophers of his generation to 'close up their Mill and Spencer' and, in his first work, *Ethical Studies* (1876), Bradley devoted a well-known chapter, the third, to the task of demolishing the ethics of 'pleasure for pleasure's sake'. There are two main themes in Bradley's critique of utilitarianism: one moral, the other logical. He invokes what he called 'the common moral consciousness', in other words conventionally edifying sentiment, to urge that utilitarianism is immoral and he borrowed an idea of Green's, that the ultimate end of conduct must be some kind of systematic whole to argue that the utilitarian *summum bonum* of the greatest happiness of all is a logical impossibility.

In seeking to show the immorality of utilitarianism Bradley says that he does not take common moral conviction to be unquestionably authoritative, but nevertheless he takes it, or a reflective version of it to be found in himself and his presumed readers, as a touchstone. In the first place, he says, happiness is not pleasure or a sum of pleasures. Secondly, the maximum pleasure of sentient beings is not the end of conduct. And neither, he goes on, is best achieved by deliberate pursuit. With something like Sidgwick's appeal to thoughtful intuition, he asks if the improvement of 'higher function', of virtue or perfection, at the cost of some increase of pain is not morally preferable to its opposite, an increase of pleasure accompanied by a deterioration of higher function. If anything is clear to the common moral consciousness it is that virtue, however much it may be a means to pleasure, is not good *because* it is such a means.

So far as there is argument here it is unpersuasive. The view that happiness is not definable in terms of pleasure derives its initial intuitive force from taking the word 'pleasure', irrelevantly, in its most elementary vernacular sense. The intuitive falsity of the principle that pleasure is the ultimate good or end is dependent, as Sidgwick argued, on taking the pleasure involved to be that of the agent and ignoring the utilitarian requirement that it should be the pleasure of all sentient beings. Much the same is true of Bradley's claim that virtue does not owe its goodness to the fact, in so far as it is a fact, that virtue is a means to pleasure. Certainly utilitarians have hoped to show that virtue is a means to the agent's pleasure, in order to provide him with a motive for acquiring it, as well as to the pleasure of all. But it is to the second of these alone, according to them, that it owes its goodness. The contrast involved in his hypothesis about improvement of higher function at the expense of pleasure is one that a utilitarian, if consistent, should be disposed to question by saying that the state of affairs envisaged is one in which one source of human satisfaction is increased while another is diminished.

More definite and original is Bradley's crucial contention that the hedonistic end of the utilitarians is a logically impossible one. The end of conduct, he says, must be 'a definite unity', 'a concerete whole', it must be systematic. All that the utilitarians have to offer is 'an infinite, perishing series'. This seems an entirely arbitrary stipulation. A continuing income of £10,000 a year is just as proper an object of aspiration as the accumulation of a capital of £200,000 and the latter would be one way of getting the former and, indeed, be principally valuable on that account. It is not, of course, obvious in the least that the greatest happiness of sentient beings is an *infinite* series. There is good reason to suppose that eventually there will be no sentient life in the only part of the universe where we know it to exist, quite apart from the familiar immediate hazards to the human part of that life. On Bradley's own level of debate it could be argued that an infinity of quantities *can* have a sum anyway: $1 + \frac{1}{2} + \frac{1}{4} + \frac{1}{8} \ldots = 2$. But it is not so much the infinity as the 'perishing', temporal nature of the utilitarian end on which Bradley lays most stress.

About this criticism there are two points to be made. The first, subsequently made by Sidgwick in answer to Green's version of the objection, is that men are, after all, temporal beings who will need to realise value over the whole temporal extent of their lives and who will, therefore, quite rationally aim at doing so. This consideration can be reinforced by an *ad hominem* argument against the alternative account of the *summum bonum* Bradley offers in place of the general happiness. This is self-realisation. The self to be realised is not, of course, the actual self which, at any moment, is necessarily realised. It must be some sort of ideal self. But a self, even an ideal self, is still a temporal thing. If an achieved perfection of character could be thought to have a kind of timelessness it must still manifest itself in temporal items of conduct. In effect Bradley is maintaining that men should not seek to *produce* something, namely the greatest possible happiness for all, but rather to *be* something, let us say perfect. But it is not enough to attain perfection. It must be maintained and preserved. The non-temporal, non-serial realisation of an essentially temporal thing like the self is a much more 'wild and impossible fiction' than the utilitarian aim of the continuous maximisation of the greatest possible happiness.

The other point is perhaps less familiar. This is that Bradley's emphasis on the necessarily serial nature of pleasure betrays a vulgar identification of pleasure and pain with thrills and pangs. A common and fundamental object of human effort is fully satis-fying employment in which the individual's powers are exercised to the limit. The achievement of this end is not a momentary kick, a climax of occupational ecstasy, but the attainment of a continuing state. Now the deep-seated and persistent desires whose satisfaction is the most important constituent of happiness are typically of this persistent kind. So, even conceived as a sum of pleasures, happiness is not of the crudely serial character that Bradley's criticism assumes.

One other objection Bradley deploys at some length to utili-tarianism is that it requires the moral agent to act on probabilities, in holding that men ought to act in those ways which, experience has shown, will probably augment the general happiness. The result, he says, is that it replaces laws by rules. What he presumably

means is that absolute specific principles of conduct are abandoned
in favour of principles that can have exceptions. Warming to his
theme, Bradley contends that, since each individual will have to
judge for himself what the probable consequences of the alternatives before him are, there will ensue 'incessant practical
casuistry'.[60] Why Bradley supposes that the individual's judgement on what the probable consequences of his action will be
must be more wavering, subjective and wilful than his judgement
of what it is his absolute obligation to do is not made clear.
But it is, no doubt, true that a consequentialist manner of reasoning
in morals leaves more scope for self-regarding distortion. On the
other hand it also leaves more room for apt and effective altruism
than a set of rigidly unconditional specific principles.

The example on which Bradley spends a good deal of time (do
not commit adultery) is worth a little attention here. Used as it is
in a criticism of Mill it may be thought to make a somewhat
malicious allusion to Mill's association with Harriet Taylor, at
a time when her first husband was still alive. That would not
be so bad if it were not for the grotesque hypocrisy involved in
Bradley's morally outraged posture on the subject. He may well
have believed that Mill's relations with Mrs Taylor were literally
adulterous, although this is now generally doubted. What is quite
beyond doubt is that Bradley was himself an inveterate adulterer
who for a long time spent a period each year with the wife of
another man. His only moral achievement in this particular domain
of human striving is that he managed to keep his misconduct
from general notice. But it was not as champion of the principle
'do not be seen to commit adultery' that he rode forth so self-
righteously against Mill.

On the point of philosophical substance, the chief defect of
Bradley's handling of this example is lack of imagination or, at
any rate, of concrete detail. Consider a standard type of late-
Victorian situation. A cruel, but not certifiably insane, husband
deserts his wife and children and fails to provide for them. Should
a man who comes to love the abandoned wife and wishes to look
after her be forbidden to live with her? Or take an actual case,

that of George Eliot and George Henry Lewes. Lewes's wife had three illegitimate children by Thornton Leigh Hunt but, since Lewes had condoned the adultery when it first began, he could not get a divorce. Did his and George Eliot's long and deeply affectionate association therefore deserve moral censure? The most relaxed utilitarianism would not have sanctioned Bradley's own adulterous habit, since it involved no acceptance of continuing responsibility for the welfare of his mistress, but then it was not, as he must have supposed, representative of all forms of adulterous relationship.

Bradley handles Mill, in *Ethical Studies*, in a consistently sneering and contemptuous fashion, referring to him, for example, with abusive quotation-marks, as 'our great modern logician'. But in 1876 Mill had been safely dead for three years. In *Mr Sidgwick's Hedonism*, a pamphlet of 1877, whose subject was very much alive, his tone is much more moderate and cautious. For the most part he is content to repeat the arguments about the logical impossibility of the utilitarian end and its unacceptability to the ordinary moral consciousness which he had used against Mill. The force of these arguments is not diminished by the more reasonable mode in which they are expressed in the later work. Some additional points are made against particular details of Sidgwick's position. The rhetorical nature of Sidgwick's description as 'Reason' of the faculty of moral intuition to which he frequently appeals is brought out. Sidgwick's account of the practical, action-guiding force of reason is questioned. It should, rather, have been applauded as drawing attention to a problem many moral philosophers had evaded. Bradley accuses Sidgwick of repeating Mill's disastrous equivocation about the desirable, as that which is and ought to be desired, from an apparent inability to recall or notice Sidgwick's plain repudiation of psychological hedonism.

More interesting is his rejection of Sidgwick's account of ethical science. Sidgwick had held that a practical science of ethics could be derived from the principle of rational benevolence together with ordinary causal knowledge about the consequences for happiness of kinds of human action. Such a hope, Bradley maintains, is 'the mere dream of a doctrinaire'.[61] A true ethics, for Bradley, takes ordinary morality as given and seeks only to understand, not to alter it. It must, he thinks, inevitably conflict with ordinary morality but, since it has no practical aim, it will have no effect on actual conduct. This is a peculiar view, more than Wittgensteinian in its passivity in the face of an established 'form of life'. Philosophical ethics, for Bradley, must leave everything as it is. It hardly conforms to the position of those like Collingwood, who have attacked analytic philosophy for its indifference to the practical implications of philosophy and have contrasted it in this respect with the idealists. Morality and ethics, thus defined, must conflict and we are to act on the former. Is this because morality is truer than ethics? If so ethics becomes a pointless speculative game. If ethics is truer than morality why should we be guided by the latter? To the extent that ethics is speculative and intellectually experimental there are, indeed, good utilitarian reasons, set out at length by Sidgwick, for not reforming morality precipitately in accordance with its findings. But if it is a philosophical, and thus critical, investigation of morality, and not a neutral descriptive science of moral phenomena, it is absurd to rule out the idea that it could exercise an influence on the everyday moral thinking from which it arises and to which it is applied.

(iv) G. E. MOORE

G. E. Moore's *Principia Ethica* of 1903 has been by far the most influential criticism of utilitarian ethics. The purported refutation of ethical naturalism, which is the book's fundamental thesis, dominated moral philosophy for the first half of this century in Britain and, to a considerable extent, throughout the English-speaking world. It has, indeed, come to be based on very different grounds from those with which Moore provided it in the first chapter of his book but in any form it is, if sound, fatal to the most natural interpretation of utilitarianism.

Its essential claim is that judgements of value, and, in particular, moral judgements, cannot be taken to be, or to be strictly deducible from, statements of ordinary, natural, empirical fact, that can be established by the senses or introspection. Moore presented this as a thesis about the meaning of terms, holding that it is evident to inspection that no ethical term is identical in meaning to any term or collection of terms that serves to describe ordinary empirical facts. The conclusion he then drew was that judgements of value report unordinary, moral facts about an autonomous realm of values.

Since the 1930s Moore's successors have agreed with him about the difference between the evaluative and the empirical, that terms in the two domains are never synonymous and statements in them never logically equivalent, but for reasons very different from his. Developed antinaturalism holds that the lack of synonymy or equivalence that Moore detected expresses a deep-seated, underlying difference of function between utterances used to describe facts and utterances used to guide action. On this view judgements of value do not describe any facts at all, ordinary or unordinary. Their task is, rather, to give universal commands ('let everyone keep promises'), to express wishes ('would that everyone kept promises') or to give vent to emotions ('hurrah for promise-keeping'). Moore's own positive account of the nature of judgements of value, as statements of 'non-natural' fact, is thus the first casualty of the revised and improved version of the critical principle from which he originally derived it.

Moore's main discussion of utilitarianism is to be found in chapter 3 of *Principia Ethica*, 'Hedonism'. His first step is to argue that utilitarianism is really a naturalistic theory and so does fall within the scope of his proposed refutation of theories of that kind. One piece of evidence he draws on is that Sidgwick differed from the classical utilitarians in not supposing pleasure to be part of the definition of good, for he was compelled to base the hedonist principle on an intuition of which nothing is heard from Bentham and Mill. More directly to the point is Mill's statement that 'to think of an object as desirable (unless for the sake of its consequences) and to think of it as pleasant are one and the same thing'. In other words the concept of that which is desirable for its own sake and of that which is pleasant is a single concept or, again, 'desirable for its own sake' and 'pleasant' are identical in meaning. He goes on to diagnose the error he takes to be involved here, not very convincingly, as arising from the fact that the approval which it is the nature of value-judgements to express is a kind of liking, in other words a kind of pleasure.

Having thus firmly settled utilitarianism on the chopping-block of his polemical guillotine he proceeds to a more detailed examination of the arguments of Mill and Sidgwick. Against Mill he makes the rather well-worn, but still cogent, objections that Mill equivocates on the word 'desirable' and inconsistently abandons hedonism in his doctrine of different qualities of pleasure. More original are his arguments against the psychologically hedonist premise that pleasure alone is desired and the connected view that objects of desire that are apparently distinct from pleasure are either means to pleasure or, where the object in question is desired for its own sake, *parts* of pleasure or happiness.[62]

The theory that pleasure is the sole object of desire, he holds, is a confused misrepresentation of the truth that pleasure is always at least part of the cause of desire. The idea of drinking some wine occurs to one and causes an experience of pleasure. This actual, felt pleasure then, in its turn, causes a desire for a glass of wine to arise. What is desired is the wine, not the non-actual pleasure that is thought of in desiring it. Where pleasure comes in is as a consequence of the thought of the wine and as the cause of the desire for the wine.

The direct response to this objection has been given already in the discussion of Mill. The fact that a desire is for a glass of wine is perfectly compatible with its being also for pleasure, in particular the pleasure expected from drinking the glass of wine. The expected pleasure is the internal accusative of the desire. There is, of course, no such thing as desire for pleasure on its own, detached from any vehicle whatever, unless pleasure be taken, as in its most vernacular sense, as a label for a group of primitive, universal sources of satisfaction. It would, perhaps, have been better if Mill had said that pleasure is what is common to all objects of desire, rather than that pleasure alone is desired for its own sake. To expect pleasure from some conceived or imagined object is at least part of what differentiates the desire for it from its mere contemplation or envisagement.

There is something, in very general terms, in Moore's alternative thesis that actual pleasure is always some part of the cause of desire. This would seem to be true at least of acquired or learnt desires, as contrasted with instinctive ones. If, from politeness or curiosity, I eat a mysterious and unfamiliar-looking item from a tray of cocktail delicacies and find it pleasant this will foster a desire for an item of that kind for its own, gastronomic, sake next time I am offered one. Experiences of pleasure and pain are, platitudinously enough, the moulders of desire. But that is not to say, with Moore, that a desire is always attended with and immediately caused by a pleasant thought or the actual pleasure caused by the idea of some possibly available thing. For the most part desires are, or are attended by, unpleasant thoughts. That is, bluntly, why we try to satisfy them. Sometimes, when we have reason to think they are soon going to be satisfied, they may be pleasant. But when we think they may or probably will not be they are unpleasant. Even when they are pleasant we do not welcome their indefinite prolongation.

Moore becomes distinctly heated when he turns to Mill's account of the way in which things that are originally desired as means to pleasure, like virtue or, in his somewhat unfortunate analogous case, money, come to be desired for their own sakes, by the truly conscientious man and the miser, respectively. Mill says that such objects change from being means to happiness into 'parts of happiness'. Moore describes this as 'contemptible nonsense'.[63] A man who desires money desires coins and banknotes. Does Mill really mean that solid material objects are literally parts of a mental state like happiness? Thinking of this degree of plainness could appeal only to a corruptly sophisticated taste for the primitive. Anyone who, for such a reason, could not make head or tail of the remark that a man's family or house or business is a great part of his happiness should move into some more practical line of work than philosophy. It would be insulting to Moore's intelligence to suppose that he was really unable to distinguish between the satisfaction one man gets from virtue, which is by way of the good opinion it causes other people to have of him, and that of another, which comes directly from the exercise of virtue, whether anyone else knows about it or not.

Moore wrote of Sidgwick: 'His personality did not attract me, and I found his lectures rather dull. From his published works, especially, of course, his *Methods of Ethics*, I have gained a good deal. . . .'[64] The aspect of Sidgwick's thought of which he is most critical in *Principia Ethica* is its insistence that ultimate good or value is only to be found in the conscious states of a sentient being. Against Sidgwick's conclusion that experienced pleasure is the only thing that is ultimately good Moore develops his thought-experiment about the two worlds, one entirely beautiful, the other entirely repellent and ugly, with regard to which it is guaranteed that no 'human being has or ever, by any possibility, *can*, live in either, can ever see and enjoy the beauty of the one or hate the foulness of the other'.[65]

Moore maintains that it is intuitively self-evident to him that it would be good for the beautiful but unexperienceable world to exist and bad for the ugly one to exist. If the guarantee that neither world can ever be experienced is acceptable, it might seem more rational to prefer that the ugly one should exist, both as a safe dumping-ground for the ugliness that composes it and because it would be a deplorable misuse of resources to waste beauty by sequestering it from any possibility of being enjoyed in the way the hypothesis proposes. In fact, the guarantee is not very acceptable, either psychologically or logically. Can the barrier be proof against all ingenuity of intrusion? If God is the contractor employed in the construction will it not coarsen him, to our long-run disadvantage, if he is commissioned to run up

an entirely repulsive world? On the logical point, if the guarantee
that the world in question cannot be experienced is more than
contingent does it even make sense to suppose that the world
exists?

Moore goes on to inquire whether it is pleasure alone or rather
the consciousness of pleasure that Sidgwick holds to be the
supreme good. He says that 'it is far more possible that we
should some day be able to produce the intensest pleasure, without
any consciousness that it is there, than that we should be able to
produce mere colour, without its being any particular colour'.[66]
Many philosophers who hold that pleasure and pain are mental
states of which we are infallibly aware and which necessarily
intimate themselves to us would deny that there is any difference
between Moore's two cases. Both, they would say, involve self-
contradiction. If pleasure and consciousness of it can be coherently
distinguished, Sidgwick, as Moore realises, would take the latter
to be the ultimate good. Unconscious pleasure could still be
significant because of its causal relations to conscious pleasure and
pain. One might say that a man derived unconscious pleasure
from the prevalence of an easy and amicable atmosphere in his
family circle, if, for instance, it was such a normal condition as to
escape his attention. It would still be preferable to the unconscious
pain produced by a persistently disagreeable atmosphere because
of the different effects of these subliminal emotional backgrounds
on the hedonic quality of the experiences of which he is conscious.

Finally Moore addresses himself to the question of whether
consciousness of pleasure is the ultimate good. Allowing that
anything that is ultimately good may *contain* consciousness of
pleasure, he denies that its goodness is constituted by the consciousness of pleasure it contains. That which is a necessary
condition of goodness need not be good in isolation. There is a
quite persuasive argument here which Moore does not develop.
J. J. C. Smart has considered the hypothesis of man sitting in a
machine which continuously supplies him with intense and
exquisite sensations of pleasure.[67] Is this the ideal mode of life for
the whole sentient creation? The practical objections to this

hypothesis are obvious. Would any exquisite sensation remain exquisite if it went on all the time? Who would keep the machines in working order and, indeed, ensure that their occupants were maintained in sufficient biological working order for them to be sensitive to pleasure? Feats of technological imagination are called for here about the reliability of automatic operation of the pleasure machines which depart rather massively from our experience of household gadgets. If the feats are performed we are confronted with an ethical analogue of Descartes' demon which is as well calculated to undermine the thesis that pleasure is what is ultimately good as the demon is to undermine belief in the overall reliability of our cognitive faculties.

In considering the view that consciousness of pleasure alone, or 'in isolation', is the only ultimate good Moore draws another distinction with much the same logical fragility as that between pleasure and consciousness of it. The possession of pleasure by persons, he says, is not the same thing as the existence of that quantity of pleasure. At first he seems to be envisaging the possibility of altogether unowned pleasure. Even if this were a coherent notion it would have little practical import since there is no way in which intentional human action could affect it. However, it seems clear that it is not coherent. Pleasure is an essentially relational idea. For pleasure to occur an experient must take pleasure in something he is experiencing. But, as the discussion proceeds, it appears, rather, that what Moore is concerned with is the way in which a given amount of pleasure is distributed between different people. He does not pick out this problem, considered above in Chapter III, section (v), clearly enough to make any useful contribution to it.

On the whole, then, Moore's specific arguments against utilitarianism, where they depart from the familiar points about desirability and Mill's theory of different qualities of pleasure, do not amount to much. The real force of his critique, and its actual effectiveness, must be attributed to his general argument against naturalism. I have examined this at length elsewhere.[68] If, as I argue there, the pleasantness of a thing is an intrinsic, non-contingent reason for pursuing it, then the practicality of moral judgements, which it is the residual element of truth in Moore's antinaturalism to stress, is not merely something with which utilitarianism is consistent (and not, as he thinks, the rock on which it comes to grief), it is also something which is more adequately catered for by utilitarianism than by any other ethical theory.

V. EPILOGUE: CONTEMPORARY UTILITARIANISM

Since Moore's *Principia Ethica* moral philosophy, at least in Britain and to a large extent in the English-speaking world, has passed through three phases. In the first Moore's own combination of a consequentialist theory of right action with an intuitionist account of the indefinable property of goodness prevailed. Because of its definition of rightness in terms of consequences it was sometimes called 'ideal utilitarianism'. But, given the strenuousness of Moore's opposition to hedonism, the label is less naturally applicable to him than to the position of Rashdall, set out in his thorough and judicious *Theory of Good and Evil* (1907), a book superior to Moore's by reason of its author's notably greater capacity to understand, and, indeed, actual knowledge of, the history of ethical speculation. Rashdall includes pleasure, along with knowledge and virtue, among the ideal ends of conduct. The Moorean view was given a brilliantly concise expression in Russell's 'The Elements of Ethics' (four essays first published in 1910 and brought together in his *Philosophical Essays* of that year). But two years later Santayana's essay 'Hypostatic Ethics', in *Winds of Doctrine,* converted Russell to a theoretically rather inarticulate subjectivism from which he at length emerged in 1954 to the qualified, tentative utilitarianism of Part One of *Human Society in Ethics and Politics.*

Between H. A. Prichard's 'Does Moral Philosophy Rest on a Mistake?' in 1912 and W. D. Ross's *Foundations of Ethics* in 1939 the prevailing academic ethical theory was one which rejected the consequentialism in which Moore had agreed with the utilitarians while accepting his intuitionist account of moral knowledge. For Prichard and his school it is the obligatoriness of action that is revealed to intuition, not the goodness of ends, and the intuitions in question are general in form, asserting the rightness of actions of a kind and not that of particular actions. Along with Kant's, of which it is a less provocatively rationalistic version, this is, of all ethical theories, that which is furthest in spirit from the doctrine of Bentham and Mill. In its pristine form it is open to the objection that the specific absolute obligations it claims we intuit are liable to conflict. Prichard's remedy was a theoretical epicycle. As well as intuitions of duty he held that there are intuitions of comparative stringency as between conflicting duties, an uncomfortable departure from the principle of the absoluteness of obligation which he was anxious to sustain. Ross, more consistently, took intuitions of duty to be only 'prima facie', to discover no more than that kinds of action *tend* to be right. To adjudicate in cases of conflict he called upon the plainly consequentialist principle that one ought always to produce as much good as possible.

In the third phase, which has not long been concluded, Moore's anti-naturalism was reaffirmed on more secure foundations, namely as a consequence of the intrinsically practical, action-guiding nature of judgements of value. The emotivism of Stevenson and the prescriptivism of Hare, in agreeing that value-judgements are not statements, true or false, and thus not possible items of knowledge, lumped utilitarianism and Moore's own positive theory together in the limbo of error. According to these theories ultimate values are chosen, not discovered. The only constraints imposed on the valuer are personal sincerity and formal universality in the expression of his convictions. There can, on such views, be no objective restriction to the ends of morality. They can be of any concrete character whatever, provided that they are sincerely and impersonally affirmed. The reaction against this ethics of pure choice was initiated by the irresistible re-emergence of the idea that morality does have a specific content, that the moral character of an action is necessarily bound up with its effects in the way of harm or injury to others.

J. J. C. Smart, in his *Outlines of A Utilitarian System of Ethics* (1961), neatly reconciles his own commitment to a utilitarian morality with admission of the validity of prescriptivist ethics. He acknowledges that the fundamental utilitarian principle is not a true or false proposition, but is rather a basic moral resolution, which is not amenable to proof. But, he says, he embraces it as his fundamental moral choice and supposes that it will recommend itself to any benevolent person. What, after all, is benevolence but the steady pursuit of the happiness of all? Of course, for those who do not wish or choose to be benevolent, his subsequent development of the details of a utilitarian morality can at best be of theoretical interest. This is less powerful an *ad hominem* argument than he supposes. Few would blithely reject altogether the choice of a benevolent style of conduct. But the serious, controversial issue is as to whether benevolence is enough, whether it is the whole of virtue. One disposed to choose the regularian style of morality associated with an ethics like Prichard's would reply that, while all in favour of benevolence, he was even more concerned to be just. Smart's ingenious rhetoric really evades the fundamental point at issue.

In 1936, when utilitarianism must have been at its lowest ebb, R. F. Harrod, in an essay, 'Utilitarianism Revised', proposed a modification to the doctrine of Bentham and Mill, at least in its usual interpretation, which has become a major topic of ethical discussion in the last two decades. Harrod proposed a remedy for what he admitted to be the defects of the utilitarian theory of obligation, its representation of what the ordinary moral consciousness takes to be hard and fast laws by rules of thumb, always liable to suspension in particular cases. Instead of defining the wrongness of an action in terms of its effects, he defined it in terms of the effects of a general practice of performing actions of that kind in relevantly similar circumstances.

The idea that considerations of utility could support the acceptance and observance of rules had been in circulation at least since Hume. Rules could be argued for in this way as required for swift action in emergencies and to establish security of expectations. But the idea that rightness should be defined directly in terms of the utility of rules, from which the rightness of particular acts would then be derivative, seemed new. J. O. Urmson, however, argued in his essay 'The Intepretation of the Moral Philosophy of J. S. Mill' (1953) that rule-utilitarianism was Mill's own position. Mill defined the rightness of actions in terms of their *tendency* to augment the general happiness. But a particular action cannot have a tendency, only a class of actions can. (Harrod had noted that such a view might be implicit in the classical texts but said that, if it was, it needed to be brought into the open.)

In the last ten years this has been the most closely examined aspect of utilitarianism. Smart, in his *Outlines* and elsewhere, has been the most fervent of those who hold that to the extent that rule-utilitarianism enjoins different conduct from its act-utilitarian alternative, the latter is self-evidently to be preferred. To follow the former would involve a loss of attainable utility and would thus be irrational rule-worship. On the other side R. B. Brandt has been an equally persistent defender of the rule-utilitarian position. The latest and most authoritative expression of his views is in his 'Toward a Credible Form of Utilitarianism' (1963).

The debate was raised to a new level of refinement and precision in David Lyon's powerful monograph *Forms and Limits of Utilitarianism* (1965). Elaborating an array of distinctions which contribute to a clearer understanding of all aspects of utilitarianism, he argues that simple or traditional utilitarianism and what he calls general utilitarianism, which holds that an action ought to be done if and only if the doing of actions of that kind in relevantly similar circumstances would make the largest contribution to utility, necessarily enjoin the very same things. What makes the circumstances of one action of the kind in question relevantly similar to those of another are just those which affect the resulting utility, for good or ill. If keeping my promise here and now will produce less utility than breaking it, my duty to keep it cannot be established in the face of this fact by the utility of promise-keeping in general, since all the many cases in which promise-keeping is the most utility-producing action are relevantly different from the present case just in respect of their productiveness of utility.

Lyons distinguishes rule-utilitarianism proper from the generalised utilitarianism he has shown to be equivalent in its particular injunctions to act-utilitarianism of the traditional kind. The doctrine that an action is right if and only if it conforms to a set of rules general acceptance of which would maximise utility (Lyons's formula for what he calls 'ideal rule-utilitarianism') is a genuine and substantive alternative to act-utilitarianism and its generalised equivalent. But, he concludes, this substantive rule-utilitarianism gets the worst of both worlds. On the one hand it is less calculated to maximise utility than act-utilitarianism; on the other it is as much exposed as act-utilitarianism to the objections about the inadequacy of utilitarianism to sustain intuitively required principles of justice and fairness.

The two foregoing paragraphs give only the barest sketch of the content of Lyons's book. Although its final upshot is unfavourable to utilitarianism, that verdict is passed on utilitarianism as a *total* account of rational moral thinking. In contrast to the complete dismissal of utilitarianism that prevailed during what may be called the period of anti-naturalism, it is now widely conceded that at least a large and central segment of rational moral thinking is utilitarian in character. The crucial issue is the one that Mill failed to confront effectively in the last chapter of his book, that of whether the principle of utility must be supplemented by a principle, or principles, of comparable generality if it is to make good its claim to be a rational reconstruction of moral thinking.

NOTES

In page references to the works of Bentham and Mill the following abbreviations are used:

H   W. Harrison (ed.), Jeremy Bentham: *A Fragment on Government and An Introduction to the Principles of Morals and Legislation* (Oxford, 1948).

E   John Stuart Mill, *Utilitarianism, Liberty and Representative Government* (Everyman edition, London, 1910).

W   M. Warnock (ed.), *Utilitarianism* (London, 1962).

1. Bentham, *Introduction to the Principles of Morals and Legislation* (*I.P.M.L.*), ch. 1, para. 2. *H.* p. 126. *W.* p. 34.

2. Bentham, *I.P.M.L.* ch. 1, para. 6. *H.* p. 127. *W.* p. 35.

3. Bentham, *I.P.M.L.* ch. 1, para. 4. *H.* p. 126. *W.* p. 35.

4. Mill, *Utilitarianism* (*U.*), ch. 2. *E.* p. 6. *W.* p. 257.

5. Bentham, *I.P.M.L.* ch. 1, para. 10. *H.* p. 127. *W.* p. 36.

6. Bentham, *I.P.M.L.* ch. 1, para 1. *H.* p. 125. *W.* p. 33.

7. Mill, *U.* ch. 4. *E.* p. 35. *W.* p. 292.

8. Mill, *U.* ch. 4. *E.* p. 36. *W.* p. 292.

9. Hobbes, *Leviathan*, ed. Pogson Smith (Oxford, 1909), part 1, ch. 6, p. 41.

10. Cf. *British Moralists*, ed. Raphael, vol. 1, 'Hobbes to Gay' (Oxford, 1969), pp. 104–18.

11. Hume, *Treatise of Human Nature* (ed. Selby-Bigge, Oxford, 1888), Book III, part 1, sec. 1, p. 457.

12. Ibid. Book III, part 1, sec. 1, p. 469.

13. Ibid. Book III, part 1, sec. 1, pp. 468–9.

14. Ibid. Book III, part 1, sec. 2, p. 471.

15. Ibid. Book III, part 2, sec. 1, p. 481.

16. Ibid. Book III, part 3, sec. 1, p. 576.

17. Ibid. Book III, part 3, sec. 1, p. 581.

18. Beccaria, *On Crimes and Punishments*, trans. H. Paolucci (New York, 1963).

19. Hume, *Treatise*, Book III, part 2, sec. 1, p. 482.

20. E. A. Burtt (ed.), *The English Philosophers from Bacon to Mill* (New York, 1939), p. 773.

21. Ibid. p. 774.

22. Paley, *Principles of Moral and Political Philosophy* (London, 1785), Book I, ch. 7, p. 36.

23. Bentham, *Introduction to the Principles of Morals and Legislation*, preface, para. 7. *H.* p. 119.

24. Ibid. ch. 1, para. 1, footnote 1. *H.* p. 125. *W.* p. 33.

25. Ibid. ch. 17, part 1, 'The Limits between Private Ethics and the Art of Legislation'. *H.* pp. 410–23.

26. Ibid. ch. 17, part 1, para. 19. *H.* p. 422.

27. Ibid. ch. 17, part 1, para. 19. *H.* p. 423.

28. Ibid. ch. 1, para. 11. *H.* p. 128. *W.* p. 36.

29. Ibid. ch. 1, para. 12. *H.* p. 128. *W.* p. 36.

30. Ibid. ch. 1, para. 13. *H.* p. 128. *W.* p. 36.

31. Ibid. ch. 1, para. 14.4. *H.* p. 130. *W.* p. 38.

32. Ibid. ch. 2, para. 19. *H.* p. 146. *W.* p. 58.

33. Ibid. ch. 4, para. 3. *H.* pp. 151–2. *W.* pp. 64–5.

34. Ibid. ch. 7, para. 1. *H.* p. 189.

35. Ibid. ch. 17, part 1, para. 7. *H.* p. 413.

36. Ibid. ch. 12, para. 34, footnote. *H.* p. 280.

37. Mill, *On Liberty*, ch. 1. *E.* p. 74. *W.* p. 136.

38. Mill, *Utilitarianism*, ch. 2. *E.* p. 7. *W.* pp. 258–9.

39. Cf. G. H. von Wright, *The Varieties of Goodness* (London, 1963) chs 4 and 5.

40. *Values and Intentions* (Stanford, 1969). pp. 33–8.

41. Mill, *Utilitarianism*, ch. 3. *E.* p. 25. *W.* p. 280.

42. Ibid. ch. 3. *E.* p. 26. *W.* p. 281.

43. Ibid. ch. 3. *E.* p. 28. *W.* p. 283.

44. Ibid. ch. 1. *E.* p. 4. *W.* pp. 254–5.

45. Ibid. ch. 1. *E.* p. 4. *W.* p. 255.

46. Ibid. ch. 4. *E.* p. 35. *W.* p. 292.

47. Ibid. ch. 4. *E.* p. 36. *W.* p. 293.

48. Ibid. ch. 4. *E.* p. 26. *W.* p. 293.

49. Cf. *The Ground and Nature of the Right* (New York, 1955), ch. 1.

50. Cf. A. Quinton, 'The Bounds of Morality', in *Ethics and Social Justice*, ed. H. E. Kiefer and M. Munitz (Albany, 1970).

51. Cf. D. H. Monro, *Empiricism and Ethics* (1967), part 3.

52. Mill, *Utilitarianism*, ch. 5. *E.* pp. 54–5. *W.* pp. 314–15.

53. Hume, *Treatise of Human Nature*, Book III, part 2, sec. 1, p. 482.

54. H. Sidgwick, *The Methods of Ethics*, Book I, ch. 3, sec. 3 (6th edn, London, 1901), pp. 31–5.

55. Ibid. Book III, ch. 11, sec. 2, pp. 338–43.

56. Ibid. Book III, ch. 13, sec. 3, pp. 379–84.

57. Ibid. Book IV, ch. 5.
58. C. D. Broad, *Five Types of Ethical Theory* (London, 1930), p. 145.
59. Sidgwick, op. cit. Book I, ch. 3, sec. 3, p. 34.
60. F. H. Bradley, *Ethical Studies* (Oxford, 1876), Essay 3, p. 109.
61. F. H. Bradley, *Collected Essays* (Oxford, 1935), p. 113.
62. G. E. Moore, *Principia Ethica* (Cambridge, 1903), ch. 3, sec. 42, pp. 68–71.
63. Ibid. ch. 3, sec. 43, p. 72.
64. P. Schilpp (ed.), *The Philosophy of G. E. Moore* (Evanston, 1942), p. 16.
65. G. E. Moore, op. cit. ch. 3, sec. 50, p. 84.
66. Ibid. ch. 3, sec. 52, p. 89.
67. J. J. C. Smart, *An Outline of a System of Utilitarian Ethics* (Melbourne, 1961), pp. 11–14.
68. *The Nature of Things* (London, 1973), ch. 12.

BIBLIOGRAPHY

I. Histories

Leslie Stephen, *The English Utilitarians*, 3 volumes (London, 1900).

Ernest Allbee, *A History of English Utilitarianism* (New York, 1902).

Élie Halévy, *The Growth of Philosophic Radicalism*, trans. M. Morris (London, 1928).

John Plamenatz, *The English Utilitarians* (Oxford, 1949).

II. The Precursors

Richard Cumberland, *De Legibus Naturae*, 1672. Selections with parallel translation in D. D. Raphael (ed.), *British Moralists 1650–1800*, vol. 1, pp. 77–102 (Oxford, 1969).

John Gay, *Dissertation Concerning the Fundamental Principle of Virtue or Morality* (London, 1731): prefixed to Archbishop King's *Essay on the Origin of Evil*. Reprinted in E. A. Burtt (ed.), *The English Philosophers from Bacon to Mill* (New York, 1939).

David Hume, *Treatise of Human Nature*, Book III (London, 1740). *Enquiry Concerning the Principles of Morals* (London, 1751). Cf. V. C. Chappell (ed.), *Hume: a collection of critical essays*, pp. 240–334 (Garden City, N.Y., 1966; London, 1968).

Abraham Tucker, *The Light of Nature Pursued*, by 'Edward Search' (1768–78).

William Paley, *The Principles of Moral and Political Philosophy* (1785).

III. The Main Texts

Jeremy Bentham, *Introduction to the Principles of Morals and Legislation* (1789). Edited by W. Harrison, with *A Fragment on Government* (Oxford, 1948). Cf. David Baumgardt, *Bentham and the Ethics of Today* (Princeton, N.J., 1952). A. J. Ayer, 'The Principle of Utility', in *Philosophical Essays* (London, 1954). H. L. A. Hart, 'Bentham', in *Proceedings of the British Academy*, vol. 48 (Oxford, 1962).

James Mill, *A Fragment on Mackintosh* (London, 1835).

John Stuart Mill, *Utilitarianism* (London, 1863). (There are many subsequent editions.) Cf. Karl Britton, *John Stuart Mill*, chap. 2 (Harmondsworth, 1953). J. B. Schneewind (ed.), *Mill: A Collection of Critical Essays*, pp. 145–250 (Garden City, N.Y., 1968; London, 1969). Alan Ryan, *The Philosophy of John Stuart Mill*, chaps 11 and 12 (London, 1970).

IV. Nineteenth-Century Criticism and Development

John Grote, *An Examination of the Utilitarian Philosophy* (Cambridge, 1870).

Henry Sidgwick, *The Methods of Ethics* (London, 1874).

F. H. Bradley, *Ethical Studies*, chap. 3 (Oxford, 1876).

G. E. Moore, *Principia Ethica*, chap. 3 (Cambridge, 1903).

V. Contemporary Writings

R. F. Harrod, 'Utilitarianism Revised', in *Mind*, vol. 45 (1936) pp. 137–56.

J. J. C. Smart, *Outlines of a Utilitarian System of Ethics* (Melbourne, 1961).

David Lyons, *Forms and Limits of Utilitarianism* (Oxford, 1965).

Jan Narveson, *Morality and Utility* (Baltimore, 1967).

D. H. Hodgson, *Consequences of Utilitarianism* (Oxford, 1967).

Michael D. Bayles (ed.), *Contemporary Utilitarianism* (Garden City, N.Y., 1968).

Cf. also the following works, which are of a broadly utilitarian tendency.

W. T. Stace, *The Concept of Morals* (London and New York, 1937).

Moritz Schlick, *Problems of Ethics* (trans. D. Rynin) (New York, 1939). (1st German edition, *Fragen der Ethik*, 1930.)

C. I. Lewis, *Analysis of Knowledge and Valuation*, Book III (La Salle, Illinois, 1946).

——*The Ground and Nature of the Right* (New York, 1955).

——*Values and Imperatives* (Stanford, California, 1969).

2

AXIOLOGICAL ETHICS

J. N. FINDLAY

I. INTRODUCTION

The aim of this monograph is to study a strand of ethical enquiry which has been present throughout the history of ethical thought, but which has in fairly recent times been given an independent development and has thereby illuminated the whole field of ethical questions. Axiology or Value-Theory began as a tailpiece to Ethics, but it arguably ought to end as the tail which wags the dog, which by illuminating the ends of practice alone makes the prescription of norms for practice itself a practicable undertaking. This monograph will study the thought of those who have done most to detach value-theory as a discipline from the practical enquiries in which it had its origin, and on which it in its turn can be used to throw light.

The word 'axiology' (like the more Germanic 'value-theory') is probably still felt to be barbaric by the best philosophical speakers in England: its value, however, lies in demarcating an enquiry, of great importance and illumination, which will probably not be explored, if its boundaries with other disciplines remain confused and blurred. The word 'axiology' was introduced into philosophy by Urban in 1906 in his heavily excellent book *Valuation: Its Nature and Laws*: it was used to translate the *Werttheorie* which the Austrian economist von Neumann had introduced into economics, and which the Austrian philosophers Ehrenfels and Meinong, concerned at all costs to follow the lead of 'science', had tried to cultivate in the field of aesthetic, moral, scientific and other values. 'Axiology' meant the study of the ultimately worthwhile things (and of course of the ultimately counterworthwhile things) as well as the analysis of worthwhileness (or counterworthwhileness) in general. Urban's book, with its elaborately stated theory of 'affective-conative meaning' was a valuable introduction of the thought-trends of Brentano, Meinong and Ehrenfels to English-speaking thinkers, and possibly a remote inspirer of the less well elaborated theories of 'emotive meaning' held later in the century by Ogden, Richards and Stevenson. Axiology, like other similar European movements, flourished faintly beyond the Atlantic, inspiring such interesting developments as Perry's behaviouristic *General Theory of Value* (1926) and Brogan's good papers on 'betterness' as the fundamental value-universal. Meanwhile, on the continent, the enquiry into value passed beyond the abstract stage represented by Lessing's work on *Wertaxiomatik* and some posthumously published work of Husserl's, and became interested in wider questions of the good life in general, and its relation to the norms of conduct which played such a preponderant role in traditional ethics. There were produced two immensely valuable systematic studies of the whole realm of values and the principles underlying its institution: Max Scheler's *Der Formalismus in der Ethik und die materiale Wertethik* (*Formalism in Ethics and the Material Value-Ethic*) (1916), and Nicolai Hartmann's *Ethik* (*Ethics*) (1926), translated into English by Stanton Coit in 1932. These are works which not only ask what worthwhileness and counterworth-whileness may be in general, but to what in detail they apply, and that not by arbitrary imposition, but in virtue of their inner sense and content. With them may be compared the British delineations of the value-realm found in G. E. Moore (especially in the last, little-read chapters of *Principia Ethica*, 1903), in Hastings Rashdall (*The Theory of Good and Evil*, 1907), and in considerable parts of W. D. Ross's *The Right and the Good* (1930) and *The Foundations of Ethics* (1939). It is with these foundational works, British and continental, that the present monograph will be mainly concerned.

The years since the initial launching and flowering of axiology have involved a profound set-back for it as for all branches of traditional philosophising. The star of Wittgenstein rose in the British and that of Heidegger in the continental firmament, and the blaze of these luminaries was temporarily such as to render the whole constellated pattern of traditional and recent problems and findings invisible. Wittgenstein thought in terms of a programme designed to bring words back from their elaborate and philosophical, to their most ordinary, commonplace uses, and in terms of such a programme talk about values and their relations became nothing but an inflated, misleading surrogate for the commendatory, prescriptive talk of ordinary life. It was this that must be studied and clarified, in a 'meta-ethical' rather than a straightforwardly ethical perspective. On the continent, likewise, Heidegger, with his determination to see all things only in the light of an agonised, barely expressible personal subjectivity, made short work of the edifices raised by the systematic value-theorists. At the level at which Heidegger's existential person lives and confronts the world and society, there can be no values in any organised, systematically discussable sense, only the tortured preferences of the individual, into whose loneliness, styled 'authenticity', the whole organised world of value and being has been absorbed. Both Wittgenstein and Heidegger emerged upon the disintegrated middle-European scene of 1918 onwards in the form of disintegration made conscious and systematic. Their utterances acted as an immense blanketing snowfall beneath which the whole pattern of ordered philosophical discourse lay for a time buried. In the hope of many, including the author of the present monograph, this snowfall is at present in process of vanishing more or less tracelessly, leaving only some extremely illuminating changes in matter and method to diversify the philosophical landscape. These large issues cannot, however, be argued in the present context.

Axiology is therefore the product of a fairly recent period in thought-history which, temporarily overwhelmed by a general disturbance, now bids fair to remain, in its essential 'problematic', a permanent field for philosophising. All this must not be taken to mean that axiology is basically a new thing, that it is not part and parcel of the whole tradition of philosophy. It has always existed, though largely subordinated to the discipline of ethics, the investigation of what ought to be done, or of what it is that something ought to be done. What is worthwhile *per se* or the contrary is, of course, something having the closest possible relation to what ought to be done, but nevertheless not so close as not to leave it possible to assert the existence or possibility of worthwhile or unworthwhile things having little or no relation to what ought to be done. The field of ethics certainly presupposes the field of axiology, but the latter, arguably, stretches out beyond the limits of the former. The relations between the worthwhile and the practically demanded are obviously of that deep, puzzling kind which form the basic material of philosophy – relations where identities suddenly show gulfs and where gulfs abridge themselves to identities – and cannot be further considered here. Suffice it to say that the concepts work differently, and are not in any simple manner interchangeable, and that it is not a service to philosophy to treat the one solely in relation to the other.

That axiology flourished among the Greeks is shown by the frequently uttered but untrue complaint that they had no concept corresponding to the modern notion of obligation. It is also shown in the well-known complaint against the Platonic Socrates that he professes a sort of 'ideal utilitarianism', in which doing as one ought is in a subtle manner *confused* with having what is worthwhile, so that being a practitioner of virtue comes to be identified with a sort of personal profit, which then assorts strangely with the ordinary personal profit of good birth, fortune, wealth, etc., and the vanishing delights of the senses. The Platonic Socrates, it is plain, is trying to cozen us into following a right way of life, and into ordering our souls correctly, by persuading us that such correctness of life and behaviour is an intrinsically worthwhile thing, and that not merely for some outside judge but for ourselves who live in this manner. And Plato emancipated from Socrates is plainly more concerned to give us an axiological hierarchy than a set of ethical precepts: thus the *Philebus* teaches us to accord supreme value to the Measure or Limit from which all excellence and all beauty derive, and secondary value to the various specifications of such Measure or Limit, while the mind and wisdom which acquaint us with such values are valuable in a third degree, the sciences and arts in a fourth and the pure pleasures which accompany the sciences and certain uses of the senses in a fifth and last degree. It is in terms of these values that our life should be shaped, and Plato is much more clear as to the factors that enter into the shaping than as to the precise, right compromise that governs their combination. If we turn to Aristotle we have a similar overweight of axiology over ethics. No question is in fact raised as to the propriety of an action or a way of living other than its subservience to a single supreme end of welfare or happiness, into whose concept, however, many distinct factors are fitted. And the subsequent history of Stoicism and Epicureanism illustrates the conflict in axiological theory of contents which are not merely both good, but good *in different ways*: both systems were, however, wedded to an axiomatic monism which meant that only one of these ways could be genuine.

If we now move to the eighteenth century, we certainly find problems of axiology equally stressed with problems of conduct or ethics. Thus Richard Price whose main concern is to prove that 'we express necessary truth when we say of some actions that they are right and of others that they are wrong' (Selby-Bigge, *British Moralists*, Clarendon Press, 1897; Bobbs-Merrill reprint, 1964, para. 616), none the less also says that 'it is not possible to contemplate and compare dead matter and life, brutality and reason, misery and happiness, virtue and vice, ignorance and knowledge, impotence and power, the deity and inferior beings, without acquiring the ideas of better and worse, perfect and imperfect, noble and ignoble, excellent and base' (Selby-Bigge, para. 640). Similarly if we turn to Hutcheson we have not only the clearly set-forth distinction of 'natural' and 'moral' good, but a variety of 'senses' acquainting us with what can only be called a series of disparate values: the agreeable and the disagreeable, the aesthetic values resident in 'uniform objects', as well as the moral values proportioned, in axiomatic fashion, to the benevolence, the ability, and the private good achieved or sacrificed by the agent (Selby-Bigge, paras 126, 127). In Kant, likewise, we have a deeply involved mixture of the ethical and the axiological, despite the widely held view that he is only concerned to specify a law or principle for rational action and not to put before us any material end to endeavour. Kant moves from laying down the Categorical Imperative in its first form, as a pure guide to ethical action, to the axiological principle that sees in the will which follows the Categorical Imperative the only unconditionally worthwhile thing in the world. Only a very confused intelligence

can imagine that acting on universalisable maxims and respecting
the will which so acts are in any way identical or even logically
equivalent postures: a stout ethical purist might in fact forbid
any idolatrous reverence for the will which conforms to the moral
law. In the same way, there are many infusions of the axiological
into Kantian imperativism, in the command, for example, to
treat persons as absolute ends, in the belief that a Divine Agent will
apportion happiness to virtue, as also in various cognitive and
aesthetic valuations which meet us throughout the Kantian
writings. Kant is in fact much nearer to setting up a comprehensive material ethic of values than Scheler and other critics have
supposed. And if, finally, we turn from Kant to the Utilitarians
we see there too an unquestioned stress on a simplified axiology,
in which all values and disvalues are concentrated into the
positive end of pleasure and the negative end of avoidance of
pain. This axiology is combined with an imperfect ethic in which,
under the guise of estimating quantities of pleasure and pain,
we in effect say how we must decide among different cases of
pleasure and pain. What we have said has made plain that questions of ultimate worthwhileness and counterworthwhileness
have been as much part of the warp and woof of traditional
ethical theory as more narrowly conceived discussions of what
ought to be done.

We shall now, in the rest of this introductory chapter, clarify
some linguistic and conceptual issues, and some questions of
principle, which will at least prepare us for the field of views and
problems that we are about to consider. We shall employ the term
'value' as a philosophical equivalent of the goodness, the
excellence, the desirability and what not which we attribute to
certain sorts of objects, states and situations: such value is very
plainly correlated, and correlated in principle, with attitudes that
we shall call 'valuations', for which well-established philosophical
term 'cherishing', 'setting store by', 'esteeming', 'prizing',
'having a pro-attitude towards' may serve as ordinary or new-
fangled equivalents. The circumscription of 'valuation' or
'cherishing' will concern us later: for the time being it is sufficiently
clear what these terms cover, though it is worth stressing that

not every passing tinge of agreeable feeling inspired by a situation amounts to a valuation or involves an attribution of value, but only one that represents a moderately stable posture of soul, and to some extent also wishes its object to *exist*, to be a stable part of the world.

It is further clear that valuation, however evanescent, is necessarily consequent on some character or specification which is capable of being distinguished from the value we find in an object, and which is what we value an object *for*, our reason for finding it precious, etc., such a character or specification being in principle such as could be elsewhere and otherwise exemplified. Even when individuals are valued for being the individuals they are, there is an obscure reference to specifications they fulfil, and occasions on which these specifications are manifest, or at least to occasions on which they can be repeatedly contemplated or assessed. Valuation clearly has a built-in generality, even if there are special problems concerned with the undoubtedly genuine valuation of individuality and of particular individuals. This built-in generality of valuations however makes it natural and proper to speak of 'a value' or of 'values' in the plural, where a value means an association of value with a particular character or specification which really reflects the valuation of a given person or set of persons, e.g. justice, Norman lineage or sportsmanship are for some persons 'values'. It is artificial, and likewise question-begging, to refer to such things merely as 'grounds of value', suggesting that valuation and value should be something amorphous and undifferentiated and externally wedded to the make-up and character of objects, whether in human experience or in reality. The so-called 'descriptive content' which can be clearly separated from the 'evaluative meaning' which seems to penetrate it may be a valuable philosophical distinction at certain levels of abstraction. It does not follow that it is so at all such levels.

Beside 'values' and 'valuations' we must of course never forget to range 'disvalues' and 'disvaluations', little as we may care for the latter pair of terms. Disvaluation covers the rejection, the spurning, the reproving and disapproving of some state or

content, a rejection likewise fairly stable in character and directed
to some more or less stable existence or non-existence in the actual
world. It is of supreme importance that in axiological considerations we should never assume that disvalues are in any sense the
mirror-image of values, that the absence of goodness is automatically very bad, or the absence of badness deeply good, etc.,
or that the principles governing valuation and disvaluation are in
any way closely parallel.

Values and disvalues, and the attitudes connected with them,
must likewise obviously admit of comparativeness or degree. A
scale or scales of degrees tending to a vague 'infinity' in either
direction and passing through a common centre of 'indifference',
is plainly part and parcel of our subject-matter. We must not,
however, assume that values and disvalues always permit of such
scalar comparison, and we must also recognise the complexities
introduced by certain quasi-values which are merely the shadows
of contrary disvalues. All these points will concern us later.

'Values' and 'valuations' must further, it is plain, permit of a
distinction, not always wholly clear, but certainly always felt even
by moderately sophisticated persons, between such values and
valuations as are freely allowed to be 'personal', peculiar to the
individual, and neither expected nor required to hold for other
persons, and other valuations and values which are felt to impose
themselves with a certain necessity or ineluctability, which it is
felt must impress itself on *anyone*, or at least on anyone who
reflects at all carefully on the matter. Thus the valuation of sitting
on beaches or eating meals in the open or wearing flowers in one's
hair are obviously by their very nature and structure matters on
which no agreement can be expected or demanded, whereas the
valuation of being happy, of enjoying freedom and power, even
of triumphing over one's adversaries, of being truly informed as
to the state of things, etc., are obviously, in varying degrees,
values disagreement with which tends to seem absurd, unfeasible,
perverse, mistaken, wrong. (These seemings may, of course, as
in the fourth case, seem open to correction.) Our impression may
be mistaken, but the utterances 'I like bondage, I rejoice in being
discriminated against, I value a state of deep unhappiness' seem

to involve a certain deep absurdity comparable to saying that A is a C because it does *not* belong to certain classes of things which are Cs. Such things can be said, they are not even formally self-contradictory, but they involve a certain vein of deep nonsense of which philosophy must take account. And while this nonsense is less evident in cases that involve *others*, the very notion of valuing things differently merely because they apply to others, seems in a deep sense arbitrary and nonsensical. Between these extreme limits of values and valuations which seem to have a cogent and mandatory quality and others which have no such character, lies a whole spectrum of intermediate cases, those which in a vague manner impress us as mandatory and cogent but in whose case we can readily be brought to doubt their cogent or mandatory character. All these distinctions are genuinely 'part of the phenomena', whether or not we decide that they can ultimately be sustained.

Valuation and values stand further, with great obviousness, as previously mentioned, in relation to various requirements, exigencies, demands, imperatives, which are most readily expressed by some case of the auxiliary verb 'ought' or 'should'. These exigencies are experienced by ourselves, and are also brought home to others, by certain manifest attitudes which can, on the one hand, be regarded as forms of valuation, though they may equally, on the other hand, be regarded as merely related phenomena. They are attitudes marked by an urgency, a dynamic pressure, which are characteristic of some, but not all manifest cases of valuation. These 'oughts' and 'shoulds' are, as has been often pointed out, as various in type as the valuations or disvaluations to which they are related: some are serious, some playful, some personal, some full of soidisant mandatoriness, some identified with a peculiar group or community, some seeming to voice the feeling of all men without restriction. Some are as much matters of degree, as much affected with comparativeness, as are certain valuations which correspond to them. There are, however, others which have a certain summary, all-or-none character which makes them quite different from valuations. That A ought to be B and ought on no account to be C, represent pure exigencies from which the value-content has, as it were, been emptied out: it is only when we enquire into the why of such impressions that value-content comes back into the picture. And the most purely summary or all-or-none of these 'oughts' or 'shoulds' are plainly the ethical 'oughts' or 'shoulds', the 'oughts' or 'shoulds' of our most serious social practice. These are not matters of degree, since whatever the importance or lack of importance of the values which condition choice or action, choice and action themselves admit no degree: one must either do or not do something. An alternative B may be nearly as choiceworthy as A, but in the actual choice the doing of A may mean the total omission of B. Not all action, however, is dominated by an ethical 'ought', and, where none is present, arbitrary preference, perhaps guided by values, personal or mandatory, takes over.

What we have so far said has sketched the main distinctions in the field of valuation and their relation to other distinctions and to one another. We have accepted a technical language because it has seemed to us to do better justice to the working of our ordinary terms and concepts in this field than the language of liking, approving, caring for, setting store by, preferring, etc., with its innumerable shifts and transitions. Philosophy must decide what distinctions are philosophically worth drawing, and while respectful to ordinary usage, particularly in the initial pinning down of its notions, it must remain magisterial in its final use of them. And a new philosophical usage can successfully hit off a distinction we wish to draw, basing itself on its own philosophical sense of ease or unease, without necessarily deferring to *non*-philosophical ease or disquiet. We have now to consider the main problems which the distinctions just drawn readily provoke, and to which the philosophers we are due to study gave very different answers.

The first and most fundamental question which an axiological ethics must confront is plainly that of the nature of the valuation, the setting store by something, which is also plainly a clearer, more graspable thing than the 'value' with which, under its influence, objects are 'credited' by us. Is this valuation primarily a stance which *we*, as agents or experients, take up to objects or states which come before us, or is it primarily a 'light' in which objects or states appear before us, much as they come before us as being about to do this or that, or as having this or that bearing on one another, etc. ? In other words, is valuation primarily an attitudinal or a phenomenological matter, a matter of how someone stands to some content or a matter of the *way* in which that content comes up or appears before him? Or is there both an attitudinal and a phenomenological side to the matter, and is there perhaps some deep relation between them? We shall see that Meinong, for example, has much to say on these matters. And if we now turn to the attitudinal side of valuation, there is a question unasked by the philosophers in our purview as to whether attitudes are to be studied as *behaviour*, in the form they take for an outside observer, or in the 'inward' form they take for the man who has them, or perhaps in both forms conjointly, and perhaps without according primacy to either. And there is the further, central question as to whether, in considering the attitudinal side of valuation, we shall lay stress on the element of *striving* for or against the realisation of something, which some have made crucial to valuation, or on the element of emotional appraisal, positive or negative, which to others has seemed equally crucial, or, lastly on some deliberate openness to the phenomena of the value-sphere by which all such emotions and practical responses are in some way provoked or triggered off. Is valuing primarily being ready to have wants, being ready to have feelings or being simply open to see things in certain 'lights'? This leads us on to consider the other side of valuation, the nature of the 'light' in which a valued object comes before us, as precious, as worthy of admiration, etc., a light which is often more evident to the valuing person than any attitude he may have to an object, and which can persist and haunt him even when the relevant attitude is quite in abeyance. Philosophers may dilate on the absurdity of attributing values to things instead of connecting them with our own reactions, but the fact remains that our own reactions are not the locus where they often appear to be: they seem to inform, to pervade, to be modally attached to objects or states of affairs. The world of our normal experience is not the neutral world of the impartial scientist: it is painted with as many axiological tinges as men have sentiments. We have therefore to consider how best to describe the tinges in question. Are they analysable in terms of some obscure readiness to evoke attitudes in persons? Or in terms of some not further analysable but relational modality of 'fitness' or 'fittingness'? Or in terms of some wholly unanalysable, simple predicate or quality? All these questions and many more have been explored by the axiologists of our period, but by none more conscientiously than Alexius Meinong in the various treatises we shall consider later. What it is important to stress is that none of these questions are in any way tractable as long as we operate with some inadequate philosophical psychology, one for instance that makes the mind a dwelling-place of elementary contents, or that lacks a properly developed analysis of observer's (i.e. behavioural) psychology, or that quite ignores the subtle twists of the concept of mental directedness or 'intentionality' which we owe to Brentano, Meinong and Husserl.

The second important matter which comes up for philosophical consideration is the claim of certain valuations to be mandatory, to be such as all who reflect enough *must* and *should* accept, and *must* and *should* apply to everyone and exact from everyone. The 'must' of sheer necessity here appears in a close marriage with a peculiar case of 'shouldness' or normativity, which to many philosophers seems the height of confusion, but which none the less always comes back in what we feel deeply disposed to say. How shall we deal with such mandatoriness? Is it merely a descriptive character of certain valuations that they thus arrogate authority to themselves, without being able to exclude a counter-arrogation of authority by contrary valuations? Or are there ways in which we can test, and by testing validate or invalidate, the authority claimed by such mandatory valuations? And if there are none such, is the whole uttering of mandatory valuations not vain and unprofitable, since finding them means no more than adopting them, and adopting them has no necessary influence on others? Or does mandatoriness involve the real presence in objects and states of affairs of obscure predicates and modalities which in non-mandatory valuations only *appear* to be present? If so, we have not merely the problem of the tests for such 'real presence', but the further problem as to why such real presence is connected with emotion or endeavour in ourselves, a connection not met with in other cases of cognition. But perhaps mandatoriness consists rather in some built-in self-restriction to what could be pursued or chosen by anyone for anyone, and perhaps such an austere notion will enable us in some way to 'deduce' the rich variety of what we ordinarily take to be mandatory values. That such a view can be sustained will be argued for in the last chapter of the present monograph. For the time being we may argue that while the concept of mandatory valuation involves profound difficulties, these need not lead to that discrediting of it as a concept that has been frequent in recent times: it should rather lead to the discrediting of the assumptions, by no means perspicuous, which have made it seem discreditable. There is nothing self-evident in the opinion that our emotions are in all cases only variable, personal reactions with nothing but a contingent relation to that which calls them forth, or to that on which they are directed: innumerable linguistic and conceptual facts belie such a simple-minded theory. The elenchus of Moore may in any case be applied to all valid mandatory valuations: we may say that we know that there are some such, and that we have much more certainty regarding them, than we have in regard to any psychological or semantic or ontological theory which would conjure them out of existence.

From questions regarding the possibility of mandatory valuations, we pass on to questions concerned with the overall structure of mandatory values and disvalues, to what we shall call in later chapters the construction of a 'value-firmament'. If mandatory values represent merely a piece of would-be legislation for all in regard to all, such questions of overall structure will at best systematise the values and disvalues of a single arrogant individual or society, but if the possibility of a validation is not merely claimed, but involved in the structure of such valuations, then we may hope to construct a firmament of values and disvalues which will be more than a mere product of personal pontification. Highly arguable firmaments of values may be held to be found in the axiologies of Scheler and Hartmann, as also of Moore,

Rashdall and Ross. We are at least here in the presence of infinitely discussable issues, and not among the mere Babel of
conflicting voices which on certain conceptions of valuation
would be all that was to be expected. Plainly the penetration to
valid mandatory values is in some manner really possible: the
only legitimate task for philosophy is to discover *how* this is the
case.

The mapping of a firmament of values, and the consideration
of the relations among them, must lead on to a further question:
the relation of mandatory values to purely personal values, of the
relation of sorts of things that everyone must value for everyone,
to the sorts of things that each individual only values for himself.
We have here the choices of trying to make the two classes of
values wholly independent, or of giving them an essential bearing
upon each other, the mandatory values being, for instance,
essentially regarded as values of higher order, which are built
upon and presuppose the existence of purely personal values
which they only order and systematise. This latter is essentially the
conception of Butler who sees the higher faculties of self-love
and benevolence, and at a further remove conscience, as ordering
the particular passions, and as having no possible content without
the latter, whereas the former is the view suggested by certain
intemperate passages in Kant where it would seem that a total
lack of non-mandatory impulses would be of advantage to pure
members of the Kingdom of Ends.

And our mapping must lead on finally to a discussion like that
in the fifth chapter of Moore's *Principia Ethica* as to the relation of
our value-map to conduct, or like many of those that occur in
Ross's *Right and the Good* or *The Foundations of Ethics*. Are values
and disvalues, mandatory or personal, sufficient to decide what
we should do in a given situation, or shall we hold that there are
practical principles which go beyond them, and which are not
formulable in terms of them? And do values and disvalues decide
what we ought to do in some simple, general manner, perhaps
involving a general metric of values and disvalues, or are the
principles that enable us to reach practical decision many and
complex? Are there perhaps practical principles, unconditional

'oughts' for conduct, to which all considerations of value and disvalue are irrelèvant? Is it further the case that purely personal factors enter into our practical decisions, and that they *should* be allowed to supplement and to give a definite outcome to our practical problems. These questions have also been considered by the philosophers we are to study, though we may be somewhat critical of some of their opinions.

We have said enough to indicate the range of concepts and problems covered by axiological ethics. Let us now consider the views actually put forward by our chosen exponents.

II. BRENTANO AND MEINONG

The present chapter will deal with the contributions to axiology and axiological ethics of Franz Brentano (1838–1917) and Alexius Meinong (1853–1920), both of whom illuminated valuation and value by placing it in the context of a truly profound, magnificently elaborated philosophy of mind. The work of both philosophers, like that of Christian von Ehrenfels, another value-theorist of the period (*System der Werttheorie – System of Value-Theory* – 1897–8), is associated with Austria: Brentano's most brilliant period of teaching was in Vienna, Meinong created and operated a small philosophical school at Graz, while von Ehrenfels taught for many years at Prague. There is something characteristically Austrian about all their work, a neat accuracy together with a fighting shy of the murky enthusiasm and the ill-justified comprehensiveness of the typical Germanic 'system'.

Brentano, with whom we shall first deal, was of course primarily a philosophical psychologist, the developer of a 'psychognosy', an analysis of mentality as such and its basic differentiations, whose empirical connections he was concerned to stress, though it seems to a modern student a severely conceptual study. This philosophical psychology was expounded in the *Psychologie vom empirischen Standpunkte* (*Psychology from the Empirical Standpoint*) of 1878 (second augmented edition in 1910), and provided the foundation of an axiological ethics, first expounded in a famous lecture entitled *The Origin of our Knowledge of Right and Wrong* (*Vom Ursprung sittlicher Erkenntnis*, 1889) and whose further development can be studied in the posthumously published *Grundlegung und Aufbau der Ethik* (*Foundations and Structure of Ethics*). The lecture on the *Origin of our Knowledge of Right and Wrong* was translated into English by Cecil Hague in 1902, and Moore wrote of it in 1903 in the *International Journal of Ethics*, vol. XIV; 'This is a far better discussion of the most fundamental

principles of Ethics than any others with which I am acquainted.
... In almost all points in which he differs from any of the great
historical systems, he is in the right. It would be difficult to
exaggerate the importance of this work.' This great lecture, thus
endorsed by a great philosopher, has long been out of print in
England, but we are glad to see it retranslated in 1969 by Roderick
Chisholm.

Brentano's psychognosy may be roughly sketched for the
purposes of the present monograph. Its great originality lay in
a subtle modification of the scholastic notion of 'intention', the
form *in* the mind which enables the mind to refer to what is not
part of itself, and to what may or may not exist in the real world
beyond itself. Only while the scholastic 'intention' was a strange
piece of machinery designed to carry out a strange task, on
which it threw not the smallest light, Brentano substituted the
task for the machinery, the performance for the instrument, so
that an intention ceased to be something that *explained* mental
transcendence, and simply became a case of transcendence itself.
In this self-transcendence, this intentionality of the mental,
Brentano refused to see anything queer or requiring explanation:
mentality is simply a plane where life is lived outside of itself,
points beyond itself, is concerned with matters 'objective' to
itself, and which need not, though they also may, be part and
parcel of their own make-up or structure. This magnificent
turning of a difficulty into a concept, and a problem into an
explanation, is one of the most astonishing, because also most
simple, philosophical feats: it simply consists in recognising what
is most deeply characteristic of 'consciousness' and the life of
mind. Psychic phenomena, acts of mind, can never be fully
described in terms of their mere characters or elements or internal
structure, but only also in terms of what they intend (and of how
they intend it), of what they are directed to, of what in a non-
linguistic sense they 'mean'.

Brentano of course was concerned to use his notion of self-
transcendence in order to demarcate the realm of 'psychic or
mental phenomena' from those that are 'physical', and it is
perhaps doubtful whether he achieved this. But whether or not

there are non-intentional states of mind, or cases of intentionality which are not mental, the notion remains of supreme importance in illuminating the higher levels of mental life, on which such performances as valuations can take place. And experienced intentionality has an importance which non-experienced intentionality (if the notion is at all legitimate) never can achieve. If animal behaviour or neural states have their own peculiar directedness to transcendent matters of concern, we can know of such directedness only through indirect, never quite reliable indices, whereas experienced intentionality has its own directly experienced directedness. We cannot in fact know that we are minding anything without knowing what we are minding. Brentano's theory of intentionality of course includes a further Aristotelian view of the way in which intentionality, while primarily directed outwards, to what is *not* part of itself, also embraces a subsidiary direction to itself, so that the intention towards X is also subsidiarily an intention to this intention, a doctrine that does not (according to Brentano) lead to an infinite regress owing to the manner in which such subsidiary, self-directed intentionality melts into and blends with its primary, outward-turned basis. And it sets in an emphatic light a point previously stressed by Aristotle and the Schoolmen: that the directedness of mind, not being a relation, does not demand the existence or being of what it intends. Its object enters into its inner description without entering it as a real part, and without needing to be a real part of anything anywhere.

The relevance of Brentano's doctrine to value-theory lies, however, not in his general demarcation of the mental, but in his peculiar classification of mental phenomena. Following Descartes, for whose insights he has a profound respect, he believes in *three* fundamental forms of experienced self-transcendence, one of which is the most simple and basic of all, the second of which is built upon and presupposes the first, while the last is built upon the second and hence indirectly on the first. The first is the *Vorstellung*, the simple Presentation or presence of something to consciousness, without any further stance towards such an object being taken up by the mind. Such presentations may be sensuous, they may also be purely cogitative, and they may be of physical things or states of things, real or imaginary, and also of psychical acts directed upon such things or upon other psychical acts. Imposed on the *Vorstellung* is the act of Belief or Judgement, characterised by a unique antithesis between acceptance and rejection. Such beliefs or judgements are for Brentano the true existential or reality-experiences: in them an object or content comes before us, not merely as being this or that, but as being truly there or not there, or as being the case or not being the case. Brentano deprecates all analyses which place the essence of judging in an association of concepts: this is a pure matter of the *Vorstellung*, of unconvinced presentation. Imposed on Judgement and *Vorstellung* alike we then have the 'Phenomena of Love and Hate', characterised by quite another kind of acceptance and rejection than that of the Judgement: they are cases in which some object is positively embraced as good (though the word 'good' may of course not be available) or rejected as bad. Brentano believes that this unique sort of acceptance and rejection, as unanalysable as that of Belief, runs through states of feeling, states of desire, and states of will alike, and this whether they are warm and excited or calm and cool. Distant approval and warm espousal (or their contraries) have precisely the same note of acceptance (or rejection), and so have the most inchoate wish and the most firmly adopted resolution. In all these cases we are, as it were, saying *Placet* or *Fiat* or their contraries, with what further overtones is a matter of basic unimportance. Plainly there is a deep introspective warrant for the affinity here noted by Brentano. The close relation of conative–affective acceptance–rejection to the acceptance–rejection of Judgement, comes out in the systematic variation of the form of Love and Hate with that of Belief: whether an attitude is one of Hope, Fear, Desire, Vague Wish or Firm Resolve, Action or mere Satisfaction or Dissatisfaction depends throughout on what we *believe* to be the case. Plainly we are dealing with axiomatic principles: it is not, for example, meaningful to resolve upon the plainly impossible or to be satisfied with what is seen not to be the case. Brentano further illuminates his concept of affective–

conative acceptance–rejection by affirming the unanalysable
character of *preference*. Preference does not consist in any relation
of superior strength or intensity among our variously directed
wants or likes – an error committed in many discussions of
voluntary freedom – but in the unique stance of liking or wanting
one thing *above* or *rather than* another. (Much as the partial beliefs
studied in probability-theory are simple stances rather than
embroiled belief-tendencies.) Plainly there is a kind of preference
which conforms to the conflict-of-strength pattern, and Brentano
has no wish to deny it, but he is utterly right in recognising that
truly interesting form of preference (of which choice is the
supreme expression) which is unitary rather than divided.

Brentano's theory now takes a new turn, of great importance
for the theory of valuation. He believes that the experiences of
Belief or Judgement, in which the reality of what we believe
seems to flood in upon us, have a limiting form in which it no
longer makes sense to question the authenticity of what one
judges to be there: its reality is itself present to us. Brentano
following Descartes believes in a clear and distinct perception
which it does not make sense to doubt: the fact, the true posture
of things, is then *evident* to us. If this Evidence (*Evidenz*) of
Brentano is interpreted as a sort of inner feeling contingently
related to the content present, the theory is of course worthless:
no experience, in the sense of mere inner feeling, if such there
can be, can amount to the evident truth or reality of anything.
But it must be remembered that Brentanos 'experiences' are not
the experiences of the empiricists and the phenomenalists, merely
states of being thus and thus subjectively. They are essentially
transcendences, states of living beyond self, and it is arguable that
transcendences which fall short of their mark, or which *may* fall
short of their mark, all presuppose a limiting transcendence in
which what is the case simply declares itself, so that only a false
philosophy of mind can make what is thus declared seem doubtful.
Brentano follows Descartes in making such cases of evident self-
declaration rare. He confines them to our assurance of the existence
and certain characters of our own inner attitudes, and of the truth
of certain simple axioms. He does not, like Meinong, spread the

net of a probabilistic self-evidence rather wide, nor like Moore maintain that we *know* many things that it would not be self-contradictory to deny.

The theory of a limiting, self-declaratory truth in the realm of Belief leads, however, to a parallel doctrine in the realm of Love and Hate and Preference. There are some cases of liking or disliking or preferring which are characterised (*charakterisiert*) by an inner rightness (*Richtigkeit*) which it is as senseless to try to circumvent or ignore as it would be to do so in the case of the inner clinch of self-evidence. These axiological clinches have not to do with the reality of things, but with the worthiness or appropriateness of our own attitudes to them or vice versa: we can as little evade (though we may of course refuse to be deflected by) the peculiar pressure of a worthy love or hate or preference, as we can evade the quite different pressure of what shows itself as evident, as being plainly the case.

Brentano's view of the precise character of this inner correctness of acts of love, hate and preference, is, however, obscure: he says that certain acts are characterised by such inner correctness, but it is not clear how such 'characterising' is to be interpreted. It might mean that *we* characterise such acts as correct in a judgement which will, of course, have to have the highest self-evidence. On such a view it will be this *judgement*, rather than the loving and hating as such, which will mediate correctness for us. Of such a view, which Meinong afterwards espoused, there is no clear trace in Brentano: it is of the essence of his theory that it is in loving and hating correctly that the good or bad is brought home to us, not by judging as to the correctness of our loving and hating: the good and bad are simply the objects of correct love and hate. What then does 'being characterised as correct' entail if it does not entail an extrinsic judgement? Two answers are possible: it may merely mean that certain acts of loving and hating *are* correct, have correctness as a *property*, though they need not, and perhaps could not meaningfully, be *experienced* as correct, or it may mean that they not only *are* correct, but are in some sense *experienced*, or capable of being experienced, as correct. If the former is assumed, some sort of a judgement or presentation will be necessary to bring this correctness into our ken, and we shall be back in our previous position. The latter is therefore what Brentano must mean, and Chisholm is therefore faithful to Brentano's intention, if not to his German, in translating the phrase 'als richtig charakterisiert' as 'experienced as correct'. Here, however, many will object that while we can intend correctness, we cannot in any sense live through it, have it as part of our lived experience. We here require a ruling as to the most suitable and in a sense true use of the verb 'to experience', and we shall here accept the view that there are and can be characters which can be thought of, intended, but which can also be livingly part of our experience, of our intimate selves, even when we do not intend them. Thus we can *experience* succession as well as project it and perceive it, and we can experience such features of succession as smooth continuity, sharp change, fragmentation into brief phases, etc. In the same way we can live through passivity and live through activity: our experiences *qua* experiences have passivity or activity as internal characters. It is arguable likewise, *pace* Hume, that we often experience our own identity in the sense of a selfsameness to which varied things happen. If all these cases of experiencing are possible, then there seems no good reason why we should not experience correctness, and there is certainly a sense of inner authority in many of our more considered valuations. But the trouble is now that if correctness can be thus experienced, we cannot be wrong about it: an act of love or hate, experienced as correct, simply is, as an experience, correct. Here we obviously require some doctrine of a simulacrum of correctness which in the limiting case fades into correctness itself, a doctrine that many would reject as absurd, but which to others would seem to have the obvious stamp of truth. Correctness and evident truth are the standards both of themselves and their contraries, and while Duessa may succeed in her deceits in the absence of Fidessa, she cannot sustain them in Fidessa's presence. God conceived as the last stronghold of the evidently correct plainly cannot require an infinite certification of His correctness. But as Brentano has not considered these questions, we shall not debate them further.

Brentano, however, buttresses his doctrine by a series of concrete examples, which are not less valuable on account of their entire obviousness. The first is that of our love for clear insight into things, and our hatred of error and ignorance. We not only feel impelled to have the attitudes in question: we also feel them to be appropriate, correct. What Brentano holds will of course arouse immense dissent: it will be pointed out that we often wish to remain ignorant of something, that some find all knowledge profitless and senseless, etc. The point of the example remains: to say that we do not care for knowledge, that we prefer error, always requires special explanation. It is in itself a perverse utterance, which requires special circumstances to justify it, whereas the contrary valuation simply make good sense, is undistorted, standard, normative. All consciousness, all speech, has a basic interest in fact and truth which only the mutely unconscious (if they could repudiate anything) could with full sense repudiate. What is here plain is even more plain in Brentano's next case: joy and sadness. To like sadness and shrink from joy, is a perfectly possible, not infrequently realised state of mind, but it involves what can only be called a perverse liking of one's own dislikes and their objects, and a perverse dislike of one's own likings and their objects. Brentano's third example is that of a love of rightness in our own attitudes of love and hate: there is something deeply perverse, though of course entirely possible, in loving to be incorrect. Other examples, seemingly tautological but not truly so, are the rightness of preferring a good, i.e. an object of correct love, to an evil, an object of correct hatred, or the existence of a good to its non-existence, or the non-existence of an evil to its existence, or a sum of several goods to only one among them, or an intense degree of something good to a weaker form of the same, etc. These apparently trivial examples are the truly basic ones, rather than such loaded instances as the evil of incest, a complex matter on which, even if the case were objectively clear, no one could possibly have a reliable experience or insight. Brentano admits that he cannot feel the correctness or incorrectness of preferring high-minded love to intellectual insight or vice versa, he even considers that it would be a reasonable inference from this lack of experience that there is *no* correctness or incorrectness in the matter. (See *Origin*, §§ 31, 32.)

We shall not here attempt to enter into the detailed pronouncements of Brentano's posthumously published *Foundations and Structure of Ethics*. It discusses most questions regarding right and wrong, good and evil, the freedom of the will, etc., that moral philosophers have discussed, including some that the scholastics discussed but which have dropped out of the straitened ethical discussions of modern times. Since Brentano believes in ethical *knowledge*, even if such knowledge is a built-in feature of our emotional and practical attitudes, he also has a place for ethical probability, and can discuss the views of the probabilists and the tutiorists, the rigorists and the laxists, moral tribes which exist now as in the middle ages, but which somehow elude the notice of moral philosophers. The main defect of Brentano is obvious: he has presented us with too many unanalysed ultimates and too many unjustified intuitions. One has a strong feeling that he has really unearthed the true foundations both of the mind and the realm of value, but one also feels that his intuitions are not enough, that one requires more clarity in his basic conceptions (e.g. correctness) and more justification for his remarkable insights. Otherwise we have nothing with which to counter Sade or Nietzsche or one or other of the dark mentors whose shrines have been recently refurbished.

If we now turn to Meinong, we have what is probably the most brilliantly elaborated of all theories of the possibility of what may be called 'emotional knowledge', and an interesting application of this theory to many of the main formal questions concerning value and disvalue, merit and demerit, rightness and wrongness· His main writings on axiology are all to be found in the recently published third volume of the new Collected Edition of his works. These are: *Psychologisch-ethische Untersuchungen zur Werththeorie* (*Psychological-Ethical Investigations into Value-Theory*) (1894), *Über emotionale Präsentation* (*On Emotional Presentation*) (1917), *Zur Grundlegung der allgemeinen Werttheorie* (*Foundations of General Value-Theory*) (1923) and *Ethische Bausteine* (*Ethical Building-Stones*) (first published in 1969). As our aim is not to set forth the history of his opinions, we shall study them in their latest stage of development, with a rearward glance at some of the earlier treatments.

Meinong builds his value-theory on the intentionalist doctrine of Brentano: that it is of the essence of mental life to live outside of itself, to point beyond itself, and to concern itself with objects that need not be part of it, and which need not have being anywhere, though, of course, they may be essential elements of reality, and known as such. The intentionalist psychology of Brentano was, however, elaborated and complicated in a large number of ways, not all of which matter from the point of view of value-theory, and some not from any point of view. Meinong introduces the novel concept of the *Annahme* or Assumption, a mental attitude which has most of the characters of the judgement, and may even imitate the conviction of the judgement, without involving any genuine conviction, without making a committed reference to what really is the case. This *Annahme* or Assumption takes the place of the *Vorstellung* or Presentation in the psychology of Brentano, the latter being treated as a merely sensational experience in which we live through contents which may indeed offer material for a Judgement or Assumption, but which do not of themselves truly present objects. The main point of the new doctrine is to make the mere entertainment of some possibility a *defective mode* of objective reference, rather than a basic mode upon which a Judgement is then built. The doctrine is interesting but not germane to our purpose: in practice there is little difference between the unconvinced contemplative assumption of Meinong and the Presentation of Brentano, except that the former expresses itself in a propositional rather than a 'thing'-directed form.

Meinong also has difficulty in accepting Brentano's belief in one psychic ground-class of Loving and Hating underlying all conative and affective phenomena: he harks back to the old dualism of Feeling and Desire, which he feels has a firm basis in introspection. But since, in his theory of valuation, he comes to admit that valuation rests jointly on both sorts of experience, he in effect admits that feeling and desire are, as it were, two modes of a single basic attitude, which is simply the point made by Brentano. Meinong therefore ends with a basic triplicity not very far from Brentano's three ground-classes of mental intention: a triplicity of unconvinced contemplation, of convinced judgement and of the affective-desiderative side of human life. And while Meinong has a more complex theory of the presupposition of the lower types of intention by the higher, he holds a similar view of the presupposition by feelings and desires of the acts of belief and contemplation which, as it were, offer them an objective material, and condition their form. Whether one desires X or is satisfied by X depends, for example, on whether one believes X to be the case or not: one cannot desire what one believes to be already realised nor be satisfied with what one believes to be unrealised. There are, however, acts of feigned belief or disbelief which make it possible for me to be as-it-were-satisfied by what I know to be unreal, or as-it-were-desirous of what I know to be the case, so that these presuppositional conditions are less restrictive than would at first seem to be the case.

Meinong, however, departs from Brentano in two fundamental respects, both important for value-theory. He teaches a new doctrine of mental 'contents', borrowed from the Polish philosopher Twardowski, which as it were reinstates the scholastic doctrine of the intention '*in* the mind' by which reference 'beyond the mind' is made possible. He also attempts an indefinite widening of the concepts of *object* to which intentional reference is possible. As regards the former of these innovations, Meinong holds that intentionality is always two-sided: it has, we may say, its me-wardness and its object-wardness, its relation to my subjective mindedness or *Zumutesein*, on the one hand, and its relation to objects of varying sorts, on the other. It is, moreover, only by having a specific me-wardness or immanent *content*, that it can have a specific object-wardness or transcendent objectivity. (The terms 'me-wardness' and 'object-wardness' are not Meinongian, but are used for elucidatory purposes.) This two-sidedness occurs even in so simple a case as that of sense–givenness, the hearing of a note, the seeing of a colour, etc. In such an experience we can distinguish the objective datum that comes before us and is given to us, e.g. the loud, high note or the bright, oblong, red patch, etc., and the specific manner in which our own experience is modified to make such a presentation possible, a manner that we can in the cases in question perhaps call a loudwise, highwise manner, or an oblongwise, brightwise, redwise manner. (The use of the termination -wise to express contents is convenient but not Meinongian.) We are otherwise minded according as we mind this or that sort of thing or state of things: there are as many nuances of immanent subjectivity as there are nuances of transcendent objectivity, and there is an absolute, necessary correlation, despite unbridgeable difference, between the one and the other. Each subjective content is the appointed medium through which an objective feature is brought home to the experiencing mind. The manner in which the painful rending of our flesh makes us aware of the sharpness of the instrument that rends it may serve as an analogy – though only as an analogy – of the essential two-sidedness which Meinong sees in all genuine conscious reference. (Except in such as is purely a symbolic substitute for the true seeing or thinking of something.)

Meinong's doctrine has been thought unplausible by many. Thus Moore in an Aristotelian Society paper of 1909–10 denied that he could detect a subjective *Zumutesein* in sensation which corresponded to, but which was not identical with, the sense-datum of which he was conscious, and the writings of Wittgenstein are full of eloquent denials that there is anything common to all the experiences in which we consider this or that feature of objects. On the other hand, the very fact that philosophers have been as ready to adopt sensation- as sense-datum language regarding sense-given qualities bears testimony to the two-sidedness Meinong believes in: we can for example, experience brightness, loudness, etc., as specific impacts on ourselves, or as characters given 'out there' in things. And there is abundant testimony, e.g. in Bradley, Wittgenstein and others, as to how the objective content of the most complex intellectual references can collapse, as it were, into a mere nuance of interior experience to which no better word than 'feeling' seems apposite. If all this is true, then all conscious references as are more than the mere readiness to use symbols appropriately – which is of course all that conscious references ever are for certain philosophers – can be condensed into nuances of interior feeling, but from this it also follows that such nuances of personal feeling are capable of a 'projection', an exteriorisation, in virtue of which they may set before us certain non-identical but necessarily correlated features of objects. The subjective variations of our personal conviction may, for example, set before us the probabilities, the likelihoods, that seem part and parcel of the perceived world. And this leaves open the yet more interesting possibility that the valuations which have their me–wardness in subjective feeling, may have a correlated, objective aspect which is, at least in some cases, a transcendent feature of the world.

Meinong further departs from Brentano, who has an Aristotelian faith in the prime reality of individual things, in believing that there are many different types of *object* which can be set up for us by differing types of intentional experience. Not only can we deal with objects of lowest order, the *things* of ordinary diction or their simple parts and aspects: we can also put before ourselves objects of higher order, such as the way first-order objects are *related* to other objects, and the complex *patterns* they thereby form, and also the *states of affairs* (called by Meinong 'objectives') which concern first-order (and also higher-order) objects, such as that this is to the left of that, this is larger than that, there is this or that actually in existence, if this were a so-and-so it would also be a such-and-such and so on. The notion of the circumstance or state of affairs as a unique kind of object of conscious reference was anticipated by the Stoic doctrine of λεκτά and by Bolzano's doctrine of Propositions-in-themselves (*Sätze an sich*), but it was Meinong who first gave them a prominent place in philosophy, coining for them the strange name of 'objective'.

From the recognition of objects treated in the incompleteness they have for our thought, there was a natural passage to the recognition of objects that have no being at all, the round square which does not and cannot exist, or the equality of Paris to London in size, which is not the case though it can be entertained in thought. It is highly arguable that human experience, even at the level of perception, is rich in objects that go beyond the concrete existent things of an individualist ontology: the world around us seems full of bearings, of suggestions, of half-formed possibilities, of pin-pointed facts or circumstances, of gaps, of vaguenesses, of generalities, of unrealized limits, and it is a matter of dogma rather than direct experience that all these higher-order things will reduce to individuals and their actual properties. It is this recognition of higher-order objectivity of various sorts which characterises Meinong's theory of objects, and which leaves a place for the values which are so unquestionably part of the ordinary look of the world, pervading things and also floating above them as standards or norms, until they are banished from the picture by the limited aims of science and the prejudices of a scientific philosophy.

Meinong of course went further than most thinkers could readily approve in giving to all his classes of objects not merely a status as objects of thought, but even a status independent of thought and mental reference. It is well known and notorious that Meinong argued that even non-existent and absurd objects needed to be *something* in order to be absent from the universe, in order to be excluded by the actual state of things. This notorious opinion is, however, neither as absurd nor as ill worked out as it is commonly thought to be, nor are the well-known attempts of Russell and others to take the legs from under it or to find substitutes for it, as successful as they are commonly thought to have been. It is not, however, necessary for our purposes to argue for the ontological position of all Meinong's higher-order entities: it is sufficient to say that they can be and often are genuine objects of our perceptual and thought-intentions as much as the individual things that are by many alone supposed to be real, and that our attitudes of valuation are as much directed to *them* as to any concrete thing that exists in the world. A mind that cannot pin-point circumstances and direct attitudes to them specifically, or that cannot see things in one-sided incompleteness as well as in concrete completeness, or that cannot treat the non-existent and even the absurd as if it were actual, is not a mind that can fully savour the values and excellences of things. The whole value of logic, for instance, is derived from a contrast with the absurd. Language enables us to perform all these feats with precision, but they are often performed less precisely at the level of unformulated perception, action and feeling.

We must, however, turn to the precise theory of valuation which Meinong fitted into his philosophy of mind, and the precise theory of values which he added to his theory of objects. On Meinong's view, valuation is primarily a matter of feeling, and only secondarily and derivatively a matter of desire. The principal reason he gives for this view is the somewhat inconclusive one that it is not because we desire (or are averse from) objects or states of affairs that we have feelings towards them, but because we have feelings towards them that we have positive or negative desires for them. Such feelings do not demand that their objects actually exist or are present, but only that they are imagined, assumed to be there. Valuation is, however, feeling (and secondarily desire) which presupposes *judgement*, rather than mere contemplative presentation, and which is, moreover, wrought up with the *content* (in Meinong's technical sense of 'content') of such judgement. In other words, when we value things, we are concerned with their *existence* or *non-existence*, their *real being* or *non-being* in the world, and we are concerned with the real being or non-being of the *specific sorts of objects* we have before us in thought, and which are set before us through the *content* of our experience. Valuation is, in other words, highly specific existence-love or existence-hatred: what we value, we want to *be* and do not want *not* to be, and are pleased to see *existing* and not to see *not existing*, and we want *it* specifically to be, and not some *other* object or sort of object.

The sense of this analysis will become plainer if we contrast valuation with other types of emotional or desirous attitude to objects. There is, Meinong says, such a thing as knowledge-love or hatred in which we indeed delight and enquire after what exists or is the case, and turn from what does not exist or is not the case, but which is not = valuation, since we do not care about the *specific content* of what exists or is the case (or does not exist or is not the case). Such an emotional-desiderative attitude is concerned with real being, and is therefore judgement-based, but it is not a case of valuation, since it is after existence and fact *whatever they may turn out to be*. It lacks a specific *bias* towards certain alternatives which is always present in valuation. Thus if I value fair dealing, I deplore its lack or its contrary, whereas a scientific student of society is as interested in an unfair as in a fair society. (Meinong does not confuse scientific interest with the valuation *of* knowledge as such: it is an interest in what is the case, not in *my* knowing it.) Valuation also stands opposed to emotional-desiderative attitudes which do not presuppose judgement, and are indifferent to the real, or to what is the case. Ordinary satisfaction and dissatisfaction are of this sort: our delight in a warm bath is unshaken by the scientific conviction that heat is merely a secondary quality. Our aesthetic satisfactions and dissatisfactions are also of this sort: questions of the reality or unreality of what aesthetically pleases or displeases us are quite irrelevant, and this is why we say we may be aesthetically pleased with something as an aesthetic spectacle or mere show whose reality would horrify us. But aesthetic satisfactions and dissatisfactions have the same close tie with *content* that valuations also have, and this differentiates them from ordinary satisfactions and dissatisfactions. The Meinongian theory of aesthetic appreciation was interestingly worked out by his pupil Stefan Witasek in his *Aesthetik*. Meinong does not speak of aesthetic valuation or aesthetic values nor of intellectual valuation or values: the aesthetic and purely scientific lack the concern with the *precise content of reality* which is characteristic of valuation and values. Meinong's analyses may seem arid and arbitrary, but have arguably lighted on a central point which other analyses of valuation often pass over. It is not merely delighting in something or urgently wanting it for ourselves, which constitutes valuation, but considering it as a contribution to the total real universe and delighting in it or wanting it in such a context. Moore plainly agrees with Meinong: he too discovers the goodness or badness of things by considering them either as being all there is, or as contributing to wider totals of existence.

It may here be noted that Meinong regards our attitude to an object's *non*-existence as having an equal importance in valuation with our attitude to its existence: if we value things we feel positively towards their existence and negatively towards their non-existence, and if we value things negatively we feel positively towards their non-existence and negatively towards their existence. But he also notes that the strength of these components is not normally equal: there are some things which we value mainly in so far as we would *miss* them if absent, without taking much positive delight in their presence, whereas there are other things which we value mainly in so far as we delight in their presence but perhaps would not miss if absent. This distinction is afterwards to recur in Hartmann's concepts of the 'height' and 'strength' of value, and is also in harmony with Meinong's own classifications of the morally good, the correct, the permissible and the morally evil. But in his posthumous *Grundlegung* he adopts the unacceptable doctrine that it would be *rational* to be just as pleased or displeased with a thing's absence as we were displeased or pleased with its presence, and vice versa, a doctrine that entails that we ought always to be infinitely sorry for all the countless good things which do not exist, and infinitely glad for all the countless bad things which do not exist, resulting in a frame of feeling that is quite indeterminate. This doctrine is a mistake in an otherwise fine analysis.

Meinong now makes use of his doctrine of 'content' to give an objective meaning to values and similar predicates. If *all* our objective references intend features of objects by a peculiar *use* (which need not be construed as at all like a causal inference) of modifications of inner feeling (in a very wide sense of the word 'feeling'), then the modifications of feeling in the ordinary, narrow sense of the word may also be used to mediate objective references, may serve to introduce us to properties perhaps transcendently 'out there' in things. If we can be made aware of extension and shape in things by being made to feel a correlative, but unbridgeably different, drawn-outness and patterning of our interior sensibility, then the pleasure, displeasure and desire with which we are affected may also serve to introduce us to suitabilities, unsuitabilities or requirements, real or imaginary, which are seen, not in ourselves, but in things. The mystery and difficulty of the use of what is 'internal' to bring before us what is 'external' is no greater in one case than the other: it is in fact, properly regarded, no difficulty at all. Meinong writes:

That we are here dealing with more than mere possibilities is shown by a group of entirely everyday attributions such as those we encounter when someone speaks of a pleasant bath, fresh air, oppressive heat, vexatious noise, beautiful colour, a gay or sad, tedious or entertaining story, a sublime work of art, excellent people, good intentions, etc. The close relations of such attributes to our feelings is not open to question, but it is just as unquestionable that they are, as attributes, completely analogous to the other properties set before us by presentative ideas in quite familiar fashion. If I say of the sky that it is blue, and again say of it that it is beautiful, I seem to credit the sky with a property in one case as in the other, and since a feeling participates in the apprehension of the relevant property in the one case while an idea does the work in the other it is natural to ascribe the presentative function to the feeling in the former case as we do to an idea in the latter (*On Emotional Presentation*, p. 33)

Meinong goes on to distinguish and name the peculiar objective features which we apprehend through our feelings and desires: he calls them *dignitatives* in the case of our feelings, and *desideratives* in the case of our desires. The basic dignitatives are four in number corresponding to the four basic types of emotional attitude: the agreeable (revealed by 'ordinary' feelings), the beautiful (revealed by aesthetic feelings), the authentically true (truth as a dignitative, revealed by 'knowledge–feelings') and the good or valuable (revealed by existence–feelings). The desideratives are various types of 'ought' (*Sollen*), revealed by various types of desire. On Meinong's view, the objective world with which we have commerce is not only peopled with things and facts, but also with dignities and requirements, which latter we can only apprehend by being emotionally or desideratively moved. The purely detached intellect, which will not permit wants or feelings to colour the objective order of things, can never see that order as it completely and truly is: it can at most see a reduced, incomplete world which is a reflex of its own heartlessness.

Meinong does not, however, espouse the view that *all* our feelings and desires reveal authentic dignities and requirements which are part of the structure of real being: only *some* of them do so. *Which* do so is, for Meinong, not a matter of wishful or emotive thinking: he is unwilling to accept Brentano's doctrine of an inwardly experienced rightness of certain acts of feeling or desire. Meinong thinks that an act of self-evident judgement, of *knowledge*, is here required: while our emotions and desires may people the world with dignities and requirements, it is a purely cognitive experience which determines which have an absolute status, which are there as part of the real structure of things. There is therefore a curious and elaborate mixture of the emotional and intellectual in Meinong's theory of true values and value-knowledge: emotions are necessary but not sufficient conditions of the latter. And, whether true or false, the theory is at least a *clear one*, not a mere muddle like the parallel accounts of Scheler and Hartmann which we shall study later. Only Richard Price, with his doctrine of a necessary tie-up between a perception of values by the understanding and a resultant affection of the heart, which that perception of necessity provokes, provides an alternative to Meinong's theory. But for Price emotion is a necessary consequence of value-perception, whereas for Meinong it is a necessary pre-condition.

If we, however, ask about the values concerning which Meinong believes himself to have firm knowledge, we shall not find that they are many: he is not like Moore, who claims clear intuitions regarding very many values. Meinong appeals vaguely to our appraisal of certain acts of military heroism and to the aesthetic dignity of certain Greek statues and German poems and musical compositions. He even suggests that the sort of self-evidence here at work is one for rational surmise rather than for uncontrovertible certainty, and that we may very well, in such a case, attach value to the judgements of *others*, and to the judgements of large numbers of reflective people.

The best example of value-insight in Meinong is, however, to be found in the careful analyses of moral value and duty which we have in the early *Psychological-Ethical Investigations into Value-Theory* of 1894, analyses which he was attempting to reformulate and modernize in the posthumously published *Ethical Building-Stones* (1969). Here Meinong distinguishes judgements of 'oughtness' from judgements of moral value, in that the former consider only the value of isolated acts, whereas the latter consider the values of permanent dispositions behind the acts. Meinong works out the logical relations of four classes of acts, the positively good, the correct, the allowable and the evil. Correct acts cover a small spectrum and pass over into positively good acts which are capable of indefinite degrees of goodness: allowable acts, likewise, cover a small spectrum and shade over into bad acts which are likewise capable of indefinite degrees. The omission of a positively good act is allowable, of a correct act positively bad, whereas the omission of an allowable act is positively good, and the omission of a bad act merely correct. Meinong further determines the goodness or badness of acts in terms of the extent to which altruism, regard for others, triumphs over self-interest. To be willing to make large sacrifices of self-interest for relatively small benefits to others has, for example, high positive goodness, provided it does not 'go to far', whereas moral evil is shown in the relatively large sacrifice of advantage to others for only a small advantage to oneself, or, more saliently, in the largeness of the personal sacrifice one is prepared to make for even a relatively small damage to others. Many axiomatic formulae are put forward and, whether or not they are quite acceptable, they at least show that the whole sphere of moral valuation has an inherent logic, and that it is infinitely far from the wholly vague pattern of emotional suasion and excuse which is alone recognised in certain modern treatments of ethical argument.

We may conclude this chapter with a brief mention of the value-system of von Ehrenfels, as expressed in *System der Werttheorie* (1897–8) in which desire, rather than feeling, serves as the primary value-fundamental, in which there is an application of the economic notion of marginal utility to the field of ethics – the *Grenz frommen* is set beside the *Grenznutzen* – and in which there is also an interesting theory of value-movement, values being held to have an inherent tendency to move 'upwards' from nearer to remoter ends, 'downwards' from ends to means, 'inwards' from objects to attitudes towards objects, and also towards *activities* of a general sort from particular objects of such activities. This theory of value-movement is extremely important, in that it highlights the sort of non-rigorous logic which causes our values to change, and in that it disposes of any equation of rational, intersubjective values with unchangeable ones. It is plainly rational for values to change according to context, and among such contexts are for example, the over-production of certain values and the under-production of others. Only a moral philosopher would think that an act of extreme kindness or a spectacle of great beauty has the same value when seen in a Moravian mission-settlement, a German concentration camp, a club of heartless aesthetes, etc., or that there is no total field in which its value must be considered. It is clear, in conclusion, that 'axiology' owes a great deal to the Austrian school which started it off, and that the neglect into which that school's writings have fallen is deeply undeserved.

III. MOORE, RASHDALL AND ROSS

The present chapter will give some account of the development of axiological ethics in England. It is not possible to pass over the contributions of G. E. Moore, who, however much his discussions of the meaning of 'good', and his teachings concerning the 'naturalistic fallacy', may have made him the father of modern 'meta-ethics', was also one of the prime founders of axiology, concerned to construct an ordered map of the main 'heads' of value and disvalue, of the main sorts of things that are purely or admixedly good or bad. His contributions to this body of theory are mainly contained in the *Principia Ethica* of 1903; his later volume on *Ethics* (1912) and his various other writings on ethical and value-problems, including his very important 'Reply to my Critics' in the Schilpp volume on the *Philosophy of G. E. Moore*, do not discuss this kind of question to the same extent. Moore's drawing up of such a map of values in the last chapter of *Principia Ethica* is not only an important philosophical effort – *Principia Ethica* together with *Some Main Problems of Philosophy* and Russell's *Principles of Mathematics* are among the supreme products of British philosophising – it also set the tone for a most brilliant intellectual and aesthetic period, the true *belle époque* of Bloomsbury, which, with its odd mixture of subtle sophistication and naïve innocence, so much in key with the *Art Nouveau* and the Peace Palace and the other fantasies of the time, now appears, from the sad vista of our present debasements, as the last happy, lucid, hopeful breathing-space of civilised man. When Moore wrote that chapter men still believed in the possibility of the 'good life', and in the possibility of saying in what it might consist.

Moore begins his study of the Good, as is well known, with a long defence of the wholly unanalysable character of the notion of goodness, of goodness as such as opposed to being this or that sort of good thing. The philosophers of the past and present had been inclined to recommend this or that good thing – being pleased, being a source of pleasure, being what one desires to desire etc. – because they thought that such conditions were part and parcel of the notion of being good, so that it did not 'make sense' to suppose that there was a good state of affairs which did not fall under such a head. In so arguing, philosophers indeed gave their pronouncements a certain indubitability, but at the cost of making them trivial. For if all 'good' means is that one is pleased, or that things are as one desires to desire them, then the statement that being pleased is good or the only good, or that this is true of being as one desires to desire things to be, becomes a mere tautology, amounting to no more than saying that being pleased is being pleased, or that being as one desires to desire is being as one desires to desire. Yet those who make such statements do so often after much furrowing of brows and cogitative sweat: while taken, no doubt, to be necessary truths, they are also taken to be truths that represent an important step in thought. Being good is therefore as unanalysable as being yellow: it may stand in necessary relation to other last characters of things, just as being yellow stands to being one of the other colours, it may stand in various inductively established relations to other things as being yellow stands for certain frequencies of vibration; it may also be causally related to innumerable things which, as we say, are instrumentally good. But 'in itself' good remains a character that must be simply apprehended, that cannot be further analysed, and only when it has been thus apprehended, and clearly put before the mind in thought, can we come to understand and know various further propositions, necessary and empirical, concerning it.

Moore's opinion as to the unanalysable character of goodness seems to deprive it of all meaning, to transform it into a surd. For what can 'good' mean if it be cut off from all relations to feeling and practice, on the one hand, or from specific objects and sorts of object on the other? We seem back with the Megarians who denied the possibility of predicating anything of anything else, so that all one could say of unity was that it was unity and of goodness that it was goodness. And in a way we *are* brought back to the Megarians, since a view of predication which makes it consist in an external bond between contents isolable in thought *does* (*pace* Butler) destroy the meaning of predication. It is odd that 'yellow' should have been seen as the analogue of 'goodness', since being yellow is above all something that is only fully anything at all in the context of the full system of colours. It may be a logical error to make a whole a part of one of its parts, but it is not a logical error to make a relation to other constituent parts, and to some whole which they all form, a part of the *analysis*, the developed content of any and every part of certain whole systems. But whatever Moore's concessions to an exaggeratedly separative mode of conceiving or rather picturing things, in actual practice he makes the meaning of 'good' the centre of a large number of necessary, and countless probable connections, which are far more important elements in its meaning than the unanalysable nucleus on which he lays such emphasis. He believes, for example, that intuition or insight, a human experience, has some sort of profound connection with the presence of goodness in things – 'a certain unique predicate can be directly seen to belong' to this or that actual or possible existent (*Principia Ethica*, p. 60) – and he also believes that a special attitude of feeling and will is part of almost all cases where we think a thing good and all cases where we think so decidedly, and that 'a perception of goodness is probably included in the complex facts which we mean by willing and having certain kinds of feeling' (ibid., p. 131). He also presumes that 'good' means what is meant by 'ought to exist' (ibid., p. 17), thus giving it an intrinsic connection with existence, like Brentano and Meinong: in later treatments this relation to 'oughtness to exist' becomes 'synthetic' and not definitory. Moore also of course recognises that many concrete characters of things, e.g. being a state of affection, are bound up with being good and necessarily so.

Moore's doctrine of the naturalistic fallacy may therefore be regarded, not so much as a contribution to axiology, as to ontology or semantics, and, as a contribution to these latter, it follows the atomising, piecemeal sort of analysis favoured by traditional empiricism which must be acknowledged, after long experience,

to be more productive of problems than of light. But in its relations
to value-theory the doctrine of the naturalistic fallacy has had
both good and bad results. It has, on the one hand, made us
deeply aware of the wholly new dimension which springs into
our ken when we value things instead of curiously and detachedly
exploring them. It has, on the other hand, tended to make it
appear that this new dimension has nothing whatever to do with
'the facts', with some sterilised sphere of pure science, a diremption which leads to many dogmatic simplifications. For it is
arguable that the 'natures' of things, even as studied by science,
are never without some relation to values and standards, which
delimit what they are and what they can do, and that there can
be no study of 'values in themselves' as divorced from necessary
trends in certain segments of the conscious psyche, and perhaps
even in unconscious and lifeless things.

If we now turn to Moore's concrete pronouncements on various
axiological connections, we have, first of all, his somewhat
sweeping, reductive analysis (afterwards mitigated) of what ought
to be done. The assertion 'I am morally bound to perform this
action' is held to be *identical* with the assertion 'This action will
produce the greatest amount of good in the universe'. The reason
for this extremely sweeping assertion is that only the greatest
amount of value in the universe has the *uniqueness* necessary to the
concept of duty: it could not be my duty to do any out of a large
number of incompatible things (ibid., p. 147). This analysis of
duty has, of course, the consequence that we can never be quite
sure what our duty really is, since no one can follow out all the
ramifying consequences of an act, and that there can be no certain
rules of duty, only such as it is reasonable in the inherently
doubtful circumstances to accept. The probabilism which is
generally thought to be connected with casuistry is therefore
connected with all practical ethics: practical ethics is essentially
concerned with instrumental values, with what are the best
means to a certain end, and in the estimation of such values
questions of causal efficacy, always infinitely doubtful and
inductive, necessarily enter. Moore's treatment is here very
valuable, since he banishes what ought to be done from its

central position in ethics, and recognizes the fact that, for all who reflect, it depends on a vast number of factors of which no sweeping account can be given.

It is, however, more than very doubtful whether Moore has given a good analysis, or even good characterisation, of what ought to be done. It is doubtful whether a strict 'ought' is a case of value at all, as it has many properties, e.g. its 'absoluteness' and lack of degree, which are not those of value. A deed that ought to be done is not necessarily a good deed, which means something more and different, and it is not even a deed that it is bad to omit, though this comes closer to the mark. Certainly, however, it has something intrinsic about it, and a certain imperative urgency, which is not explicable in terms of mere instrumentality. It is, further, extremely doubtful whether what ought to be done is ever to produce the greatest amount of good possible in the universe. Such an account assumes without argument that the bad can be weighed against the good, and it assumes without argument that the different kinds of good and bad can be weighed against one another, and it assumes, contrary to what we ordinarily hold, that it is our duty to produce the greatest possible addition of good for the universe, when the ordinary notion of duty plainly pledges us to much less, and has plainly a place for 'works of supererogation'. To depart so widely from ordinary notions plainly requires more argument than one based on the mere *uniqueness* of the notion in question.

The second interesting axiological contribution of Moore is his doctrine of Organic Wholes. While objects considered as what they are in themselves always and necessarily have the same value or disvalue, the wholes that they form may have values and disvalues which are in no sense the sum of, and not even plainly proportionate to, the values that enter into them. Thus pleasure, *per se* a thing of little worth, when associated with the awareness of what is worthy of admiration, *per se* also a thing of little worth, gives rise to the new whole of well-justified aesthetic pleasure which is one of the most valuable things in the universe. In the same way great pain, a very evil thing, associated with great wickedness, or choice of what is for other reasons evil, creates an

evil which is decidedly less in amount than the evil of the pain plus
the evil of the wickedness: wickedness requited, though it adds
one evil to another, produces a result which mitigates both evils.
Moore's principle is obviously fundamental in value-theory, but
it is odd that it did not lead him to a related principle of context,
which would have enabled him to make better sense of the
'organicism' of Hegel. Plainly a thing in a given context does *not*
have the value or disvalue that it would have in isolation or in
another context, and yet this contextual value or disvalue is *not*
the same as the value of the whole in which it belongs. Thus a
certain speech may be particularly gorgeous at a certain place in a
tragedy, yet the tragedy need not therefore be particularly gorgeous
and may, despite the speech, be a rather poor tragedy *on* the
whole. Value *in* a whole is, in fact, not the same as value *on* the
whole, and one would think the penetration of Moore would have
reached down to this fact.

Moore further gives a rather interesting analysis of what he
calls the beautiful, though he admits that it is not quite what is
ordinarily meant by beauty, and is rather analogous to what
Brentano meant by the 'good': the beautiful is what ought to be
admired, or what, on the treatment of 'ought' Moore accepts, it
is good to admire. Moore's definition of beauty enables him to
explain why many unconscious natural objects, which he finds it
hard to hold are *very* valuable apart from the aesthetic admiration
they excite, are none the less truly beautiful. Their admiration is,
or would be if it existed, a truly good thing. Obviously Moore's
definition of beauty covers unillustrated abstractions like a
mathematical theorem as much as things worked out in sensuous
imagery, and it covers anything that is impressive, salient,
remarkable, whether in the world of fancy or of fact. It is this
curious definition of the beautiful which explains why aesthetic
satisfactions occupy such an important place in Moore's account
of the 'ideal', of the pure and supreme good. Most of what it is
worth while knowing, e.g. the table of Mendeléeff, the theory
of general relativity, the life of Ho Chi Minh, etc., is impressive
and beautiful in Moore's sense, and Moore is right in holding that
the existence, or reality, or truth of what is thus known is only,

as it were, a last crowning touch of value added to the other items of value there present. In itself truth is of small importance: it is not facts, but meaningful facts, that are worth knowing. In this judgement Moore concurs with the judgement of those who set and assess examinations at Oxford and Cambridge.

Moore's attempt to sketch a map of the firmament of values is audacious but somewhat eccentric. He opines that

> by far the most valuable things which we know or can imagine are certain states of consciousness, which may be roughly described as the pleasures of human intercourse and the enjoyment of beautiful objects. No one probably who has asked himself the question, has ever doubted that personal affection and the appreciation of what is beautiful in Art or Nature, are good in themselves; nor, if we consider strictly what things are worth having *purely for their own sakes*, does it appear probable that anyone will think that anything else has nearly so great a value as the things which are included under these two heads ... what has not been recognized is that it (this) is the ultimate and fundamental truth of Moral Philosophy. That it is only for the sake of these things that anyone can be justified in performing any public or private duty; that they are the *raison d'être* of virtue; that it is they ... that form the rational ultimate end of human action and the sole criterion of social progress: these appear to be truths that have been generally overlooked (*Principia Ethica*, p. 188)

All Bloomsbury is implicit in these utterances: the pleading is gorgeous, but it fails wholly to persuade. That these are goods for which nothing can be bartered is not in doubt, but they are not the pre-eminent constellations in the value-firmament. It is impossible to exclude from that firmament, or admit merely on quasi-aesthetic grounds, the knowledge, the mind's self-transcending submission to what actually is, to which Plato and Aristotle accorded so high a place: we cannot endorse Moore's supercilious judgement (ibid., p. 199) that 'knowledge, though having little or no value by itself, is an absolutely essential constituent in the highest goods, and contributes immensely to their value'. Nor can we say of the habitual virtue commended by Aristotle 'that to maintain that a virtue which includes no more than this, is good in itself is a gross absurdity. And of this gross absurdity, it may be observed, the Ethics of Aristotle is guilty' (ibid., p. 176).

Nor can we agree that the value of certain surpassing cases of courage and compassion is not such as definitely to outweight the evils that call it forth. We cannot say 'There is no reason to think that any actual evil whatsoever would be contained in the Ideal' or that 'we cannot admit the actual validity of any of the arguments commonly used in theodicies' or believe that the supreme good would be attained if we only had to contend in imagination against non-existent evils (ibid., pp. 220-1). Obviously there is something Arcadian, something redolent of the Cambridge backs, in all this, and one can only be struck dumb by the unargued dismissal of so much that other reflective men have thought precious. 'No Cross, no Crown', and 'The unexamined life is not worth living' are valuations as deeply experienced and persuasive as any of those of Moore.

On great evils Moore is more completely persuasive. The first class of these consists in the admiring contemplation of things which are themselves either evil or ugly, and here cruelty and lasciviousness are given as salient instances. We may agree with Moore that cruelty is the most absolute of all evils, and that no theory of valuation can be listened to which subverts or even questions such a judgement, but lasciviousness would require a stronger case to be made against it than that given by Moore who is content to say that 'there are cognitions of organic sensations and perceptions of states of the body, of which the enjoyment is certainly an evil in itself' (ibid., p. 209). The second class of great evils are all cases of the hatred of what is good or beautiful, and that these are great evils, and not in virtue of a tautology, is quite plain. In the third class of great evils Moore puts pain, which rightly occupies a more eminent place among evils than pleasure does among goods. We may, in conclusion, admire Moore for his fine voyage of discovery among the varied territories of value, even if he has failed to explore some thoroughly or has drawn their contours all awry, and even if he has not provided us with anything of a rational method, other than mere intuition, by means of which such exploration can be carried out.

Hastings Rashdall is the second of our chosen British moral philosophers who has developed an axiological view of ethics:

his opinions are set forth in the two impressive volumes of *The Theory of Good and Evil* (1907). Writing at a time when the influence of Bradley hung like a pall over Oxford, neither permitting common-or-garden analysis or genuine Hegelian dialectic, Rashdall was as clear a thinker as the nebulous subject-matter of value would allow him to be, while avoiding the exaggerated atomism of Moore's treatments. Like Moore, Rashdall held that the notion of value or good was the fundamental idea for ethics, and without the trappings of the naturalistic fallacy or the harshly posed distinction between goodness and good things, he refused to identify the good with Pleasure, Virtue, Knowledge, etc., by making it pervade them all alike; there are in fact quite a number of distinct good things which morality must bring together and compare and fit into the ordered pattern of the good life.

The rightness of acts Rashdall explains, like Moore, in terms of productivity of a maximal amount of good, though he avoids the pitfall of saying that this is what 'rightness' means, or of giving any bad reason to show that this is what the content of duty must be. It would, he thinks, be self-evidently immoral to think we can do more than our duty – yet many good men have thought just this – and this must mean that we are always obliged to produce the largest amount of good that it seems possible for us to produce. On the avoidance of evils Rashdall has little or nothing to say, not entering into the question, as Moore does in the case of pain, whether evils may not in some respects behave differently from goods and be governed by distinct principles: the principle tacitly accepted is that evil is simply good in reverse and can in all circumstances be simply cancelled out by countervailing good.

To the whole view that the rightness of acts consists in promoting, or seeking to promote, the greatest possible amount of good open to the agent to produce, Rashdall gives the excellent name of 'ideal utilitarianism', a name much used for a time in describing the thought of Plato and Aristotle. This ideal utilitarianism did not have the unpalatable consequence that right acts and virtuous efforts have a merely instrumental value as producing

valuable consequences beyond themselves, as is taught in all
forms of hedonistic utilitarianism. A right act or a virtuous effort
may contribute its own quota of value to the overall situation,
and this may, in many cases, be much more important than the
pleasure or just distribution that it effects. It is overall goodness in
all its forms, immediate or consequential, which decides rightness
or obligatoriness, and there is no reason why an ideal utilitarianism may not sometimes place so high a value on certain
actions and efforts as to let them outweigh all consequences that
are in any way likely.

As regards our mental access to goodness Rashdall, like Meinong
and Moore, makes it a matter of intuitive judgement, and a
judgement involving the '*a priori* and purely intellectual idea of
value' (*Theory of Good and Evil*, I 156). But this intuitive judgement is rooted in facts of feeling in a not merely contingent and
empirical manner. *At least* it is the case that feelings are the
'subjective index' by means of which we recognise value–
properties in things, but it is more than that: 'moral judgements
imply facts of feeling as part of their ground' and 'value cannot
be recognised as attributable to anything in consciousness which
can excite no feeling of pleasure in its possession' (ibid., pp.
153–4). On the other hand, Rashdall also says that value–terms
would not mean *nothing* to one incapable of a variety of value-
concerned emotions, and that what they meant would still be the
'very essence of the moral judgement' (ibid., p. 170). Rashdall
further refuses to believe in *one* specifically moral emotion (ibid.,
p. 171), and thinks that there are great dangers in believing that
there is or must be one. It will lead us to look only to emotionally
stirring cases of value and ignore the humdrum commonsensical
ones (ibid., p. 173). These statements do not add up to any clear
and satisfactory theory of the relations of 'reason and emotion'
in the value-judgement, but they at least recognise the unique
and peculiar status of a rationality which works through emotions
and of an emotionality which has the dispassionate, revelatory
quality of an act of reason.

As regards the concrete goods to which Rashdall's *a priori*
category of value attaches, they are all held to be actual states of

consciousness: 'it is in actual consciousness that value resides and in nothing else' (ibid., p. 65). This account excludes from value anything merely facultative or dispositional, as the virtues, on certain accounts, have been held to be. 'Those who make virtue an end mean by "virtue", virtuous consciousness. . . . And the virtuous consciousness means a consciousness whose volitions and desires are controlled by a rational ideal of life, together with the feelings and emotions inseparably accompanying such volitions and desires' (ibid., p. 65).

The actual states of consciousness to which value attaches are of a wide number of different sorts, or they exhibit a large number of aspects in virtue of which they are more or less valuable. In general, however, they fall into three main groups, of which the highest group consists of a wide number of forms of virtuous consciousness, most of which have been named by tradition, while the lowest group consists of a wide number of forms of pleasurable consciousness, of which pleasure and happiness are the broadly distinguished varieties. But between the virtuous and the pleased forms of consciousness, lie what, for lack of a better word, we may call its cultured states, its states which are part of the 'life of the mind', which revolve about Art, Letters, Learning and the like. The educated Victorian–Edwardian world in which Rashdall moved certainly believed in Morality, Culture and Entertainment as the three distinct forms of what is individually and socially desirable, and they certainly ranked them much as Rashdall does.

Rashdall is, however, very keen that we should not ignore *any* of these main differentiations of value even though there may be some with little capacity to participate in one or other of them. Man is Reason, Feeling and Will and the ideal state for man, and hence also for society, is an ideal state of *all* the three elements in human nature in their ideal relation to one another. Rashdall's utilitarianism is accordingly organic and will not permit simple substitution of one sort of good for another. It is not the human ideal to live only in states of pleasure regardless of their source, nor to eschew all pleasures but those which form part of the highest mental activities: pleasure *qua* pleasure, and the lower as well as the higher pleasure, is indefeasibly part of the human good. In the same way it is not the human ideal to cultivate only the higher forms of virtue and to neglect culture or happiness or both, and Rashdall also makes a point afterwards stressed by Scheler and Hartmann that there can be no virtues of generosity, fairness, courage, etc., unless there are other goods than virtue which these virtues can dispense, distribute, defend, etc. This does not of course mean that the value of these virtues is in any way a function of the more elementary values with which they are concerned. Culture and pleasure without virtue are not, of course, an admissible choice at all, and the sort of value that we call 'aesthetic', while having a peculiar autonomy that Rashdall finds difficult to analyse, can none the less not set itself up against values as a whole – as some aesthetes have tried to make it do – but has a place assigned in that pattern, and one must on each occasion judge how far it can be allowed to go.

But despite his organicism and his doctrine of the non-substitutability of values, Rashdall still professes himself a believer in the 'commensurability' of all values. Though values may to some extent be relative to context, yet in a determinate context it is possible to compare them, and to compare them quantitatively. One valuable goal can in given circumstances be rated as more or less valuable than another, and this sheer quantity of value can in some cases outweigh difference of values which involve 'height'. Thus the integrity of a Chinese mandarin is a higher thing than the freedom from torture and dishonour of a number of European prisoners: none the less it may be right to corrupt the Mandarin to save the Europeans, since there is *more* value thus realised. (It is strange how the forgotten prejudices of the period intrude into an impartial treatise.) Rashdall entirely deprecates the view that there are some values or disvalues so immensely exalted that no amount of a lower value or disvalue can compensate for them. Cardinal Newman tried to defend the Catholic conception of lying as venial, by holding that it would be better for the whole human race to die in agony than for one man to commit a venial act of lying. This judgement, Rashdall mildly asserts, is unacceptable (*Theory of Good and Evil*, II 43). It may be noted that Rashdall's doctrine of the commensurability of all values does not entail commensurability in terms of a common unit. He thinks, however, that there are cases where it *does* make sense to say that A is n times better than B.

Rashdall mitigates the harshness of the over-rigorous doctrine of the obligatory maximisation of values, and of the denial of works of supererogation, by a doctrine of vocation. It is not everyone's duty to strive for the higher values above the lower on every occasion, since not everyone has a vocation to produce these higher values, or to maintain production of them on all occasions. Those who aspire to heights of culture or of virtue beyond their capacity will bring less value into being than if they had aimed lower: their vocation is in fact to produce and enjoy lower types of value. On this ground and on this alone can we justify the reduction of a man's level of aspiration in the field of duty: it is always one's duty to produce the best of which one is capable in the whole situation of persons and things of which one is a part. This stress on vocation is, of course, very important, but one may doubt whether it deals with the obstinate feeling that one is *not* obliged to maximise value even within the limits of one's vocation, and that the view that one is so ignores the higher kinds of merit.

A remaining point of interest in Rashdall's theory is his excellent treatment of distributive justice in volume I, chapter VIII. Rashdall points out that it is not sufficient that we should maximise good: it is also necessary that we should do so fairly, justly, impartially, without arbitrary inequality. The immense obscurity of the egalitarianism which seems part of the notion of justice is recognised by Rashdall when he says that justice involves no more than 'equality of consideration'. It need not in all circumstances involve equalisation of well-being, nor equalisation of possession of the instruments and opportunities of well-being, nor any sort of straightforward equalisation. Differences of capacity render all this impossible, and so do differences of individual taste and preference, and so too, of course, do abundances and shortages in what is desired. But the sheer vagueness of the general notion of justice does not affect the validity of its inspiration nor the possibility of giving it a concrete meaning in frameworks made definite by nature or by social convention.

Rashdall, however, feels that justice constitutes a grave problem for ideal utilitarianism. For if the maximisation of good is the sole criterion of duty, why should we lay stress on the way good is distributed? Shall we say that the just distribution of good is itself a good of higher order? This view Rashdall rejects, since a higher-order good would be a mere abstraction, and not an actual state of anyone's consciousness. This objection would, however, touch all those higher patterns of good which are spread out over a whole society or even over the consciousness of the same person at different times: a happy life for example, is not concentrated into a single state of consciousness. If there can be genuine welfare of this distributed sort, it is not clear why justly distributed welfare should not be a genuine form of good. Rashdall prefers to balance his books by stressing justice as a *virtue*; an unjust society may realize more good for its members except in respect of the justice of some or all of those members. But Rashdall's doctrine conflicts with his own principle that virtue is always founded on values beyond itself. If there were no such evil as an unjust allocation of good (in a non-willed sense of 'unjust' and 'allocation'), then there could no moral evil in the wills which tolerated such an unjust allocation.

Sir David Ross, the third British moral philosopher we are to study, built his views on the treatments of Moore and Rashdall: he is not, however, a pure axiologist, an ideal utilitarian as they are, but his system none the less includes a considerable infusion of ideal utilitarianism on which we shall mainly lay stress. His two works on ethics, *The Right and the Good* (1930) and *The Foundations of Ethics* (1939) have a certain dull greatness which shines through the crudity of certain of his formulations and the pettifogging character of some of his arguments. The influence of Aristotle and Butler, as well as an unusually wide and deep study of contemporary British, American and continental thought, gives his work a classic quality: he is not afraid to say of certain moral axioms that 'the moral order expressed in these propositions is just as much part of the fundamental nature of the universe (and, we may add, of any possible universe in which there were moral agents at all) as is the spatial or numerical structure expressed in the axioms of geometry or arithmetic. . . . . In both cases we are dealing with propositions that cannot be proved, but that just as certainly need no proof' (*Right and Good*, pp. 29–30).

The doctrine with which the name of Ross is mainly associated is that of *prima facie rightness* or *prima facie duty*. On that view, what we ought to do on a given occasion is always the outcome of a number of distinct 'claims' upon us, each of which would become our full-fledged duty if it were the only claim in the field. Some of these claims are axiological and are rooted in different values and disvalues that we recognise and of which we feel the attraction or repulsion. Among all these we have to seek the ideal utilitarian accommodation recommended by Moore and Rashdall: we must weigh the goods and evils inherent in, or springing from, various possible lines of conduct open to us at the moment, and opt for the line of conduct that will, we consider, contribute the greatest amount of additional good to the universe and the least amount of evil. This ideal utilitarian claim is very important, and is in fact the general background of the life of duty, which develops into our unconditional duty when other special claims are not present.

There are, however, a number of special claims which Ross does not think reducible to any addition of value or reduction of disvalue, but which are felt as right without regard to any amount of good or evil they may contribute to the universe. These claims may be overridden by utilitarian claims of sufficient weight, but there are circumstances in which they will override such utilitarian claims. In *The Right and the Good* Ross lists among such non-utilitarian requirements those (*a*) which demand fidelity to a promise or engagement or tacit understanding arrived at with others; (*b*) those which demand gratitude, and expressions of gratitude, for benefits previously conferred on us by others; (*c*) those which demand the upsetting of a distribution of pleasure or happiness which is not in accord with the merit of those among whom there is such a distribution. Ross also points to such non-utilitarian anomalies as that we are much more stringently bound to avoid injuring others (duty of non-maleficence) than we are bound to promote their positive well-being, and to the curious fact that while we have a duty to improve our own condition as regards virtue and knowledge (duty of self-improvement) we are not obliged to promote our own pleasure. All these special claims relating to whom we have special relations or to special forms of good, are not easily dealt with by the general utilitarian formula of endeavouring to maximise good and minimise evil, but seem to involve an added note of sacredness or stringency: this may be overridden by merely utilitarian claims, which in such a case have a higher, more stringent *prima facie* rightness, but they have in all cases to be considered.

It is not our task here to go into all the arguments for and against the non-axiological claims on which Ross lays such stress. It is arguable that Ross finds it hard to deal with them in an axiological framework because he fails to see that the sort of values with which our more stringent duties are concerned are essentially disvalues rather than positive values, and disvalues of an entirely intrinsic and very grave sort. They are disvalues which as it were question and place in jeopardy the whole fabric of mutual adjustment and accommodation which is the foundation of the moral order, a foundation which all positive values require for their security, and which are not to be put on a level with values and disvalues of the occasion which are as it were, only a loose, changeable superstructure built on the basis in question. Breaches of faith, acts of ingratitude, grossly unequal distributions in a sense rend the whole fabric of our mutual social commitment, defy the moral order and therefore involve an evil much greater than any transitory inconvenience or personal discomfiture. This evil tends to pass unnoticed, since the duties of fidelity, gratitude, veracity, common fairness, etc., which guard against them, do not, if fulfilled, yield goods of any particularly high order. They provide only the foundations, not the pinnacles of the axiological order. Seen in this light, as being concerned with the avoidance of grave underminings and questionings of the whole order of values, the duties in question can be held to have their roots in the grave disvalues which they seek to avoid. They are part of the grave need to minimise evil rather than augment good, which Ross too recognises when he acknowledges the more stringent character of the obligation not to harm over the obligation to benefit or improve. If ideal utilitarianism is allowed to recognise and give full weight to the profound gulf between the good and the bad, and to recognise that the avoidance of evil is in some deep sense more fundamental than the achievement of good, then it will perhaps be possible to bring Ross's duties of special obligation into the fold of an amended ideal utilitarianism.

Ross stresses the non-deducible character of the accommodation of the various duty-claims upon us: we have *prima facie* duties of various sorts, but there is no general principle according to which we can decide which should prevail in a given case. A certain moral perception, to make use of a notion of Aristotle's, alone can cut the Gordian knot. The principle that the more stringent *prima facie* duty should prevail, affords no guidance, and is in fact little more than a tautology, and so is the ideal utilitarian principle that one should always produce the better of two alternative goods. 'When we have to choose between the production of two heterogeneous goods, say knowledge and pleasure, the "ideal utilitarian" theory can only fall back on an opinion, for which no logical basis can be offered, that one of the goods is the greater; and this is no better than a similar opinion that one of two duties is the more urgent' (*The Right and the Good*, p. 23). (One wonders whether there is here even any genuine difference of meaning between the ideal utilitarian and Ross's deontological mode of speaking.) Ross further says that 'the sense of our particular duty in particular circumstances, preceded and informed by the fullest reflection we can bestow on the act in all its bearings, is highly fallible, but it is the only guide we have to our duty' (ibid., p. 42). Where all is so extremely without principle one is inclined to wonder whether Aristotelian talk of 'perception' and the suggestions of a differing amount of value or differing degree of stringency, always present but not always rightly apprehended, are really in place at all. One is inclined to feel sympathy with the modern talk of a *decision* among various general duty- or value-claims. However this all may be, Ross's conception of *prima facie* duty does justice to an all-important fact in the phenomenology of choice: that we are always liable to be faced by a number of distinct calls to realise good or avoid bad, not capable of being reconciled in practice, and not subject to any principle which determines their preferential order. Conflict among such claims and the sheer overriding of one by the other, are part of the structure of value-experience, which is perhaps much what Hartmann meant when he spoke of the 'antinomic' character of the realm of values.

We must turn, however, from Ross's conceptions of 'rightness', to his conceptions of value or goodness which are more central for our purpose. *Part*, at least, of our moral life consists in deciding which is the more valuable or less disvaluable of a number of realisable or avoidable states of things, which may all be our 'objectives' of pursuit or avoidance. Ross believes that *both* rightness and goodness are unanalysable properties, the former pertaining specifically to acts, the latter to states of affairs generally. We can specify the various possible *grounds* of rightness and goodness, but this is not to say what these properties themselves are. We need not repeat our criticisms of Moore's doctrine of the naturalistic fallacy: obviously they apply here. Ross holds that our judgement as to the goodness or relative goodness of various sorts of things always *expresses* our personal attitudes to the things concerned but that it never *means or refers to* those attitudes: what it means or refers to is a property that has nothing to do with anyone's attitude to anything, and which belongs purely to the state of affairs under consideration. 'What we *express* when we call an object good is our attitude towards it, but what we *mean* is something about the object itself and not about our attitude towards it. When we call an object good we are commending it, but to commend is not to say that we are commending it, but to say that it has a certain character, which we think it would have whether we were commending it or not' (*Foundations of Ethics*, p. 255). The peculiar use of 'expression' and 'meaning' which here occurs is borrowed from Meinong, but Ross does not develop anything like Meinong's full doctrine of emotional presentation.

He only says that an emotional attitude is *in some manner* essential to a judgement of value, but that such a judgement is none the less purely intellectual, fact-stating, truth-directed. Ross, like Moore, thinks that so much is required to make value-dispute and argument possible.

If we now turn to Ross's views as to the main sorts of things that are good, we find him more or less following Rashdall in first accepting *three* main divisions of goodness: the goodness of virtuous disposition, the goodness of knowledge and opinion, and the goodness of being pleased or happy. But fourthly and more hesitantly Ross accepts, as Rashdall was not willing to accept, as an independent, higher-order good, 'the apportionment of pleasure and pain to the virtuous and the vicious respectively', a non-moral good upon whose recognition and pursuit the moral good of justice depends (*The Right and the Good*, p. 138). Ross's view of the relations of these various sorts of good is more abstractly moralistic than Rashdall's: he conceives that, while there can be graded comparisons of value *in* each of the three main departments of value, there is only a total difference of grade among the three departments themselves. This means that all cases of virtue are more valuable than all cases of knowledge and pleasure, and that all cases of knowledge are more valuable than all cases of pleasure. The weakest virtuous stirring is necessarily worth more than the most powerful act of intellectual penetration and the greatest of pleasures. One is reminded of Cardinal Newman's preference of universal but innocent agony to a single venial sin, and of Rashdall's rejection of it. It is, however, the logic of the doctrine which on reflection, disquiets Ross: he does not see how one scale of magnitude can begin totally above the infinite levels possible on another, a problem which a mathematician would not find serious. He therefore takes the view that the impossibility of grading items belonging to different scales lies in the fact that they embody different *senses* of goodness or value. The goodness of virtue and knowledge consists in (or is at least bound up with) the fact that they are fit objects of *admiration*, whereas the goodness of certain pleasures, which Ross restricts to the pleasures of *others*, is that they are fit objects of satisfaction. These doctrines are far from clear. That the goodness of virtue and knowledge is indefinable and yet is capable of being 'paraphrased' as being a fit object of admiration (*Foundations of Ethics*, p. 253) is not wholly easy to comprehend, nor yet why pleasure, which is a fit object of satisfaction, should be without such an indefinable property. But by these doctrines Ross maintains his moralism, even if he is forced to put intellectual values into the same class as moral values, and is also able to draw a very moralistic distinction between one's own pleasures and those of others, the former not being good in any ethically significant sense, and so something that we are not obliged to produce at all.

Ross then goes on to many interesting analyses of moral value, grading virtue according to the *motives* which inspire conduct. The highest of such motives is the desire to do one's duty, the next highest the desire to achieve something good, in so far as it is good, beneath which lie many motives directed to valuable ends but without any conscious direction to their value. Ross does not think that mixed motivation necessarily detracts from moral excellence provided the highest motives could do the trick alone: if this is the case, the addition of other good motives augments the virtue. And Ross does not think that moral value diminishes if a choice comes wholly easy, provided that the same choice would have been made had circumstances *not* made it easy.

Our criticism of many details of Ross's teaching must not be allowed to obscure the impressive coherence of the whole, and its faithfulness to many of the finer shades of valuation. Ross is at all times alive to the most minute nuances of the moral judgement, and to complex distinctions which it is only too easy to ignore or minimise. His treatment, like that of Moore and Rashdall, certainly shows that, despite endless points of controversy, there is an ordered system of values and disvalues which comes to light in moral reflection and discourse, and that there is a worthwhile philosophical enterprise which investigates this ordered system.

IV. SCHELER AND HARTMANN

In the present chapter we shall sketch the contents of two major German contributions to value-theory, works which not only study the general logic of value-discourse, but which also draw up a comprehensive map of the value-firmament, an ordered setting forth of the different sorts of things that can be held to be good or bad in some cogently valid fashion, and which can arguably be placed in cogently valid relations to one another. These works are Max Scheler's *Formalism in Ethics and the Material Value-Ethic*, first published in Husserl's *Jahrbuch für Philosophie und phänomenologische Forschung* (*Journal for Philosophy and Phenomenological Research*) in 1913 and 1914, but not as yet translated into English, and Nicolai Hartmann's *Ethics*, published in German in 1926, and in an English translation by Stanton Coit in 1932. Both works have a certain sweeping splendour: they consider many questions that Anglo-Saxon moral philosophers never raise (though ordinary Anglo-Saxons often consider them) and they see all these questions in a systematic interrelatedness which is also largely foreign to Anglo-Saxon thought. On the whole they leave one with the impression that, however difficult it may be to lay bare the rationale of value-research, it is none the less something that *can* be undertaken, and that can be made to yield results neither emptily analytic nor arbitrarily personal. Both abound in loosely stated and poorly substantiated insights, which do not always form a coherent pattern. Their analyses do not, however, remain obstinately on the fringe of what is worth considering, attached to the false dogma that the most obvious truisms are also those that will yield the richest harvest of truth and light, and their easy inconsistency means that they do not remain obdurately wedded to wrong methods and basic misconceptions, which lead repeatedly to the same *impasse*. Socrates and Moore were both philosophers of the most august greatness, but we may be glad that not all philosophers chopped logic as finely and as vainly as they did. Scheler and Hartmann both think darkly and nebulously, but since the realm of values is itself darkly nebulous rather than classically clear, and resembles a Teutonic Valhalla more than a Greek Olympus, we have perhaps more to learn from them than from moral philosophers all too obstinately clear-cut and consistent.

Max Scheler's work on ethics is only one of his immensely original, penetrating studies of the human person in relation to the world, to other human persons, and to a supercosmic, eternal something, which, whether real or unreal, transcends the cosmos and the conscious beings in it. The foundations of his thought lie in Husserl, and he is everywhere concerned to describe matters as they appear or are given to consciousness, and not to allow scientific of metaphysical theories to undermine or overturn the conscious appearances. Thus whatever the obscure processes, physical, physiological and psychological, that may have led to our complex vision of the world as it stands arrayed around us, the fact is that it is a world that includes things as well as sensations, situations as well as things, other conscious beings as well as ourselves, inner states as well as outer acts, values as well as valueless facts, and a numinous culmination which gathers together and unifies all phenomena, whether or not we treat it as an illusion. Towards such appearances we must be loyal, however much theorists may assure us that 'all they really are' is movements of atoms, excitations of neurons, patterns of behaviour, linguistic constructions, etc: the content of such theories is less solid than the appearances they set out to explain. Scheler was, however, an early pupil of Husserl's, much more influenced by the *Logische Untersuchungen* (*Logical Investigations*, trans. J. N. Findlay (Routledge, 1970)) of 1899–1901 than by the phenomenological writings that began to pour forth in 1913. His point of view is accordingly realistic rather than idealistic, and while the phenomena which make up the experienced world are necessarily set up for the subject in certain characteristic psychic acts, there is no suggestion that what is thus set up may not also, in limiting cases, coincide, and be known to coincide, with things as they in themselves authentically are. Scheler's whole book is in fact part of an attempt of German thought to free itself from the influence of Kant, from Kantian 'constructivism' in epistemology and from Kantain rigorism and imperativism in ethics. The attempt may be adjudged vain, since these sides of Kant still dominate German thought.

Scheler, like Hartmann, is concerned to put emotion, rather than cold intellectual grasp, at the centre of value-experience: it is in and through our feelings that objects and states come before us as endowed with worthwhileness and counterworthwhileness, and without feelings this essential side of things could not get through to us at all. It is all-important, however, that we should have a correct theory of the sort of feelings that are concerned in value-experience, and that we should not assimilate them to the states, conditions, *Zustände*, sensational modifications that we merely live through, without intrinsically directing ourselves to objects in and through them, or which, if they are afterwards connected with objects, are so connected in a merely extrinsic, causal manner. The feelings that are important for value-experience are essentially 'intentional', directed feelings: they discharge themselves upon objects rather than are merely produced by them. And this intentional directedness is never casual nor at random, but is always the appropriate *answer* to what the object is given to us as being, so that the same situation in which we direct feelings towards an object is also one in which the object reveals itself as being in some way suited to the feelings we direct towards it, or in other words as having a value. The connections between intrinsically directed feelings and objects having something that suits them have, further, the universal cogency which stamps them as *a priori*: they are not grounded inductively on what we uniformly find to be the case in beings like ourselves, but are lived through as ineluctable, as appropriate, as having the same sort of force as pure logic. To quote Scheler:

It is our *whole* spiritual life – not merely our objective cognition and thought in the sense of a knowledge of being – that involves *pure* acts and pure act-principles, i.e. acts and principles independent of the facts of our human organization, in essence and content. The emotional side of our spirit, our feeling, preference, love, hate, willing, also has its own *a priori* content, which it does not borrow from thinking, and which ethics must set forth in entire independence from logic. There is an *a priori ordre du cœur* or *logique du cœur* as Blaise Pascal tellingly puts it. (*Formalism*, p. 59)

Or again:

A feeling of anger arises in me and runs its course, a feeling which certainly has no intentional, original bond with the thing *about* which I am angry. The idea, the thought, or rather the objects given in them, that I at first perceived, conceived or thought, arouse my anger, and only afterwards – very quickly in normal cases – do I relate my feelings to these objects, always through my idea of them. I certainly 'apprehend' nothing in such anger . . . The situation is quite different when I rejoice or grieve over or about something . . . The words 'over' and 'about' reveal in speech that in such rejoicing or grieving objects are not first apprehended, *over* which I rejoice, etc., but that they rather have stood before me already, not merely as things perceived, but as things coloured by certain value-predicates given in feeling. The value-qualities given in the valuation in question intrinsically *demand* certain qualities in such 'response-reactions', just as these last in their turn achieve their target in them. (Ibid., p. 268)

The passages quoted reveal all the penetration and confusion of Scheler's treatment. There is no developed theory, as in Meinong, as to how an emotional reaction, merely because it is directed or appropriate, can mediate an apprehension of value in that to which it is directed. Nor is it clear that anger is not often as intrinsically directed and appropriate as rejoicing and grieving. Moreover the whole analysis proves too much. Intentionality is not necessarily the same as justifiability: to be specifically directed to some object, is not to be nor to seem justifiably so directed. One good reason for believing in objective value-predicates is that we do not *always* feel that our emotional intentionality has anything justified about it: sometimes it appears merely 'personal'. The fact that we *sometimes* feel a peculiar correctness and appropriateness in our directed emotions at least provides an argument (if not a truly clinching one) for holding there to be some objective peculiarity in what we feel about in such cases.

It is interesting, in view of Scheler's emotional theory of valuation, to note his reaction to the emotive theory of value-discourse which, though only launched in Anglo-Saxon countries in the thirties, is clearly set forth and pondered by Scheler in the second decade of the century, and given the name of 'ethical nominalism'. Scheler writes: 'If after experiencing a pain I cry "Ow", this "Ow", is not directed to the experienced pain as when I say "I am feeling pain": it simply expresses such pain. . . . Just so the sentences "This is good (bad)" do not report the content of an inner experience as taking place or as having taken place nor communicate it to others: they only *express* certain acts of emotion and desire' (ibid., p. 169). And again: 'In place of the involuntary expressions of desire and feeling, which make up the most primitive sense of the so-called value-judgement, we later encounter the *voluntary intimation* of such acts with the intention to arouse a similar desire and feeling in others' (ibid., p. 170). Scheler refutes such emotivism by holding that there is a 'distinction of essence' between merely responding emotionally to something or desiring others to do so (on the one hand), and really judging something to be good, beautiful, etc. (on the other). This distinction points to a value-predicate in the objects which, though essentially evocative of feeling, is not the same as any feeling it evokes, or any power to evoke such feeling (ibid., pp. 173–4).

We must, however, turn from Scheler's general doctrine of *a priori* emotionality, to the detailed content that he connects with it. He first states such simple-minded axioms as that the existence of a value is itself a value, the non-existence of such a value being (presumably) an equal negative value, whereas the existence of a negative value is itself a negative value, its non-existence being (presumably) an equal value. The writing-off of negative values (disvalues) as the mere absence of values, enables Scheler to work out his whole map of values in terms of positive values. Clearly Scheler has not realised the positive nature of badness, and its non-equivalence to the mere absence of good. Some inkling of this truth, however, filters through in the doctrine that an 'ought', an obligation, while it always derives from a value, is none the less *primarily* concerned with the non-existence of the *disvalue* whose absence is tantamount to the value in question. 'It is therefore the case that a positive value underlies every ought-proposition, a value that it itself never can embrace. For what ought in general to be is never primarily the being of what is good, but only the non-being of what is evil' (*Formalism*, p. 213). This proposition would only make full sense if the non-being of an evil were something different from the being of a good, as it in fact plainly is.

From this doctrine Scheler goes on to make many points in opposition to Kant. An ethics, he holds, that makes 'ought' or duty central, must always of necessity have a merely negative, critical character. 'We see from this', he says, 'that every imperativistic ethic, i.e. every ethic that starts out from the thought of duty as the *most original* ethical phenomenon, and endeavours to reach the ideas of good and bad, virtue and sin, from this starting-point, must throughout be of a merely negative, critical and repressive character' (ibid., p. 215). There are natures that like to approach the sphere of value from this indirect, negative, dutiful angle, but Scheler considers it a defect that they have to do so. (As does Kant also, we may remark, in his doctrine of a holy will.) All this being assumed, it is only to be expected that Scheler will be unfavourable to a need- or desire-analysis of value or valuation. 'It is not the case', he writes,

as the need-theory of value and valuation supposes . . . that anything, an X, only has value in so far as it satisfies a need. The valuableness of anything does not mean that a mere lack, the objective-correlate of the need-experience, is removed, that a value-vacuum is as it were filled, a hole stopped up. Rather does the feeling of lack presuppose that the *positive* value of the missing good is first given in feeling, in so far, that is, as we do not have a merely *undirected* pressure that does not at all qualify to be called a need. (Ibid., p. 364)

Scheler has of course not proved his point. Plainly there are cases where something is primarily missed rather than positively cherished, and cases where something is primarily cherished and only secondarily missed, if indeed it is missed at all. The most positively precious things are all arguably dispensable. In the absence of any previous, thoroughgoing discussion of these matters, other than that of Meinong, whom Scheler did not read carefully, we may pardon Scheler for his rather poor axiomatisation.

At a stage more concrete, Scheler holds that values form a one-dimensional continuum unambiguously ordered as higher and lower: like Brentano he believes in an irreducible act of *preference* (*Vorziehen*) which is the appropriate medium through which this difference impresses itself on us. He then gives a series of criteria, of somewhat doubtful acceptability, of the higher or lower standing of certain values. Higher values are more enduring than lower ones – a counter-argument for the fleeting, dependent character of higher values might very well have been offered – they are less plainly anyone's special property and so are less diminished when shared, they are more fundamental – again an argument in the opposite direction would have been possible – they yield a *deeper* sort of satisfaction without which lower satisfactions do not really satisfy, and they are less relative to person and situation, more truly absolute, than lower values (ibid., pp. 88–98). The bearers of value are divided into a large number of classes: there are values attaching to persons and values attaching to things, values for self and values for another, values of acts, functions and reactions, of dispositions, deeds and consequences, of intentional and non-intentional experiences, of fundaments, forms and relations, of things for their own sake and of things for something else's sake, etc. As Aristotle would say, all these are good in differing but related senses. Scheler further elaborates an ascending scale of 'value-modalities' which is not unlike the scales of Ross. At the bottom of the scale are the values of the agreeable, ranging from those of mere coenaesthetic bodily agreeableness, through those of unlocalised 'mind-joys' and 'mind-sorrows', up to very lofty forms of spiritual blessedness or despair. Above these hedonic values lie the very Germanic values of *vitality*, values of activity and repose, of energy and exhaustion, of health and disease, as also of the noble and the ignoble: the distinction between nobler and baser forms of existence runs through the whole biological order. Above the vital values lie spiritual (*geistige*) values, which divide familiarly into values of aesthetic enjoyment, of moral participation and of intellectual penetration, and above these again lie the values which express different forms of personal *sanctity*. It is worth while pointing out, as Scheler does, that

holiness is an ineliminable upper limit to the value-continuum:
it helps to inspire and justify dogmatic religion, rather than being
a mere offshoot of the latter. We look in the direction of the holy
before some object, often quite inadequate, seems to exemplify it.

In his practical use of this ascending scale of values, Scheler
stresses an important principle afterwards taken over by Hartmann:
that the higher values cannot be independently pursued, but that
they arise 'on the back' of a pursuit of lower values. It is not by
seeking to be virtuous or cultivated or scientific, least of all by
seeking to be holy, that we become these excellent things: we
become them by pursuing and diffusing the lower goods in which
it is proper to 'lose ourselves'. Not to achieve such a loss of self,
is to corrupt, not to realise, the higher values: in the moral sphere,
it is to achieve *Pharisaism* rather than true moral goodness. To
Scheler the whole Kantian cult of pure duty is definitely Pharisaic:
if one cannot be zealous about other lesser things than duty and
purity of will, e.g. the happiness and equal opportunity of others,
one cannot be zealous about these latter things at all. Scheler's
doctrine is, of course, as exaggeratedly puritanical as the Kantian
doctrine: if Kant pushes us towards common kindness while
directing us to keep our will fixed on higher moral abstractions,
Scheler pushes us towards higher moral abstractions while directing us to keep our will firmly fixed on soup-kitchens or ventures
in adult education. Plainly it is possible to aspire to personal
culture, virtue and sanctity without rending them from their
necessary soil in the pursuit of lower, more foundational goods.
But that all such higher goods presuppose lower, foundational
goods is an important moral theorem which has been only too often
ignored in the long past history of emptily formal treatments
of duty or virtue, and of crudely material hedonistic systems.

In the concluding Sixth Section of his work on Ethics Scheler
writes abundantly regarding the nature of a person, and of the
relation of value to personality. A person is much more than an
epistemological subject, and is not merely an abstract point from
which mental acts radiate. It is a kind of unity which is *itself*
differentiated and totally present in all the acts that we attribute
to it, and outside of which they would not be conceivable: it is

also a kind of unity which diffuses itself through bodily as well as mental acts, and thereby acquires a seeming diremption into parts external to parts. The essential *Ineinander* or mutual interpenetration of the acts of the person, means, further, that the person is not only *not* intrinsically diffused in space, but also *not* intrinsically successive in time. Its relations to temporality, like those it has to spatiality, are due to its immersion in body. The person is, further, never present to itself in the sense of being an object to its own acts: it *experiences* its unity and pervasive identity rather than envisages these in objectified fashion. These positions are by no means new, and, even if they are in some sense unquestionably true, Scheler has certainly not given them an acceptably lucid sense nor freed them from absurd exaggerations.

It is in the ethical sphere, however, that the person, as opposed to the subject plays its full part, and all values are values for, or of the person. Scheler puts the responsible, adult, sane, normal person in the centre of the axiological picture, and is even prepared to talk as if, in certain phases of value-development, women and slaves, not to mention children and animals, are rightly regarded as sub-persons. There are, of course, certain values which are universal in the sense of not being geared to the distinguishing peculiarities of this or that person or sort of person, but Scheler, like Rashdall, holds to the doctrine of an essentially vocational aspect of truly concrete values, a being tailored to the needs and capacities of the individual person. In this doctrine Scheler is of course setting himself up against the formal universalism of Kant. Scheler writes:

If every 'ought' can only be a genuine moral 'ought' in so far as it rests on insight into objective values, there is also the possibility of evident insight into a good which has reference to an individual person written into its objective essence and value-content, and whose accompanying 'ought' therefore *calls upon* this person and this person alone, regardless as to whether the same call is heard by others or not. ... What is intrinsically good is good 'for me' in the sense that, in the specific material content of this intrinsic good (descriptively put), there is an experienced reference to me, an experienced index that proceeds from this content and points to 'me', that as it were says 'For you'. (*Formalism*, p. 510)

What holds for the individual, holds also for a given moment in the individual's life, or for the particular society to which the individual belongs: all have individual vocations, which are not subsumable under any general principle.

Scheler devotes a great deal of space to the values which are the vocation of *social* as opposed to individual persons: though they realise themselves in and through individual persons, he thinks it right to grant them their own personality. This is even true of the atomistic type of society in which every individual mistrusts and uses every other, though here there is an element of fiction in the 'personality' in question. This is not, however, the case in regard to the highest society, the universal communion of sanctified persons, which remains a necessary idea, whether or not it is satisfactorily embodied in this or that actual church. 'The unity of the church, despite the possible contemporary plurality of social culture-persons. . . . is likewise an *a priori* proposition. The inclusive solidarity *of all possible* finite persons in my salvation, and of my salvation in the salvation of all finite persons, lies in the essence of a total intention directed to the value of all things in the absolute sphere of being and value' (ibid., p. 571).

Such extended construction in spheres deemed mystical and reactionary will not be pleasing to the liberal Anglo-Saxon mind: it is, however, questionable whether this mind, with its hundred clear-cut, dogmatic diremptions, could ever achieve a comprehensive understanding of the firmament of values, or of any inclusive or ultimate matter. More serious questions arise in regard to Scheler's method of investigation. How can we justify the innumerable intuitively based utterances which make up his book, utterances for which so little supporting argument is offered? And how can Scheler explain the existence of maps of value widely differing from his own? Scheler's intuitive method admits the existence of value-delusions and errors, but there is no systematic treatment of their types and sources. At one point only does he indicate a principal source of value-error: the *resentment* which leads one to overvalue one's own achievements and enjoyments, and to undervalue achievements and enjoyments which lie beyond one's range. It is this resentment which makes those who do the right thing with difficulty and sacrifice, undervalue the achievements of those who do it with ease, which makes men see merit in difficulty, sacrifice and even weakness. It is this resentment which prefers acts done painfully out of duty to acts done freely out of love, again a point scored against Kant. It is this resentment which exalts struggle, and connects civilization with the facing of challenges. Scheler, like Nietzsche, from whom the notion of resentment is borrowed, will have none of all this. The luminous values of his empyrean require no dark shadows to set them off. But it is by no means clear that the need for challenge and contrast in the value-world can be wholly set down to the malign workings of resentment: without them, it may be argued, there could not be values at all.

Hartmann's work on *Ethics*, to which we now turn, is divided into three main parts, the first concerned with valuation and value in general, the second with the detailed pattern of the value-firmament, and the last, riddled with inconsistencies, with the problem of Free Will. We shall confine ourselves to the first two parts of the work, which alone concern axiological ethics.

Hartmann takes over, without much added analysis or criticism, Scheler's doctrine of a logic of the heart. The organ through which the rich distinctions and structure of the world of value come home to us is Feeling, and there is an emotional *a priori*, parallel but not reducible to the *a priori* governing theoretical fields. Hartmann tellingly points out, much as Hutcheson had done in the eighteenth century, how widely ranging is the scope of our feelings, and how vastly wider than the scope of our action or practical decision. We react approvingly or disapprovingly to acts, characters and states of affairs remote in space and time which it is quite beyond our practical power to affect, we react similarly to things imaginary or even impossible, and we are always emotionally sensitive to strains of good or bad, better or worse, in the things around us, even though what we feel about has nothing to do with us, and does not fall within the range of our practical business. Nor is it by constituting ourselves imaginary heroes or policemen or busybodies or creators that we thus respond to the light and shade in the world: we may remain inert, but we

continue to feel, and sometimes feel seriously about things, as
seriously as when practical issues are at stake. Hartmann is far
from approving the Anglo-Saxon opinion, plainly having its
roots in a particular temperament, that it is only committed
action that shows what we *sincerely* value or care for. Hartmann
then glides, with little more difficulty than Scheler, to the view
that the emotional impressions which objects make upon us are
also in some way revelations of their intrinsic nature, and that the
peculiar stirrings we discharge upon objects also set before us,
sometimes in illusory fashion, values and disvalues and 'oughts'
which are in no sense matters of feeling, but which inhere in the
cosmos or in the possibility of a cosmos. The fact that we only
sometimes feel that our emotional responses have this objective
warrant, that there are purely-personal-seeming as well as objec-
tive-seeming values – the preciousness of some keepsake as
opposed to the preciousness of truth – and that objects are frequently shifted from one of these cadres to the other, is a point
on which Hartmann lays no stress, all-important as it is for the
whole of value-analysis.

Hartmann is as entrenchedly opposed to Kant as is Scheler, and,
while believing profoundly in an emotional *a priori*, he is concerned to strip this notion of any subjective associations. The
axiological *a priori* is all 'out there', an ideal framework of self-
existent generalities which we discover and do not make, and
which imposes itself on our feeling as the particularities of nature
do on our senses or as the generalities of mathematics do on our
understanding. Hartmann borrows from Husserl the Platonising
belief that there is a direct experience or vision of species, of
eidetic universals, as much as of concrete particulars, and that,
while our insight into such species and their relations rests in the
first instance on experience of particulars and their various
'sides' or aspects, it in no sense reduces to the latter. To understand what it is to be angry or good is an act of pure *ideation*
which is quite independent of our ability to illustrate or even
recognise anger or goodness in particular cases, a view which
has the unmistakable warrant of introspection. It is through our
emotional responses that we can become aware, in the first

instance, of values in things, and, at a higher remove, of values as such. This doctrine needs to be supplemented by the view that it is through a peculiar psychological tension or pressure that we become aware of the 'ought-to-beness' which derives from and attends upon values, a tension or pressure which is not to be confused with the ought-to-beness which it makes evident to the mind.

Hartmann has a variety of deeply interesting, if not always wholly convincing, views regarding the realm of values which we must now set forth very briefly. He does not, in the first place, believe in a single, uniform essence of value or goodness which acquires specificity only through association with specific 'materials' or descriptive contents, the typical view of Anglo-Saxon analysis. He believes in an infinite variety of *species* of goodness or value (and of course of disvalue) which go with certain variations in material or descriptive content. In this opinion he accords with certain Anglo-Saxon intuitionists, e.g. Ross, who thinks that pleasure and virtue are good in different senses. But for Hartmann there are not merely these broad differences of sense in our value-references, and differently virtuous men will, e.g. the Hellenic and the Christian, be virtuous or good in radically different manners, these differences in virtue being differences in what we may call their axiological aura and not merely in what they do or tend to do. Hartmann further adheres to the somewhat exaggerated view, also defended in Plato's *Lysis*, that what one is really feeling about in a given case shows itself, on reflection, to be always a value *in specie* and never any instance or 'bearer' of such a value. This would entail that it is only *for the sake of* her generic or specific wifely virtues that one can value one's wife, and not as being the individual *bearer* of such excellences. The term 'bearer' is characteristically chosen: the individual becomes a mere peg, as it were, upon which valuable characters hang, a position remote from the extreme 'personalism' of Scheler.

Hartmann believes, like Scheler, that some values are 'given to axiological feeling' as unquestionably 'higher' than others. Thus moral values, the values of voluntary acts and dispositions, are unquestionably higher than 'goods-values' or values of welfare, and some moral values, e.g. those of friendship or loyalty, are unquestionably higher than others, e.g. those of mere veracity. Hartmann stresses the fact that this dimension of 'height' is correlated with peculiar emotional differences: higher values exact a different *Wertantwort* or value-response than do lower ones. There is plainly a deep deference, a Kantian *Achtung*, in our attitude to the higher values which is absent from our attitude towards lower ones. Hartmann leaves it an open question whether there are any general criteria of this valuational 'height', but he rejects as too simple the criteria enumerated by Scheler. It is further clear to Hartmann that 'height' does not represent the *only* dimension in which values order themselves. Many values fall into entirely different orders, and regarding these it is not possible to say that one is higher or lower than the other. There is no clear sense, for example, in saying that aesthetic values are higher or lower than moral values. Hartmann further points out that the realm of value is dominated by a dimension which is to some extent the inverse of the dimension of height, and to which he gives the name of the 'strength' of value. Strong values are those whose *non*-realisation represents a graver disvalue than that of weaker values, and whose ignoring or violation by a voluntary agent represents a graver offence than is the case with weaker values. But such strong values are also in general *lower* values, whereas weaker values tend to be higher. As Hartmann sensibly says: 'A loss of material good is in general a more serious matter than a loss of spiritual goods. A threat to life and limb is the gravest threat, but mere life is not on that account the highest good. . . . Aesthetic is far higher than material pleasure . . . and yet a man strives much more for the latter as long as he does not have it.' Turning to moral value he writes 'that murder, theft and all real crimes are felt to be the most grievous moral transgressions is due to this, that the justice they violate is based on the most elementary of goods-values . . . Hence the unique moral importance of justice. The importance does not attach to its height but its strength.' And again: 'If we compare the highest moral values, for instance radiant virtue or personal love with justice, the twofold relation becomes immediately evident. A neglect of radiant virtue and love exposes no one to radical dangers, a person who is incapable of them is not on that account a bad man.' Hartmann holds therefore that there is a dimension of strength of value concerned not so much with 'the actualization of positive values as with the avoidance of disvalues', and that this dimension is to a large extent independent of the dimension of height, though in general it operates inversely. 'It is this dimension of strength of value which is mainly considered in the severe prohibitions of certain moral codes, and which many philosophers seek to extend to all morality. But morality,' says Hartmann, 'shows a double face – its symbol is the head of Janus. It sets up a backward looking claim to the more elementary values, and a forward looking claim to the higher values.' Perversion results if *either* of these dimensions is exclusively regarded. It is as wrong to think only in terms of crying positive evils and their obligatory avoidance, as to think only in terms of 'higher things' and to ignore such crying positive evils. Would that this Janus-wisdom had filtered down to the conventional puritans of our ethical tradition. (See *Ethics*, vol. II, English translation, pp. 449–59.)

The many-dimensional realm of values has, however, a necessary relation to realisation which Hartmann expresses in terms of the notion of 'ought' (*Sollen*). Whether or not values are instantiated, it is part of the being of all values in some sense to demand instantiation, and this part of their being Hartmann calls their ideal ought-to-beness. Values, *qua* values, have an interior content distinct from such ideal ought-to-beness – being valuable is, in other words, not simply being what ought to be – but the two notions entail one another. Such ideal ought-to-beness is not always a case of ought-to-be-doneness, since many values are not realisable by action, and some even transcend the possible, and are in principle unrealisable whether by action or in any other manner. This ideal ought-to-beness, however, gives rise to what Hartmann calls a positive ought-to-beness whenever the real sphere is out of step with the ideal sphere of values, and this positive ought-to-beness is experienced as a *tension* by conscious practical beings, a tension which may take the form of a more or less ardent wish or, in some cases, of a practical resolution or an actual performance. This tension, which in certain cases amounts to the voice of duty, is the medium, but only the medium, through which positive ought-to-beness is apprehended: those who experience the tension also know the nature of the ought-to-beness which is what is given in and through the tension, and it does not make sense to ask what in itself such an ought-to-beness is or means.

Hartmann believes, further, that though the ought-to-beness of values is in no sense subjective, it is only through subjects, and in fact only through the special subjects called 'persons', that it gains any purchase on the world. Conscious practical subjects become aware of values through feeling, they experience their ought-to-beness in the tension of necessary desire, they may then be moved to think out plans for realising such values in actual situations, and such plans may then be put into action so that what ought to be comes to coincide with what actually is. Outside of conscious practical persons the realm of values is, however, held to be without influence on the actual world. Hartmann does not believe in a Platonic influence of the Good on the arrangement of things in nature, nor in any form of unconscious Aristotelian teleology. He puts before us the very Germanic picture of Man as having a unique 'demiurgic' vocation, as being *the one channel* through which what is good can become part and parcel of what actually exists. And not only is this the one channel for such influence, it is also a channel that may or may not be used, according as a man freely decides to realise or not to realise such values as he feels. (Hartmann's views on freedom are, however, a sad nest of obscure contradictions.)

Values, moreover, according to Hartmann, are radically different from categories, since it is never the case that they *must* be embodied in the world, only that they make a claim, inspire an effort, suggest a line leading to such embodiment. If nature worked unconsciously toward what is good, or if man necessarily realised the highest when he saw it, and was able to realise it, then values would be categories, part and parcel of the structure of the universe. The non-categorial nature of values is, further, shown by *their intrinsically antinomic character*. What is good, Hartmann tells us, necessarily lies in a large number of incompatible directions, and it is intrinsically impossible that *all* of these should be followed out into realisation. One cannot, for example, achieve pure simplicity and variegated richness in the same thing or occasion, and yet *both* incontestably make claims upon us, and ought *both* to be realised. The realm of values, in fact, always imposes a logically impossible task upon us: we are to achieve each and all of a large number of things which yet *cannot* all be achieved together. In practice, of course, we sacrifice one good to another, or we make compromises and accommodations among goods, or we realise one here and another there, and so on. This does not affect the fact that all such practical accommodations necessarily override the claims of certain values, and everywhere consummate something that in some respects ought not to be. And Hartmann even thinks that there is a sense in which we are always 'guilty' in such antinomic situations, guilty for not having realised *all* the good things which are yet such that they *cannot* all be realised. What Hartmann here teaches would to many seem absurd, and certainly he uses the term 'guilt' in a curious, unacceptable, Germanic manner. It remains arguable that the doctrine of the antinomic character of all values is profoundly true to our value-experience. What is self-contradictory certainly makes no sense in theory: there are no states of affairs that can ever make it true. But, contrary to what is generally thought, what is self-contradictory makes sense in practice: we are in fact obliged to strive towards value-accommodations to which full reality can never be given. Even Kant saw this when he held that only in eternity could we conform to the demands of the categorical imperative. The whole of our moral life is riddled with situations where we have to behave as if something were the case which probably is not and cannot be so, and only a very shallow morality results from full adaptation to what is actual or possible. (Not that this last is not also a necessary part or 'side' of morality, not fully reconcilable with the other part.) To be a 'knight of the ideal' may not accord with contemporary Marxist and similar fashions, but it may be argued that one will not achieve any morality at all if one aspires to less.

Hartmann, further, attempts a curious analysis of 'oughtness' in its relation to actuality and necessity, thereby making an eccentric but illuminating contribution to modal logic. An 'ought' is a necessity that has, by some strange mischance, been loosed from that close connection with actuality and possibility that other necessities entail. Two plus two *must* amount to four, and it is also a fact and a possibility that they should in all cases do so. A man must (in the sense of 'should') be wise as a serpent and gentle as a dove, but this does not mean that he will in fact be both of these things, or even that it is *possible* for him to be both of them. 'Ought' in fact goes with 'cannot' as often as 'can', and the ultimate 'oughts' are cases of 'cannot' rather than 'can'. Modal logicians are unlikely to incorporate Hartmann's suggestions into their treatments of deontic logic: the fact remains that he has pointed to a profound analogy between two senses of 'must' which also goes paired with an equally profound difference.

Hartmann couples his view of the strange, complex topography of value with a special view as to why we map it so inadequately. We do so because our feeling for value has a narrowness, an *Enge*, like the narrowness of conscious attention. To be deeply cognisant of the worthwhileness of certain things is necessarily to let the worthwhileness of other things become lost in the margin, and this is particularly so when the things in question are widely disparate or perhaps practically incompatible. If our whole life is built around certain values, it is unlikely that we shall be highly sensitive to values remote from these or even tending in a contrary direction. But the focus of valuation, like the focus of conscious attention, compensates for its narrowness by its tendency to shift, and it is by such a 'wandering' of the valuational focus that Hartmann accounts for the profound 'transvaluations' that occurred when the Greek world passed over into the Christian world, or the Christian world into the Renaissance world, and so on: all are by-products of an intense consciousness of new values whose swimming into the focus has pushed out the old. Such values are not really new, only hitherto ignored, and they are certainly not the creations of those who suddenly feel them, as Nietzsche thought them to be. This wandering of the value-focus, rather than malign resentment, is the cause of most value-errors and perversions, and it is these that the philosopher, with his balanced sympathy for all periods and societies, must therefore seek to correct. Hartmann has here certainly pointed out an important source of value-disputes. Nothing is more common than the assumption that if A and B exclude one another in practical realisation or in social cultivation, they necessarily exclude the possibility of each other's having value. This is plainly not the case: that A and B cannot both be does not mean that A and B cannot both be excellent. And though the impossible realisation of both sides of a contrary opposition might be the most valuable thing of all, it may still be the case, in this sorry, logical world, that realising one side of such an opposition may be better than realising nothing at all.

Hartmann's doctrine of the antinomic character of value comes out well in his treatment of what he calls the most elementary value-antitheses, an interesting, almost pre-Socratic collection of items. There is, he points out, a value in what must or should be the case (the law of nature or the holy will) but there is also a value in what may or may not be the case, the contingent, the variable and the free. There is an obvious value in the realisation of values in the actual world, but there is also a value in their perpetual non-realisation, their essential transcendence of what is or can be. There is a value in moving *towards* valuable ends, and there is a value in desisting from movement in actual *achievement*. There is a value in constancy and uniformity, and a value in change and variety, a value in intensive purity and a value in many-sided richness, a value in harmonious poise and a value in exciting conflict, a value in simplicity and a value in complexity. There is a Kantian value in universality and a Schelerian value in individuality, there is a value in subordinating the individual to the community and a value in subordinating the community to the individual, and so on. To ordinary people all these antitheses involve homiletic truisms: only philosophers see them as para-doxes, or try to explain them away.

Above these pre-Socratic oppositions Hartmann ranges a series of values which lead up to and prepare the way for moral values. The most basic of these is the value of life, and above this the values of consciousness, of activity, of endurance, of power, of freedom, of foresight, of practical success: there are also supporting values of the environment with its many facilities and opportunities, values of the varying powers we dispose of, of the fortunate turn of occasions, of such social supports as friends, reputation, good birth, money, etc. Aristotle would have recognised all these as necessary ingredients of the good life: modern moral philosophers, concerned only with narrow, detailed problems of immediate duty, do not discuss them.

When we proceed to Moral Goodness, the summit of value in the Hartmannian scheme, the Schelerian principle is accepted that such moral value cannot be divorced from the pursuit of non-moral situational and goods-values, and in fact normally arises 'on the back' of this. Hartmann does not, however, accept the Schelerian exaggeration that the conscious pursuit of virtue is necessarily a case of corrupt Pharisaism. He rightly maintains that it is possible to cultivate virtue in oneself and in others, *provided* such cultivation goes with the committed, not merely instrumental cultivation of other goods. He also emphasises, as against any form of utilitarianism, that moral values do not, *qua* values, depend on the amount or degree of the lower values they realize or that they aim at: they are incomparably higher and better. The value of active justice in moral agents is, for example, much higher than the mere goods-value of the apportionments they effect.

In his treatment of moral values, Hartmann not only has a chapter on humdrum moral 'goodness', but on the more rarefied values of nobility, of *Fülle* or moral breadth, and of purity in its various contexts and senses. Unquestionably these are ethical modalities that merit attention and circumspection. Hartmann then discusses the characteristic ethical discoveries of the Hellenic world, of the Christian world and of that Germanic modernity which is represented by Nietzsche. He dwells at length on the four cardinal virtues of Plato's *Republic*, and gives an illuminating

reinterpretation of Aristotle's doctrine of the Mean. He dwells on
the specifically Christian discoveries of the value of neighbourly
love, of humility, sincerity, fidelity and trust, and other great and
deep virtues. He finds something to admire in Nietzsche's introduction of such new value as *Fernstenliebe* or Love of the Remote,
and in *Schenkende Tugend* or Radiant Graciousness: the former
contrasts with Neighbourly Love, without really discrediting it,
and the latter with such Christian virtues as Humility. This part
of the book has a richness and a truth to value-experience which
renders it comparable to Aristotle's *Ethics* or Hegel's *Phenomenology of Spirit*. Hartmann does not write well. He in turn exhorts,
sobs, spumes, pronounces, perorates, divagates and contradicts
himself, and his work, even when well translated, gives small
pleasure to Anglo-Saxon readers. But what he puts forth so
poorly is often better worth meditating than the writings of far
more lucid and temperate moralists. The firmament of values is
not merely mapped in his writings: it springs up before us in
remarkable, sparkling life.

V. FINAL SUGGESTIONS

We have now completed our short study of certain recent British and continental thinkers who have contributed importantly to the analysis of valuation and values, and who have also sketched an overall map of the value-firmament, of things good or bad in their order of hierarchical precedence or coordination, to the extent that any such order can be established among them. In the course of our study we have seen lively discussions arising in regard to questions upon which, according to certain opinions, only persuasion and not true discussion is possible, and we have also seen theorems winnowing themselves out which should be part of any well-considered treatment of value-issues: such as that there are radically different sorts or senses of value between which quantitative or even ordinal comparison is not readily possible, that there is a deep distinction between values that appear purely personal and those that claim cogency or validity, that values and disvalues have a close and necessary relation to feeling, but that the values which claim validity cannot be exhaustively analysed or even explained in terms of mere feeling, that the main 'heads' of impersonal, 'valid' valuation, freedom, fairness, happiness, etc., are moderately clear and quite readily agreed upon though their detailed specification or correct practical implementation is infinitely controversial, that value and disvalue have a close connection with various senses of 'ought', but that the central senses of the latter reveal it as a much more restricted conception, much more closely concerned with disvalues and their avoidance than with values, that values are not merely 'higher' than other values but also 'stronger', and that the 'strength' of value is connected with the disvalue of omitting something, that the values called 'moral' presuppose all other types of value as objects of pursuit, but that their value does not depend on the latter values, that moral value has a close connection with the readiness to sacrifice personal for impersonal good, etc. These and a large number of similar theorems can be said to have distilled themselves from the views we have examined, or they have remained over as a common precipitate. There is plainly 'something' in axiology as an analysis of soi-disant cogent valuation, and there is plainly 'something' in the systematic mapping of values and disvalues to which this analysis serves as a prelude.

Can we, however, get a better understanding of what is being done in all this elaborate value-cartography? Are there principles which explain how it is a possible and meaningful enterprise, one not merely based on a vague appeal to diffused, civilised sentiment? The way it has been conducted by the thinkers we have examined has not been very satisfactory. For Brentano, Meinong, Moore, Rashdall, Ross, Scheler and Hartmann have, in the main, appealed to intuition rather than argument. They have simply asked us to *agree* to such propositions as that knowledge is better than error, that readiness to make personal sacrifices increases merit, that enjoyment of beauty and personal affection are the highest of goods, that moral goodness excludes the deliberate pursuit of moral goodness and entails the pursuit of ends other than moral goodness, and so on. Some of these propositions are of great translucency, and there would certainly be great perversity in rejecting many of them. But philosophy is a tough game and a man should be allowed to espouse perverse positions if their perversity cannot be demonstrated or at least shown up as plausible. The emotivist theory that value-pronouncements merely register personal feelings and seek to impose it on others, may be a gross travesty of our value-experience, but it certainly fits many of the procedures of the philosophers we have been examining.

It is first necessary to clear out of the way any crassly 'objective' theory of values, such as is set up, for example, in Hartmann's account of the *ansichseiende*, self-existent value-world. It is not that such theories are demonstrably wrong: it is merely that it would not help us if they could be proved true. It is not illuminating to treat the ordering of values like the topography of the moon which can be established by simply training a telescope on

one's object, or, more satisfactorily, by going there. The sort of
values that one is concerned to establish in a systematic axiology
are ineluctable, framework values, things presupposed in all
rational choice, and indispensable to a complete account of anything whatever. The sort of 'objective' values in which some
value-cartographers have believed have been merely empirical
objects that we *find* to be there: they are in no sense framework
conditions of possible existence or experience or endeavour.
Such things as we find out there are by definition contingent,
things that might also not have been there or that could be
replaced by other things. Their relation to our feelings and desires
is likewise contingent: it would be a mere fact of human nature
that they appealed to us. Whereas a framework of cogent values
cannot be a set of things that we merely happen to like or find
inspiring: our liking or need of them must in some deep sense be
necessary, and if there are no such objects of necessary liking or
wanting then there are no such framework values at all.

This does not mean that to be necessarily liked or wanted is
all that there is to being a cogent value: the emotivist analysis
may have this amount of truth that it is only in feeling them, in
being actually drawn to them, that we can fulfil or realise our
understanding of what values are. They are not to be fully understood at a distance, in a framework of detached description: they
must be experienced as making an actual impression on us for
them to be fully there for us at all. But this need for direct
emotional encounter does not mean that we cannot afterwards
detachedly analyse what such encounter involves, and so frame
an indirect characterisation, if not a true definition or description,
of what such values are. Nor will it be wrong to attribute such
values thus pinned down and characterised, to the framework of
the universe. The mere 'seeing of values out there in things' is
trivial: the most purely personal, the most superstitiously arbitrary
values are quite readily seen 'out there'. The arguments of a
phenomenology turned towards idealism are likewise inadequate:
we cannot give values a place in the objective universe by the unacceptable ruse of arguing that the whole so-called objective
universe has no more than an 'intentional inexistence' in our con-

scious references, and that the values perceived in it have therefore as secure a place in the objective universe as any other part of its structure. We may concede the metaphysical transcendence of the natural world as what our references to it always imply and some-times see, or claim to see, with assurance, but this does not mean that we need regard it as an external accident that this world declares itself to our perception and judgement, or that in a still more intimate encounter it declares what it is to our emotions. To feel about something may in certain privileged cases be the last, most penetrating way of knowing what the thing is, and what stands before us as the 'objective correlate' of such feelings may be in truth the very 'nucleus' of the things themselves.

It is not, however, our task in the concluding chapter of this monograph, to make out a case for all these murkily stated con-tentions. What will be suggested is that we do require something like the Transcendental Deduction of Kant to show why value-research and value-cartography should be possible, why it is not nonsensical to set up a framework of 'heads of value' within which our emotional endeavours and practical responses can be channelled, in so far, that is, as they can come to have the authority and internal correctness which some of them are certainly experi-enced as having. Kant tried to show, with very imperfect success, that there are certain framework conditions of what can be brought home to perception and judgement as objective, as having the kind of being that can be successfully investigated and established, and he also tried, with still smaller success, to show that there are certain framework conditions, certain categorial limitations, in what can be recommended as a possible line of action to someone who not only acts, but also reflects rationally on how he should act. If Kant's transcendental broodings on morality only led him to the empty puritanical formalisms that have been so often criticised, is it arguable that a more penetrating transcendentalism will establish something like that rich tapestry of values that we have studied in the philosophers of our choice, and so rescue us from the mere dogmatism and intuitionism which these philosophers have practised? It is a belief in the possibilities of such a transcendentalism that has inspired the present writer to produce his *Values and Intentions*, as well as many papers on Ethics such as 'The Methodology of Normative Ethics', 'The Structure of the Kingdom of Ends' and others. All these writings had their source in the axiological thinkers we have studied, and have sought to find a rational basis for their intuitive conclusions. The contents of these writings will not here be set forth, but we shall try to set forth the line of transcendental explanation they contain in supplementation and criticism of the philosophers in question.

The kind of transcendentalism we are trying to expound is one that has roots in the moral philosophy of the eighteenth century, and particularly in the ethical writings of Adam Smith, which have had important modern echoes in Meinong's discussion of the moral value-subject in his *Psychological-Ethical Investigations into Value-Theory*, as well as in Scheler's important work on the *Essence of Sympathy (Das Wesen der Sympathie)*. It lays stress on the fact that to be a conscious experient is not merely to have commerce with objects, but also to have commerce with other subjects, into whose subjective approaches one sympathetically enters, and in association with whom one not only establishes an acceptable view of the world but also arrives at acceptable practical ways of coping with that world. Such sympathetic entry is not merely some curious psychological capacity which human organisms happen to have, and which rests precariously on a more basic relation to physical objects: it is a capacity that conscious thinking beings cannot be without, if they are to be confronted with any objects at all. Through the caprices of a stepmotherly nature one might indeed be stranded in a situation without fellows *with* whom one could face, and could act on, nature, but the *place* for such fellows would always be present: it is a categorial, a necessary place. And it is categorial not merely in its observable physical aspects but also in its unobservable, interior aspects: through sympathy, which is not necessarily based on one's own personal experiences, one enters into the not straight-forwardly observable inner life of others, which always has a necessary place in our world, though its precise content may be filled in, often with grave need of correction, by experience, imagination or inference. This necessary being-with-others, and with others *given* from the first as having an *ungiven* dimension as well as a straightforwardly given one, is something for which we shall not here argue. The use of personal pronouns in language, with its unmysterious though deeply metaphysical passage from 'I' to 'you' and vice versa, nothing being more evident than the at least partial secrecy of what 'you' experience to what 'I' experience and vice versa, is evidence for it, as is also the strange fact of Wittgenstein's conversion, in the course of his philosophical development, from an exaggeratedly solipsistic theory of meaning to an exaggeratedly public one. We are not concerned to defend this last, nor to maintain more than the necessary presence of a possible public dimension to the possibility of object-directed experience and of language in the full sense of the word. Fellows and objects are necessary to one another, and it is only in relation to both that we ourselves can be subjects and can make significant references to things, people and our own mental and bodily life.

All this being presupposed, the entry into other people's, and into other sentient beings', feelings and interests is a necessary part of our experience of a possible world and of our ability to talk significantly and testably about it. It is important not to understress the metaphysical oddity of the sympathetic performance. For it is in a sense the divesting of ourselves of the specificity of our interest and our conscious content and the particularity of our person, and the imagining ourselves in a position that is, on many views, totally unimaginable, and because thus unimaginable, also totally unmeaning. How can Octavius imagine what it would be like if *he*, Octavius, were Cleopatra, and how can a convinced Nazi put *himself* into the shoes of a hounded Jew, all performances recommended by certain modern metamoralists, and yet involving an apparent logical absurdity that would make the endeavour quite vain? We shall not dwell on this point, for the absurdity plainly has its roots more in current concepts of personal identity, and of identity generally, and of the so-called 'criteria' of the same, than in anything in the undoubted performance which we all can and very often do carry out. The sort of sameness possible for a person is plainly not a sameness that excludes the *possibility* of being in *some* sense quite a different person. Obviously, however, the beings who often perform whatever may be meant by putting themselves into other people's shoes, and who have acquired some skill and zest in this performance, must in the end tend to move to a new, higher level of interest where what they concern themselves with is not what this one or that one likes or is interested in, but only with what *survives* all such laborious translation of oneself into everyone else's shoes, so that one then, at that level, only desires and likes what everyone must desire and like, and desire and like for everyone, and desire and like everyone to desire and like for everyone, and so in unending complication. Such beings, who are of course ourselves, must become concerned with the new, higher-order objects of interest of what Adam Smith called the impartial spectator but who is better described as the impartial judge or agent: the man who desires not to want or like for anyone, at least in his impartial capacity, what he cannot want or like for all. The logical structure of such impartiality is much more teasingly complex than the above characterisations might suggest, and much care is required if one is to avoid inconsistency and circularity and to achieve fruitfulness. All this cannot, however, be argued in this place. But what must be stressed is that some rising to this impartial standpoint is not only involved in all practical cooperation but also in the developed form of the discourse which goes with it. Without some rising to invariances of aim which are unaffected by the specificity of personal interest or the particularity of persons, it would not be possible to consult or advise or plan in concert. Practical discourse of this developed sort can have purchase and sense only if it is in some sense addressed *to anyone* and prescribes *for anyone*, even if that *anyone* is at first merely anyone in some limited group, or anyone having some property, or anyone conceived in this sheer separate particularity. To counsel is to suggest what anyone in a given position should do: it is to tell a man what anyone in his position should do, not merely what I want him to do or what someone else wants him to do or what he himself wants to do. I must to some extent put him into the position of anyone, or anyone into his position, if I am to advise and not merely to hector or defer. And from the *anyone* of the tribe or the *anyone* of the conspiratorial conclave or the *anyone* concerned solely with that anyone himself, we progress to the anyone concerned with anyone by the same unlimited freeing of variables which we also encounter in the sphere of logic, and which makes it natural to say that the wholly free variable is *implicit* in the restricted one. We may say therefore that without some implicit relation to the total body of possible persons, whether as agents, patients or judges, practical discourse would not make sense: one cannot significantly ask what one ought, or what it would be reasonable to do. And the *impersonal authority* of the interests which pursue only what everyone must desire for everyone is quite unmysterious: it is merely a consequence of what impersonal interests as such are. In them speaks the voice of Everyman addressing himself to Everyman, beside which the voices of particular interests belonging to particular persons necessarily shrink back, as not having the unboundedly general appeal that is in question. And if they do not shrink back, they do so only as being the powerful personal interests that they are and not as involving anything like an impersonal 'authority'.

What we have, however, to show is that – this exalted higher-order interest in what anyone could and would find interesting for anyone having been formed – it must of necessity generate just such a system of higher-order values as Moore, Ross, Scheler, Hartmann, etc., have sketched for us so elaborately. It seems possible, *prima facie*, that there are *no* universal objects which conform to the requirements in question, that what everyone could or would desire for everyone is an emptily unspecifiable notion. It is arguable, however, that such is not the case, and that while, no doubt, we can play about with 'logical possibilities' which are not genuine possibilities at all, there in fact are, and must be, higher-order objects which satisfy the condition of being what everyone could or would desire for everyone, and would desire everyone to desire for everyone, and so on.

It is arguable, first of all, that the traditional hedonic goals of universal pleasure and happiness are in this condition. They ignore, without overriding or eliminating, the specificity of personal interest and the particularity of the person. They involve in short, that everyone, no matter who he may be, should have whatever he likes or wants, whatever this last may be – clashes of interest of course involve complications, which we need not here consider – and that he should want everyone to have the same. Universal malevolence, though logically consistent if higher-order interest be separated from lower-order interest, would involve an uncomfortable policy of self-frustration at lower levels, and, if carried up to higher levels, would involve a yet more uncomfortable malevolence towards one's own malevolence, and malevolence towards this second malevolence, and so on indefinitely. In a similar manner, if one attempts to answer Adam Smith's difficulty as to why one should sympathise with the victims of aggression and not with the aggressors, the answer lies in the fact it would be infinitely uncomfortable and rent with conflicts to sympathise with all aggressors, whereas sympathising with those who do not aggress, would if all adopted such a stance, involve no internal discrepancy or conflict. A conflict of inner attitudes does not involve a logical contradiction, but it does involve the same sort of inner disquiet that a contradiction does in those who try to accept it. It is arguable, likewise, that the goals of power and freedom are goals which ignore specificity of first-order interest and personal particularity, and are accordingly goals that (with due restrictions for conflict) can and would be desired by everyone for everyone.

Having argued all this, it is not hard to see a track of argument leading to the valuation of impartial justice, to evade which must involve difficult perversity. For the whole self-divestment of the particularity and specificity of interest has nothing partial about it, and partiality could only be added to it by some wanton, extrinsic addition. In the pursuit of impartial justice we merely set up as a conscious aim what is already followed in principle, we make into a new, higher-order goal what is already involved in the impartial pursuit of lower goals. Such an erection of impartiality into a higher-order aim of course results in many refinements: it is one thing to be unbiased in one's treatment of persons, it is another more scrupulous thing to pursue lack of bias as an end in itself. What it-is important to note is that the development of this new, higher-order interest is in a sense logical and inevitable, though not so in a purely formal sense. There is a step involved in passing from merely acting in accordance with a principle and making an end of that principle, and it is a step that it would be possible not to take, and one that one is not compelled to take. There is nothing formally inconsistent in being indifferent to differences of person and character of interest, without erecting such indifference into a conscious end. But to take this step is, in a quite ordinary sense, 'natural', 'logical' and 'consistent'. It would be odd and strange not to esteem a principle that one already follows in one's estimations.

It is not necessary to explain how a tendency to rise above the specificity and particularity of interest should lead one on to valuing that imperfect but more intense rising above the specificity and particularity of interest which is involved in the deeper forms of unselfish personal love. The step in question could, with formal consistency, be evaded: it remains, however, deeply consequent. In a similar manner it is not hard to follow Kant in the *Critique of Judgement* when he recognises a profound homology between aesthetic and ethical disinterestedness, so that the beautiful becomes in necessary fashion a 'monogram' of the good. In both aesthetic and properly axiological interest there is a rising above the specificity and particularity of first-order interest: arguably, therefore, in virtue of such an affinity, aesthetic interest and its objects become of concern to our 'practical' value-interests. And the same applies to the disinterestedness of the cognitive sphere, and the various values that develop from it, values so richly recognised by Kant in his consideration of regulative principles at the end of the *Critique of Pure Reason*. The last stone in the arch is of course the moral value or virtue of pursuing all these variously specified values: it would be inconceivably perverse and in a deep sense inconsequent to value certain ends and not to value the will which bends itself to realise these, and which in a sense comprises them all in its intentions. Our valuations of the good will must, however, be Schelerian rather than Kantian: it will presuppose all the lower values which give it content and meaning, while not exhaustively depending for its value on these last. What we see emerging in all this is an organised body of values, the authentic membership of the Absolute Good. And it is plain that all these members are to be found recognised and honourably mentioned somewhere or other in the writings of Kant: only his official pronouncements on Ethics reveal the restrictive impress of his pietistic forebears.

One comment is necessary on the whole method of our undertaking: that it throughout exploits a loose logic of analogy or affinity, similar to the logic of inductive arguments, and not at all a rigorous formal pattern of deduction such as some philosophers would alone consider 'logical'. Sometimes this logic works simply by extending to a case B an attitude already directed to a *closely similar* case A; sometimes it takes on a wider sweep, and generalises an emotional attitude confined at first to a limited class of cases. This last is illustrated by the passage from the limited benignity and limited impartiality which follows from close entry into the interests of certain others, to the wider benignity and impartiality which is extended to all sentient beings, etc. It is a well-known fact that there is no easy way of formalising analogical arguments, or distinguishing on paper between a profound and relevant resemblance and one superficial and of small relevance. All this of course applies *a fortiori* to the resemblances relevant to valuational attitudes.

But the kind of analogy which is most important for cogent value-formation is not, however, entirely an ordinary movement along lines of resemblance: it is also what Ehrenfels calls a movement *inwards*, a movement from valuing an object X towards valuing the attitude which values X. This is not an ordinary case of analogy since the valuation of X does not resemble X at all. This movement is illustrated by the transition from being impartial to valuing impartiality as such, or from being benign to being concerned with benignity, or from being concerned with certain good objectives to being concerned with one's own or with other people's concern for them. Plainly it is in a deep sense 'natural' and 'consistent' to like the liking of X if one likes X: even at the level of purely personal taste we behold, for example, ardent fishers liking other ardent fishers. This elementary tendency is, of course, exploited to the full in Stevenson's emotivistic analyses of value-judgements. What does not, however, appear at the Stevensonian level is the *logical* character of the move from favouring X to favouring the favouring of X. It is not a logical move in the sense of an obligatory entailment – one need not take it, and may even *refuse* to take it – but it is none the less 'reasonable' in the paradigmatic sense in which inductive and analogical arguments are 'reasonable'. It is thus by a loose logic of straightforward analogy combined with the 'movement inward' just examined, that the whole firmament of values necessarily arises, and builds up its form and its force: it is, in fact, as inconceivable that the pattern of 'highest heads' of value set up by ourselves will not arise in every reflective society as that men in such societies will not develop a largely similar number-system or a calculus of probabilities.

It is obvious from our arguments that the 'highest heads' of value are not only established by an exceedingly lax if all-important logic, but that they are also exceedingly vague in outline and content. To seek happiness, freedom and opportunity for all, and to be impartial in seeking them, and to value the attitudes involved in such seeking and in such impartiality, and also to value certain cognitive, aesthetic and affectionate attitudes having some affinity with the attitudes just mentioned, all yield unexceptionable, copybook ideals from which hardly any well-thinking person would dissent, but it remains infinitely hard to say what these ideals mean in the concrete, and particularly so in the many cases in which their claims conflict with one another. Here the wrong approach is to hold, as the philosophers of our choice all hold, that there is some one correct implementation of all the values in question in each concrete case, and that the difficulty of arriving at such a correct result is merely like that of determining, from simple physical principles, the course that a stone will take as it bounds down some complicated hillside. But the two difficulties are not alike since the laws which govern the movement of stones are not vague, nor are the contours of the most complicated hillside, whereas in the realm of values everything has blurred edges: mist is as much part of the picture as in a Chinese painting. It is absurd to drag in an Aristotelian perception αἴσθησις, to solve one problem, for such αἴσθησις is useless where there is nothing to perceive. Plainly a cutting of the Gordian knot after full contemplation of all values and disvalues present or possible in a situation, is all that remains open to the practical agent: it is a decision, not insight, that is required. Yet in a sense the doctrine of αἴσθησις makes sense, since a conscientious decision among incompatible value-claims is always felt to be right for the individual in question, and felt to be right not by that individual alone but by all who consider his case. For them, otherwise oriented and circumstanced, another decision might have been correct, but his decision, representing the deepest response of his practical being, is right for him, and, as limited to him, right for all. The doctrines of vocation on which Rashdall and Scheler have laid such stress here come into their full right. We are not free to determine the points of the compass in the realm of values, but remain free, within wide limits, to steer a course among them.

We have now come to the end of suggesting ways of improving axiological ethics by giving it something like a transcendental deduction to rest on. It is not maintained that these ways are mandatory, but only that they are suggestive. There really is, it would seem, an organised framework of values and disvalues within which our practical decisions must be made, and philosophy must give some account of the structure of this framework and of the principles guiding its construction. A transcendental deduction need not, further, be regarded as the last word in the matter. It may only be a first step leading to a metaphysical deduction that is far more profound and far-reaching. For the self-transcendence of consciousness involved in our intentional references, and the further self-transcendence of consciousness in the sympathetic entry into the inner life of others, are amazing, paradoxical performances: though they form the very warp and woof of our conscious existence, we must still ask how they are possible. Possibly in reference to a Unity which, like the Platonic Good or Neoplatonic One, transcends Being and Knowledge, and yet necessarily gives rise to both and draws them back from their imperfection to its more than perfect self ? Whatever we may decide on such ultimate issues, the construction of a value-firmament remains a worthwhile, and not impracticable, philosophical task.

BIBLIOGRAPHY

Brentano, F. *Vom Ursprung sittlicher Erkenntnis* (1889). Trans. Roderick Chisholm, as *The Origin of Our Knowledge of Right and Wrong* (1969).

Dewey, J. *Theory of Valuation* (Chicago, 1939).

Eaton, H. O. *The Austrian Theory of Values* (Oklahoma, 1930).

Ehrenfels, Chr. von. *System der Werttheorie* (*System of Value-Theory*) 2 vols (Leipzig, 1897–8).

Ewing, A. C. *The Definition of Good* (Cambridge, 1947).

Findlay, J. N. *Meinong's Theory of Objects and Values* (Oxford, 1963).

——, *Language, Mind and Value* (1963).

——, *Values and Intentions* (1961).

Hartmann, N. *Ethik* (Berlin, 1926). Trans. Stanton Coit, as *Ethics*, 3 vols (1932).

Laird, J. *The Idea of Value* (Cambridge, 1961).

Lepley, R. *Value: A Co-operative Inquiry* (New York, 1952).

Lewis, C. I. *An Analysis of Knowledge and Valuation* (La Salle, Illinois, 1946).

Meinong, A. *Psychologisch-ethische Untersuchungen zur Werththeorie* (*Psychological-Ethical Investigations into Value-Theory*) (Graz, 1894).

——, *Über emotionale Präsentation* (*On Emotional Presentation*) (Vienna, 1917).

——, *Zur Grundlegung der allgemeinen Werttheorie* (*Foundations of General Value-Theory*) (Graz, 1932).

——, *Ethische Bausteine* (*Ethical Building-Stones*) (Graz, 1969). All republished in vol. III of Meinong's *Gesamtausgabe* (Collected Works) (Graz, 1969).

Moore, G. E. *Principia Ethica* (Cambridge, 1903).

Perry, R. B. *General Theory of Value* (New York, 1926).

Rashdall, H. *The Theory of Good and Evil*, 2 vols (Oxford, 1907).

Ross, W. D. *The Right and the Good* (Oxford, 1930).
——, *The Foundations of Ethics* (Oxford, 1939).
Scheler, Max. *Der Formalismus in der Ethik und die materiale Wertethik (Formalism in Ethics and the Material Value-Ethic)* (Halle, 1916).
Stevenson, C. L. *Ethics and Language* (New Haven, 1944).
Urban, W. *Valuation: Its Nature and Laws* (1906).
Wright, G. H. von. *The Varieties of Goodness* (1963).

3

EVOLUTIONARY ETHICS

ANTONY FLEW

With the one exception of Newton's *Principia* no single book of empirical science has ever been of more importance to philosophy than this work of Darwin.

JOSIAH ROYCE,
The Spirit of Modern Philosophy (p. 286)

The Darwinian theory has no more to do with philosophy than has any other hypothesis of natural science.

LUDWIG WITTGENSTEIN,
Tractatus Logico-Philosophicus (4.1122)

I. INTRODUCTION

The obvious and the right place from which to begin a study of evolutionary ethics is the work of Charles Darwin. For, primarily, it is his ideas — or what have been thought to be his ideas — which advocates of evolutionary ethics or evolutionary politics have tried to apply more widely. This is not, of course, to say that Darwin had no intellectual ancestors; any more than it is to suggest that biological theory has since his death stood still. To say or to suggest either thing would be absurdly wrong.

It would not even be true to say that nothing was published with any claim to the label 'evolutionary ethics' until after the appearance in 1859 of *The Origin of Species*. For Herbert Spencer was strictly correct when, in the General Preface to *The Principles of Ethics*, he claimed, 'as a matter of historical truth, that in this case, as in other cases, the genesis of ideas does not follow the order of logical sequence; and that the doctrine of organic evolution in its application to human character and intelligence, and, by implication, to society, is of earlier date than *The Origin of Species*'.[1] He is referring here to his *Social Statics*, first issued at the end of 1850 and containing the outline of the ethical ideas which he is about to develop. He could also, and elsewhere does, claim to have been the first to use the notion of the survival of the fittest in an evolutionary context — in the *Westminster Review* for 1852. Again, as has been pointed out long since,[2] the very phrase 'a struggle for existence', which epitomises the gladiatorial view of human life so often taken to be the true moral of Darwinism, is to be found already in a similar context in 1798 in Malthus's *First Essay*,[3] a work to which — as Darwin acknowledged, though he would never have used so portentous a phrase, especially of himself — 'I owe in large measure the stimulation of my thoughts.'[4]

Nevertheless, after all due cautions have been given, it is *The Origin of Species* which is, and must be, the reference point. It is the ideas of this book which the forerunners foreran. It is what this book said or suggested that later evolutionary thinkers tried to develop. It was the triumph in biology of the theory which it presented that lent vicarious prestige to whatever could be put forward as Darwinian.

This explains why the second of the four Sections into which the present monograph is divided will deal with Darwin's theory. The reason why these preliminaries will be fairly extended is that it is essential to master Darwin's general ideas in biology before attempting to consider their application, or misapplication, elsewhere; just as it should be a precondition of either a search for his precursors, or an investigation of the character and extent of later developments, first to get quite straight about what those precursors are supposed to be precursors of, and what the developments are developments from. Although these are all points too obvious to be denied, they are certainly not always acted upon.

After these preliminaries the main treatment in the later sections will be systematic rather than historical. There has been no spokesman for an evolutionary ethic of sufficient stature as a moral thinker to warrant the full individual treatment required by an Aristotle, a Hume, or a Kant. Nor does there seem to have been in such ethics any line of development which it would be philosophically profitable to pursue. Nevertheless — in defiance of all the strict academic compartmentalists, insisting that nothing must have anything to do with anything else — attempts to bring ethics and politics into some sort of relation with the facts of evolutionary biology are perennial; and there has certainly been far too little careful and sympathetic philosophical investigation of what the possibilities and impossibilities here actually are. We shall be having many sharp things to say about some particular sorts of attempt at an evolutionary ethics. So it is the more important to emphasise right from the beginning that the desires to connect, and to see microcosms in relation to the macrocosm, are in themselves excellent; and quite certainly should be shared, and not despised, by anyone who aspires to the title of 'philosopher'. It is, therefore, neither surprising nor discreditable that in every generation since Darwin some of the liveliest and least blinkered of students of biology — Darwin himself included — should have wanted to explore the possibility of connections between evolution and ethics.

The main reason why professional philosophers are apt very brusquely to dismiss all such efforts is that they mistake that they must involve what they call the Naturalistic Fallacy. The nerve of this is an attempt to deduce a conclusion about what *ought* to be, or *ought* to have been, from premises stating only what in neutral fact *is* the case, or what *has been* or what *will be*. Once this fallacy has been recognised for what it is, it may seem that with evolutionary ethics this is both the heart of the matter and the end of the affair: 'There is a temptation for the logician to point out the fallacy and to leave it at that.'[5]

This is not good enough. Nor to finish the job is it sufficient, as the author of that last quotation seems to have thought, straightway to seek for psychogenetic explanations of the supposed mistake in logic. The first thing is to show in some detail precisely what if anything is going wrong in the particular case, or perhaps in several specimen cases, and to identify and to expose any other associated errors and confusions which may have made it easier to effect the illegitimate transition. The second and the more important thing, before the philosopher thinks of launching out into psychogenetic speculations, is to enquire whether there may not after all be something else involved besides this old familiar Naturalistic Fallacy.

Once this question is put, and pressed, it soon becomes obvious that other things are involved. Our Section III therefore raises the questions of whether Darwin's theory could provide a foundation for, or whether it itself contains, a law of progress; in each case arguing for the negative answer. This provides a first occasion to analyse precisely what is and what is not involved in the idea of natural selection, and to distinguish different sorts of law (senses of 'law'). The same section examines extensively two bold attempts. The first is that of Julian Huxley, who began by trying to detect in the actual course of biological evolution trends we could scarcely refuse to count as progressive, and then conscripted these to serve as a reassuring prop such as could in fact be provided only

by a natural force or by Divine Providence. The second is that of
the Marxist biologist Joseph Needham, who began by discerning
in that same actual development the appropriate fulfilment of a
universal law of progress, and then tried, despite the supposed inevitability of the socialist apocalypse, to make some room for a
measure of historically relevant human choice.

It will perhaps be remarked that both these spokesmen of different sorts of evolutionary ethics, and indeed most of the others
considered elsewhere in this monograph, are not merely English-
speaking but English. This limitation is an expression of a considered policy. We have deliberately chosen to treat a few fairly
fully — and those few the ones most likely to have been read by
English-speaking, and particularly British, students — rather than
to give a breathless series of mentions of many more. It is in any
case hopeless to think of forestalling the complaints of reviewers
about the comparative or total neglect of some favoured contri-
butor to what has long since become an unmanageably abundant
international literature. What can reasonably be aspired after is
that this restrictive policy will make for a more adequate treatment
and illustration of the main general issues; and certainly, in a less
conciliatory vein, the present writer cannot regret the consequence
of having to ignore Teilhard de Chardin in favour of such forth-
right and immensely more readable authors as Needham and the
early Julian Huxley.

Section III, as we have seen, will thus consider the quest in biological evolution for some immanent substitute for Divine Providence. It is only after this that we shall proceed in Section IV to
look in a concentrated way at the hardy perennial attempts to proceed directly from the purely factual premises supplied by the
science of biology to evaluative conclusions. One key distinction
here, often neglected, is that between trying to deduce such conclusions directly from such premises — a move which must involve the Naturalistic Fallacy — and attempting after first somehow establishing a biological criterion to reach them indirectly —
an enterprise which might perhaps succeed in escaping this stock
objection.

In Section IV too we notice the remarkable variety of moral and political conclusions which their protagonists have believed to be warranted by Darwin's theory. The very diversity, and often mutual incompatibility, of such supposed implications must constitute a strong reason for challenging the legitimacy of the sort of derivation proposed — a type of direct deduction which should already and independently have been seen to be invalid.

Two examples here will sufficiently illustrate this diversity. First, Darwin has been taken, or mistaken, to have provided a knock-down justification for just that same intensely competitive economic system whence, according to Engels and others, he had himself abstracted those ideas of natural selection and of a struggle for existence which he proceeded to employ so triumphantly in his own scientific field.[6] Thus J. D. Rockefeller, who was certainly an expert both on big business and on no-holds-barred competition, in one of his Sunday-school addresses declared: 'The growth of a large business is merely a survival of the fittest. . . . The American Beauty rose can be produced in the splendour and fragrance which bring cheer to its beholder only by sacrificing the early buds which grow up around it. This is not an evil tendency in business. It is merely the working out of a law of nature and a law of God.'[7]

Second, Darwin has also been taken, or mistaken, to have provided the premises to sustain the opposite conclusions of collectivism. Such a moral seems to have been suggested, albeit cryptically, by the other founding father of Marxism when he read the *Origin* at its first publication.[8] By the turn of the century it had become a commonplace of socialist propaganda. Thus in 1905, in an Editor's Preface to a work on *Socialism and Positive Science* first published in Rome in 1894 and already widely circulated on the Continent, James Ramsay MacDonald stated that 'the Conservative and aristocratic interests in Europe have armed themselves for defensive and offensive purposes with the law of the struggle for existence, and its corollary, the survival of the fittest. Ferri's aim in this volume has been to show that Darwinism is not only not in intellectual opposition to Socialism, but is its scientific foundation.'[9] MacDonald goes on to conclude that 'Socialism is naught but Darwinism economised, made definite, become an

intellectual policy, applied to the conditions of human society'.[10]
It is noteworthy, both as one of those paradoxical reversals which
are so common in the history of ideas, and as a further indication
of the unwisdom of trying directly to deduce norms from facts,
that Ferri himself begins by proclaiming himself 'a convinced
follower' not only of Marx but also of both 'Darwin and Spencer'.
He allows 'that Darwin, and especially Spencer, stopped short
half-way from the final conclusions of religious, political and social
order, which necessarily follow from their indisputable premises'.[11]
But, notwithstanding his recognition that 'Herbert Spencer
affirmed aloud his English individualism', Ferri still insists on
concluding that 'Marx completes the work of Darwin and
Spencer'.[12]

Finally, Section V is about 'Seeing in an Evolutionary Perspective'. Sections III and IV discuss fairly strong views of the 'philosophical implications' of Darwin's theory. Section V is concerned
with the weaker, more defensible, and unduly neglected conten-
tions, that the practical thinker needs ever to remember that
ethical ideas have evolved and will presumably continue to evolve,
and that all human life — and questions of public and private
conduct in particular — can fruitfully be seen in an evolutionary
perspective. It is, we shall argue, in the development of such relatively mild and vegetarian notions — rather than in those of a
reinforcement by a surrogate Providence or of the deduction of
morality from biology — that we have to seek whatever residue of
merit there may be in the bolder programmes of evolutionary
ethics.

II. DARWIN'S THEORY

Darwin is so often thought of as the sponsor of 'the Theory of Evolution' that it is salutary to recall the full title of *The Origin*. It is *The Origin of Species by Means of Natural Selection*; and to this is added a sub-title, which has since acquired a sinister ring: *or the Preservation of Favoured Races in the Struggle for Life*. Darwin's claim to originality does not lie in his having been the first to entertain the possibility of the evolution, as opposed to the special creation, of species. 'The general hypothesis of the derivation of all present species from a small number, or perhaps a single pair, of original ancestors was propounded by the President of the Berlin Academy of Sciences, Maupertuis, in 1745 and 1751, and by the principal editor of the *Encyclopédie*, Diderot, in 1749 and 1754.'[13] Nor was Darwin the first to introduce into a biological context the ideas of natural selection and of a struggle for existence. These can be found in Lucretius in the first century B.C., although he combines them with a notion of natural kinds detached from that of special creation — or indeed any creation by any genuinely personal agency. Lucretius describes how in the infancy of the earth it 'put forth herbage and trees first, and in the next place created the generations of mortal creatures, arising in many kinds. . . . Wherefore again and again the earth deserves the name of mother which she has gotten, since of herself she created the human race, and produced almost at a fixed time every animal that ranges wild over the great mountains, and the birds of the air at the same time in all their varied forms. . . . Many were the monsters also that the earth then tried to make, springing up with wondrous appearance and frame: the hermaphrodite, between man and woman yet neither, different from both; some without feet, others again bereft of hands; some found dumb also without a mouth, some blind without face. . . . So with the rest of like monsters and portents that she made, it was all in vain: since nature denied them growth, and they could not attain the desired flower of age nor find food nor join by the ways of Venus.' Lucretius concludes: 'And many species of animals must have perished at that time, unable by procreation to forge out the chain of posterity; for whatever you see feeding on the breath of life, either cunning or courage or at least quickness must have kept that kind from its earliest existence.'[14] And of course, Lucretius was himself a disciple, clothing in Latin verse ideas which he had learned from the fourth-century Greek Epicurus, who was here himself using such fifth-century sources as Empedocles of Acragas.[15]

Yet none of this diminishes either the originality or the importance of Darwin's work. What he did was to bring the key ideas together into an argument, and to illustrate that argument with an enormous mass of evidence, much of it the product of his own observations. As he himself remarked, in a typically modest and engaging passage of the *Autobiography*, '*The Origin of Species* is one long argument from the beginning to the end, and it has convinced not a few able men.'[16]

One recent interpreter goes so far as to say: 'The old arguments for evolution were only based on circumstantial evidence. . . . But the core of Darwin's argument was of a different kind. It did not make it more probable — it made it a certainty. Given his facts his conclusion *must* follow: like a proposition in geometry. You do not show that any two sides of a triangle are very *probably* greater than the third. You show they *must* be so. Darwin's argument was a *de*ductive one — whereas an argument based on circumstantial evidence is *in*ductive.'[17] This statement is certainly correct in so far as it insists that Darwin's argument has a deductive core, although it surely exaggerates the amount which this core by itself establishes.

Consider Darwin's Introduction. He first presents his problem: 'In considering the origin of species, it is quite conceivable that a naturalist, reflecting on the mutual affinities of organic beings, on their embryological relations, their geographical distribution, geological succession, and other such facts, might come to the conclusion that species had not been independently created, but had descended, like varieties, from other species. Nevertheless such a conclusion, even if well-founded, would be unsatisfactory, until it could be shown how the innumerable species inhabiting this world have been modified, so as to acquire that perfection of structure and coadaptation which justly excites our admiration.'[18] Then, after a sharp paragraph, excised from later editions, about 'the author of the *Vestiges of Creation*', Darwin continues: 'It is, therefore, of the highest importance to gain a clear insight into the means of modification and coadaptation. At the commencement of my observations it seemed to me probable that a careful study of domesticated animals and of cultivated plants would offer the best chance of making out this obscure problem. Nor have I been disappointed. . . . I shall devote the first chapter . . . to "Variation under Domestication". We shall thus see that a large amount of hereditary modification is at least possible.'[19]

Chapter ii is to deal with 'Variation under Nature'. 'In the next chapter the "Struggle for Existence" amongst all organic beings throughout the world, which inevitably follows from the high geometrical ratio of their increase, will be considered. . . . As many more individuals of each species are born than can possibly survive; and as, consequently, there is a frequently recurring struggle for existence, it follows that any being if it vary however slightly in any manner profitable to itself, under the complex and sometimes varying conditions of life, will have a better chance of surviving, and thus be *naturally selected*. From the strong principle of inheritance, any selected variety will tend to propagate in its new and modified form. This fundamental subject of "Natural Selection" will be treated at some length in the fourth chapter; and we shall then see how natural selection almost inevitably causes much extinction of the less improved forms of life, and leads to what I have called divergence of character. In the next chapter I shall discuss the complex and little known "Laws of Variation".'[20] The five following chapters consider the most obvious and serious difficulties in the way of accepting the theory, and the final one is a 'Recapitulation and Conclusion'.

This sketch of the argument and plan of the book indicates both what the deductive core of that argument was, and that Darwin

himself was not inclined to think that that core constituted a demonstration of his main conclusions. He does not claim to have
demonstrated, and did not in fact demonstrate, 'the conclusion
that species had not been independently created, but had descended, like varieties, from other species'. Nor did he claim
to have demonstrated 'how the innumerable species inhabiting this world have been modified, so as to acquire that
perfection of structure and coadaptation which justly excites
our admiration'. But what he did succeed in demonstrating
was that, granted as premises certain very general and scarcely
disputable facts, then some natural selection must also be a
fact.

Thus in chapter iii Darwin argues: 'A struggle for existence inevitably follows from the high rate at which all organic beings
tend to increase . . . as more individuals are produced than can
possibly survive, there must in every case be a struggle for existence, either one individual with another of the same species, or
with the individuals of a different species, or with the physical
conditions of life. It is the doctrine of Malthus applied with mani-
fold force to the whole animal and vegetable kingdoms, for in this
case there can be no artificial increase of food, and no prudential
restraint from marriage.'[21] Just as the idea of the struggle for
existence is derived as a consequence of the combination of a
geometrical ratio of increase with the finite possibilities of survival, so in chapter iv 'Natural Selection' is itself derived as a consequence of the combination of the struggle for existence with
variation. Darwin summarises his argument: 'If . . . organic beings present individual differences in almost every part of their
structure, and this cannot be disputed; if there be, owing to their
geometrical rate of increase, a severe struggle for existence at
some age, season, or year, and this certainly cannot be disputed;
then . . . it would be a most extraordinary fact if no variations had
ever occurred useful to each being's own welfare, in the same
manner as variations have occurred useful to man. But if variations
useful to any organic being do occur, assuredly individuals thus
characterised will have the best chance of being preserved in the
struggle for life; and from the strong principle of inheritance they

will tend to produce offspring similarly characterised. This principle of preservation, or the survival of the fittest, I have called natural selection.'[22]

Yet to prove this strictly is not strictly to prove that all species are 'descended, like varieties, from other species'. Darwin proceeds in the next paragraph but one to state: 'Whether natural selection has really thus acted in adapting the various forms of life to their several conditions and stations, must be judged by the general tenor and balance of evidence given in the following chapters.' This advice is clearly correct. For the demonstration as given leaves open such theoretical possibilities as that there might turn out to be comparatively narrow limits on the amount of change which could in practice come about in this sort of way, or that a Creator might have chosen to create some or all species specially — perhaps also, and perhaps inevitably, arranging at the same time for false clues which would discomfit the incautious infidel.[23]

Nor, even when these arbitrary suppositions have been suitably disposed of, can it be allowed that Darwin has demonstrated that natural selection operating on chance variations has been solely and entirely responsible for all 'that perfection of structure and coadaptation which justly excites our admiration'. He himself makes no such claim. In the last sentence of the Introduction, after a cautious statement of an evolutionary view and a repudiation of his earlier belief that 'each species has been independently created', he writes: 'I am convinced that natural selection has been the most important, but not the exclusive, means of modification.'[24] Indeed, to the surprise of some of those who know the ferocity with which neo-Darwinians are apt to reject anything which smacks of Lamarck, Darwin himself, though — and perhaps partly because — he insisted that 'Our ignorance of the laws of variation is profound',[25] always allowed the possibility that the effects of use and disuse may be inherited: 'my critics frequently assume that I attribute all changes of corporal structure and mental power exclusively to the natural selection of such variations as are often called spontaneous; whereas, even in the first edition of *The Origin of Species* I distinctly stated that great weight must be attributed to the inherited effects of use and disuse, with respect both to the body and the mind.'[26]

What Darwin did do was to bring various very general facts and key notions together into a deductive argument, showing by this and by appeal to other more direct considerations that natural selection must be and is going on. This granted, he is able to deploy a massive case for saying that species have evolved, and that natural selection has been — and is — the main instrument of this evolution. The variations upon which this selection works are, he always insists, all individually small: 'As natural selection acts solely by accumulating slight, successive, favourable variations, it can produce no great or sudden modifications . . .'; and this squares well with 'the canon of "Natura non facit saltum" [Nature does not make leaps] which every fresh addition to our knowledge tends to confirm'.[27] Darwin is already in the *Origin* cautiously willing to extend his account to all species, except apparently the first: 'I believe that animals are descended from at m os only four or five progenitors, and plants from an equal or lesser number. Analogy would lead me one step farther, namely, to the belief that all animals and plants are descended from some one prototype. But analogy may be a deceitful guide. Nevertheless . . . we must . . . admit that all the organic beings which have ever lived on this earth may be descended from some one primordial form.'[28]

III. A LAW OF PROGRESS?

One great advantage of starting, as we have insisted on doing, from Darwin himself is that this helps to bring out the fundamental difference between evolution and natural selection. Another is that it focuses attention on the deductive core of Darwinism. No one who has failed to appreciate these two things can hope to do precise justice to the nature and the originality of Darwin's contribution. For our present purposes they are equally important, but in other ways. It is the notion of evolution, and the consequent discrediting of the idea of special interventions in the biological sphere, which promises to reinforce our suspicions of those who would claim that supernatural activity endorses (favoured) moral intuitions and the deliverances of (privileged) consciences. It is similarly this same notion of evolution which applied to ethical ideas must discourage any assumption of an authoritative finality, in principle beyond all criticism and reappraisal. It is the fact that the core of Darwin's theory is a compulsive deductive argument which makes it possible to misplace the idea of necessity, and then perhaps to mistake its character: where a conclusion follows necessarily it can be all too easy to assume that that conclusion must itself be logically, or even morally, necessary. When an appreciation of the deductive character of this argument is combined with a failure fully to understand how restricted is the meaning in this context of such phrases as 'the survival of the fittest' and 'natural selection', it may appear as if Darwin has established some sort of law of progress — a misconception from which Darwin himself was not, as we shall soon find, quite emancipated.

(i) THE MEANING OF THE EXPRESSION 'THE SURVIVAL OF THE FITTEST'

This expression — as has been noticed already — was originally coined by Herbert Spencer. But when employed within the context of Darwin's theory its meaning is restricted. For that theory provides no independent criterion of fitness. It is, as has very frequently but too often ineffectively been pointed out, a theory of the survival of the fittest only and precisely in so far as actual or possible survival is to be construed as the sufficient condition of fitness to survive. If some further and independent criterion were to be introduced the deductive argument would no longer be valid: natural selection is necessarily selection only for exactly what at precisely the time in question it in fact takes to survive; and where anything else seems to be being picked it is because that something else then happens to be linked contingently with what at that time happens to be required for survival. The Darwinian guarantee that it is always the fittest who have survived, the fittest who do survive, and the fittest who will survive is by itself neither an assurance that any particular thing which has survived so far will continue to do so, nor an undertaking that everything which is most worth while must survive. If anyone were to complain, using this present Darwinian criterion of fitness, that some particular social arrangement encourages the multiplication of the unfit and the extermination of the fit, then his complaint would be plainly self-contradictory. It seems to be peculiarly difficult to keep this last observation clearly and consistently in mind. Even so shrewd a commentator as Professor D. G. Ritchie, in his *Darwinism and Politics*, at least seems to lapse in the remark that the 'prudential restraint' of Malthus 'would mean that the most careful and intelligent part of the population would leave the continuance of the race mainly to the least careful and least intelligent portion — thus bringing about the survival of the unfittest'.[29] This uncharacteristic lapse, if it really is a lapse, is all the more noteworthy in that the author had earlier been at pains to point out, following T. H. Huxley, that 'the fittest' here means only 'those "best fitted to cope with their circumstances" in order to survive and transmit offspring'; and had even himself gone on to make, against Herbert Spencer, the further point that it must be contradictory 'to blame governments simply because they "interfere" with natural laws'.[30] (Perhaps in this particular case it would be not merely charitable but also correct to construe Ritchie's 'the survival of the unfittest' here as an elliptical equivalent of '(what by any sane standards of human worth would be) the survival of the unfittest'.

The same and further difficulties arise about 'natural selection', which in Darwin is an alternative expression for 'the survival of the fittest': 'This principle of preservation, or the survival of the fittest, I have called natural selection.'[31] For here we have also to recognise not only that the occurrence of natural selection necessarily guarantees, because it is logically equivalent to, the survival of the fittest, but also that the achievement of Darwin's theory is precisely to show that such selection, as a matter of fact, constitutes an immensely effective instrument which — given the necessary variations, and in inordinate time — has produced fabulous results. When we also take into the reckoning the fact that many people are inclined to believe, that whatever is in any sense natural must be as such commendable, and that Nature is a deep repository of wisdom, we need not be surprised to discover that for many the process of evolution by natural selection becomes a secular surrogate for Divine Providence; and that for some the possibility, or even the duty, of relying on this benign and mighty force presents itself as a decisive reason why positive social policies must be superfluous, and may be wrong — indeed almost blasphemous![32]

(ii) THE MEANING OF THE EXPRESSION 'NATURAL SELECTION'

In this the wheel turns full circle. For the greatest philosophical significance of Darwin's work — in a sense of 'philosophy' both much wider and more usual than that affected by the Wittgenstein of the *Tractatus* — lies precisely in the fact that Darwin showed how the appearances of design among living things might come about without actual design.[33] The whole point about natural selection is, one is tempted to say, that it is not selection at all. Indeed someone might well have urged — someone probably has — that natural selection is really an empty idea, because strictly the expression 'natural selection' is self-contradictory. Here one may recall and compare the argument, which was at one time used against Freud, that the notion of an unconscious mind is self-contradictory, because a mind is essentially something which thinks and because, on a similarly Cartesian definition, 'thinking' is a generic term for all and only modes of consciousness. With natural selection the line would be that choice or selection is essentially artificial, as opposed to natural; and it is both as such and for independent reasons necessarily a prerogative of persons.

In either case such arguments, even if strictly correct, are as objections pedantic and perverse. For both Freud and Darwin were drawing attention to enormously fruitful analogies: on the one hand between certain patterns of behaviour which are and others which are not accompanied by consciousness;[34] and on the other hand between the intentional activities of animal- and plant-breeders, and the unplanned and undirected operations of living nature in general. Certainly in the Darwinian case much of the pungent appeal of the label 'natural selection' derives from the very fact that the expression is strictly contradictory. The tension between its two elements gives it the appeal of such a paradoxical idiom as 'the evidence of my own eyes', which makes the point that I, having actually seen it myself, have something much more direct and better than what usually counts as evidence. Yet there should be no doubt, despite some recent suggestions to the contrary,[35] that in its Darwinian employment the expression 'natural selection' does have content; and that the assertion that natural selection occurs is none the less contingent and empirically falsifiable for being beyond all reasonable doubt true.

To state that natural selection occurs is to make at least three claims: first, that not all offspring survive to reproduce; second, although most creatures reproduce after their kind, variations do nevertheless occur; and third, the character of these variations is relevant to questions about which offspring will survive to reproduce. The factual character of the first, and the difference to be made by the conjunction with it of the equally factual second and third, can be illustrated by some famous lines from *In Memoriam* (1850), in which we see the first clearly without a glimmering of the other two:

> So careful of the type she seems,
> So careless of the single life;

> . . . of fifty seeds,
> She often brings but one to bear,
> I falter where I firmly trod, . . .
> 'So careful of the type'? but no,
> From scarped cliff and quarried stone
> She cries, 'A thousand types are gone:
> I care for nothing, all shall go'.[36]

The danger of Darwin's pointedly paradoxical expression 'natural selection' — and this danger has often been realised — is that it may mislead people to overlook that this sort of selection is blind and non-rational; precisely that is the point. Once this point is missed it is easy, especially if you are already apt to see Nature as a mentor, to go on to take natural selection as a sort of supreme court of normative appeal; and this despite — or in many cases doubtless because of — the time-serving character of the criterion of fitness by which this sort of selection operates. Such ideas may then be, and often have been, regarded as the biological application of the Hegelian slogan 'World history is the world's court of judgment'.[37]

(iii) PROGRESS IN DARWIN'S THEORY?

These apotheoses of natural selection take many forms. Perhaps the most interesting and important of such misconceptions, and one from which Darwin himself is not altogether free, is that the deductive argument which is the core of the theory proves some sort of law of progressive development. Thus he concludes the chapter on 'Instincts' with the sentence: 'Finally, it may not be a logical deduction, but to my imagination it is far more satisfactory to look at such instincts as the young cuckoo ejecting its foster-brothers, — ants making slaves, — the larvae of ichneumonidae feeding within the live bodies of caterpillars, — not as specially endowed or created instincts, but as small consequences of one general law leading to the advancement of all organic beings, — namely, multiply, vary, let the strongest live and the weakest die.' Again in the penultimate paragraph of the whole book, he writes: 'As all the living forms of life are the lineal descendants of those which lived long before the Cambrian epoch, we may feel certain that . . . no cataclysm has desolated the whole world. Hence we may look with some confidence to a secure future of great length. And as natural selection works solely by and for the good of each being, all corporeal and mental endowments will tend to progress towards perfection.'[38]

The first of these two passages is not, perhaps, as clear and explicit as one could wish. But in the light of the unhesitating concluding sentence of the second we may perhaps take it that 'what may not be a logical deduction' is not 'the one general law leading to the advancement of all organic beings', but rather its suggested implications as regards the more unattractive instincts. Certainly Darwin is offering natural selection as a guarantee of progress, and as both a descriptive and a prescriptive law. Equally certainly this guarantee is not in fact warranted by his theory. Indeed, neither of the conclusions of the second passage can be justified as deductions from the theory alone.

The first was on the evidence available to Darwin an entirely reasonable inductive extrapolation. It is only since the beginning of the atomic era that we have acquired any serious grounds for anxiety about the immediate survival prospects for our own species. The second conclusion never was justified. To choose is necessarily to exclude, and there would seem to be no reason at all, and certainly none within the theory, for saying of every individual organism which loses out in the struggle for existence that this must be for its own good. Applied not to individuals but to species of beings, the statement might seem to find some justification in the now notorious fact that most actual variations are unfavourable. But since survival is in the theory the criterion of fitness, and hence of what counts as favourable, the only good which is guaranteed is the survival of whatever makes for survival; and this good is not necessarily good by any independent standard. Nor, of course, does natural selection guarantee that any particular species, or even any species at all, will enjoy even this purely biological good of having what it takes to survive.

Again, while presumably it does follow that, all other things being equal, the more efficient, and in that sense the more perfect,

forms of any advantageous organ will tend to replace the less perfect forms, this is only guaranteed in so far as the organ in question does at the crucial times confer some decisive selective advantage upon the organism of which it is a part, and in so far as
efficiency is defined in terms of survival value in that particular
context. This more cautious and more correct formulation leaves
open various discouraging possibilities, all of which would have
to be disposed of before it could be allowed that the second of the
present conclusions is warranted by the theory. This latter conclusion, it must be stressed, is much stronger than the first. Whereas that involved only a modestly confident extrapolation of an
immemorial trend, this purports to find a theoretical basis for a
boldly optimistic claim about a long-term tendency. The foundation is inadequate, for two reasons: first, because of the nature of
the criterion of fitness which is involved in natural selection; and
second, because that process operates on organisms and not on
organs. Unless an organ is, directly or indirectly, relevant to the
survival or the multiplication of the organism of which it is a part,
natural selection will not engage with it at all; while an organism
may labour under and be ruined by all sorts of other disadvantages
which more than offset the selective promise of one particular
organ. An individual, therefore, or a species can perfectly well
have many splendid corporeal and mental endowments without
this ensuring that it has what is in fact needed for survival: men
who are wretched specimens, both mentally and physically, may —
and all too often do — kill superb animals; and genius has frequently been laid low by the activities of unicellular creatures
having no wits at all.

(iv) TRENDS, FORCES, AND LAWS OF DEVELOPMENT

Although it is thus wrong to think that Darwin's theory implies
a general law of progressive development, the idea that it does has
been and remains perennially tempting. Since it surely is the case
that in every epoch of the fossil record fresh possibilities of life
have been realised, since it also seems that the most complex of
these in each epoch have been more elaborate than the most

sophisticated achievements of the previous period, and since we ourselves are among the latest products of the development, it is easy to pick out a trend which we can scarcely regard as anything but progressive.

> . . . to have come so far,
> Whose cleverest invention was lately fur;
> Lizards my best once who took years to breed,
> Could not control the temperature of blood. . . .[39]

To pick out such a progressive trend is, of course, made still easier if we allow ourselves to misconstrue in a normative sense the palaeontologists' purely spatio-temporal use of the terms 'higher' and 'lower' to characterise first the strata and then the creatures whose fossils first appear in these strata. (It was not for nothing that Darwin pinned into his copy of *Vestiges of the Natural History of Creation* the memorandum slip: 'Never use the words *higher* and *lower*.'[40]

Once a trend has been thus identified it may seem a short step from a trend to the trend, another equally short from the trend to a law of tendency, and so again finally from a law of tendency to the universal overriding law of development. The slippery slope is greased by the facts that the crucial mechanism is called natural selection or the survival of the fittest, and that the core of Darwin's theory is a deductive argument which certainly does prove that natural selection is operating and is ensuring this survival of the fittest. But a trend is a very different thing from a law of tendency. There is a trend if there has been a direction in the development so far, whether or not there is any reason to think that things will continue to develop along this line. But to assert a law of tendency is to say that something always has occurred and always will occur, except in so far as this tendency was or will be inhibited by some overriding force. Furthermore, a law of tendency is a very different thing from an absolute law of development. The former may obtain even though the tendency in question is never in fact fully realised: the First Law of Motion and Malthus's Principle of Population are not disproved by the observations that in fact there always are 'impressed forces' and countervailing 'checks'.

But an absolute law of development would state that some particular line of evolution is absolutely inevitable, that it neither will nor could be prevented by any counteracting causes.

Darwin himself seems never to have gone further than to suggest, as in the two passages quoted, that his theory might warrant a law of the first and weaker kind — that there is in the evolution of all living things an inherent tendency to progress. It was left to others reviewing evolutionary biology in the light of their own various preconceptions about the destined lines of human development to discern in Darwinism the deeper foundation for or the wider background of their supposed absolute laws of human progress. By far the most interesting and most important case is that of Marx and Engels. In his Preface to the first German edition of *Capital* Marx writes: 'when a society has got upon the right track for the discovery of the natural laws of its movement — and it is the ultimate aim of this work to lay bare the economic law of motion of modern society — it can neither clear by bold leaps, nor remove by legal enactments, the obstacles offered by the successive phases of its normal development. But it can shorten and lessen the birth-pangs.'[41] And in his speech at Marx's graveside Engels claimed: 'Just as Darwin discovered the law of development of organic nature, so Marx discovered the law of development of human history.'

The crucial distinctions between actual trends, laws of tendency, and absolute laws of development can be illustrated from the writings of Julian Huxley and Joseph Needham; and the distinctions themselves are in turn essential to a proper critical appraisal of these writings. Thus Julian Huxley takes as one of the mottoes of his famous essay on 'Progress, Biological and Other' one of the sentences which we have just quoted from Darwin: 'As natural selection works solely by and for the good of each being, all corporeal and mental endowments will tend to progress towards perfection.' It is, I think, clear that Huxley if pressed would never claim to be showing more than a law of tendency, and usually only an actual trend.

He starts by urging that the most fundamental need of man as man is 'to discover something, some being or power, some force or tendency . . . moulding the destinies of the world — something not himself, greater than himself, with which [he can] harmonise his nature . . . repose his doubts . . . achieve confidence and hope'. He then offers 'to show how the facts of evolutionary biology provide us, in the shape of a verifiable doctrine of progress, with one of the elements most essential to any such externally-grounded conception of God'. He later concludes that 'the fact of progress emerging from pain and battle and imperfection . . . is an intellectual prop which can support the distressed and questioning mind, and be incorporated into the common theology of the future'.[42]

All this would seem to require at least a law of tendency — a force — if not and preferably an invincible law of development. But in the intermediate small print Huxley attempts to establish only an actual trend, although he is later inclined to slip from this to the far stronger conclusion of a supporting tendency. Thus in that small print he claims: 'It will, I hope, have been clear, even from the few examples which I have given, that there has been a main direction in evolution.' He then defines this direction under six heads: 'During the time of life's existence on this planet, there has been an increase, both in the average and far more in the upper level, of certain attributes of living things.' However, in a concluding polemical paragraph against Dean Inge, Huxley both employs and neglects the distinction between such an actual trend and a supporting force: 'He has been so concerned to attack the dogma of inherent and inevitable progress in human affairs that he has denied the fact of progress — whether inevitable we know not, but indubitable and actual — in biological evolution: and in so doing he has cut off himself and his adherents . . . from by far the greatest manifestation in external things of "something, not ourselves, that makes for righteousness".'[43]

Although Huxley is certainly not adequately insistent upon the first crucial distinction between an actual trend and a force, he does in the following essay on 'Biology and Sociology' fairly clearly repudiate the suggestion that the actual progressive direction of development to be discerned in evolutionary biology and elsewhere necessarily reveals an absolute law of progressive development: 'When we look into the trend of biological evolution, we find as a matter of fact that it has operated to produce on the whole what we find good. . . . This is not to say that progress is an inevitable "law of nature", but that it has actually occurred. . . .'[44] This strongest idea of a law of inevitable development, rejected by Huxley, is in fact urged, eloquently and unequivocally, by Needham in two books of essays, *Time: the Refreshing River* and *History is on Our Side*. Generations which knew not the Spanish War may need to be told that the first of these titles is drawn from a stanza of Auden's since disowned 'Spain':

> And the poor in their fireless lodgings, dropping the sheets
> Of the evening paper: 'Our day is our loss, Oh, show us
> History the operator, the
> Organiser, Time the refreshing river.'[45]

It is worth quoting fairly extensively from these two Needham books, which are not as well known as they deserve to be, and which surely constitute both one of the most colourful and one of the most distinguished contributions to the often rather shabbily pedestrian corpus of evolutionary ethics and evolutionary politics. Much of their interest lies in the attempted synthesis of biological science, Marxist historical pseudo-science, and ritualistic Christian religion; the author was at the time of writing a leading biochemist, an active member of the Communist Party, and a practising Christian.

Thus Needham is able to write: 'The historical process is the organiser of the City of God, and those who work at its building are (in the old language) the ministers of the Most High . . . the curve of the development of human society pursues its way across the graph of history with statistical certainty . . .'; or 'the new world-order of social justice and comradeship, the rational and classless world state is no wild idealistic dream, but a logical extrapolation from the whole course of evolution, having no less authority than that behind it, and therefore of all faiths the most rational'; or 'the organisation of human society is only as yet at the beginning of its triumphs, and . . . these triumphs are *inevitable*, since they lie along the road traced out by the entire evolutionary process. . . .' (A footnote quotes the *Communist Manifesto*: 'The downfall of the bourgeoisie and the victory of the proletariat are equally *inevitable*.'[46]) Again, in the second book Needham urges: 'Whatever force hinders the coming of the world co-operative commonwealth . . . that force is ultimately doomed. Against the world-process no force can in the end succeed.'[47]

(v) LAWS AND INEVITABILITY

We have already argued, earlier in the present Section, that Darwin's theory does not provide a foundation adequate to sustain a general law of progress (III (iii) above); notwithstanding that it certainly is possible to pick out from the record of biological evolution so far trends which we human beings could scarcely fail to rate as progressive (III (iv) above). There is, therefore, no call for any further argument here to show that no absolute law of progressive development, which must as such be much stronger than any mere law of tendency, can possibly be derived from that theory; and, of course, there can be no question of deriving directly any sort of law at all from the observation only of an actual trend in the developments to date.

However, it is perhaps worth pointing out parenthetically that the spokesman for absolute laws of historical development must have difficulty in allowing room for effective human action; for, in so far as anything is absolutely inevitable, it would seem that attempts to prevent it must be futile and efforts to bring it about redundant; and this consequence is fatalism. It is this difficulty with which Marx — who had no wish whatsoever to become a 'remote and ineffectual don' — was trying to deal by introducing the idea of shortening and lessening the birthpangs; and which Needham — characteristically drawing on both the Chinese sages and Mr. R. Palme Dutt — tries to meet rather more fully.[48]

The line of approach actually taken here by Marx is importantly different from that of Needham and Palme Dutt. For, in effect, Marx is providing some — surely rather limited — scope for effective human action only by conceding that his law of development is imprecise. Development through the successive phases is inevitable and hence, it might seem, independent of any human wishes and decisions, although the speed, and the roughness or the smoothness, of this development can be affected by human choice. Palme Dutt on the other hand — and here he is perhaps being more faithful to the spirit and intentions of Marx than Marx himself — insists that all history is made by men, and hence that its course is always the outcome of human choices: 'It is the very heart of the revolutionary Marxist understanding of inevitability that it has nothing in common with the mechanical fatalism of which our opponents incorrectly accuse us. This inevitability is realised in practice through living human wills under given social conditions, consciously reacting to those conditions, and consciously choosing their line between alternative possibilities seen by them within the given conditions.'[49]

But now in so far as this is allowed it becomes thoroughly misleading to talk of any outcome as, without qualification, inevitable. For to say that something is, without qualification, inevitable is, surely, to imply that it is going to happen quite regardless and quite independent of any or all human decisions and human efforts; whereas Dutt's point is the entirely different one that, knowing — thanks to our Marxist analyses — what the situation is going to be and knowing too what people are like, we are entitled to be sure that they will react in ways which will effect such and such an outcome. Thus he continues: 'We are able scientifically to predict the inevitable outcome, because we are able to analyse the social conditions. . . . We are able to analyse the growth of contradictions, and the consequent . . . ever greater revolutionary consciousness and will in the exploited majority, till they become strong enough to overcome all obstacles and conquer. . . . But the human consciousness of the participants . . . is the consciousness of living, active, human beings, revolting against intolerable evils, deliberately with thought and passion choosing a new alternative, doing and daring all to achieve a new world. . . .'

The crux lies in the misplacement of the word 'inevitable'. It is one thing to say that, granted various truths or alleged truths about certain people and the situations in which they find themselves, then it necessarily follows that they will in fact act in such and such a way, and that the outcome will in fact be thus and thus. It is a very different thing to say that, granted these same truths or alleged truths, then the persons concerned will inevitably act in such and such a way, and that the inevitable outcome will be thus and thus. The point is that in the first case the necessity is logical, belonging only to the inference: here any 'inevitably' can qualify only the word 'follows', which links the premise propositions to the conclusion proposition. But in the second case the word 'inevitably' appears within the conclusion itself; and there it must carry a totally different, an empirical, sense. If the outcome is, without qualification, inevitable, then there can be nothing which anyone at all could do or could have done which would have prevented or would prevent that inevitable outcome. In a sentence: from 'Whatever will be will be' it follows necessarily that 'Whatever will be will be'; but it does not follow at all that 'Whatever will in fact be will have been inevitable'.[50]

One word more on Marxism and inevitability, before we return to Julian Huxley and his search for 'an intellectual prop which can support the distressed and questioning mind, and be incorporated in the common theology of the future'. It seems that Marxists, or at least those of the Muscovite obedience, are now inclined to abandon any idea of an absolute law of development towards a world socialist commonwealth, and instead to fall back on much weaker but still very strong laws of tendency. Thus the present writer was recently assured by the leading Marxist theoretician in Poland, himself a member of the Central Committee of the ruling Party, that socialism in one form or another was on its way — unless of course an all-out nuclear war produced universal ruin. Again, in England the Marxist philosopher Mr. Maurice Cornforth is now both stressing this same proviso and insisting — obviously rightly — that the defeat of the Axis powers in the Second World War was by no means inevitable.[51] If the point which we have just been making is accepted, this development will have to be characterised as a sensible shift: from the claim that, given a full Marxist understanding of man and society, we can know that the old original Clause 4 of the British

Labour Party will inexorably become the basic law for all mankind; to the rather more cautious contention that, granted that same understanding duly revised to take account of the facts of a new age, we can know that this supreme consummation will be effected unless a global nuclear catastrophe intervenes. In place of (what at any rate often looked like) an absolute law of development we now have (what quite clearly is) only a very strong law of tendency. All roads may still lead in the direction of socialism; but arrival at this destination is no longer so absolutely guaranteed.

(vi) EVOLUTION NOT 'SOMETHING, NOT OURSELVES, WHICH MAKES FOR RIGHTEOUSNESS'

The immediate relevance of all this to us here lies in its indirect bearing on hopes, such as we have seen expressed by Julian Huxley, of finding in evolutionary biology some sort of 'intellectual prop which can support the distressed and questioning mind'; or, more boldly, in the words of the definition of the moral function of God which Huxley quotes from Matthew Arnold, the hopes of finding 'something, not ourselves, that makes for righteousness'. There is a fundamental reason, which has so far been no more than hinted, why it must be misguided to seek such support in pre-human evolutionary biology alone, and without any special and particular reference to the peculiarities of the period of man. One hint lay in the contrast, which we developed early in this present Section, between natural selection and selection (III (ii) above). Ordinary literal selection always involves rational agents whereas natural selection typically does not. Another hint is to be found in our reasons for challenging Darwin's perhaps too optimistic presumption that 'we may look with some confidence to a secure future of great length'. Such confidence would be inductively justified only if we could discount the impact of man within the evolutionary process; only, it might therefore seem and paradoxically, if we were not here to be looking forward to anything at all.

The crux is, simply, that the future not only of mankind but of the entire evolutionary process on this planet is in our hands. The point is made with salutary brutality by Mr. A. M. Quinton, writing on 'Ethics and the Theory of Evolution'. He first notices how confidence in the possibility of discerning a progressive trend in the course of evolution so far 'seems to be based on the general agreement amongst biologists about the ordering of the evolutionary hierarchy'. He then remarks: 'One feature . . . which might be used is the unanimous opinion that man is the most evolved species, the one which shows the highest degree of biological progress. He has certainly won the contest between animal species in that it is only on his sufferance that any other species exist at all, amongst species large enough to be seen at any rate.' [52]

The same points are involved when Huxley himself, writing thirty years after his *Essays of a Biologist*, claims with visionary eloquence: 'In the light of evolutionary biology man can now see himself as the sole agent for further evolutionary advance on this planet, and one of the few possible instruments of progress in the universe at large. He finds himself in the unexpected position of business manager for the cosmic process of evolution.' [53]

We shall be considering in a later section this idea of seeing human life in an evolutionary perspective, an idea which becomes more and more prominent in Huxley's later essays (Section V below). But here the important thing to get clear is that, precisely in so far as it is true that the future both of mankind and of the entire evolutionary process on this planet — indeed in the whole solar system — is in our hands, to that extent there can be no question of finding any guarantee of future progress, either in the actual course of evolution before the emergence of man, or in its hypothetical development supposing there were to be no further human participation.

In the previous subsection we were insisting that men make history (III (v) above). One relevant consequence of this is that any predictions or assurances about the future course of that history require to be founded upon investigations of human nature and human society in particular, rather than upon a study of (prehuman) organic evolution in general. This is something which Marxists have always recognised: 'Just as Darwin discovered the law of organic nature, so Marx discovered the law of development of human history'; but each made his own discovery by enquiring in the appropriate area. Again, and typically, the dominant theme of Dr. John Lewis's *Man and Evolution* is the enormous difference between modern man and the other animals; and hence the equally enormous difference between human and pre-human evolution. Needham, because of his frank concern to retain some form of Christian belief, however Modernist, is atypical; yet he too insists repeatedly that the universal and progressive world-process proceeds through successive integrative levels each of which has its own laws requiring direct and independent study.[54]

The further point which we are now making is that not only do men make history — with the implication just indicated — but that the future course of the evolution of all other species is, or soon will be, in human hands — with the further implication that any substantial and particular predictions about developments there need also to take account of the peculiar powers and proclivities of our unique, and uniquely destructive, species.

The upshot of the present subsection is that the kind of reinforcement or guarantee sought by the author of *Essays of a Biologist* could be found only either 'outside' the universe, in an old-fashioned Divine Providence, or 'inside' the universe, in absolute laws of historical development. If the former could somehow be discovered then it would, presumably, follow that the course of biological evolution up to and including the emergence of man must have been — like everything else in the universe — a manifestation of that Divine Providence; and that, presumably, must imply that all manner of things are and were and will be well. Again, if there were absolute laws of historical development, and if the development which they determined could be rated as progressive, then Huxley might have found in these laws that outside support which he craved. (It would be outside support — 'something, not ourselves' — since it is an essential feature of any such Juggernaut view of history that any development determined by its absolute laws is altogether outside human control. Precisely that is what makes the Juggernaut a Juggernaut; and it is this feature which makes Popper's phrase 'the Juggernaut view of history' apt.)

But either recourse ought to be suspect in a supposedly secular context. There is, surely, something very odd, indeed pathetic, in Huxley's attempt to find in evolutionary biology 'something, not ourselves, which makes for righteousness'. For this quest is for him a search for something, not God, which does duty for Divine Providence. Yet if there really is no Divine Providence operating in the universe, then indeed there is none; and we cannot reasonably expect to find in the Godless workings of impersonal things those comfortable supports which — however mistakenly — believers usually think themselves entitled to derive from their theistic beliefs. Nor, in so far as we insist — as indeed we must — that men make history, can any laws of tendency which we may be able to discover in history fill Huxley's bill. For, in so far as such laws either epitomise or presuppose our human tendencies, they very obviously cannot, whether or not they make for righteousness, constitute a 'something, not ourselves'.

There cannot, therefore, be the answer longed for to the heartcry: 'Oh, show us / History the operator, the / Organiser . . .'. Still less is there any profit in our

> . . . invoking the life
> That shapes the individual belly and orders
>   The private nocturnal terror:
> 'Did you not found the city state of the sponge
>
> Raise the vast military empires of the shark
> And the tiger, establish the robin's plucky canton?
>   Intervene . . .'

No doubt it is in part because Auden himself now hopes that there is, after all, someone who might 'descend as a dove or / A furious papa or a mild engineer, but descend', that he has become so averse from any reprinting of 'Spain'. Nevertheless, the author's own backslidings notwithstanding, the final stanza is the last word on the early Huxley's hopes:

> The stars are dead. The animals will not look.
> We are left alone with our day, and the time is short, and
>   History to the defeated
> May say Alas but cannot help nor pardon.[55]

IV. FROM *IS* TO *OUGHT*

The panorama presented by evolutionary biology is, though often terrible, magnificent; and to have brought the development of all living things within the scope of a single theory constitutes one of the greatest achievements of the human mind. 'Thus', in the concluding words of the *Origin*, 'from the war of nature, from famine and death, the most exalted object which we are capable of conceiving, namely, the production of the higher animals, directly follows. There is grandeur in this view of life, with its several powers originally breathed by its Creator into a few forms or into one; and that, whilst this planet has gone cycling on according to the fixed law of gravity, from so simple a beginning endless forms most beautiful and most wonderful have been, and are being evolved.'[56] There is indeed.

It is, therefore, as we insisted at the very beginning, neither surprising nor discreditable that people should want to adjust their ideas to this vision, and to seek possible wider applications for the concepts of evolutionary theory. In the previous section we considered one kind of suggestion about 'the philosophical implications of Darwinism'. In the present section we shall run through some major variations on the theme of the Naturalistic Fallacy. This has certainly been central in much which has been called evolutionary ethics; so much so that it has often, but wrongly, been thought to be the essential and polymorphous error which must both constitute and vitiate everything so labelled.

(i) A SPECIAL CASE

The first move is to distinguish what is peculiar to one special case from what is common to all such attempted deductions. Their general character, as has been indicated already, is determined by the fact that all the premises are, or should be, purely descriptive;

whereas the conclusions obtained are to be taken as prescriptive. The peculiarity of the special case is that here the premises are universal propositions the truth of which is dependent upon their being consistent with the facts that we do do whatever it may be that we do actually do. But it must be radically preposterous, not but what it has been and is common, to try to generate some mandate to do this rather than that from propositions which, to be truly what they pretend to be, must either be equally consistent with the choice of either alternative or be wholly inconsistent with our having any alternatives at all. It would be idle and absurd to seek prescriptions for our behaviour where we are not confronted with options for choice, and unless the prescriptions sought are to require some of these and to forbid others.

We have already noticed one instance of the special case (III (i) above). We also, later in that Section (III (v) above), approached from a rather different direction the presently crucial point. D. G. Ritchie was there quoted as trying to rebut the policy of prudential restraint urged by Malthus, by urging that this must lead to 'the survival of the unfittest'. Yet this is a conclusion which must be, in Darwinian terms, contradictory. For survival, or — strictly — survival to reproduce, is not the reward but the criterion of biological fitness. But, of course, in so far as we maintain — and rightly — some standard of human excellence other than mere reproduction or multiplication, there may indeed be all too much reason for us to fear and deplore the present and likely future outcome of high reproductive rates among the backward, the improvident, and the fanatical.

Further examples of what we are distinguishing as the special case can be generated wherever we have what is supposed to be a law of nature including human action within its scope. For if it really is a law of nature, then it follows that nothing which has happened, is happening, or will happen can be inconsistent with it; any occurrence inconsistent with it constitutes a sufficient reason for disallowing its claim to express a law of nature. There is, therefore, a further special absurdity — over and above whatever general fallacy may be involved in any attempt to deduce normative conclusions from neutrally descriptive premises — in appealing to a premise of this sort as if, simultaneously, it could both express such a law of nature and constitute a reason for acting in one way rather than another.

The crux can be illustrated, light-heartedly but very aptly, by referring to a crisp exchange recorded in Mr. Raymond Chandler's *Farewell, My Lovely*. Philip Marlowe is conversing with Anne Riordan: "You take awful chances, Miss Riordan." "I think I said the same about you. I had a gun. I wasn't afraid. There's no law against going down there." "Uh-huh. Only the law of self-preservation." With his accustomed acuteness Marlowe, returning the gun, corrects himself: "Here. It's not my night to be clever." [57] Certainly, interpreted as other than a wisecrack, his remark would be foolish. For, precisely in so far as there were a psychological law of self-preservation under which all our actual actions could be subsumed, there could be no point in appealing to this law as a reason for acting not in one way but another; while if after all no such law holds, then it cannot provide any reasonable ground for anything. All those who in martyrdom witness to their conviction that survival can sometimes be too dearly bought do not thereby rebel against Nature's law of self-preservation. Rather they demonstrate that no such law obtains; or, at any rate, that if it does, the human animal does not fall within its scope.

Various misunderstandings of and ambiguities in the key terms and expressions have in the Darwinian context helped to conceal this absurdity; notwithstanding that, as we suggested in the Introduction, the great diversity and the frequent mutual inconsistency of the practical morals actually drawn ought surely to have made the supposed method of derivation suspect. Since the major misunderstandings and ambiguities have been noticed already in passing, we need here only to review them and to provide further illustrations.

First, and certainly not confined to our present biological context, is the failure to distinguish two kinds of law of nature — or, better, two senses of 'law of nature': the descriptive, in which such a law cannot have any genuine exceptions, since the occurrence of any event inconsistent with the truth of a proposed law constitutes a sufficient reason for failing the candidate; and the prescriptive, in which the occurrence of violations constitutes no reason at all for maintaining that the law originally propounded does not really obtain. The point of the passage just quoted from *Farewell, My Lovely* lies in its wisecracking exploitation of this ambiguity. But, as is shown by other examples which we have given and shall give, the fact that one can draw an illustration from such a source must be interpreted not as evidence of the universal obviousness of the crucial distinction but as one more indication of the quality of Chandler.

Second, the expression 'natural selection' seems to be used in two crucially different senses: both, more narrowly, in an incompatible contrast with '(artificial) selection' and, comprehensively, in such a way that the latter is just a special case of the former. It becomes absolutely essential to make this distinction the moment we wish to take account of the actual or possible impact of human choice upon the course of biological evolution. We have already tried, in the previous Section (III (vi) above), to show how the past, present, and potential impact of our own species upon and within this development rules out any possibility of discovering at the sub-human levels some comfortably reassuring substitute for Divine Providence. We can now appreciate, in the light of everything which has been said in this present subsection, why it is even more fundamentally misguided to hope to make a law of natural selection into the arbiter or the scapegoat on to which we can shuffle off the burdens of human decision and human responsibility. For in so far as the law applies to us at all it can only be because 'natural selection' is being construed in the comprehensive second sense in which there can be no antithesis between natural and artificial selection, because whatever we do in fact select is by that token shown to have been selected naturally.

With all the advantages of hindsight we may well regret that Darwin himself did not in the *Origin* explicitly make, and make much of, this distinction between a narrower and a wider sense of 'natural selection'. But it is much more regrettable, and far less excusable, that a writer on *Darwin and the Darwinian Revolution* now, a full century later, should still fail altogether to seize the points involved. Thus we read that: 'Francis Galton, Darwin's cousin and great champion, who made it his mission, as he thought, to give practical content to Darwin's theory, was by this very enterprise denying that theory. The science of eugenics, devoted to the improvement of the human stock, was designed "to further the ends of evolution more rapidly and with less distress than if events were left to their own course".' Darwin's own sympathetic yet pessimistic reactions to one of Galton's eugenic proposals are then mentioned, and the occasion grasped to rebuke poor Darwin because 'It did not seem to have occurred to him that it vitiated his essential principle, making survival independent of the natural struggle for existence.'[58] On this scandalous bit of commentary we may comment in turn, equally superciliously but with justification, that it does not seem to have occurred to the authoress that a programme for the improvement — by reference, presumably, to some human standards of excellence and fitness — of our own human stock could be no more and no less inconsistent with Darwin's theory than are the activities of those throughout the centuries who have selected for desired varieties of plants and animals and against others — activities to which he himself gave the most careful attention in the first chapter of the *Origin*, and elsewhere.

Third, the two logically connected expressions 'natural selection' and 'survival of the fittest' are within the theory implicitly so defined that whatever is in fact 'selected' and survives must necessarily be the fittest, regardless of all other merits or demerits, and notwithstanding that both expressions contain terms which are often or always elsewhere employed for commendation (III (i) above). Granted this Darwinian criterion of fitness it becomes a necessary truth that whatever survives to reproduce is fit, and must have been naturally selected; although this, it is just worth reiterating, does not imply, what is not true, that to say that natural selection occurs is to utter a tautology.[59] When a failure to take account of the difference between the Darwinian and other more ordinary criteria of fitness for selection is combined with a blindness to the equivocation between two senses of 'law', it becomes easy, first to misplace the idea of necessity, and then to misconstrue it. A logical necessity is thus unwittingly transmogrified

into, and hence appears to reinforce, a moral necessity: compare
the way in which, as we have seen (III (v) above), the logical necessity of an implication may be alchemically transmuted into the
practical inevitability of an event. To say within the terms of
Darwinian theory that in natural selection the fittest must survive
is to utter only a tautology. But this can be mistaken to be an
urgent practical imperative, categorically demanding that we make
every sacrifice to ensure that they in fact do.

Thus — to go straight to the bottom — consider the savage
'Social Darwinism' which Adolf Hitler assimilated in the Vienna
of his youth: 'If we did not respect the law of nature, imposing our
will by the right of the stronger, a day would come when the wild
animals would again devour us — then the insects would eat the
wild animals, and finally nothing would exist on earth except the
microbes'; or again, 'By means of the struggle the élites are con-
tinually renewed. The law of selection justifies this incessant
struggle by allowing the survival of the fittest. Christianity is a
rebellion against natural law, a protest against nature. Taken to its
logical extreme Christianity would mean the systematic cult of
human failure.'[60]

These passages from an outrageous source very effectively
underline the present point: actual survival to reproduce is itself
within Darwin's theory the sole and sufficient criterion of fitness
thus to survive; and the mere capacity to survive and to reproduce
is the only and often humanly very questionable merit for which
natural selection necessarily selects. An 'élite' selected simply on
this basis could be, literally as well as metaphorically, the scum
which rises to the top. But the same passages also illustrate the
crucial confusions between the two senses of 'law' and the two
senses of 'natural selection'. The anti-Christian moral which
Hitler draws may be salutarily compared with Rockefeller's
Sunday-school claim, quoted already in our Introduction: 'The
growth of a large business is merely a survival of the fittest. . . .
This is not an evil tendency in business. It is merely the working
out of a law of nature and a law of God.'

We end this subsection with two further illustrations: one to
show that the same misconceptions have been accepted by more

disinterested protagonists, the other to reveal that a first-rate philosopher is not necessarily immune. First, from the founder and first General of the Salvation Army: 'In the struggle of life the weakest will go to the wall and there are so many weak. The fittest, in tooth and claw, will survive. All we can do is to soften the lot of the unfit and make their sufferings less horrible than at present.'[61] Although we have provided already all the instruments required for the dissection, it is perhaps just worth adding that many of those who, by Booth's human and humane criteria, scored as the weakest who went to the wall would, by the biological criterion of mere survival to multiply, not have counted as weak at all. For in Booth's day as today high fertility was often both a cause and a consequence of poverty.

Second, from C. S. Peirce: '*The Origin of Species* of Darwin merely extends politico-economical views of progress to the entire realm of animal and vegetable life. . . . As Darwin puts it on his title page, it is the struggle for existence; and he should have added for his motto: "Every individual for himself, and the Devil take the hindmost!" Jesus, in his Sermon on the Mount, expressed a different opinion.' Peirce goes on to tell us that 'The Gospel of Christ says that progress comes from every individual merging his individuality in sympathy with his neighbours', and Peirce contrasts this with what 'may accurately be called the Gospel of Greed'. It was not one of Peirce's good days, for only a page or two later, in the same article, on 'Evolutionary Love', he says: 'Another thing: anaesthetics had been [in 1859] in use for thirteen years. Already, people's acquaintance with suffering had dropped off very much; and, as a consequence, that unlovely hardness, by which our times are so contrasted with those that immediately preceded them, had already set in and inclined people to relish a ruthless theory.'[62]

(ii) THE NATURALISTIC FALLACY AS SUCH

In (i) above, although most of our distinctions and arguments had some wider application, we were primarily concerned with one special case of the attempt to deduce normative conclusions

from the purely descriptive premises provided by evolutionary
theory. We now proceed to consider the Naturalistic Fallacy in
general, although always of course with special reference to its
application in our context. The label 'Naturalistic Fallacy' derives
from G. E. Moore's *Principia Ethica* (1903). It is an apt label, since
one very typical way of committing this fallacy is by offering some
supposedly neutral descriptive statement about what is allegedly
natural as if it could by itself entail some conclusion about what is
in some way commendable. Yet Moore's own account is so
wrapped up in various unfortunate assumptions that — all other
reasons apart — it is wise to begin from the now much-quoted
passage from Hume, noting by the way that *Principia Ethica* neither
quotes nor mentions this earlier classical authority.

Hume presents his remarks as an important afterthought to the
first Section of Book iii of his *Treatise of Human Nature* (1740),
under the section title 'Moral Distinctions not Derived from
Reason': 'In every system of morality which I have hitherto met
with I have always remarked that the author proceeds for some
time in the ordinary way of reasoning, and establishes the being of
a God, or makes observations concerning human affairs; when of
a sudden I am surprised to find, that instead of the usual copulations of propositions, *is* and *is not*, I meet with no proposition that
is not connected with an *ought* or *ought not*. This change is imperceptible; but is, however, of the last consequence. For as this
ought or *ought not* expresses some new relation or affirmation, it is
necessary that it should be observed and explained; and at the
same time a reason should be given, for what seems altogether
inconceivable, how this new relation can be a deduction from
others, which are entirely different from it.'

This observation is so important — and one is tempted to add,
mischievously, so clear and so clearly sound — that there is now
no lack of well-girded champions eager to contest both its accepted
interpretation and its truth. We can here eschew most of the details of Hume scholarship, doing so the less reluctantly for having
ourselves participated vigorously in the recent discussion in the
journals.[63] Yet it is relevant to our present purposes to warn the
unwary not to be misled by Hume's irony. It would be completely

wrong to take him absolutely literally, as if he were modestly claiming only to have noticed, and to have become seized of the vast importance of, a distinction which, however unwittingly, everyone was always and systematically making already. If that really had been Hume's contention it would, of course, have been quite obviously false, and could have been disposed of even more briskly than some of his most impatient critics have thought to be rid of it.[64]

However, Hume was not that — or any — sort of a fool. His immediate thesis was not that a distinction always is made, and that it is invariably marked by those different copulations of propositions, *ought* and *is*; but rather that it always ought to be made, because it is 'of the last consequence'. And why it is of the last consequence is, in Hume's view, that it is an expression and an implication of what he thought to be the great fundamental truth — and one of his own prime insights in philosophy — that values are not any sort of property of things in themselves, but that they are in some way a projection out on to the things around us of human needs and human desires. (One resulting problem, more obvious perhaps to us than to Hume, is that of explaining how values can be in some such fundamental way dependent on, and some sort of function of, human needs and human desires, without its thereby becoming the case that some purely descriptive statements about what people do want or would want must entail consequences about what ought to be. It is more than enough here for us simply to notice this problem, and to remark that it is at least not obvious that Hume completely forgot his point of the last consequence when he came to give his positive accounts of morals and aesthetics.)

Once Hume's ostensibly afterthought observation is understood, the first question is whether such a distinction, with a logical Grand Canyon between its terms, really can be made and maintained. It must be entirely beside the point to preen oneself — as some have done — upon having rustled up a herd of words which combine elements of both sorts in their meanings, or of expressions which can be ambiguous as between one and the other. For what has to be shown is not that this basic distinction is not in fact always made, but that in principle it cannot be.

Another recent approach calls attention to a 'class of unquestionably descriptive practical statements, namely what I shall call *appetitive utterances*, which indicate the objects or states of affairs that the person addressed will most enjoy or like or will get most satisfaction from. "You will most like or enjoy the Red Lion" is as good, sufficient and direct an answer to the question "Which hotel shall I stay at?" as "Stay at the Red Lion" or "The Red Lion is the best hotel". It is like them and different from "The Red Lion is the smartest or largest or quietest hotel" in that no contingent presumption needs to be made about the special tastes or requirements of the questioner in order to predict the action that will follow on his sincere acceptance of the advice, or at any rate to be assured of its relevance to his enquiry.'[65]

Yet neither that you would most enjoy the Red Lion, nor that it is the best hotel, constitutes an indefeasibly good reason for your staying there. You may, for instance, not be able or willing to afford the best, just as you may have some special reason, moral or other, which forbids indulgence on this (or any other) occasion. What is special about these appetitive utterances is, not that they make no contingent presumption about the requirements of the person addressed, but that the presumption involved is in fact almost always correct. But even if it were correct, not just usually but absolutely invariably, the conclusion to be derived from any appetitive premise would still be purely factual: if it is enjoyment you are after — as in fact, like everybody else, you are — then this is what in this particular case will serve your turn. So the subsistence of appetitive truths seems to have in itself no tendency to show that an *ought* can, after all, be deduced from an *is*.

A third and very plausible approach — persuasively suggested within the present volume by Mr. G. J. Warnock in sections v and vi of his *Contemporary Moral Philosophy* — urges that at least part of what distinguishes moral ideals and moral values from ideals and values of other sorts is that morality is always supposed to be directed towards the welfare of those concerned. Now if this is indeed so, and assuming that no one's welfare could be consistent with the wholesale frustration of all his desires, it might seem that one should be able to deduce some moral conclusions from some collections of flawlessly factual premises about what is or would be desired. Certainly from premises about what people want we can hope to deduce conclusions about what would satisfy or frustrate them; while equally certainly we can, if we like, characterise the promotion of their satisfaction as moral. Such a characterisation can probably be justified both by an appeal to (much of) the common usage of the term 'moral' and its associates, and also by reference to the point and purpose of moral discourse. Yet no such attempt, however successful, to construe 'moral' in terms of what is or would be desired by any individual or group could even begin to show that we can validly deduce, from the proposition that something is in this way and by these persons desired, the totally different conclusion that it is indeed desirable (in the sense of being what ought to be desired). For the crucial difference will still warrant the crucial distinction: between, on the one hand, simply stating quite neutrally that these are the things which would satisfy such and such desires; and, on the other hand, going on to prescribe that these particular desires are desires which ought to be satisfied.

However, the present occasion no more demands an exhaustive defence of Hume's thesis in its accepted interpretation than it calls for an attempt to show that that interpretation embodies the correct reading of Hume; and here again we can disclaim the task with a better conscience for having already taken a part in discussion in the journals. The main reason for making those remarks which we have made is further to clarify what the Naturalistic Fallacy is supposed to be, before proceeding to examine some particular moves — moves which can be seen to be fallacious without the support of any fully worked-out and impregnably defended general characterisation; and yet moves the unsoundness of which will need somehow to be taken into account by those philosophers who propose to deny that the Naturalistic Fallacy is a fallacy. The need to allow for this should give pause; as, in another way, should the recognition that though the label was a philosopher's coinage the idea itself is not peculiar to our notoriously fallible and perverse profession. Einstein, for instance, took it as obvious that 'As long as we remain within the realm of science proper, we can never meet with a sentence of the type "Thou shalt not kill". . . . Scientific statements of facts and relations . . . cannot produce ethical directives'.[66]

When we come to particular cases the most notable thing is precisely the lack of precision as to what the connection between the biological facts and the ethical directives is supposed to be. For instance, Julian Huxley tells us that 'in the broadest possible terms evolutionary ethics must be based on a combination of a few main principles: that it is right to realise ever new possibilities in evolution, notably those which are valued for their own sake; that it is right both to respect human individuality and to encourage its fullest development; that it is right to construct a mechanism for further social evolution which shall satisfy these prior conditions as fully, efficiently, and rapidly as possible.'[67]

It would be hard to dispute either that this is a statement 'in the broadest possible terms', or — as he goes on to say — that 'to translate these arid-sounding generalities into concrete terms and satisfying forms is beyond the scope of a lecture'. Again, after our earlier stress on the enormous difference between saying that something is desired and saying that it is desirable, we are bound to notice the tendency to equate the valuable with what is in fact valued: 'that it is right to realise ever new possibilities in evolution, notably those which are valued for their own sake'. But it is not necessarily an objection, although it is no doubt true, to say that the directives indicated seem in no way distinctively evolutionary. Certainly they might have been — indeed they often were and are — accepted without benefit of Darwin. Yet the claim to be propounding an evolutionary ethics might still have been abundantly vindicated if only Huxley had spelt out, as he never did, the steps of the logical deduction which, as 'the evolutionary moralist', he maintained was possible: 'He [the evolutionary moralist] can tell us that the facts of nature, as demonstrated in evolution, give us the assurance that knowledge, love, beauty, selfless morality, and firm purpose are ethically good.'[68] Well, no doubt he can tell us. But that, in default of any less elliptical exposition, is no sufficient reason for agreeing that what he tells us is true.

Again, if we turn to Spencer we find a similar indeterminacy about precisely what supposed evolutionary facts are to be connected with the desired ethical directives, and how; an indeterminacy which, in his case, cannot plausibly be excused by reference to any restriction of space. It is significant that in the Preface to the second heavy volume of *The Principles of Ethics* he is ready to concede that, in the last two parts, 'the Doctrine of Evolution . . . helps us in general ways though not in special ways'. But, even in a part to which this is supposed not to apply, a section which begins with the bold promise that 'Acceptance of the doctrine of organic evolution determines certain ethical conceptions' ends with only the unshattering and uncommunicative conclusion that it is 'an inevitable inference from the doctrine of organic evolution, that the highest type of living being, no less than all lower types, must go on moulding itself to those requirements which circumstances impose'.[69] One may perhaps recall here the statement which once introduced the lead story in an international news magazine notorious for the breathless urgency of its house style: 'Last week, as in every week in human history, in the best of times and in the worst of times, the leaders of the world's nations played out their separate parts.'

The proper objection to this is that it suffers not so much from a surfeit of generality as from a deficiency of substance. But there are other claims against which the same charge could not be laid. Consider three: first, 'that the conduct to which we apply the name *good*, is the relatively more evolved conduct; and *the bad* is the name which we apply to conduct which is relatively less evolved'; second, that 'no school can avoid taking for the ultimate moral aim a desirable state of feeling . . . gratification, enjoyment, happiness. Pleasure somewhere, at some time, to some being or beings, is an inexpugnable element of the conception'; and third, that 'the process of evolution must inevitably favour all changes of nature which increase life and augment happiness: especially such as do this at small cost'.[70]

Now, as we argued at length in Section III, Darwin's theory

provides no basis for concluding that there is any such law of progress as Spencer seems to be proclaiming in the third of these passages. Nor will it do to say, what the first passage seems to be suggesting, that moral behaviour is somehow more sophisticated biologically, or more a product of evolution, than immoral. For even if we allow 'the origin of the moral sentiments, in the same way as other natural phenomena, by a process of evolution', still 'as the immoral sentiments have no less been evolved, there is, so far, as much natural sanction for the one as for the other'.[71] The temptation, compounded by the strong suggestion of ordinary usage that any evolution must be from the inferior to the superior, is to mistake it that evolution in the Darwinian context must be ever towards more and better. Then, conjoining this misconception with the second less exceptionable claim, we bring forth the comfortable conclusion that the process of biological evolution must be a progress towards the supreme good of the classical Utilitarians, the greatest happiness of the greatest number.

In this argument, which can at best be a reconstruction of only one strand of Spencer's thinking, the conclusion is mediated by an ambiguity in 'evolution': between, on the one hand, the neutral scientific sense, and, on the other hand, a sense in which any evolution necessarily tends in a direction which must be rated as good. Even supposing, what we earlier urged is not and cannot be the case, that there really were some immanent guarantee that as a matter of contingent fact evolution in the former sense does produce these good results, still it must be quite wrong to try to equate the evolved with the good or the good with the evolved. The crucial point was made forcefully by Russell over fifty years ago, in words which read piquantly today: 'If evolutionary ethics were sound, we ought to be entirely indifferent as to what the course of evolution may be, since whatever it is is thereby proved to be the best. Yet if it should turn out that the Negro or the Chinaman was able to oust the European, we should cease to have any admiration for evolution; for as a matter of fact our preference of the European to the Negro is wholly independent of the European's greater prowess with the Maxim gun.'[72] And, it is fair to add, the same could with the appropriate alterations be said of Russell's own present preference for the Chinese and the Vietcong.

Russell's argument is decisive against any attempt to define the ideas of right and wrong, good and evil, in terms of a neutrally scientific notion of evolution. It can, as we shall see, be equally effective against the rather different suggestion that Darwin's theory can supply us with a, or even with the, satisfactory moral criterion. But before moving on to that we must break a lance with the shrewd and scholarly author of *The Moral Theory of Evolutionary Naturalism*. For, notwithstanding that he himself notices and cites earlier and better formulations by Hume and others, what seems to be the main thesis of his book constitutes an instructive example of an ideologically important misconception encouraged by one of the peculiarities of Moore's treatment. This thesis is that 'in so far as the evolutionary moralists' treatment of ethical questions is naturalistic, it is not normative; and that in so far as normative considerations are introduced it is not naturalistic'. He refers, approvingly, to Guyau: 'Most Evolutionary Naturalists, he declares, have made the great mistake of giving a naturalistic account and "also pretending to have rendered it . . . imperative in its precepts".'[73] Quillian's conclusion is that by introducing the normative the evolutionary naturalists have tacitly acknowledged the inadequacy of a naturalistic world-view.[74]

To understand both why this should be thought and why it is mistaken it is necessary to go back first to Moore and then to Hume. Moore, as we have said, introduced the label 'Naturalistic Fallacy', but, as we also mentioned, he characterised the mistake in a most unfortunate manner (a way, incidentally, which would make it a mistake in introspective psychology and not in logic — and hence not, strictly speaking, a fallacy at all). It was for him the error of believing 'that when we think "This is good", what we are thinking is that the thing in question bears a definite relation to some one other thing'. But then immediately, and without perhaps fully appreciating the possibilities of confusion opened up by thus using the word 'naturalistic' both in a peculiar and also in a less peculiar sense, he goes on to distinguish two sorts of view: on the one hand, 'Naturalistic Ethics'; and, on the other,

'Metaphysical Ethics'. In Moore both equally are taken to involve the Naturalistic Fallacy. The former is distinguished by the fact that here the value words are implicitly or explicitly defined in terms of something natural. This too is duly explained: 'By "nature" . . . I mean . . . that which is the subject-matter of the natural sciences and also of psychology.'[75]

So far it might seem that Quillian had simply misread his Moore, however excusably. But Moore straightway proceeds to introduce a distinction between natural and non-natural properties, and asks: 'Which among the properties of natural objects are natural properties and which are not?' He insists that goodness — for Moore *good* is always the key term in ethics — is just such a non-natural characteristic: 'For I do not deny that good is a property of certain natural objects: certain of them, I think, *are* good.'[76] Now if this were all right, then there would be certain things in the universe possessing properties which must necessarily be beyond the range of 'the natural sciences and of psychology'. And if to introduce the normative is, as this suggests, tacitly to recognise the subsistence of such non-natural properties, then indeed the evolutionary naturalists — and everyone else too who does the same — is thereby implicitly acknowledging the inadequacy of a naturalistic world-view.

This shows how Quillian, by following Moore, could be led to think what he did. To appreciate why this thought is mistaken it is helpful to go back further still, to Hume. As everyone must know, it was Hume's ambition 'to introduce the experimental method of reasoning into moral subjects',[77] and thereby to effect a sort of Copernican revolution in reverse. For Hume the paradigm for this exercise was the achievement of the new optics, construed as showing that colours are not truly qualities of the things which we uninstructedly describe as coloured. Rather they are somehow projections from our own 'sensoria'.[78] It was in these terms that Hume would have us see 'that morality is nothing in the abstract nature of things, but is entirely relative to the sentiment or mental taste of each particular being, in the same manner as the distinctions of sweet and bitter, hot and cold arise from the particular feeling of each sense or organ'.[79]

But now if, as Hume suggests, putting a value on something or commending some course of action neither is nor presupposes the ascription of any supposed non-natural characteristics to anything, then there is no longer any reason for thinking that anyone who — as we all must — values, commends, recommends, prescribes, and so on, must thereby be — however unwittingly — acknowledging the existence of some reality of which a naturalistic world-outlook cannot take account. For except in so far as some Moorean account is correct, none of these proceedings seems to present any insuperable obstacle to tough-mindedly naturalistic description. Certainly many spokesmen of a naturalistic world-outlook, including most of Quillian's Evolutionary Naturalists, have also been, like many of their opponents, committers of the Naturalistic Fallacy. But there is no necessary connection between naturalism, in the sense in which the word refers to a sort of world-view, and naturalism, in the rather artificial sense in which a naturalist would be one who tried to deduce *ought*s from *is*es. Hume, for instance, and in this he was not inconsistent, was as surely a naturalist in the first sense as he was committed to rejecting naturalism in the second.

(iii) NOT THE MEANING BUT THE CRITERION?

In the previous subsection we considered the possibility of deducing ethical conclusions directly from premises supplied by evolutionary biology. For any such move to be sound the prescription in the conclusion must be somehow incapsulated in the premises; for, by definition, a valid deduction is one in which you could not assert the premises and deny the conclusion without thereby contradicting yourself. A more modest suggestion, not always properly distinguished as such, is that, although the present meanings of our moral words cannot be explicated either wholly or partly in evolutionary terms, still evolution somehow supplies a necessary criterion. This seems to be the view of, for instance, Needham. For he welcomes the 'expulsion of ethics from biology and embryology' and notes: 'That *good* and *bad*, *noble* and *ignoble*, *beautiful* and *ugly*, *honourable* and *dishonourable*, are not terms with a biological meaning is a proposition which it has taken many centuries for biologists to realise.' Nevertheless, elsewhere he urges: 'The evolutionary process itself supplies us with a criterion of the good.'[80]

Now, assuming that our reading is correct, this move involves no crude attempt to deduce a moral *ought* from an evolutionary *is*. But Needham is still exposed to Russell's objection: 'If evolutionary ethics were sound, we ought to be entirely indifferent as to what the course of evolution may be, since whatever it is it is thereby proved to be the best.' The decisiveness of this objection was no doubt concealed from Needham by two things: first, the by now familiar ambiguity in the word 'evolution' (IV (ii) above); and second, his own conviction that, as a matter of contingent fact, biological evolution has a direction which he was prepared to rate as progressive (III (iv) above). The shift from the neutral to a commendatory sense of 'evolution' is well illustrated in the paragraph from which our second quotation is taken: in that particular sentence the sense must be the former. But two or three sentences further on it is equally clearly the latter: 'The kind of behaviour which has furthered man's social evolution in the past can be seen very well by viewing human history; and the great ethical teachers, from Confucius onwards, have shown us . . . how men may live together in harmony, employing their several talents to the general good.'[81]

It might perhaps be suggested that Russell's point really would lose its force if once it were to be conceded that, as a matter of contingent fact, evolution is tending to move, and is perhaps actually moving, in a commendable direction. If only, it might be urged, this were to be conceded, then there could be no objection to adopting some evolutionary criterion of the good; and we might proceed to argue that 'when we have found our Ten Commandments in general evolution' we can go on to 'discover our *Deuteronomy* in political analysis'.[82]

The one grain of truth in the main suggestion is that anyone equipped with such a mixed factual-cum-evaluative premise would be in a position to make valid inferences from purely factual evolutionary premises to evaluative conclusions. But, precisely because of the mixed character of this second premise, this must be without prejudice to anything so far said about inferences from purely factual premises to evaluative conclusions. What is not true in this suggestion is the heart of the matter, the idea that Russell's objection can be escaped by appealing to such a mixed premise. It cannot. For consider how the exchanges must go. The protagonist says that his criterion of the right is found in the actual direction of evolution. The deuteragonist replies that in that case the protagonist is committed to approving the direction of evolution quite regardless of what it may turn out to be. The latter then triumphantly appeals to his happy discovery that, as a matter of fact, the direction of evolution is as it ought to be. But now, on the protagonist's own chosen terms, this discovery must be wholly lacking in factual content. For, in so far as his criterion of the right lies in the actual direction of evolution, it becomes necessarily true that the actual direction is as it ought to be. The contingent fact to which the protagonist appealed thus disappears; but not before the very making of any such appeal has tacitly conceded Russell's point.

Waddington's striking employment of Biblical terms may usefully provoke the reflection that all the moves and counter-moves which we have been discussing here can be paralleled in discussions as to whether moral ideas can be defined in terms of the will of God, or whether — failing that — God's will could serve as an acceptable criterion of the right and the good. It might indeed even be urged that a main justification for going through all these moves and counter-moves at length here is as a training for recognising and dealing with mistakes of the same form made in other contexts.

Be that as it may, there certainly are some remarkable formal analogies between evolutionary ethics as expounded by Waddington and the arguments of those moral theologians who have tried to derive their often peculiarly clerical norms from the supposed intentions of nature: for instance, the argument — rather less frequently heard in the last year or two — that all 'artificial' contraception must be wrong because it involves a frustration of the natural function of sex, and so on.

Such comparisons will no doubt be disconcerting to both parties, but they surely ought to be more embarrassing to the secular. For if you are, however mistakenly, committed to the belief that the whole universe is an expression of the intentions of an omnipotent and righteous author, then this belief provides you with a positive reason both for accounting nature good and for speaking of intentions in this connection. But, for anyone who disowns such beliefs, to look to nature as his moral arbiter must be as incongruous and gratuitous as it is for the same person to hope to find some natural law of progress to do substitute duty for Providence (III (iv)–(vi) above). T. H. Huxley in his famous Romanes Lecture on 'Evolution and Ethics' may well have gone too far, particularly in replacing a positive connection by a negative rather than by no connection at all. But for an atheist or an agnostic his sort of approach is, surely, more appropriate: 'Let us understand, once for all, that the ethical progress of society depends, not on imitating the cosmic process, still less in running away from it, but in combating it.'[83]

Waddington has made several essays towards an evolutionary ethics. Indeed he was largely responsible for a revival of interest in the possibilities in Britain during the early 1940s: first by provoking a discussion in *Nature*; and then by editing a consequent book on *Science and Ethics*. We have noticed, and shall notice, his contributions to that book only incidentally: partly because Professor D. D. Raphael has already dealt very faithfully with them as part of his philosopher's contribution to a commemorative volume of *A Century of Darwin*; but mainly because Waddington has since made it clear that he would prefer to be judged by his later work on *The Ethical Animal*. In his contributions to *Science and Ethics* he seemed to be wanting to read norms off immediately from biological descriptions: 'It is a complicated matter to describe what is normal, as opposed to abnormal growth, but it can be done; and, once it is done there is a generally valid criterion of goodness in food. . . .'[84] But in the latter he advocates a rather more sophisticated operation: 'if we investigate by normal scientific methods the way in which the existence of ethical beliefs is involved in the causal nexus of the world's happenings, we shall be forced to conclude that the function of ethicising is to mediate the progress of human evolution. . . . We shall also find that this progress, in the world as a whole, exhibits a direction. . . . Putting these two points together we can define a criterion which does not depend for its validity on any pre-existing ethical belief', and he is most insistent that what is distinctive about his view is that this criterion is 'a criterion for deciding between alternative systems of belief'.[85]

It is hard to determine whether one ought to be more surprised or more distressed that Waddington should think that, by thus making his evolutionary criterion not directly a criterion of the right but rather a criterion for judging which is the best among rival systems of belief about what is right, he escapes objections of the kind we have been deploying. But, once the key passages have been picked out for attention, it is surely obvious that it does not. For what is a criterion for deciding which is best among rival systems of belief about what is right if it is not a means of deciding which set of beliefs is, on balance, the most correct (which exercise obviously necessitates some prior criterion of what is right)? If in reply it is suggested that Waddington's criterion is intended only as a criterion of the efficiency or otherwise of different systems of ethicising [*sic*] in their supposed biological function, 'to mediate the progress of human evolution', then the further question arises, whether the putative direction of human evolution is being taken to be commendable as such, or only in so far as the actual direction satisfies some other standards. If the former, then — in a catch-phrase of the old pre-television era — this is where we came in. If the latter, then, as far as our present sort of evolutionary ethics is concerned, that's that.

V. SEEING IN AN EVOLUTIONARY PERSPECTIVE

It might therefore seem that the conclusions of our long discussion should be what Mrs. Carlyle suggested at the beginning: in her emphatic way she 'did not feel that the slightest light could be thrown on my practical life for me, by having it ever so logically made out that my first ancestor, millions of millions of ages back, had been, or even had not been, an oyster'.[86] Yet even if we discount — as is nowadays generally and perhaps too easily done — any sort of possible implication for questions of religion, Mrs. Carlyle's conclusion is far too abrupt. For we have still to consider a third way of trying to bring the facts of evolutionary biology into relation with practical conclusions for morals and politics.

This third way consists in the relatively modest but nevertheless substantial contention that such practical and present questions can and should be seen in an evolutionary perspective. Julian Huxley, for instance, has in his time — as we have seen (III (iv) and (vi), and IV (ii), above) — explored other and stronger versions of evolutionary ethics. But it is this third contention which has survived and which is the guiding and unifying idea of both *Evolution in Action* (1953) and *Essays of a Humanist* (1964). The Preface to the former urges: 'It makes a great difference whether we think of the history of mankind as wholly apart from the rest of life, or as a continuation of the general evolutionary process, though with special characteristics of its own.'[87] Again, in the latter he writes: 'It is in large measure due to Darwin's work on biological evolution that we now possess this new vision of human destiny . . .'; which destiny 'is to be the chief agent for the future of evolution on this planet'; for, in the striking phrase already quoted from the earlier book, man 'finds himself in the unexpected position of business manager for the cosmic process of evolution'.[88]

But now, if the challenge of Mrs. Carlyle is to be met, two related questions have to be answered, and answered satisfactorily: first, why should the rest of us, who are not by training and inclination biologists, strive to think of things in this way; and second, what 'great difference' is it supposed to make if we do? Certainly, it is entirely natural for a professional biologist to see everything in this sort of perspective; and no doubt it is good for all of us to try from time to time to see things from such other points of view. But is there any reason for thinking that this evolutionary perspective is any more, or any less, valid than whatever might come naturally to someone else schooled in a different discipline? To an astronomer, perhaps, it might be equally natural to see things on scales by which man and life would not appear at all. And to the sort of eloquence about man's cosmic insignificance provoked by such considerations we may recall the robust response of Frank Ramsey, in the spirit of Mrs. Carlyle: 'My picture of the world is drawn in perspective, and not like a model to scale. The foreground is occupied by human beings and the stars are all as small as threepenny bits.'[89]

The first things which need to be said in reply to the challenge is that this evolutionary sort of way of looking at things presupposes various general propositions, and that these are in fact true. There may be some ways of looking at some things, or at all things, with regard to which no issues of truth or falsehood arise at all. But where, as here, they do arise, we surely must insist, as a necessary though not necessarily a sufficient condition of the acceptability of the way in question, that the propositions concerned are either known or reasonably believed to be true (or, of course, justifiably entertained for some legitimate speculative or imaginative purpose). We must not with a too easy catholicity allow, without ever first examining the truth of all their would-be factual presuppositions, that the professional points of view of the astrologer, the psychoanalyst, the theologian, and the evolutionary biologist are all equally valid and acceptable.

For us the relevant general propositions are the claim that the history of mankind is a continuation of the general evolutionary process, and the claim that the future of this entire process — the future of all other living things as well as of mankind — lies largely or wholly in human hands. We have already said something about the second of these two claims (III (vi) above). The first requires a little exposition. For it involves a certain extension and development of the ideas of the *Origin*, the sort of extension and development which Darwin himself began in *The Descent of Man*. The crux is the generalisation of the insistence on the continuity of evolution, the denial of any sort of special creation at any stage, and the application of this to man: 'He who is not content to look, like a savage, at the phenomena of nature as disconnected, cannot any longer believe that man is the work of a special act of creation.'[90]

The full significance of this first claim can, as so often, be best brought out by considering what is being rejected. Darwin wrote, in the final paragraph of his concluding chapter: 'Man may be excused for feeling some pride at having risen, though not through his own exertions, to the very summit of the organic scale. . . . We must, however, acknowledge . . . that man with all his noble qualities . . . with his god-like intellect which has penetrated into the movements and constitution of the solar system. . . . Man still bears in his bodily frame the indelible stamp of his lowly origin.'[91] That qualification 'in his bodily frame' produces an understatement. For the whole argument of the book is against any such limitation which would leave room for the idea of the special creation of incorporeal souls as potentially immortal subjects of the distinctively human attributes. Darwin as much as Huxley was therefore committed to rejecting what is surely an essential doctrine of the Roman Catholic faith: for while — generously — 'the teaching of the Church leaves the doctrine of evolution an open question, as long as it confines its speculations to the development, from other living matter already in existence, of the human body'; nevertheless, 'That souls are immediately created by God is a view which the Catholic faith imposes on us.'[92]

It is nowadays unfashionable to draw attention to such conflicts. Yet they do have to be recognised if we are going to understand how much may be involved in seeing in an evolutionary perspective. This particular conflict is one of the grounds to which we must look to appreciate the soundness of Royce's assessment, quoted on page 216, of the 'importance to philosophy' of Darwin's work: 'Once man himself was accepted as a natural product of the evolutionary process, the rest of the Cartesian compromise could hardly be maintained. It was this obvious extension of the Darwinian theory, rather than the actual argument of the *Origin*, which was the occasion for Bishop Wilberforce's scurrilous attack at the British Association meeting of 1860.'[93] And that Wittgenstein should have even seemed to be denying the importance of these 'philosophical implications of Darwinism' is an indication of an obsessively narrow conception of philosophy: 'The history of ideas is', as one of its masters has remarked, 'no subject for highly departmentalised minds; and it is pursued with some difficulty in an age of departmentalised minds.'[94]

Darwin is thus himself developing in the *Descent* a thesis implicit already in the *Origin*: that man is wholly a part of nature; and that there is no need or warrant to appeal to special interventions to account for any stage or aspect of his origin and development. As applied to ethics in particular this involves that all moral ideas and ideals have originated in the world; and that, having thus in the past been subject to change, they will presumably in the future too, for better or for worse, continue to evolve.

Something must now be said, both about the sense of 'imply' in which the general thesis, as applied to man, is implicit in the *Origin*, and about what is and is not necessarily involved in such a claim that moral ideas and ideals have evolved and will presumably continue to evolve.

First, it is a weak but widespread sense of 'imply', one of special importance in the history of ideas, yet one which because it has had so little attention from philosophers is hard to characterise satisfactorily. We shall try briefly to suggest the sort of thing which is and is not involved, though this weak kind of implication does need far more thorough examination than it can have here. To assert any proposition commits you, on pain of self-contradiction, to accept all the logical consequences of that proposition: for the simple but sufficient reason that 'logical consequence' is defined as something which cannot be denied without contradicting the original assertion. Now the theory of the *Origin* certainly could without difficulty be formulated, even if it is not already, in such a way that an adherent of that theory was not logically required, not required on pain of self-contradiction, to accept the application of its key ideas to our own species — on the lines indicated in the *Descent*. There need, that is to say, be no formal logical inconsistency in at one and the same time asserting the origin of all other species of animals ('the brutes') and of plants by natural selection, while nevertheless denying such an origin for men — or perhaps only for their supposed incorporeal souls.

Nevertheless, even though the application of the original theory (or of the original theory suitably amended) to our species may not in the stronger sense be logically implied, it certainly is in a weaker sense implicit. For, unless some very potent positive reason can be produced for granting a special exemption, the refusal to include mankind in the scope of the theory must be in the last degree arbitrary, and thus unreasonable right up towards the point of, even though it may not actually involve, self-contradiction. Similarly, though it is again surely not actually contradictory to maintain that evolution by natural selection is the means chosen by Omnipotence in order to produce our own privileged species, the contention is at least at first sight — what shall we say? — incongruous. To that extent, and in that sense, a radical and comprehensive naturalism must appear to be implicit in Darwinism. (A few paragraphs back we said that one reason for denying that Darwin's theory had any philosophical implications was a concentration on a very narrow sense of 'philosophy'. We can now add, and a very strict sense of 'implication'.)

Both the positions mentioned in the previous paragraph may instructively be compared with that developed in Philip Gosse's too easily ridiculed and too rarely read book, *The Natural History of Creation* (*Omphalos*). Gosse was writing at a time when uniformitarian and evolutionary views had long since become the almost universally accepted orthodoxy in geology, but when — incongruously, but strictly not inconsistently — most biologists still believed that each species had been independently created. *Omphalos* was in fact published just two years before *The Origin of Species*, in 1857. What Gosse emphasised, and what most of his scientific colleagues chose to forget, was that any special creation of any creature which is to be truly a member of whatever particular species is in question must be a creation at some particular stages in various cycles. Gosse also urged that the same sort of thing applies to geological and other phenomena too. But in so far as this is true, any specially created thing must at the moment of creation contain 'traces' of a past which it has not in fact had. Just as the trunks of specially created trees must, if they are to be true adult specimens of their kinds, have growth rings indicating their annual progress through the years they never had, so also specially created rocks, if they too are to be true specimens of their kinds, must contain their own appropriate 'traces' of their past which never was — including in particular, in some cases, fossils.

To the whole-hearted scientific naturalist such consequences of doctrines of special creation are bound to be altogether incredible; and no doubt Gosse should have seen that he had produced a triumphant reduction to absurdity of an idea incongruous with the whole spirit and method of science. Yet no one who was prepared — as almost all Gosse's contemporaries at the time of the publication of *Omphalos* were — to go on accepting the conventional wisdom about the special creation of species had any business to despise him — as they mostly did — when with learning and candour he presented these consequences as they applied to things organic and inorganic both, and when he honestly and boldly accepted and proclaimed them for true as being indeed clear consequences of other and more fundamental things which he also held for true. *Omphalos* is, of course, the book of a deluded fanatic. But it is neither mean, nor evasive, nor time-serving, nor muddleheaded.

Returning to the *Descent*, our second question is about the bearing of the Darwinian claim that moral ideas and ideals have evolved and presumably will continue to evolve. One thing which is certainly not a necessary consequence of this claim, though it is too often thought that it is, is that all or any moral claims are unimportant and lacking in any sort of authority. Thus to Hume — the first considerable philosopher in the modern period to develop a world-outlook which was through and through secular, this-

ANTONY FLEW

worldly, and man-centred — to argue that morality is rooted in human needs and human inclinations, and these needs and inclinations which we in some measure share with the higher animals, was the very reverse of depreciatory. This point was taken by Darwin too. It was seen as a sign of grace in him by some of the Victorian first reviewers of the *Descent*.[95] What and all that may be implicit, in the weak if not the strong sense, in the discovery that moral ideas and ideals have evolved, is that moral claims cannot possess any supernatural authority. But that is a very different thing from being unimportant, or lacking any sort of authority at all.

Again, it is not, though it is too often mistaken to be, a part or a consequence of the argument of the *Descent* that human phenomena must be equated with their sub-human origins. It is, therefore, quite wrong to complain: 'Thus, as he earlier reduced language to the grunts and growls of a dog, he now contrived to reduce religion to the lick of the dog's tongue and the wagging of his tail.'[96] Not merely is such an equation not a part or consequence of, it must be strictly incompatible with, an evolutionary doctrine. For evolution entails change and, unless the process of change has turned full circle, this entails difference — which means that, with that one biologically irrelevant exception, if A has evolved from B, A cannot be the same as B.

On the other hand what is, surely, at least in the weak sense, implicit in a vision of ethics as subject to evolution is, first, a critical approach to all first-order moral issues and second, an insistence on completely naturalistic answers to second-order questions about the nature of ethics. No doubt one could, without any strict and formal inconsistency, allow moral evolution, for better and for worse, to be a fact, while still insisting that some favoured actual moral norms are not merely right — which some indeed surely are — but somehow in principle beyond all need for justification and all possibility of criticism. The epistemological correlate of such a view will usually be that the favoured norms are recognised as the right ones by (favoured) intuition. No doubt too it could similarly be strictly consistent to admit the same general fact while still maintaining that some particular known standards are in some way divinely revealed and endorsed. Yet either or both these positions must surely be awkward and uncomfortable — wide open to charges of arbitrariness and special pleading.

By contrast, other approaches to moral questions and accounts of their nature — those of Hume, for instance — can accommodate themselves very comfortably with the fact of general and moral evolution; and indeed some — Hume again provides an example — might almost seem to demand an evolutionary background. An example of the other sort would be *Principia Ethica*. For Moore's book, though he presumably had the advantage of knowing and accepting the main lines of Darwin's thought, is, as has frequently been observed, curiously parochial. The argument proceeds as it were in suspense outside space and time; and, incidentally, in complete isolation from the progress of the natural and the human sciences. The values which were to prove so acceptable to Bloomsbury seem to be taken as luminously self-evident.[97] Such 'Intuitionist ethics is a kind of secularised version of the ethics of Divine command in which the supernatural lawgiver is internalised . . .';[98] and in this it, like its unsecularised original, is incongruous, though not necessarily incompatible, with the facts of human evolution.

This then provides the first and most extensive part of the answer to Mrs. Carlyle. The case for urging the need to see morality — or anything else — in an evolutionary perspective must, of course, start from the contention that an evolutionary account of its genesis and future is in fact correct; and in this philosophical context we have throughout been taking the truth of that surely not very seriously disputatious scientific contention for granted. But if once we do grant this, and — to adapt a phrase used by Mrs. Carlyle's husband — 'Gad! we'd better!', then it has certain implications both for ethics and for meta-ethics, in the weak but important sense of 'implication' rather sketchily explained above.

Two other lines of justification can be dealt with here very shortly, though the relative brevity is not necessarily an indication of relative unimportance. Both are the sorts of justification which can be, and tediously but none the less truly often are, offered for 'taking the wider view'. The first is that it may enable us to see things which do not emerge so easily, or perhaps at all, if we limit ourselves to a more parochial survey. Julian Huxley again constitutes an excellent example. For it was precisely his evolutionary vision which enabled him to recognise clearly, long locust years before this was even as widely admitted as it now is, that human fertility represents the number-one threat to the present and future welfare of the human race. It is this same evolutionary vision, rooted in the facts of biology, which links this human concern with a driving anxiety for the conservation of wild life, and which also opens up an awareness of the possibilities of eugenics as a challenge to research and action.[99]

The second is that some men have a longing 'to see things as a whole', to find some deep, comprehensive, unifying perspective against which they may set their everyday lives. No philosopher can afford either to despise or not to share such yearnings; and the evolutionary vision possesses the certainly neither universal nor despicable merit of being based upon, and not incompatible with any, known facts. The passage of Julian Huxley from which we have quoted already will bear repetition in full: 'In the light of evolutionary biology man can now see himself as the sole agent of further evolutionary advance on this planet, and one of the few possible instruments of progress in the universe at large. He finds himself in the unexpected position of business manager for the cosmic process of evolution. He no longer ought to feel separated from the rest of nature, for he is part of it — that part which has become conscious, capable of love and understanding and aspiration. He need no longer regard himself as insignificant in relation to the cosmos.'[100]

NOTES

The references in these notes are for the sake of brevity all given by the name of the author only, followed where necessary by an arabic number in brackets to indicate which work is referred to, and then the page number or the number of the chapter and/or section in point. The Bibliography provides the key needed for the interpretation of these references.

I should also like here to thank Dr. W. D. Hudson, the General Editor of the present volumes, Professor R. F. Atkinson, at that time still a colleague at Keele, Mr. John Grundy, and Miss Faith Heathcote for reading this whole study in draft and for making a large number of suggestions. These have in sum led to a substantial improvement in the final version as now published.

1. Spencer, vol. i, p. viii; punctuation adjusted.
2. Ritchie, § 1.
3. Malthus, p. 17.
4. Wittgenstein, p. 29.
5. Toulmin, p. 465.
6. Engels, pp. 19, 208–10; but cf. Willey, pp. 14 ff.
7. Quoted in Hofstadter, p. 31. It is wholly appropriate that this quotation should be found in a chapter on 'The Vogue of Spencer'. For Herbert Spencer too was an advocate of self-reliant individualism in a freely competitive economy, always boasted of being an evolutionary thinker, and had an enormous influence in the U.S.A. Hofstadter's source is W. J. Ghent, *Our Benevolent Feudalism* (Macmillan, New York, 1902), and Ghent's, as I know, thanks to my colleague Mr. Francis Celoria, who examined the British Museum copy for me, is anonymous: 'Mr. Rockefeller appeals both to evolution and to divine sanction . . . he is reported as declaring in one of his Sunday-school addresses. . . .' (Ghent, p. 29).
8. Marx (1).
9. Ferri, p. v.
10. Ibid., pp. vii–viii.
11. Ibid., p. 1.
12. Ibid., pp. 136, 140.
13. Lovejoy (2), p. 268; cf. Lovejoy (1), *passim*.
14. Lucretius, v. 790–2, 832–5, 837–41, 845–8, 855–9.

15. Kirk and Raven, pp. 336–40.

16. Darwin (3), p. 140.

17. Pantin, p. 137; italics in original. In the next few paragraphs I re-traverse some, but only some, of the ground covered in an earlier essay on 'The Structure of Darwinism' (Flew (2)).

18. Darwin (1), p. 2.

19. Ibid., p. 3.

20. Ibid.; the italics are as in the original, but here and elsewhere the capitalisation and inverted commas in quotations have been made to conform with the conventions followed in the rest of the present study.

21. Darwin (1), p. 50.

22. Ibid., pp. 102–3.

23. E. Gosse, pp. 66 ff.; cf. P. Gosse, *passim*.

24. Darwin (1), p. 4.

25. Ibid., p. 131.

26. Darwin (2), p. viii.

27. Darwin (1), pp. 413–14.

28. Ibid., pp. 424–5.

29. Ritchie, p. 76.

30. Ibid., pp. 12–13, 28.

31. Darwin (1), pp. 102–3.

32. See, for instance, Spencer, vol. ii, *passim*; and cf. Hofstadter, ch. 2.

33. See, for supporting argument, Flew (6), ch. 2.

34. See, for supporting argument, Flew (1).

35. Manser; and cf. Flew (5).

36. Tennyson, p. 243.

37. Hegel, p. 216, and cf. p. 375; the phrase is actually an un-acknowledged borrowing from Schiller.

38. Darwin (1), pp. 234, 428.

39. Auden, p. 119.

40. Darwin and Seward, vol. i, p. 114 n.

41. Marx (2), p. xix.

42. J. S. Huxley (1), pp. 17, 19, 58.

43. Ibid., pp. 34, 35, 59.

44. Ibid., pp. 78–79.

45. Spender and Lehmann, p. 56.

46. Needham (1), pp. 16, 41, 266; italics in both cases original.

47. Needham (2), pp. 209–10.

48. Needham (1), pp. 266 ff.

49. Dutt, in *The Communist International* for 1935; quoted in Needham (1), p. 267.

50. For further development of this theme in this and similar contexts see Flew (3), ch. 6.

51. Cornforth, pp. 332–3.

52. Quinton, p. 120.

53. J. S. Huxley (3), p. 132.

54. Needham (1), pp. 32 ff., 160 ff., 243 ff., and *passim*.

55. Spender and Lehmann, pp. 56, 58.

56. Darwin (1), p. 429.

57. Chandler, p. 46.

58. Himmelfarb, p. 351.

59. See Manser; and cf. Flew (5).

60. Trevor-Roper, pp. 39, 51; and cf., perhaps more accessibly, Bullock, pp. 36, 89, 398–9, 672, 693.

61. Booth, p. 44; T. H. Huxley, perhaps a trifle unfairly, drew attention to this passage in a letter to *The Times* on 29 December 1890.

62. Peirce, vol. vi, pp. 293, 298.

63. See MacIntyre, Atkinson, Hunter, and Flew and Hunter; the whole controversy is now conveniently collected in Chappell, pp. 240–307.

64. See Searle; and cf. Flew (4).

65. Quinton, pp. 110–11; punctuation made to conform.

66. Einstein, p. 114.

67. J. S. Huxley (2), p. 124.

68. Ibid., pp. 125, 214.

69. Spender, vol. ii, pp. vi, 25, 260.

70. Ibid., vol. i, pp. 25 (italics supplied), 46; vol. ii, p. 432.

71. T. H. Huxley (2), p. 80.

72. Russell, p. 24.

73. Quillian, pp. 78, 95.

74. See especially ibid., p. 137; and cf. p. 109.

75. Moore, pp. 38, 39–40.

76. Ibid., p. 41; italics in original.

77. Hume (1), title-page.

78. Newton, especially pp. 124–5; the same, idea is, of course, found earlier — in Galileo, for instance, and among the Greek atomists.

79. Hume (2), p. 23 n.

80. Needham (1), pp. 151 (italics supplied), 56.

81. Ibid., p. 56.

82. Waddington (1), p. 125. Entirely by the way: if we are going to bring in pre-Columbian Mexico — or anything else — let us get it right. The author on the previous page conjures up 'an Aztec of Chicken [*sic*] Itza', whereas in fact Chichen Itza was founded by the Maya, was later taken over by the Toltecs, but was never Aztec.

83. T. H. Huxley (2), p. 82.
84. Waddington (1), p. 41.
85. Waddington (2), pp. 59, 173.
86. Carlyle, vol. iii pp. 20–21.
87. J. S. Huxley (3), p. vii.
88. J. S. Huxley (4), pp. 37, 132.
89. Ramsey, p. 291; and cf. Flew and Hepburn.
90. Darwin (2), p. 927.
91. Ibid., pp. 946–7.
92. Pius XII, p. 30.
93. Toulmin and Goodfield, p. 240.
94. Lovejoy (2), p. 22.
95. For the references, see the notes to pp. 294–5 of Himmelfarb.
96. Himmelfarb, p. 307.
97. Moore, especially ch. 6; and cf. Keynes.
98. Quinton, p. 128.
99. J. S. Huxley (4), *passim*.
100. J. S. Huxley (3), p. 132.

SELECT BIBLIOGRAPHY

We have tried to notice in the text all the works which in compiling the present study we have found useful, and some others too. This Select Bibliography therefore draws special attention to a few of these works, marked with an asterisk in the General Bibliography, where their full particulars will be found. The basic points of reference should, for reasons given in the text, be two works of Darwin: first, *The Origin of Species*, especially chap. xiv; and second, *The Descent of Man*, part i, especially chapts. iii and iv.

For a survey of the actual impact of Darwinian ideas, or ideas thought to be Darwinian, on moral and political thinking in one country see Hofstadter's *Social Darwinism in American Thought (1860-1915)*. Two other historical studies can also be recommended: first, Quillian's *The Moral Theory of Evolutionary Naturalism*; and second, Wiener's *Evolution and the Founders of Pragmatism*. A useful secondary source for accounts of the ideas of a baker's dozen of nineteenth-century contributors to *Evolutional Ethics* is part i of the book of that title by C. M. Williams; and its part ii constitutes a specimen of the sort of thing usually involved, a specimen none the less valuable for this purpose for being from the pen of a writer very definitely not of the first rank.

Such primary sources as Spencer's *The Principles of Ethics* or Stephen's *The Science of Ethics* generally make protracted and unrewarding reading. But this certainly does not apply to T. H. Huxley's Romanes Lecture on 'Evolution and Ethics', re-issued along with various pieces by his grandson as a book under the same title. T. H. Huxley's acceptance of a gladiatorial view of sub-human nature, and his deliberate rejection of this as a human ideal, can be most interestingly contrasted with Kropotkin's stress on *Mutual Aid* at the sub-human as well as the human level, and the contention in his *Ethics* 'that not only does Nature fail to give us a lesson of amoralism . . . but . . . *the very ideas of bad and good . . .*

have been borrowed from Nature' (p. 16; italics original). In studying Bagehot's curiously titled *Physics and Politics* it is salutary to read the author's remarks on 'unfit men and beaten races' aloud in a German accent. Among works wholly of our century we can for the various reasons indicated in the text recommend Needham's *Time: the Refreshing River*, Julian Huxley's *Essays of a Humanist*, and Waddington's *Science and Ethics*.

GENERAL BIBLIOGRAPHY

Atkinson, R. F., '"Hume on *is* and *ought*": a Reply to Mr. MacIntyre,' *Philosophical Review*, vol. lxx (1961).

Auden, W. H., *Collected Shorter Poems* (1930–1944), (Faber, London, 1950).

Bagehot, W., *Physics and Politics*, ed. J. Barzun (Knopf, New York, 1948).

Booth, W., *In Darkest England, and the Way Out* (Salvation Army, London, 1890).

Bullock, A., *Hitler: a Study in Tyranny* (Penguin Books, Harmondsworth, 1962).

Carlyle, J. W., *Letters and Memorials* (Longmans, Green, London, 1883).

Chambers, R., *Vestiges of the Natural History of Creation* (12th edn., 1844; W. & R. Chambers, London and Edinburgh, 1884).

Chandler, R., *Farewell, My Lovely* (Penguin Books, Harmondsworth, 1949).

Chappell, V. C. (ed.), *Hume, a Collection of Critical Essays* (Doubleday–Anchor, New York, 1966; Macmillan, London, 1968).

Cornforth, M., *Marxism and the Linguistic Philosophy* (Lawrence & Wishart, London, 1965).

*Darwin, C. (1), *The Origin of Species* (6th edn., J. Murray, London, 1872).

—— (2), *The Descent of Man* (new edn., J. Murray, London, 1901).

*Darwin, C. (3), *The Autobiography of Charles Darwin*, ed. N. Barlow (Collins, London, 1958). It is important to use this first complete edition, since all earlier — and some later — editions omit various remarks about religion.

Darwin, F., and Seward, A. C., *More Letters of Charles Darwin* (J. Murray, London, 1903).

Denzinger, H. (ed.), *Enchiridion Symbolorum* (29th rev. edn., Herder, Freiburg-im-Breisgau, 1953).

Einstein, A., *Out of My Later Years* (Thames & Hudson, London, 1950).

Engels, F., *Dialectics of Nature* (paperback edn., International Publishers, New York, 1963).

Ferri, E., *Socialism and Positive Science* (Independent Labour Party, London, 1906).

Flew, Antony, (1), 'Motives and the Unconscious', in *Minnesota Studies in the Philosophy of Science*: I. *The Foundations of Science and the Concepts of Psychology and Psychoanalysis*, ed. H. Feigl and M. Scriven (Minnesota U.P., Minneapolis, 1956).

—— (2), 'The Structure of Darwinism', in *New Biology 28* (Penguin Books, Harmondsworth, 1959).

—— (3), *Hume's Philosophy of Belief* (Routledge & Kegan Paul, London, 1961).

—— (4), 'On not Deriving *ought* from *is*', *Analysis*, vol. xxv (1964–5).

—— (5), '"The Concept of Evolution": a Comment', *Philosophy*, vol. xli, no. 155 (1966).

—— (6), *God and Philosophy* (Hutchinson, London, 1966).

—— and Hepburn, R., 'Problems of Perspective', in *The Plain View*, vol. vii (Ethical Union, London, 1955).

—— and Hunter, G., '"The Interpretation of Hume" and a Rejoinder to the Same', *Philosophy*, vol. xxxviii (1963).

Ghent, W. J., *Our Benevolent Feudalism* (Macmillan, New York, 1902).

Gosse, E., *Father and Son* (Four Square Books — Landsborough, London, 1959).

Gosse, P. H., *The Natural History of Creation* (Van Voorst, London, 1857).

Hegel, G. W. F., *Hegel's Philosophy of Right*, trans. and ed. T. M. Knox (Oxford U.P., London, 1942).

Himmelfarb, G., *Darwin and the Darwinian Revolution* (Chatto & Windus, London, 1959).

*Hofstadter, R., *Social Darwinism in American Thought* (*1860–1915*) (Pennsylvania U.P., Philadelphia, 1944).

Hume, D. (1), *A Treatise of Human Nature*, ed. L. A. Selby-Bigge (Oxford U.P., London, 1896).

—— (2), *An Inquiry Concerning Human Understanding*, ed. C. W. Hendel (Liberal Arts Press, New York, 1955). The passage quoted is a note to § 1, found only in the first and second editions of Hume's lifetime.

Hunter, G., 'Hume on *is* and *ought*', *Philosophy*, vol. xxxvii, no. 140 (1962).

Huxley, J. S. (1), *Essays of a Biologist* (1923; Penguin Books edn., Harmondsworth, 1939).

*—— (2), contributions to J. S. and T. H. Huxley, *Evolution and Ethics* (Pilot Press, London, 1947).

—— (3), *Evolution in Action* (Chatto & Windus, London, 1953).

*—— (4), *Essays of a Humanist* (first paperback edn., Penguin Books, Harmondsworth, 1966).

Huxley, T. H. (1), 'The Progress of Science', in *Collected Essays*, vol. i (Macmillan, London, 1894).

*—— (2), 'Evolution and Ethics', in J. S. and T. H. Huxley, *Evolution and Ethics* (Pilot Press, London, 1947).

Keynes, J. M., 'My Early Beliefs', in *Two Memoirs* (Hart-Davis, London, 1949).

Kirk, G. S., and Raven, J. E., *The Pre-Socratic Philosophers* (Cambridge U.P., Cambridge, 1957).

*Kropotkin, P. (1), *Mutual Aid: a Factor in Evolution* (Heinemann, London, 1907).

*—— (2), *Ethics: Origin and Development* (Harrap, London, 1924).

Lewis, J., *Man and Evolution* (Lawrence & Wishart, London, 1962).

Lovejoy, A. O. (1), 'Some Eighteenth-Century Evolutionists', in *Popular Science Monthly*, vol. lxv (Science Press, New York, 1904).

Lovejoy, A. O. (2), *The Great Chain of Being* (Harper Torchbooks, New York, 1960).

Lucretius, T., *de Rerum Natura*, trans. W. H. D. Rouse (Loeb Classical Library: Heinemann and Harvard U.P., London and Cambridge, Mass., 1947).

MacIntyre, A. C., 'Hume on *is* and *ought*', *Philosophical Review*, vol. lxviii (1959).

Malthus, T. R., *Population: the First Essay* (Michigan U.P., Ann Arbor, 1959). There is so great a difference between the first and all later editions of the *Essay on Population* that the convention has been introduced, and is here followed, of referring to the former as the *First Essay* and to the latter as the *Second Essay*.

Manser, A. R., 'The Concept of Evolution', *Philosophy*, vol. xl, no. 151 (1965).

Marx, K. (1), Letter to F. Lassalle, dated 16 January 1861.

—— (2) *Capital*, translated from the third German edition by S. Moore and E. Aveling; reprinted as re-edited by D. Torr (Allen & Unwin, London, 1938).

Moore, G. E., *Principia Ethica* (Cambridge U.P., Cambridge, 1903).

*Needham, J. (1), *Time: the Refreshing River* (Allen & Unwin, London, 1943).

—— (2), *History is on Our Side* (Allen & Unwin, London, 1946).

Newton, I., *Opticks* (paperback edn., Dover, New York, 1952).

Pantin, C. F., 'The Origin of Species', in *The History of Science*, ed. Jean Lindsay (Cohen & West, London, 1953).

Peirce, C. S., *Collected Papers*, ed. C. Hartshorne and P. Weiss (Harvard U.P., Cambridge (Mass.), 1931–5).

Pius XII, Pope, *Humani Generis* (False Trends in Modern Teaching), trans. R. A. Knox (Catholic Truth Society, London, 1953). The Latin text of the passage quoted can be found as Denzinger, § 3027.

Popper, K. R., *The Poverty of Historicism* (Routledge & Kegan Paul, London, 1957).

Quillian, W. F., *The Moral Theory of Evolutionary Naturalism* (Yale U.P., New Haven, 1945).

Quinton, A. M., 'Ethics and the Theory of Evolution', in *Biology and Personality*, ed. I. T. Ramsey (Blackwell, Oxford, 1966).

Ramsey, F. P., *The Foundations of Mathematics* (Routledge & Kegan Paul, London, 1931).

Raphael, D. D., 'Darwinism and Ethics', in *A Century of Darwin*, ed. S. A. Barnett (Heinemann, London, 1958).

Ritchie, D. G., *Darwinism and Politics* (2nd edn., Sonnenschein & Scribner, London and New York, 1890).

Royce, J., *The Spirit of Modern Philosophy* (Houghton Mifflin, New York, 1892).

Russell, B. A. W., *Philosophical Essays* (rev. edn., Allen & Unwin, London, 1966).

Searle, J. R., 'How to Derive *ought* from *is*', *Philosophical Review*, vol. lxxiii (1964).

Spencer, H., *The Principles of Ethics* (Williams & Norgate, London, 1892–93).

Spender, J., and Lehmann, J. (eds.), *Poems for Spain* (Hogarth Press, London, 1939).

Stephen, L., *The Science of Ethics* (2nd edn., Smith, Elder & Co., London, 1907).

Tennyson, A., *The Poetical Works of Tennyson* (Oxford U.P., London, 1953).

Toulmin, S. E., 'World Stuff and Nonsense', *The Cambridge Journal*, vol. i (1947–8).

—— and Goodfield, J., *The Discovery of Time* (Hutchinson, London, 1965).

Trevor-Roper, H. R. (ed.), *Hitler's Table Talk* (Weidenfeld & Nicolson, London, 1953).

*Waddington, C. H. (1) (ed.), *Science and Ethics* (Allen & Unwin, London, 1942).

—— (2), *The Ethical Animal* (Allen & Unwin, London, 1960).

*Wiener, P. P., *Evolution and the Founders of Pragmatism* (Harvard U.P., Cambridge, Mass., 1949).

Willey, B., *Darwin and Butler* (Chatto & Windus, London, 1960).

*Williams, C. M., *Evolutional Ethics* (Macmillan, London and New York, 1893).

Wittgenstein, L., *Tractatus Logico-Philosophicus* (Routledge & Kegan Paul, London, 1923).

4

MARXISM AND ETHICS

EUGENE KAMENKA

ACKNOWLEDGEMENTS

Work on this study was begun in the Institute of Advanced Studies of the Australian National University in Canberra and completed in the Research Institute on Communist Affairs in Columbia University in the City of New York; I owe much to the excellent conditions for research and writing offered by both Institutes. Mrs E. Y. Short of the Australian National University gave me a great deal of help with bibliographical problems and references; I am very grateful to her. The Research Institute on Communist Affairs in Columbia University offered me a senior fellowship during my sabbatical leave (January 1968–January 1969) so that I might complete this and another study. Mrs Christine Dodson and the staff of the Institute have helped me to prepare the manuscript for publication.

EUGENE KAMENKA

I. INTRODUCTION

Readers of a series devoted to the various types of ethical theory from the Greeks to the present day may well have expected this component study to bear the simple title, *Marxist Ethics*. Such a title would have been misleading. Marx himself wrote nothing substantial or systematic on the problems of ethical theory or moral philosophy as such; his disciples, beginning with Engels, have distinguished themselves in this field mainly by their philosophical dilettantism and consequent *naïveté*. At a time when serious philosophers were beginning to see that further progress in ethics required careful logical analysis, the disentangling of issues and the solution of certain quite fundamental logical problems, Marxist writers approached the subject with complete disdain for technical questions and a fundamental inability to grasp the difficulty of the problems they were pretending to tackle. Much, indeed most, of their writing was popular in character and pamphleteering in spirit, directed against the moral pundit and the street-corner revivalist, against 'Christian' or 'bourgeois' ethics in their crudest form. In relation to the genuine logical concerns and insights of a Plato, a Butler, a Hume or a Kant most of the Marxist arguments were simply part of a tedious *ignoratio elenchi*.

The penalty imposed on the amateur is that he relives, unwittingly, the history of the subject. He sincerely presents as his own discoveries views that have already been held, elaborated, discussed and exposed at a higher level; he jumbles together what the professional, with care and devotion, has long since shown to be distinct and mutually inconsistent. Marxists, in fact, have failed to develop an original or comparatively coherent view of ethics that can be ranked as 'a type of ethical theory' finding its natural logical place beside utilitarian ethics, ethical intuitionism, existentialist ethics, or even Greek ethics. In the work of the

Marxists and, to a lesser extent, in the work of Marx himself, we find an uncritical conflation of ethical relativism, evolutionary ethics, the ethic of self-determination and self-realisation, utilitarian strains, the ethic of co-operation and a kind of social subjectivism, all assumed or proclaimed rather than argued for. The work of disentangling these strands, and of assessing the place of each strand in Marxist thinking about ethics, has been left almost entirely to those examining the Marxist position from outside. When such examination is carried out, the illusion of a coherent and worked-out Marxist position in ethics disappears, together with the illusion that the works of Marx and Engels, let alone those of their professed disciples, form a single and unambiguous intellectual system. We are left, as this study will attempt to show, with what is at most a number of insights, noticeably provided by Marx and not by his disciples. These insights might be relevant to someone else's attempt to deal with the problems of ethics in a serious and professional way. They constitute *reminders*, things ethical theorists should not forget, rather than propositions on which an ethical theory can be based. It is for this reason that I have chosen to call this study *Marxism and Ethics*.

To say that Marxism has nothing worthy of being called a serious position in ethical philosophy is not to say that ethics is peripheral to Marxism, or to Marx's own thinking about society. In a book written some years ago – *The Ethical Foundations of Marxism* – I attempted to bring out the ethical beliefs and hopes that lay at the centre of Marx's position and made him a radical critic of bourgeois society. Marx's primitive ethic, as I called it then, was in my view utopian and involved certain fundamental logical confusions, but it was by no means a mere set of unworked-out moral preferences and moral prejudices, as some of Marx's more old-fashioned or less scholarly critics sometimes still maintain. Marx's own ethical impulse stems from Rousseau and Kant and the ethic of German romanticism; his roots lie in an important ethical and intellectual tradition. As Marx the philosopher became somewhat submerged beneath Marx the social scientist this ethical impulse was to some extent hidden from view by accretions from other sources – by the materialist critique of moralities, by Darwinian strains, by a concentration on material needs that bore a superficial resemblance to utilitarianism. To some, perhaps even to most, of his disciples, these accretions seemed the very essence of Marxist ethics. In this study I shall therefore attempt to combine history and analysis, a discussion of the varieties of ethic in Marxism with a discussion of the significance of Marxism for the theory of ethics. I shall distinguish between the various ethical strains found in the work of Marx and Marxists and between the various periods in the life of Marx and in the life of the movement erected in his name. We should especially guard against conflating and confusing the views of Marx with the cruder, more naïve versions of his thought publicised by Engels. The primitive ethic of Karl Marx and its revival in the current cult of alienation and the young Marx form the subject of Chapters II and III, the more traditional Marxist attempt to deal with ethics in terms of the 'materialist interpretation of history' is discussed in Chapters IV and V, while Soviet attempts to create a formal, philosophical discipline called 'Marxist ethics' are examined in Chapter VI. Marxism as a distinctive intellectual view is disintegrating in ethics, as in all other fields; it has left behind it a legacy of 'reminders' rather than a foundation for moral philosophy or a key to the solution of ethical disputes. The importance of these reminders at any particular time is directly proportionate to the social *naïveté* and lack of historical sense of those who write about ethics.

II. THE ETHICAL IMPULSE IN THE WORK OF KARL MARX

Until recently, the important implications of classical Marxism for moral philosophy have been taken to lie in its critique of objectivism in ethics, in its 'exposure' of the pretended impartiality and universality of moral injunctions and codes. 'Reason', Hume had said, 'is the slave of the passions'; morality, Marx and Engels appeared to be claiming, is the slave of interest. Marx's 'materialist' conception of history, according to his disciples, showed that moral codes and beliefs were man-dependent, born of man's social situation and varying as that situation varied. Since there was no 'man in general', since there were only specific men belonging to this or that specific social class, there was no morality in general. There were only specific *moralities*, reflecting the specific interests, demands and situations of specific classes, conflicting as these classes conflict. Moral codes or beliefs could therefore not be treated as true or false, valid or invalid, *in themselves*. They belonged to a particular historical time and expressed the concerns of a particular historical group; only in this context could they be understood and appraised. It was possible to speak in the name of the slave-owning morality or the slave morality, in the name of feudal morality, or bourgeois morality, or proletarian morality. It was not possible to speak in the name of *morality as such*; to do so was to utter nothing but empty sounds, to assert a common interest where there was no common interest, to speak in the name of a consensus when there simply was no consensus.

The rejection of any appeal to 'abstract' moral principles was for many decades one of the best-known features of the work of Marx and Engels. Marxism was distinguished from utopian socialism precisely by reference to its *scientific* character, to its refusal to confront society with moral principles and moral appeals. 'Communists preach no morality at all', Marx wrote (characteristically) in the *German Ideology* (1845–6).[1] 'They do not put to people the moral demand: Love one another, be not egoists, etc.; on the contrary, they know very well that egoism, like sacrifice, is under specific conditions a necessary [inevitable] form of the individual's struggle for survival.' Throughout the remainder of his life Marx would object bitterly to any attempt to base a socialist programme on 'abstract' moral demands embodied in such terms as 'justice', 'equality', etc. Marxism was a science; it did not advocate socialism, it showed that socialism was inevitable. It did not ask for a 'just' wage, it showed that the wage-system was self-destructive. Marxism did not confront society with moral principles, but studied the 'laws of motion' that governed social change. It did not tell the proletariat what it *ought* to do, but showed the proletariat what it would be *forced* to do, by its own character and situation, by its position in 'history'.

Moral philosophers, however, have long been aware of what seems to be an important underlying inconsistency in the Marxist view. Marxists, including Marx himself, have not merely predicted socialism, as a scientist might predict earthquakes, they have worked for the coming of socialism and made it clear that they will welcome its coming. They have been committed to the moral superiority of socialism over preceding systems. This *ad hominem* criticism can easily be supplemented by showing the same *prima facie* inconsistency in the theoretical writings of Marx and Engels. In the 'philosophical' writings of Engels, indeed, there is no doubt that the inconsistency is more than apparent. It breaks out sharply in the proclamation which Engels put side by side with his somewhat crude relativist treatment of moralities, the proclamation that proletarian morality is the ultimate, highest, 'truly human' morality destined to become the morality of all mankind. For Engels, it is clear, moralities do themselves progress; they pass, like society in general, through successively 'higher' stages until they reach the ultimate rational, truly human condition. Clearly implicit in all this is an (unexamined and unspecified) eternal, immutable, non-relativistic standard by which historical moralities are judged – precisely the sort of standard, in fact, that Engels has been concerned to reject. Karl Marx was too able and subtle a thinker to fall into Engels's flagrant inconsistencies;[2] we shall not find Marx obviously contradicting himself in the one breath. But it is clear that Marx, too, saw the coming society of Communism as ethically higher than its predecessors, even as the *first* truly ethical society. He was prepared to denounce exploitation, privilege, servility and the divided class society – though not the exploiters, the privileged, the servile, the classes themselves[3] – in terms which were unmistakably ethical, or at least moral-advocative, in tone. It has not always been clear to his critics whether Marx was implicitly appealing to a worked-out though unpublished ethic consistent with his exposure of class moralities and meant to supplement it, or whether he was merely giving vent to unexamined moral preferences and prejudices unaccounted for in his theory.

(i) DIFFICULTY OF INTERPRETATION

One of the great difficulties for the critic, as for the student wishing to tackle Marx's ethical theory seriously, is the lack of any extended or systematic discussion of ethics in any particular place in the whole corpus of Marx's work. An anthology entitled *Marx on Ethics* would contain no passages that continue to be strictly relevant for more than three or four sentences. The passages would come from diverse sources and unexpected contexts, making it hard to gauge their intended scope or to be sure that they are not polemical overstatements or simplifications. Marx, of course, had been educated as a philosopher, but with the 'discovery' of his materialist conception of history in the spring of 1845, followed by his collaboration with Engels on the *German Ideology* (1845–6), he wrote *finis* – it seemed – to the philosophical style and concerns of his youth. From 1848, when he was thirty, to his death in 1883, he devoted himself almost exclusively to his economic studies and to political pamphleteering and analysis. His style grew more empirical and his pretensions increasingly 'scientific' in the Comtean and Victorian English sense of the word. 'Philosophy' he left to Engels – unfortunately so, for it is

difficult to believe that anything other than Marx's great sense of
material and psychological indebtedness to Engels's friendship,
coupled with Marx's immersion in other work, can account for
his failure to express dissatisfaction with Engels's performance or
to repudiate Engels's claim to be presenting a joint view. From
those of Marx's works that were known to socialists and social
thinkers in the hey-day of classical Marxism between 1870 and the
1920s therefore, from such works, for example, as the *Contribution
to the Critique of Political Economy* and *Capital*, the *Communist
Manifesto*, the *Critique of the Gotha Programme* and *The Civil War in
France*, one could only speculate concerning Marx's outlook on
ethics, or on most other philosophical questions. The typical
discussion of Marx's outlook on ethics in this period proceeded
either by way of deduction from his general theory of history and
society or by imaginative exegesis of a few scattered remarks.
Then, in the late 1920s and early 1930s, came the first systematic
publication of Marx's earlier and more philosophical writings and
notes, sponsored by the Marx–Engels Institute and initially edited
and planned by the serious and devoted Communist Marx
scholar David Riazanov. The impact of these newly discovered or
rediscovered writings, especially in the English-speaking world,
was much delayed by the Nazi persecution of culture and cultured
men, by Stalin's only significant 'contribution' to Marxist
scholarship (the dismissal, arrest and execution of Riazanov) and
by the difficulties facing international communication and
scholarly discussion in the Second World War. In consequence,
only in the 1950s and the 1960s has the significance of Marx's
early writings been fully appreciated in any country, and only in
the last few years have some representative selections from these
writings become available in English. Especially important for an
understanding of the ethical background of Marx's work are his
doctoral thesis on the philosophy of nature of Democritus and
Epicurus (1841), his incomplete critique of portions of Hegel's
Philosophy of Right (1843), his contributions to the *Deutsch-
französische Jahrbücher* of 1844 and the *Economico-Philosophical
Manuscripts* that he jotted down later that year. It is in the light
of these writings, many modern philosophical writers agree, that

the ethic running through Marx's work is best understood, though the emphases to be placed on various strands and periods in Marx's work are – understandably enough – still the subject of dispute. There is especially sharp disagreement about the question of continuity in the development of Marx's thought, but this question, too, can now be approached much more knowledgeably and seriously through a consideration of the drafts, couched in remarkably philosophical language, which Marx prepared in 1857–8 while working on his *Contribution to the Critique of Political Economy*. These drafts, first fully published in two parts, in the original German, by the Foreign Languages Publishing House in Moscow in 1939 and 1941, were almost unnoticed at that troubled time. Their republication in East Berlin in one volume in 1953, under the 1939 title *Grundrisse der Kritik der politischen Ökonomie* has since brought them into the purview of Marx scholarship and has helped to demonstrate further that Marx took his early philosophical views on economics seriously well after he had become a Communist and a 'materialist'. A small section of the *Grundrisse* is now available for the English reader in the volume *Karl Marx, Pre-Capitalist Formations*, edited by E. J. Hobsbawm and translated by Jack Cohen, published in London in 1964.

(ii) MAN AS A 'SUBJECT'

Karl Marx [I have written elsewhere[4]] came to Communism in the interests of freedom, not of security. In his early years, he sought to free himself from the pressure exercised by the mediocre German police state of Frederick William IV. He rejected its censorship, its elevation of authority and of religion, its cultural Philistinism and its empty talk of national interest and moral duty. Later he came to believe that such pressures and such human dependence could not be destroyed without destroying capitalism and the whole system of private property from which capitalism had developed.

Professor Popper sensed the same moral commitment to freedom from a consideration of Marx's mature work alone.

Marx's condemnation of capitalism [he writes[5]] is fundamentally a moral condemnation. . . . The system is condemned because, by forcing the exploiter to enslave the exploited, it robs both of their freedom.

Marx did not combat wealth, nor did he praise poverty. He hated capitalism, not for its accumulation of wealth, but for its oligarchical character; he hated it because in this system wealth means political power in the sense of power over men. Labour power is made a commodity; that means that men must sell themselves on the market. Marx hated the system because it resembled slavery.

Marx's early writings have confirmed this. Underlying the whole of his work, providing the ethical impulse that guided his hopes and his studies, was a vision and a theory of human freedom, of man as master of himself, of nature and of history. It was a vision of the fully social man who has developed all his potentialities, made himself the aim and measure of all things, subsumed them to his human needs and purposes. It is this vision and this theory that modern philosophical writers refer to when they speak of Marx's *humanism* or, to emphasise the element of rebellion, of his *Promethean ethic*. This ethic was reinforced by Marx's leading character trait – his tremendous concern (in reaction against his prudent father and the humiliations invited by his Jewish origin) with *dignity*, seen as independence and mastery over obstacles. As late as 1873, asked to state the vice he detested most, Marx replied: 'Servility.' But this line also has its roots in the history of Europe, and especially in the history of Germany in the period 1770–1848.

As the scientific rationality of Western civilisation began to bear its full fruit [Professor Marcuse writes in an interesting work [6]] it became increasingly conscious of its psychical implications. The ego which undertook the rational transformation of the human and natural environment revealed itself as an essentially aggressive, offensive subject, whose thoughts and actions were designed for mastering objects. It was a *subject* against an object. This *a priori* antagonistic experience defined the *ego cogitans* as well as the *ego agens*. Nature (its own as well as the external world) were 'given' to the ego as something that had to be fought, conquered and even violated.

This concept of man as a *subject* – implicit, to some extent, in Cartesian philosophy with its sharp ontological distinction between consciousness and matter, that is, user and used – reached its first theoretical culmination in one strain in the philosophy of Kant. In the *Critique of Pure Reason* Kant had striven to show that the necessary structure of the phenomenal world was imposed upon it by the knowing mind. Even the concept of God was merely one of the 'regulative ideas' of pure reason, a product of the rational mind's search for a single principle of explanation and for an ultimate unity in nature. In the *Critique of Practical Reason* he had argued that morality presupposes, behind the phenomenal human being subject to the laws of nature and of reason, a pure rational will moving freely in the intelligible, noumenal world. This will was self-determined, subject to no laws but the self-imposed rational law 'to treat humanity in every case as an end, and never as a means'. In the *Critique of Judgment* Kant had continued his vindication of man, attempting to show that man is the measure of all things beautiful, that aesthetic appreciation arises from the harmony between the object of cognition and the forms of knowledge. It is man, as the bearer of a rational faculty and as a knowing subject, who gives nature its supreme end and divine form, who organises its materials, and in morality proclaims himself as the highest end and being. Small wonder that Marx saw Kant as representing the French Revolution in the sphere of ideas, the declaration of the rights of man translated into philosophy (and thus made practically impotent). Two, three generations of young Germans, from Schiller and the young Fichte onwards, were to fight religious and political censorship and oppression in the name of the (Kantian) autonomy of man. Was it not Kant himself who had only one portrait in his study – that of Rousseau – and who was (wrongly) suspected of having written the young Fichte's *Critique of All Revelation*?[7] Did not the whole new moral critique of religion and the authoritarian state, from Fichte to Feuerbach, take its departure from the Kantian proposition that morality rests on the autonomy, religion (like political authoritarianism) on the heteronomy, of man? Was man the creator, the focal point of the universe, the condition of all knowledge, to be degraded into a dependent and externally determined creature? 'The criticism of religion' (i.e. Feuerbach's *Essence of Christianity*), the young Karl Marx wrote in the *Deutsch-französische Jahrbücher*, 'ends in the teaching that *man is the highest being for man*, it ends, that is, with the categorical imperative to overthrow all conditions in which man is a debased, forsaken, contemptible being forced into servitude, conditions which cannot be better portrayed than in the exclamation of a Frenchman at hearing of a projected tax on dogs: "Poor dogs! They want to treat you like men!" ' *'Punishment, coercion,'* Marx writes in the *Holy Family*, 'is contrary to *human* conduct', because, as he had written earlier elsewhere, 'where the law is true law, i.e. the existence of freedom, it is the true existence of the freedom of man. . . . Law retreats before man's life as a life of freedom.' Or again: 'Every emancipation consists of leading the human world and human relationships back to man himself.' Or: 'A social revolution . . . is the protest of man against the dehumanised life . . . the fellowship against whose separation from himself the individual is reacting is the true fellowship of man, the fellowship of being human.'

This is not the place to go on multiplying texts from Marx in order to document, step by step, the development and the details of Marx's concept of the free man as the basis of ethics, philosophy and, ultimately, of the whole of social science.[8] Neither can we consider at all carefully here the materials from which Marx fashioned his doctrine, that is, the easily demonstrable influence on him of aspects of the thought of Kant and Fichte and, more obviously and directly, of the writings of Hegel, the Left Hegelians and Feuerbach. But in the formative years of his life, between 1841 and 1845, Marx did emerge with a doctrine that represented as worked-out a position on ethical philosophy as he ever reached, and which remained – I believe – implicit in the rest of his work, shaping not only his moral outlook, but his whole conception of human history, its problems and its destiny. That doctrine may be summarised as follows:

The *presupposition* and the true *end* of ethics, of philosophy, of all human activities, is the free, truly human man. Man is potentially the only *subject* in a world of objects, and anything that turns him into an object, subordinates him to powers outside himself, is inhuman. To Marx, as to so many other eighteenth- and nineteenth-century European radicals, there was something especially monstrous about an alleged type of *self*-abasement, about the situation in which man fell slave to things or institutions that he had *himself* created, to human forces severed from humanity, the situation in which man humiliated himself before an idol of his own making. This process Marx, following Hegel, called (self-)alienation and estrangement, or later, *fetishism* and *dehumanisation*, and it represented for him the ultimate in self-degradation. Ethics, for Marx, then, was concerned with freedom, and freedom meant human self-determination; it meant that man was governed by his own nature and its requirements, and by that alone. Man's nature consisted of a set of potentialities; freedom allowed him to go about the task of realising them to the full. It enabled him to subordinate nature and his environment to his will, to realise himself in work and in his intercourse with others instead of subordinating himself to demands confronting him as alien requirements, as limitations on his being and not as fulfilments of it. (This is what one can call the Kantian strain in Marx, though one must remember that it is a simplified, Prometheanised Kant – a Kant without the conflict between duty and inclination, without the frank elevation of the noumenal will over man's empirical nature, and without Kant's recognition of the independent requirements of logic or 'reason'.)

From the logic of Hegel Marx derived further content for the conception of freedom, and hence of the good. Conflict and 'contradiction' may be the necessary condition of change (and hence of progress), but they are also the marks of that inadequacy, one-sidedness, incompleteness which produces a necessary instability. 'That which is the Best', Marx had quoted approvingly (from Aristotle) in his doctoral thesis, 'has no need of action but is itself the end.' The truly harmonious, the stable, the ultimately durable, is the truly real as against that which is dependent and therefore to some extent unreal, contingent, temporary. To change in conflict is to be determined from outside; to suffer contradiction is not yet to be free. Thus 'contradictions' (practical and theoretical incoherence, conflict, instability) become for Marx moral criteria. The 'contradictions' of capitalism are not mere signs of its impending collapse, but also symptoms of its *in*humanity, of its (historically conditioned) failure to make the free man, consciously controlling his fate, the basis of the whole system. The importance of this conception in Marx's thinking becomes evident when we compare his *Economico-Philosophical Manuscripts* of 1844 with an otherwise similar criticism of capitalist economics published by Engels a few months earlier, his 'Outlines of a Critique of Political Economy'. Engels's article, which Marx praised highly and which helped to bring about their friendship, criticised political economy both morally and logically – but the two criticisms were distinct. Marx, on the other hand, insists that ethical deficiency and logical 'contradiction' are necessarily connected. No criticism is complete until the two have been shown to arise from a single cause, a 'one-sided' treatment of man or a failure to grasp the human content of social and economic institutions. The whole point of the *Economico-Philosophical Manuscripts* is to proclaim that political economy cannot be an ethically neutral study of so-called 'objective relations' between non-human economic categories. The fundamental categories of political economy, Marx insists, are not labour, capital, profits, rent, land. The fundamental category is man, man and his human activities. These activities must not be abstracted from man; they must be seen as integral expressions of his humanity. It is when these categories are abstracted, objectified, reified, given independence vis-à-vis man, that man falls into servitude and the system of political economy into theoretical contradictions expressed in actual conflict and instability. Only by bringing economics back under the control of man can the subject be made coherent, the economic system stable and man become free.

What, however, of man's relation with other men? Here Marx begins with a (quasi-Hegelian) conception drawn from Feuerbach, that of man as a *Gattungswesen*, a species-being. In the *Essence of Christianity*, first published in 1841 and causing an immediate sensation, Feuerbach had argued that man cannot be treated as an abstract individual, in the way in which Christianity treats him. Human beings belong to one of two sexes, and the concept of 'humanity' cannot be accounted for, or formed, without recognising that any individual is *incomplete* as a human being without another, especially of the opposite sex. Love, which Feuerbach treats as the central human characteristic, requires two people, an *I* and a *Thou*, and so does man's recognition of himself as a member of a species, as a universal and not merely a particular being. The distinctive species-characteristics of man cannot be imagined to exist unless there is a second human being in interaction with whom man develops love, speech and the knowledge of himself and his (common) humanity, that is, becomes human. Marx, who had no high opinion of Feuerbach's somewhat metaphysical preoccupation with love and sexuality, treats the concept of humanity more socially in the political sense of the word. Man is part of a community; he cannot do everything himself, he cannot realise his potentialities, or come to know his capacities, except in contact and co-operation with others. (Robinson Crusoe is logically possible only as a castaway, as one reared in society and *then* severed from it.) When society is truly human, other men appear before man as complements of his being, as collaborators in common human purposes, as 'himself once more'. Society becomes truly human when man ceases to be an abstract individual confronted by other abstract and therefore hostile individuals, when each man recognises himself as a universal, social being, a *Gattungswesen* in whom the community speaks and acts. For Marx, at least in 1844, this was what Communism was all about:

Communism . . . [is] the real *appropriation of the essentially human* by and for man; . . . the complete and conscious return of man to himself as a *social*, i.e. human, man. This Communism . . . is the genuine resolution of the conflict between man and nature and between man and man – the true resolution of the conflict between existence and essential being, between reification and self-confirmation, between freedom and necessity, between the individual and the species. Communism is the riddle of history solved, and it knows itself to be the solution.

What one is to make of all this we go on to consider in the next chapter.

The Marxian system, I have been arguing, begins with a 'philosophy of man'. It proclaims man to be the presupposition and the end of all philosophy, all science and all human activity; for Marx man is the *subject* in terms of which these latter are to be understood and judged. Ludwig Feuerbach, an understanding of whose earlier work forms an indispensable precondition for the appreciation of Marx's aims and methods, summarised his own philosophical development from his beginnings as a theological student, through his Hegelian period to his *Essence of Christianity* thus: 'God was my first thought, Reason my second thought, man my third and last thought.' In the *Essence of Christianity*, Feuerbach added: 'There is no other essence which man can think, dream of, imagine, feel, believe in, wish for, love and adore as the *absolute*, than the essence of human nature itself.'[9] Marx, as philosophical critics now increasingly recognise, took seriously and actually tried to carry out the programme which Feuerbach had only been able to sketch in his *Preliminary Theses for the Reform of Philosophy* – the dissolution of philosophy in its traditional (German idealist) form, its negation and preservation at a higher level in a new and complete *science of man* as a creative, social being, destined to become master of himself and the universe. Ethically, this means that, for Marx as for Feuerbach, man is the sole and ultimate standard, the absolute in terms of which all else is to be judged. ('Marxism', the Soviet philosopher A. M. Deborin wrote in 1923, 'is thus a continuation of Feuerbachianism',[10] and the contemporary Polish Marxist, Adam Schaff, entitles his interpretation and defence of Marxism *A Philosophy of Man*.)

Professor Robert C. Tucker, in an interesting though often one-sided and philosophically cavalier book,[11] has argued that one necessary consequence of the Promethean ethic is a 'neurotic' bifurcation of man: the romantic, utopian (according to Tucker,

typically *neurotic*) elevation of man as subject, creator, Absolute
(which can only take place in fantasy) brings with it a strongly
emotional (neurotic) rejection of man's actual life in the real world;
empirical man is felt to be dependent, forsaken, humiliated,
frustrated, fallen from grace. Whatever we may think of Tucker's
charge of neurosis, it is certainly true that this *is* how Marx portrays man in this world. The servitude of man in all past human
societies and the coming liberation from this servitude provide
the basic plot of the Marxian conception of history which is a
moral drama (though it is not only that). Those things which
Marx sees as enslaving man are the primary targets of Marx's
criticism and the main object of his study.

(i) THE ROLE OF MONEY

'The critique of society which forms the substance of Marx's
work', a leading French Marx scholar, Dr Maximilien Rubel,
correctly reminds us,[12] 'has, essentially, two targets: the State and
Money.' The State, for Marx, was the visible, institutionalised
expression of political power over men; money, both the visible
means and the secret but indispensable ground of the more
fundamental and pervasive economic power over men. If Marx
was concerned with the critique of politics and economics, it was
because he saw in these critiques the key to understanding the
human condition and grasping the necessary foundations for the
elimination of power over men. Throughout his work, Marx
makes it clear that he does not see man enslaved simply by other
men: the citizen by a dictatorial police state, the worker by a
greedy and grasping capitalist. All past and present social systems
may resolve themselves, from one point of view, into systems
made up of masters and slaves – but the masters are no more
free than the slaves, both live in a relationship of mutual hostility
and of insurmountable mutual dependence, both are governed by
the system that makes them play out their allotted roles, whether
they will or not. Marx sees this dependence as arising 'naturally'
from the division of labour and the consequent introduction
of private ownership. But the possibilities of intensifying

dependence, of alienating man from his work, his products and his fellow human beings, are vastly increased with the rise of money as a universal medium of exchange. Money – into which everything can be converted – makes everything saleable. It enables man to separate from himself not only his goods, the product of his work, but even his capacity to work itself, which he can now sell to another.

Money lowers all the gods of mankind and transforms them into a commodity. Money is the universal, self-constituting value of all things. It has therefore robbed the whole world, both the human world and nature, of its own peculiar value. Money is the essence of man's work and existence, alienated from man, and this alien essence dominates him and he prays to it.[13]

Man's alienation, for Marx, is expressed in the fact that man's forces, products and creations – all those things that are extensions of man's personality and should serve directly to enrich it – are split off from man; they acquire independent status and power and turn back on man to dominate him as his master. It is he who becomes their servant. As the division of labour, the use of money and the growth of private property increase, man's alienation becomes more acute, reaching its highest point in modern capitalist society. Feudalism enslaved the whole man; capitalism splits man's functions off from man and uses them to enslave him. In capitalism the worker is alienated from his product, from the work that he sells on the 'labour market', from other men who confront him as capitalists exploiting his labour or as workers competing for jobs, and from nature and society which confront him as limitations and not as fulfilments of his personality. It is this alienation – expressed in the intellectual field by the compartmentalisation of the science of man and society into the 'abstract' study of economic man, legal man, ethical man, etc. – which Marx portrays vividly in his *Economico-Philosophical Manuscripts*:

The more riches the worker produces, the more his production increases in power and scope, the poorer he becomes. The more commodities a worker produces, the cheaper a commodity he becomes. The devaluation of the world of men proceeds in direct proportion to the exploitation of the values of the world of things. Labour not only produces commodities, but it turns itself and the worker into commodities. . . .

Not only the products of man's work, but the very activity of this work are alienated from man. The alienation within the worker's activity consists:

First, in the fact that labour is external to the worker, i.e. it does not belong to his essential being, in the fact that he therefore does not affirm himself in his work, but negates himself in it, that he does not feel content, but unhappy in it, that he develops no free physical and mental energy but mortifies his body and ruins his mind. Therefore the worker feels himself only outside his work, while in his work he feels outside himself. He is at home when he is not working and when he works he is not at home. His work, therefore, is not voluntary but coerced; it is *forced* labour. It is, therefore, not the satisfaction of a need, but only a means for satisfying needs external to it. . . .

The result therefore is that man (the worker) no longer feels himself acting freely except in his animal functions, eating, drinking, procreating, or at most in his dwelling, ornaments, etc., while in his human functions he feels more and more like an animal. What is animal becomes human and what is human becomes animal.

Drinking, eating, and procreating are admittedly also genuinely human functions. But in their abstraction, which separates them from the remaining range of human functions and turns them into sole and ultimate ends, they are animal.

At the end of his *Economico-Philosophical Manuscripts* of 1844, Marx painted a picture of the Communist society, the society of true and ultimate human freedom. Sympathetic critics have called it the picture of a society of artists, creating freely and consciously, working together in spontaneous and perfect harmony. In such a society, Marx believed, there would be no State, no criminals, no conflicts, no need for punitive authority and coercive rules. Each man would be 'caught up' in productive labour with other men, fulfilling himself in social, co-operative creation. The struggle would be a common struggle: in his work, and in other men, man would find not dependence and unpleasantness, but freedom and satisfaction, just as artists find inspiration and satisfaction in their own work and in the work of other artists. Truly free men rising above the very conception of property will thus need no rules imposed from above, no moral exhortations to do their duty, no authorities laying down what is to be done. Art cannot be created by plans imposed from outside; it knows no authorities and no discipline except the authority and discipline of art itself. What is true of art, Marx believed, is true of all free, productive labour. Just as true Communism, for Marx, is not that crude Communism which 'is so much under the sway of *material* property, that it wants to destroy everything which cannot be owned by everybody as *private property*; it wants *forcibly* to cut away talent, etc.'; so free labour, for Marx, 'is not mere fun, mere amusement, as Fourier thinks with all the *naïveté* of a *grisette*. Truly free labour, for example, composition, is damned serious at the same time, it is the most intensive exertion.'[14]

(ii) FOUR ASPECTS OF ALIENATION

Alienation for Marx, then, occurs when man falls into servitude to and dependence upon his own powers or the institutions and goods he has himself created; it is overcome when man makes all his activities free expressions of his nature and full satisfactions of his needs. In its consummate form (i.e. in bourgeois society), alienation takes place at four levels, or in four ways:

(1) Man is alienated from the things he produces and his own labour in producing them. Instead of serving his needs, these come to dominate him and his life. (Marx, in the conditions of his time, would have taken as an example the seamstress, whose life is determined by and is an adjunct to the need for producing dresses, instead of the production of dresses being determined by the needs of the seamstress.) Socialists today often use as an example the cult of mass consumption and built-in obsolescence, the manipulation of the consumer to buy and to orient his life to buying, because in our economic system 'things demand to be bought', production needs more and more consumers, not because anyone thinks the *consumer* needs the things produced.

(2) Man is alienated from other men through the competitive character of the economic system based on private property, which forces everyone to live at someone else's expense and

8 EUGENE KAMENKA

which, in particular, divides men into classes with irreconcilable
interests. Man's fellow-beings therefore confront him as *hostile*
beings; they *limit* his exercise of his capacities instead of extending
it.

(3) Man is alienated from nature, which does not confront him
as a field for the creative exercise of his powers, but as a source of
difficulty and drudgery, as a limitation on his creative powers.

(4) Man is alienated from society as the expression of social,
collective power. In so far as a political interest is possible in
capitalist or any class society, it confronts men as an external,
separate interest, as the state interest distinguished from and
conflicting with private interests. (It is in reflection of this that
moral rules appear as external, alien rules laid down by a 'higher'
authority.)

Alienation in the practical, 'material' life of man is reflected in
man's theoretical life, in the creation of 'abstract' sciences such as
traditional philosophy, economics, ethics, etc. Each of these
sciences deals with a feature of man or of human activity in isolation, as though it were independent of the whole man and his
entire social history and circumstances. It thus subjects man to
'laws' that stand outside himself – to the law of barter, which is
one law, to the law of morality, which is distinct and separate
from it, to the laws of reason, treated as eternal and immutable
and 'above' man's actual wants and desires. Each of these 'abstract' sciences, as the young Marx – following Feuerbach – would
have put it, takes one of man's predicates and converts it into a
subject, tears it out of the context without which it cannot be
understood.

We are now in a position to see how Marx could resolve the
apparent tension between his ethical vindication of Communism –
his man-centred ethico-logic – and his materialist critique of
moralities. The materialist conception of history, at least in its
emphasis on the historical laws that determine man's development independently of his will, is the law of man's development
in the *period of alienation*, in what the later Marx called the
prehistory of mankind. Moralities are sectional, class-bound,

conflicting, dependent on economic interests, not truly ethical or truly human, because *man* is still sectional, class-bound, in mutual conflict, dependent on economic interests and not truly human or free. As long as man cannot be himself, as long as man is forced to play out a social role cast for him by the system, he cannot become the subject of ethics. His moralities are not expressions of his humanity, but reactions to his (inhuman) condition; individuals are not ethically culpable because their actions are not free, they are forced upon them by the conditions of their life. When man recognises the inhumanity of his condition, he leaves behind the field of moralities and enters upon a human ethic; he stands on the threshold of consciously gained and consciously exercised freedom; he becomes an ethical subject who judges himself by the standards of his own nature instead of being a moral object judged by external standards imposed upon him.

Viewed as a *morality*, judged in terms of its ethical *content*, the Marxian proclamation of the moral primacy of man obviously forms part of an important (modern) moral tradition. It is not the mere personal eccentricity of some romantic philosopher, fallen under the spell of Hegel and Feuerbach and taking it upon himself to project on to man the qualities that past generations had thought to be typically and exclusively proper to God. Marx's view has strong and deep roots in the culture created by the Reformation and strengthened by the scientific and industrial revolutions; it is an extreme, radical, thoroughgoing expression of that elevation of man and his concerns that began with Luther, gained strength with the French Revolution and forms the basis of most 'progressive', social democratic and ethical humanist agitation and reform since the revolutions of 1848. It is the implicit assumption behind the intensified struggle for religious and political liberty, and social and economic dignity, which marks off the modern from the medieval world. It is, and has been, especially effective wherever the impact of science, education and technical progress is vitiated by political and religious impediments to modernisation, where man's actual subordination to authority and need is felt to be sharply, intolerably at variance with 'the human spirit', with man's potentialities as the user of science and technology, as the destined sovereign of nature and free creator of literature and art. This is why Marxism has appealed especially to the intelligentsia – the rather special class produced by the (limited) spread of knowledge and education from industrial societies into backward, traditional, agrarian societies in which knowledge and education of the western kind act as revolutionary forces and their bearers become a special revolutionary class. It is not surprising either, then, that Marxian humanism has had an important impact on the intellectuals of Communist-dominated eastern Europe, where Party control and authority are felt to provide such impediments. Nor is it surprising that it has had far less direct impact in Communist China and much of the rest of Asia and Africa, where the belief in man's unlimited potentialities is still basically weak, where moralities, outlooks and expectations are still in the main pre-industrial, and where nationalism is currently a *substitute* for humanism. Marxian humanism shares the man-centredness of utilitarian ethics, but it is much more effective than utilitarianism in registering protest against those conditions in which modernisation is hindered (as in India) by the continuing modesty of human wants, by the self-imposed limitation of desires and expectations, by the acceptance of hardship, suffering and waste of human resources as 'natural'. For utilitarianism takes the desires and expectations of man at any given moment as an ultimate; Marx's morality seeks to transform and 'enrich' his wants, to increase his expectations, to prevent him from finding 'happiness' by tailoring his demands to his satisfactions, by learning to like what he gets. Utilitarianism works within a given social and political system and criticises it only where it fails to satisfy demands expressed within the system; Marxian humanism is prepared to transcend the system, to criticise the system itself for the wants and demands it creates.

In recent times, especially in advanced industrial countries and among men whose outlook was moulded by the horrifying excesses of Hitler and Stalin, there has been a marked revulsion from the Promethean ethic of human liberation on the ground that it provides no in-built check against such horrifying excesses. In the work of Karl Popper, with its emphasis on the dangers of

historicism and utopianism and its vindication of piecemeal
social engineering, in the 'Christian realism' of Reinhold Niebuhr,
in the political theory of Michael Oakeshott, this revulsion has
provided the psychological impetus and political foundation for
a return to 'the ethic of prudent mediocrity' of a Burke, a Pope
or a Goethe. Man's potentialities are for great good or for great
evil; it is best if he does not become drunk with his own power,
but proceeds little by little, respecting the actual, empirical desires
of others and keeping within rules meant to restrain his passions
and his experiments. This is the – anti-Promethean – message of a
great deal of contemporary moral and political writing. It appeals
greatly to the increasing number of (middle-class non-'coloured')
men who are reasonably comfortable in their own existing society
and believe in the capacity of a system that has institutionalised
change and technological progress to deal with strains and in-
justices without major dislocation or revolutionary outbursts.

For the moral philosopher, however, the historical popularity
or unpopularity of Marx's ethic and its relation to types of
society and social change is not the main point. Moral philosophy,
notoriously, is plagued by certain fundamental logical problems –
the problem of the status and character of ethical propositions and
of the nature and foundations of moral argument or justification.
For some moral philosophers, too, the *raison d'être* and the final
test of a moral philosophy lie in its ability to provide rational,
convincing and workable criteria for resolving the problems of
choice, for enabling men to choose among possible alternatives
within a given human situation. 'To preach morality', Schopenhauer wrote, 'is easy, to give it a foundation is difficult.' Does
Marx succeed where others have failed?

It is quite clear that Marx does not see ethics as providing a set
of rules or criteria by which men can resolve the dilemma of
moral choice in their day-to-day lives in society as we know it.
'Rights and duties', Marx wrote in the *German Ideology*, 'are the
two complementary sides of a contradiction which belongs only
to civil society' (i.e. to the society in which men pursue individual
interests in conflict with each other and have not yet internalised
the concept of community or created the material foundations for

such a community). As long as men face moral uncertainties, dilemmas of choice, they are facing situations that are inherently evil, situations in which interests conflict, in which one satisfaction can only be gained at the expense of another. The moral dignity of man requires something other than principles of arbitration between competing interests and demands, something other than principles which assume the existence of conflict and evil. Man's dignity requires the *overcoming* of those situations in which interests conflict, the creation of a society in which men have common purposes and agree naturally and spontaneously, as members of a family or a collective (allegedly) might agree, on what is to be done. Morality is not a question of rules, but a question of habits. Truly moral habits can only arise when man is free, free of superstition and external compulsion, free of the pressure of divisive classes and interests, free of property and free of compelling, soul-destroying need or the fear of need. True morality, in fact, is what free, rational, self-determined men acting without external compulsions would do. If there has been no true, spontaneous, natural morality in the past, this is only because men have never been able to realise themselves in free, rational, uncompelled social activity.

Marx thus attempts to sidestep the whole problem of justification in morals and the conflict between 'ought' and 'is'. Morality is not a question of what 'ought to be done'. The logical dilemma faced by moralists arises from the fact that they are trying to impose external principles of co-operation on societies that are by their nature incapable of producing spontaneous, rational and lasting co-operation, or from the fact that they abstract men and human activities from concrete social situations and lay down rules and requirements that ignore the realities of human life in that situation, ignore what a concrete man needs and can do. The reader should note the extent to which this view of Marx's is in tune with much of modern criminology, with the treatment that most sensitive contemporary writers give to juvenile delinquency or the 'culture of poverty'. 'Where the necessities of life are absent', the ageing Feuerbach wrote in the 1860s, long after Marx had ceased to read him, 'there [the consciousness of] moral necessity or obligation is also absent.' Moral indignation, as Feuerbach and Marx both saw, certainly comes most easily to those who are capable of treating the whole of mankind as though it were made in their own image and placed in their own (usually comfortable) situation. To say 'it is no use preaching at the juvenile delinquent, the point is to remove the poverty, sense of deprivation, alienation from the rest of society that produce the vast majority of delinquents' is to concede the validity of much that Marx is saying.

Nevertheless, Marx is not merely giving us a sociology of morals. Implicitly, at least, he is trying to justify his passionate and advocative pleading by pretending that his moral distinctions are in fact logical distinctions, that the denial of his morality would be the self-contradictory rejection of logic. He does not say this explicitly, but he creates an aura of logical necessity by the use of such terms as 'essence' (distinguished from mere 'existence'), 'truly human' (distinguished from empirical man), 'pre-history' (distinguished from 'true history'). It is this conception of a 'true' man, a 'true' history and a 'true' reality which is quite vital to Marx if he is to elevate a certain way of life, or a certain way of behaving, above others. This position rests on the (false) Hegelian idealist view that ordinary, empirical reality can somehow be logically deficient, lacking true or real reality. This logical deficiency, for Marx as for Hegel, is expressed in 'contradiction', where such contradiction is not true logical contradiction at all, but the existence of conflict and the empirical lack of complete self-sufficiency. To say that man, in his present state, is not 'truly human' is not to make a logical point but to make a moral one, to set up moral criteria of humanity that do not follow from the mere use or meaning of the word 'man'. In other words, Marx, like many moralists, is driven from the postulation of moral hierarchies to a postulation of logical hierarchies, to the conception of good as a 'higher', 'more real' type of existence.

Many critics have drawn attention to features of the Marxian view of history that raise the suspicion that it is an Hegelian theodicy, portraying mankind as evolving towards an ultimate messianic kingdom and history as containing a moral and logical end to which all else is a necessary but in itself inadequate and incomplete prelude. Certainly Marxism is one (particularly subtle) version of the cult of the perfectibility of man and of progress in history, and the arguments that could be opposed to such optimism are never seriously examined, in fact hardly even conceived of. But more fundamental than the conflation of the historical and the moral end (which is more blatant in the writings of Engels and of Stalinist Communists than in the writings of Marx) are the confusions inherent in Marx's conception of man as destined to become the *subject* of history. Here Marx, through Hegel and other sources, has clearly been influenced by scholastic logic. Man, as Marx in his metaphysical moments portrays him, is (potentially) the *unconditioned being* of the scholastics (i.e. God), whose unconditionedness is one of his *perfections*, essential to his (true) nature, and therefore to be deduced from it. It is from the scholastic view of God that Marx unconsciously derives the conception of man as (properly) always a subject and never a predicate. It is from scholastic logic that he gets the otherwise unsupported notion that the self-sufficient, the self-determined, the always active, is morally superior to the conditioned, the determined, the also passive.

Now the simple answer to this is that man is neither wholly active nor wholly passive, neither (by his nature) always subject nor always predicate, neither self-determined nor wholly determined from outside. As the later Marx saw much more clearly, man interacts with his environment; he determines (affects) it and it determines (affects) him. That it is morally better to act than to be acted upon is never, in Marx or anywhere else, more than an unsupported assumption. It is not an uncommon assumption (providing one basis for feelings of male superiority and an ethic for Milton's Satan), but it is no better established for all that. There is nothing to show logically, without moral assumptions, that it is 'human' to act and 'inhuman' to be acted upon or even to be treated as a means or object; it is not 'contrary to human nature' to make oneself a beast of burden, an object of pleasure or part of the rat-race. Men and women have done so for many generations; to say that in doing so they have behaved as though they were not human is to load the term 'human' with a moral content that cannot be deduced from its empirical denotation.

Marx's difficulties in this connection come out clearly in his treatment of 'alienation' as a fundamental ethical concept. It was a happy accident (and one that has proved rather temporary) that Marx could run together, in dealing with the vast mass of European mankind, dependence on wage-labour and the capitalist system, extreme poverty and suffering, and a feeling of utter lack of control over the conditions of one's life and work. For Marx, in consequence, several possible meanings of alienation became fused and blurred, even though Marx had himself admitted that the alienation which produces a feeling of misery and denial of his self in the worker produces a feeling of well-being and self-affirmation in the capitalist. In one sense of alienation, man is alienated whenever his actions, his circumstances, his whole life are determined by circumstances beyond his control. We have argued that such circumstances will always exist, that man can never be entirely self-determined. Alienation in this sense, therefore, is not 'alienation', a particular (evil) state of existence, but is simply what is naturally involved in all existence, which is always conditioned and never unconditioned. A second, somewhat less obviously utopian sense in which Marx seems to use alienation is when man's purposes are not determined by himself. Man's actions, even within the limitations set by events completely beyond human control, are not expressions of his desires, they are forced upon him by his external situation. But here, too, one has to say that there is no logical distinction between human purposes and human actions and conditions: what a man wants or purposes, as Marx himself argued, is the product of the man's past history and his environment, of the interaction between his character and his surroundings; our purposes are our own only in the sense that it is we who have them, not in the sense that they spring entirely out of an internal, self-contained history. If our purposes are to be looked at *objectively*, then they are never self-determined in the causal sense; they are only self-ratified, if you like, and such ratification also has a causal history. We are thus, in the objective sense, all alienated in all our purposes. Marx cannot attempt to avoid this difficulty by treating alienation *subjectively*, as so many contemporary American sociologists do, and as Marx himself does in emphasising the worker's *feeling* of dehumanisation. It is possible to draw a distinction between men who *feel* that their purposes are their own and men who feel that they are dominated by circumstances or other people or 'the system'. It may then be an empirical fact that the former feel satisfaction in their lives and the latter do not. (This would be a matter for empirical investigation; Marx avoids the need for this by linking alienation with poverty, which is no longer plausible.) But the whole point of Marx's critique is to discount the subjective criterion of the worker's feelings, to say that the slave is no less a slave because he feels himself to be free. Marx's whole argument, then, rests on his vacillation between the various possible meanings of alienation or on the implausible view that the three stand in relations of mutual implication. Even then, it requires for its moral impact and initial plausibility a further unsupported assumption. This is the assumption that from the point of view of ethics, of human freedom, there is a crucial distinction between limitations that result from 'natural' necessity and limitations that result from the actions of other human beings, whether they confront the individual as the demands of other people, of impersonal institutions, of social forces or of machines and commodities. Even if it were true that many men felt such a distinction to be morally relevant, this might be merely the result of romantic illusions, of their reluctance to concede that objects and institutions created by men acquire a life of their own. *Fetishism*, one might argue, lies not in being dominated by machines, but in thinking that because they were built by humans machines should somehow remain human, or subject to human control. Behind all this, one suspects, lurks another fallacy of scholastic logic, the view that the effect is somehow contained in, and properly subservient to, the cause. This accounts for one invalid argument of remarkable longevity, that children should respect their parents because the parents gave birth to them, and for another more modern version, that it is monstrous for man to be governed by machines because he made them.

For most people, without doubt, Marx's contribution to ethics will be most seriously vitiated by the patent utopianism of his conception of the truly human society with its spontaneous co-operative morality. The basis on which Marx predicts the flowering of such a morality is at times viciously metaphysical, at other times embarrassingly slender. Marx's confidence seems to rest on a mixture of the following propositions, each of them false:

(1) Man, when truly and fully human, when conscious of his nature, his potentialities and his relations with other men, is naturally co-operative. In Marx's early work this rests on a confused logical doctrine – the notion that an essence is truly universal and that man, in recognising his essential humanity, therefore necessarily recognises all other human beings as aspects of himself, or as himself once more and cannot, from his humanity, derive any ground for conflict with them. In Marx's later work, there is some, rather half-hearted, attempt to deduce such co-operation from the requirements of modern industry and to argue empirically that industrial workers are beginning to display such 'natural' co-operation. Engels, half-supported by Marx in the *Critique of the Gotha Programme* – as though conscious of the weakness of this – ultimately seems to come down on the view that the *abundance* of material goods produced under Communism will remove the grounds for conflict – as though men quarrelled only over material goods and as though marginal wants did not acquire greater urgency as other satisfactions come to be taken for granted.

(2) Man, in becoming truly human, is able to exercise untrammelled rationality. Given the common human purposes that Marx assumes, reason can and does provide the basis for complete agreement on all questions, from the allocation of resources to the priority of tasks. It is in line with this that Marx speaks, in the Preface to *Capital*, volume 1, of all social relations under Communism becoming rational and intelligible relations.

(3) All social conflicts can ultimately be derived from the institution of private property and the class structures created by it. With the abolition of that institution social conflict loses its

essential base. It is this which leads Marx to the view that in a society in which private property has been abolished and its existence forgotten the State, law and the criminal will wither away, men will see in each other their natural collaborators and colleagues and significant social conflict will become impossible.

For the philosopher all this, without question, will not do. Nor is it particularly convincing for the social theorist, who is well aware of the conflicts and tensions within and between those countries that have abolished private ownership of the means of production. And despite the popularity of the concept of alienation in recent radical writing, it seems to me clear that it is a concept useful to the moralist, to the littérateur and social critic, rather than to the serious ethical theorist. It is a dramatic way of bringing out the disparity, in contemporary post-industrial society, between man's technological and scientific powers and his ever-increasing degree of social dependence; it is also a way of liberating socialism from the necessity of predicting poverty. But in so far as the use of the term 'alienation' implies that such a disparity is somehow unnatural or in a more than moral sense inhuman, it is simply wrong. Alienation, in other words, is not a logical concept or a category on which a theory of ethics can be founded without further examination and analysis; in Marx and recent neo-Marxists it is a moral-advocative term deriving its force from moral assumptions it does not seriously examine and from the disparity between existing social conditions and some of the hopes and expectations born of the optimism of the scientific and industrial revolutions. This is not to say, of course, that any given society must be accepted as it is; it is to deny that logic and the nature of man prove it ought to be different. Let us admit frankly that moral and social reform are political activities, springing from and utilising existing (strictly historical) expectations, traditions and moral attitudes with their allied frustrations and dissatisfactions. To be morally adult is to be able to take a stand without demanding that history and logic be rewritten to support it, without demanding that the nature of the universe guarantee our 'rightness' and/or our prospects of success.

IV. ETHICS AND THE MATERIALIST INTERPRETATION OF HISTORY

'A philosophy of man', Adam Schaff writes,[15] 'can start off from two opposite principles: (1) that man's existence is the realisation of some superhuman conception of plan, external to man; (2) that man's existence is the creation of man himself – man makes himself, and the starting point of all considerations about man should be that he is autonomous.' The upshot of our criticism of the young Marx's humanism was to deny that these *are* the two alternatives for a consideration of man's position, either logically or ethically. Man's existence is neither the realisation of some superhuman conception, nor is it the work of man himself. To use Hegelian language, man is both subject and predicate. There is no logical discontinuity between man and his environment, no actual or ideal truly human and unconditioned essence against which the whole of empirical human existence is to be set and judged. Human nature, human purposes and human conceptions are the product, at any given stage or in any given place, of the continuous interaction between actual existing men and their environment. They are to be understood neither in terms of 'man' alone, nor in terms of his environment alone. Man is thus neither autonomous nor heteronomous; what he is, at any time in history, is neither his own work nor that of another. While we can say that there are certain (e.g. physiological) features of man that have changed less drastically in the last two or three thousand years than other (e.g. cultural) features, there is no basis for proclaiming the existence of an underlying human nature that persists through and underlies all change and seeks to determine it. Such a human nature would have to become, like 'substance' in Locke, 'an uncertain supposition of we know not what', an empty and question-begging set of potentialities knowable only after the event.

Marx himself, in the 'materialist interpretation of history' which he develops after 1845, helps to lay the foundations for our criticism. 'All history', he argues against Proudhon in the *Poverty of Philosophy*, 'is nothing but the continuous transformation of human nature.' In notes criticising Feuerbach that he jotted down a little earlier (the *Theses on Feuerbach*), he writes: 'Feuerbach resolves the religious essence into the human. But the essence of man is no abstraction residing within each individual. In its real form, it is the ensemble of social relations.' In the *German Ideology* he elaborates: '[The] sum of productive forces, forms of capital and social forms of intercourse which every individual and generation finds in existence as something given is the real basis of what the philosophers have conceived as "substance" and "essence" of man.' Man is born into a specific society which shapes his outlook, capacities and hopes – he cannot be understood or discussed apart from the social arrangements in which he lives and the place which he occupies within those arrangements. Thus Marx went on to argue, in passing, in 1848, that 'conscience is related to the knowledge and whole way of life of a man. A Republican has a different conscience from a Royalist, a propertied man has a different conscience from one who is propertyless, a thoughtful man a different one from a man without thought.' In other words, as we suggested at the opening of this study, there is not morality, there are historically conditioned *moralities*. Conscience, Reason and Will are not ahistorical faculties confronting man as the voice of an inner essence or a transcendent truth; they are human functions and activities, products of the continuous interaction between changing men and their changing environment. It is precisely for this reason that each generation and social group reinterprets the meaning and significance of human history and of special histories – the history of philosophy, of science, and so on – in terms of the concerns, insights and attitudes born of its own historical situation, and it is for this reason that seemingly dispassionate, disinterested and well-informed men find themselves engaged in far-reaching moral and intellectual conflict.

Marx's naturalism, however, as we have hinted, was never

completely thoroughgoing; behind his materialist treatment of man the older Marx still strove to maintain his youthful belief in man as the ultimate subject in terms of which everything was to be understood. Thus Marx insists, with Vico, that man makes his own history; thus Marx attacks, in the *Theses on Feuerbach*, all previous materialism for treating the material world as given, for failing to see it as the product of human praxis; thus Marx ends with the slogan that man's task is to revolutionise and humanise the world: so far, 'philosophers have only interpreted the world differently, the point, however, is to change it'. Because Marx is wedded to the view that man is the ultimate ground and point of all history and existence, even his materialist account tends to emphasise the social (human) as against the natural (non-human); he is much happier reducing an intellectual phenomenon to a social situation (classes and economic production) than seeing it as the product of a natural (e.g. geographical) situation. There are times, notably in his account of despotic Asiatic society and in his acceptance of the 'mongolising' and 'tartarising' influence of the Russian terrain as a reason for Russian backwardness, when Marx does concede and use the direct influence of the natural world in shaping man. But generally, and in terms of his theory as a whole, Marx is anxious to avoid any form of direct geographical determinism (such as we find in Plekhanov) or any account in which man figures purely as an object acted upon by something else than other men and human products. Man's relation with 'nature' for Marx is always dialectical; man shapes it as it shapes him, there is no understanding one without the other. For Marx nothing that enters into relationship with man remains simply non-human. This is why the motive forces in the Marxian conception of history are characteristically human products – inventions and the class struggle, not rivers, mountains, trees or fields, which to Marx are nothing until they become objects of human intentions and purposes. Here the influence of classical idealism, with its view that mind permeates 'nature' and thus gives it significance and form, is still strong, though Marx's transformation of the doctrine makes it much more concrete, plausible and intellectually fruitful.

Nevertheless, in its most general tendency, Marx's materialist interpretation of history might well be taken as laying foundations – when taken together with the work of Feuerbach, Darwin and Freud – for a *naturalistic* view of man, for the recognition that man occupies no special logical place within historical, empirical processes and that he is neither logically nor causally discontinuous with them. The study of the human is not logically different from the study of the non-human; social development is not in principle different from non-social development. Man is part of the subject-matter of zoology, biology, physics and chemistry just as he is part of the subject-matter of economics, politics, sociology and the history of culture. He is *part* of these subjects and not a manipulator or organiser or 'presupposition' or 'end' standing outside them. The notion that man's purposes are independent ultimates controlling his life and his history is an illusion: we can study human purposes just as we study the purposes (drives and reactions) of primates or any other living organisms. While purposes may be causes, they are also effects. With the decline of mechanism, unfortunately, these have once again become (in different formulations) controversial questions among philosophers. In recent writing – in the work of such philosophers as Ryle and the later Ayer – they have been discussed at a level of sophistication and with an emphasis on close analysis undreamt of by Marx and ignored by his more recent disciples. It is not likely that any competent philosophers will find in Marx and the Marxists new insights into the logical problems raised by such recent writing. But it is important to beware of the unexamined and highly questionable assumptions that underly much of the new scholasticism – with its manipulative view of logic, its instrumentalism in relation to language and its extreme individualism in ethics and politics. Marx helps to remind us that human history creates a *prima facie* case against these assumptions, that they may be and have been questioned with force and insight.

At the same time, the materialist interpretation of history, with its emphasis on historical change and class conflict, helped to lay the foundations for a pluralist view of man and society – for the recognition of competing moralities and outlooks within society and within the individual man himself. It taught us that society was not a harmonious whole and that men were not harmonious wholes. Just as there was no total social interest, subsuming and reconciling all individual interests, so there was no total individual interest – a man could be part of many traditions, confront himself and others in many roles, be torn between allegiances to competing groups and ways of life. Marx himself and his disciples, it should be noted, were never thoroughgoing in this pluralism: they did tend to treat any individual man as belonging to a single class and to think of society as being made up of a finite number of classes. Marxian pluralism has to be, and has been, carried further than Marxists have been willing to carry it: we have to recognise the individual man, and the individual society, as infinitely complex, as the battle-site of an infinite number of traditions, outlooks and ways of life, as an *economy* of motives and interests which can never be exhaustively enumerated. None of the components of such an economy can be treated as atomic simples, confronting other components as monads without windows. Within each society there is an infinite number of sub-societies; component traditions and interests have points of affinity as well as points of conflict; they enter into alliances, change allegiance, split up into further components and so on. The complexity of individuals and 'their' interests has long been recognised in literature, especially in the novel; it is time that it was more clearly recognised in ethics.

If the materialist interpretation of history has helped (primarily non-Marxists) to work towards a philosophy of naturalism and pluralism, it has had a seriously stultifying effect on the further working out of such a philosophy, especially among Marxists, and as much in the field of ethics as anywhere else. One of the well-known *misuses* to which the materialist interpretation was put was to substitute a genetic account of the origin of a view, or a reference to the interests it allegedly serves, for examination of the truth or falsity or internal coherence of the view itself. Thus an attempt to supplement 'scientific Marxism' with neo-Kantian morality might be denounced as 'petty bourgeois', or philosophers, scientists and historians might be attacked, as they were under Stalin, on the grounds of their 'class-origin'. (The most important fact about Berkeley, in Stalinist writings, was his being – in fact becoming – a bishop, and Russell was for years treated as an aristocrat philosopher.) The view that intellectual enquiry was itself necessarily the battle-ground of competing class-bound ideologies not unnaturally helped to introduce the dishonesty of political polemics into Marxist intellectual production and to create an atmosphere (amid the conditions of sharp political struggle) in which labelling a view as 'bourgeois' was an acceptable substitute for serious criticism. It was this trait which turned the work of so many able socialist writers into little more than political pamphleteering, and which makes the reading of most Marxist writing on ethics between 1880 and 1950 such an unrewarding task.

The position here was further obscured by Engels's proclamation, in his *Ludwig Feuerbach* and his *Anti-Dühring*, that all truth is relative. Engels's discussion is a particularly confused one and cannot be recommended to any serious student of philosophy for its contribution to the problem. Engels confuses absolute truth in the sense of what is unambiguously so or not with 'absolute truth' in the sense of complete knowledge, the sum of all possible knowledge. He concludes from the fact that we cannot ever exhaust all possible knowledge and that we can find later that our knowledge was 'inadequate' (or false), that we cannot ever say 'X is (absolutely and unambiguously) Y'. He has to concede, of course, that we do assert some propositions to be true *absolutely*, unambiguously, without a 'later-developing false side' but – he says – they are always trivial. Now, if propositions cannot in principle state an unambiguous issue, then we cannot talk or discuss at all.[16] It should be said, however, that this kind of relativism can be put forward more coherently in the field of ethics. If we leave aside the Marxist commitment to an ultimate morality, or an ultimate moral end, we might treat the materialist interpretation of history (especially in Engels's hands) as saying that there are no ethical truths – there are only moral outlooks. Such outlooks are produced historically – they are the outlooks, interests, demands of specific social groups (classes) in specific periods. It makes no sense to ask whether they are true or false. We can only ask what conditions produced them, what makes people subscribe to them, what conditions militate against their continued importance in society. In other words, we should treat moralities as we treat religions (other than our own) – as wishes, illusions, fantasies, demands, that acquire independent force, clothe themselves in principles, institutions, enforcement agencies, take up associated empirical material, etc. This is the view that I have referred to as a kind of social subjectivism, and that has also been called ethical relativism. It is popular among anthropologists, who do in fact treat the moral codes of the peoples they are studying in precisely this way. It has recently been defended again in Professor D. H. Monro's *Empiricism and Ethics* and seems to me to be a possible and coherent basis for approaching the problem of ethics. It is inconsistent with other aspects of Marxism, but it is not inconsistent in itself. The apparent objectivity of morals would, on this view, be an illusion – stemming from the fact that our moral outlook is not an individual creation but 'forced upon us', as it were, by our education, our social background, our immersion in various activities and ways of life. The sociologist Émile Durkheim, in his book *The Elementary Forms of the Religious Life*, gave one such naturalistic account of the feeling of transcendence, of objectivity, associated with moral beliefs. He saw it as resting on the recognition that the tribe precedes the individual and will go on after him, and that tribal ceremonies produce in the individual feelings, ecstasies, etc., beyond his conscious control. For the working out of details in this way, then, we once again have to look outside Marxism.

There is one other point of ethical interest suggested by the materialist interpretation of history which again has not been developed by Marxists themselves. (It was taken up, or at least hinted at, in the work of the French syndicalist Georges Sorel, with his distinction between the producers' morality of heroic dedication, work for its own sake, co-operation and emulation, as distinct from the prudential, utilitarian, competitive and individualistic morality of the consumer concerned with profit and reward, seeing all activities as means to an individual end.) This is the suggestion that moralities and moral demands are not those of individuals or groups of individuals, but the demands and requirements of a productive process or of a social activity, which carries with it certain norms in which people are caught up as part of carrying on the activity and which they come to accept as their own. (We do speak of the morality, or outlook, of military officers or commercial salesmen and of the morality, or outlook, of academic enquiry.) The existence of moralities as moralities required by an *activity*, or social province, in which individuals are caught up, is widely recognised in literature and in much political and historical writing, but it has not made the impact it should have made on ethics and political philosophy. There the tendency is still to think of the individual, and not of an activity, as the bearer of a morality and the subject of rights.

All this, however, is to look at the materialist interpretation of history imaginatively, a way in which orthodox Marxists have not looked at it. To them, it has been a 'law' of historical development and a canon of historical explanation; a reductive theory that provides a simple but complete and adequate account of morality and of all other ideological phenomena. As such, it derived what plausibility it had from the considerable ambiguity with which it was formulated and the noteworthy lack of precision or consistency in the way in which it was applied. True, Marx and Engels seemed to think that the whole thing came down to a simple preposition enunciated by Marx in the introduction to his *Contribution to the Critique of Political Economy*: 'the mode of production in material life determines the general character of the social, political and spiritual processes of life'. Within this material process of production Marx (and Engels after him) distinguished two separate, if related, factors: the *productive forces* and the *relations of production*. The productive forces are the skills, knowledge and tools (all of them social products) existing at any given period of society. The relations of production are the ways in which different factors of production (land, domestic animals, tools, machines, labour) are appropriated and in which economic returns are secured – in other words, the class structure of society.

Systematising and bringing together various scattered remarks by Marx and Engels, subsequent Marxists (Plekhanov and Kautsky) expressed the theory thus: each society has an *economic base*, consisting of productive forces and relations of production. The state of development of the productive forces determines the relations of production, the class structure of a society. This class structure (or, in an alternative formulation, the economic base as a whole) determines the *superstructure*, the political and legal arrangements, moral, religious and other ideological beliefs of the society. As it changes, they change. In line with this, Marx and Engels wrote in the *German Ideology*:

Morality, religion, metaphysics, all the rest of ideology and their corresponding forms of consciousness thus no longer retain the semblance of independence. They have no history, no development; but men, altering their material production and their material inter-course alter – along with these – their real existence and their thinking and the products of their thinking.

The proletarian, Marx and Engels said in the *Communist Manifesto*, sees law, morality and religion as 'so many bourgeois prejudices, behind which lurk in ambush just as many bourgeois interests'. And a few pages later they added:

Does it require deep intuition to comprehend that man's ideas, views and conceptions, in a word, man's consciousness, changes with every change in the conditions of his material existence, in his social relations, and in his social life? What else does the history of ideas prove, than that intellectual production changes its character in pro-portion as material production is changed? The ruling ideas of each age have ever been the ideas of its ruling class.

When people speak of ideas that revolutionise society, they do but express the fact that within the old society the elements of the new one have been created, and that the dissolution of the old ideas keeps even pace with the dissolution of the old conditions of existence.

Completely in line with this Engels was to write many years later, in *Anti-Dühring*:

We maintain . . . that all former moral theories are the product, in the last analysis, of the economic stage which society had reached at that particular epoch. And as society has hitherto moved in class antagonisms, morality was always a class morality; it has either

justified the domination and the interests of the ruling class, or, as soon
as the oppressed class has become powerful enough, it has represented
the revolt against the domination and the future interests of the
oppressed.

There have been remarkably few sustained Marxist attempts to
apply this doctrine in detail to ethical theories and the history of
moral philosophy. Engels, in *Anti-Dühring*, gives a rough and
unconvincing sketch in which he distinguishes Christian-feudal
morality (subdivided into Protestant and Catholic moralities and
into further subdivisions that Engels does not attempt to connect
with class structure at all), bourgeois morality and 'the proletarian
morality of the future'. He concedes that there are some moral
injunctions, such as 'Thou shalt not steal', which are common to
all periods of history in which society is based on private property,
precisely because these periods have the existence of private
property in common. Karl Kautsky, in his *Ethics and the Materialist
Conception of History*, makes an honest but dilettantish attempt to
take the Marxist account of morality seriously and apply it *in
concreto*. He turns his attention to classical Greek moral philosophy. In the ancient world, he argues, the ethical question first
emerged clearly as a result of the class tensions that followed the
Persian wars. These wars placed the Greeks at the centre of
widespread commercial activity and produced three leading types
of morality: the Epicurean, representing those connected with
private production; the Platonic and Neo-Platonic, representing
the section of the aristocracy not engaged in personal control of
production; the Stoic, representing several of the remaining
classes and acting as a mediating ethical theory. (The logical
concerns of the *Republic*, of course, or of the *Euthyphro*, find no
real recognition in Kautsky.) Since then, we rarely meet with any
Marxist analysis of the connection between a moral theory and a
class position more profound than a reference to Aristotle's
contempt for slaves and women or to Locke's exaltation of private
property. (Professor I. S. Narsky, of Moscow, has just reminded
us, in an otherwise serious book on Hume, that Hume's moral
theory should be seen as Whig and not as Tory, as though that
helped us to understand the subtle manner in which Hume wends

his way between utilitarianism, a theory of moral sentiment and
the requirements recognised by a man with an acute eye for
logical difficulties.)

This lack of concrete application of the materialist interpretation of history should not cause surprise. It is precisely in the
process of concrete application that the theory loses its plausibility and that the ambiguities in it become apparent. Marx himself, as I have striven to show elsewhere,[17] sat to it very loosely
indeed in his own detailed account of economic history and in his
political analyses and intellectual criticism. A number of recent
critics have shown very clearly the difficulties and imprecision
involved in the notion of an economic base to be distinguished
from an ideological superstructure. Not only can we show, as
Engels admitted and later Marxists now again admit, that ideological factors can and do react back on economic production and
technical organisation. We can show even more fatally, as John
Plamenatz did in his *German Marxism and Russian Communism*, that
the distinction between the economic base and the ideological
superstructure simply cannot be drawn in the way required by the
theory. Ideological factors do not merely act on the base, they
become part of it (feudal law is essential to the definition of feudal
classes, for example). The 'base' thus becomes simply the whole
social situation in which a person or movement finds itself. This
can be demonstrated from the few concrete remarks that Marx and
Engels make about moralities. It is never made clear precisely
what they are to be reduced to or precisely what they 'express'.
In the *Communist Manifesto* and in Engels's *Anti-Dühring* intellectual theories – especially law, political philosophy and ethics –
are reduced directly to class interests, but what such interests are
and precisely how they would be determined is never discussed.
In his well-known epigram on Kant, on the other hand, Marx
reduced Kant's doctrine of the good will not to the hypocritically
concealed interests of the German bourgeoisie but to its *political
impotence* coupled with its *aping of the French model* – that is, to the
'conditions' of the class, conditions in which 'material' and
'non-material' factors are jumbled together and no social factor is
in principle excluded. Elsewhere – in the *German Ideology*, as we

have seen – Marx goes beyond classes altogether by reducing the conflict of rights and duties in moral theory to the incoherence of a civil society based on private property and 'abstract' individuals. And in his theory of ideologies generally Marx seems to vacillate between treating ideologies as expressions of social interests on the one hand, and as compensations, fantasy-supplementations of social reality, on the other.

The materialist interpretation of history, in its allegedly concrete formulation, then, does not provide us with a key to the problems of moral philosophy. It may help us to ask questions; it does not itself provide any satisfactory answers. Anyone tightly bound to its dogmas is unlikely to find real answers. The history of moral philosophy *does* have a certain integrity: there are logical problems in ethics that worried a Plato, a Butler, a Hume, a Kant and a G. E. Moore independently of their moral sympathies. These logical problems cannot be removed or side-stepped merely by reference to the class-allegiance these philosophers had or to the conditions in which they lived. (It is when we believe the philosophers to have been wrong that we look for the distorting influence of time and place.) If moralities are to be interpreted as systems of demands or attitudes (which *are* historically conditioned, and the 'truth' or 'falsity' of which is not at issue), then the account to be given of them will have to be very much subtler and more careful than that suggested by the materialist interpretation of history or given by any Marxist. The distinction between moral demands and other demands has not been discussed by Marxists in any illuminating way; the foundation on which moral demands arise or the interests which they express has not been stated clearly. The complexity of moral beliefs and of problems about morality has simply not been recognised by Marxists. Those who want to work out a subjectivist ethic based on social movements and groups rather than individuals will have to go well beyond Marxism and discard much of it. Those who believe in an objectivist ethic will find nothing in the materialist interpretation of history that *proves* them to be wrong – though it does raise a strong presumption against the belief that there is an unhistorical voice of Conscience, or Reason, or the Good Will, that men have heard even if they have not heeded it. And Marxists themselves cannot proclaim ethical relativism in the same breath as that in which they set up the moral duty to the Revolution and the 'truly human morality' of socialism. This latter inconsistency only Marx himself avoided, and not always clearly.

V. HUMAN WELFARE AND HUMAN NEEDS

'Marxist–Leninist ethics', says a Soviet textbook on the subject,[18] 'also contains a normative aspect. It not only explains the social essence of morality and the laws of its development, but also provides a theoretical foundation for the moral goal of Communist society, for the norms and principles of Communist morality.' In other words, it gives ethics a *foundation* in Schopenhauer's sense; it allegedly provides a 'scientific' principle of justification for Communist morality. (In the Russian text, the Hegelian word *moment* is used where I have put 'aspect'. The use of this word makes it clear, and is meant to make it clear, that the normative aspect of Marxist–Leninist ethics is no accidental accretion, but an essential phase or aspect in Marxist–Leninist ethics, one that helps to determine its structure and development.)

Such a claim to derive normative principles from the Marxist science of society immediately attracts the attention of the moral philosopher and causes him unease. We have argued that the materialist conception of history, modified, reinterpreted, 'diluted' to a sociological naturalism, can be used to develop an internally consistent relativist or subjectivist view of ethics. On this view, 'moralities' would be ideologies in the strict Marxist sense, projections – in universalised or distorted form – of particular historical interests or demands, or empirical wishes that social life and human relations might be otherwise, or – most plausibly – a combination of both. Marxists would thus deny, as they have indeed often denied, that imperatives can ever be other than hypothetical, that the dictates of conscience or morality can ever be treated as eternally valid absolutes, that *values* exist independently of valuations. Such ethical relativism, however, seems at best difficult to reconcile with belief in the *objective* moral superiority of socialism, in the scientific basis (i.e. justification) of

Proletarian or Communist morality, or in moral progress (a conception which seems to imply underlying or meta-criteria logically independent of the actual historical moralities judged in terms of these criteria). While clear differences of approach to this problem can be detected among Marxists, both today and in the earlier history of Marxism, it is generally true that the issues involved have not been clearly grasped or distinguished by Marxists. The resultant tendency has been to have things all ways, to emphasise different approaches at different stages of the one work, and to say that they are all part of Marxism. The prestige of science in the late Victorian era and the first decades of the twentieth century led western European Marxists in the social democratic tradition to come down most heavily on the scientific, 'value-free' pretensions of Marxism. Thus the Austro-Marxist Rudolf Hilferding distinguished between *Marxism*, a *science* of society predicting the coming of a Communist society, and *socialism*, a *moral outlook* that welcomed this coming. Others, for example, Kautsky and Bernstein, were led to a 'moral supplementation' of Marxism – Kautsky by taking from Darwin an evolutionary ethic, Bernstein by appeal to the Kantian and neo-Kantian principle that all men must count equally and that man must never be used as a means. The Communists, concerned with revolutionary struggle and Party authority, tended to make their norms even more frankly imperative on the one hand but even more flexible on the other. True morality lay in obeying the dictates of history; since history was working towards the Revolution, the primary moral imperative was to aid the Revolution. In the light of this end, all else was to be judged. A gun, as Trotsky put it, is good in the hands of a proletarian fighting for the Revolution and evil in the hands of a *bourgeois* opposing it.

The point, however, is whether Marxists can with any plausibility derive such norms from the Marxist science of society and its 'materialist' conception of history. There are, in effect, only two ways in which this has been seriously attempted. One way was by arguing that norms are implanted in, or provided by, history itself. The other consisted of seeing man as the 'scientific' foundation for norms. The approach by way of history need not

delay us long, though it was for many years the most influential
and widespread approach within Marxism. It drew for authority
primarily on Engels, who had conflated Darwin and Hegel (and
in the process vulgarised Hegel and his dialectic into a doctrine of
evolutionary progress through conflict and contradiction). To
Engels, each stage of historical development was, at least in some
respects, 'higher' than that which preceded it and the final stage
of history was therefore the highest of all – an implicit end towards
which all history, blindly and unconsciously, had been working.
(It was in just this way that Darwinians saw man as the Crown of
Creation, the *end* towards which evolution had unconsciously
worked and in which it had surpassed itself. It should be noted,
however, that this strain is also present in Hegel and Marx, even
if it is expressed less simple-mindedly than in Engels.)

The difficulty here, of course, is obvious – in what sense, other
than 'later', is each stage of history 'higher' than its predecessor?
In moral Darwinism, notoriously, 'better' really meant only
'fitter to survive under given conditions' and in Hegel the slogans
'whatever is real is rational' and 'world history is the world court
of justice' seemed, to a careless reader, pompous ways of saying
that whatever triumphs is right. To show that the later is *morally*
better, we should need an independent criterion in the light of
which historical stages are judged. Hegel and the young Marx
had such a criterion, whatever difficulties it may in turn raise.
Engels did not, at least explicitly. When he writes, in *Anti-
Dühring*, that in the process of historical change 'there has on the
whole been progress in morality, *as in all other branches of human
knowledge*' (my italics), he characteristically misses the point. We
may be able to make some sense of the notion that later *science* is
higher than earlier science – that is, that it incorporates, amends
and corrects the knowledge gained by the former, and adds more
knowledge. But how a series of *relativistic* moralities (expressions
of interests, not truths) can suddenly become *truths*, or how one
interest can be higher than another, is not shown and cannot be
shown without making independent moral assumptions. Surely
the whole point of Engels's preceding paragraph had been that
each morality is *not* a branch of knowledge, but an ideology.

The appeal to man remains, then, as the only possible solution. An increasing number of Marxists, indeed, are taking this path – not only such quasi-Marxian humanists as Marcuse and Fromm, and the Yugoslav philosophers, but also such contemporary 'old-style' Marxists as Howard Selsam and Donald Clark Hodges, not to speak of the 'socialist humanism' now proclaimed by Soviet propagandist philosophers. Here the argument would run something like this: Man, as an empirical being, has certain purposes, needs and requirements which form part of the description of man and which must be recognised by any science that has man for its subject. Man's moral demands are the attempts to fulfil these requirements, to realise these needs. Provided the attempts are realistic and take into account objective conditions and realities, they are norms that any detached, honest and impartial human enquirer must accept as built into the nature of man. There is no point in asking for some further, metaphysical criterion by which man's requirements can be shown to be good – there is, after all, no ultimate or absolute for man more ultimate or absolute than his own needs.

This approach may be put more metaphysically (generally by those under the influence of the young Marx) or less metaphysically (by those who see themselves as 'materialists'). Marcuse attempts to ground the humanist ethic in logic by arguing that 'man' as a class-concept or universal necessarily involves criteria or principles by which we distinguish the human from the non-human. 'Man' is thus a normative concept from the start; to describe or define man is already to recognise goals towards which man works or ends towards which he strives. One such normative defining characteristic, emphasised by both Marx and Marcuse, is *consciousness* – for both, man is not truly human until he is able to act consciously, rationally, in the full knowledge and understanding of what he is doing. (Engels's use of the Hegelian slogan 'Freedom is the insight into necessity' is connected with this view of man.) Anything that interferes with man's exercise of his rationality thus makes man to that extent non-human and is therefore bad. On this view, there could be progress in morality, the progress consisting in its increasing rational practicality, its increased understanding of obstacles to the satisfaction of human needs and of the means that will result in the removal of such obstacles.

The more empirical Marxists tend to come much closer to utilitarianism, to think primarily in terms of happiness and suffering, satisfaction and deprivation, though also maintaining the emphasis on consciousness and practicality. Thus Adam Schaff writes:

Scientific socialism is essentially humanist, and the essence of its humanism is its conception of the happiness of the individual. Everything in Marxism – its philosophy, political economy and political theory – is subordinated to this. For Marxism is the sum of theoretical instruments which serve one practical aim, the struggle for a happier human life. This is how Marx understood the question while still young, when he said that a revolutionary philosophy is the ideological weapon of the proletariat. Such is the meaning of the Marxist postulate of the unity of theory and practice. And this is why the theory of happiness takes on a specific form with Marxism – not as the abstract reflection of the meaning of happiness or of its subjective components, but as the revolutionary idea of that transformation of social relations which would make possible the creation of the conditions for a happy life by removing the social obstacles to such a life. Marxist socialism approaches the problem of individual happiness from its negative side, that is to say, it investigates the social obstacles to human happiness and how they can be removed. It is this approach which brings positive results, because of its realism.[19]

Howard Selsam, in his *Ethics and Progress*, puts it thus:

The warp of ethics lies in man's ability to see a contradiction between what he is, how he lives, and what he could be and how he should live.[20]

Throughout the world men are today turning away from old established standards and are creating richer, fuller human ethics by envisioning and seeking a life free of poverty and ignorance and offering the fullest possible development of man's limitless potentialities. Men make their moral codes and their ethical theories, and in the world today masses of people are making them, consciously or unconsciously, with blood and sweat, and with a deeper, securer sense of what human life on this earth should be than in any previous period of the world's history.[21]

Donald Clark Hodges, in a lengthy discussion of my *Ethical Foundations of Marxism*,[22] modifies some of his earlier pronouncements on Marx's ethics and now argues that Marxism provides no philosophical foundation for ethics, just as it itself does not rest on any ethical foundation. Marx is merely a sociologist of morals and a social critic who shows people how their moral demands can be satisfied. But Hodges, too, goes on to write:

> One difference between the materialist and idealist approaches to human conduct is that the former bases itself upon the economic interests of individuals, which are necessary conditions of the full flowering of the personality, while the latter bases itself upon abstract principles, feelings and imaginary projections that provide little more than psychological comfort and the illusion of personal integrity. For those who have made their accommodation to poverty, as for those who have adjusted to physical and mental illness, self-interest consists in preserving the *status quo*. However, such people are not qualified judges even of their own interests. To judge one's own interests correctly is tantamount to knowing the assumed or conventional limits. Although disagreements arise from efforts to moderate conflicting aims and to implement them in the face of concerted opposition, there is much less reason for disagreement by qualified judges concerning the desirability of various forms of economic, social and political advancement over corresponding forms of degradation. As Engels notes in a critique of the humanistic ethics of Feuerbach, the happiness of man depends not upon moral but upon material considerations, especially economic instrumentalities, including the leisure affluence affords for enjoying members of the opposite sex, books, conversation, art, music, outdoor activities, and the like. . . . Instead of a moral struggle to rise above the pressures of the social environment, it is far more consonant with self-interest to struggle to bring economic and social conditions into conformity with human needs.[23]

The reader will hardly have failed to notice the tangle of unexamined moral-philosophical presuppositions that runs through this type of Marxist writing. There is a clear assumption of a life 'proper to man', constantly appealed to but quite inadequately discussed. In spite of all the play with empiricism, there is the distinction – made explicit by Hodges – between men's true or rational interests and their apparent, diseased, limited interests which are not to be counted as providing moral norms. Allied with this is the distinction, common in Marxist propaganda, between real 'needs' and mere irrational desires. Morality, in other words, is based on what men want, but we are to include only their rational, real (read approved?) wants. This is as true for the metaphysical Marxian humanist, with his rationalist conception of what is fitting for man, and his ultimately arbitrary singling out of some potentialities in place of others, as it is for the more empirical 'materialist'. Both, in concentrating attention on the practical tasks of social transformation, have tended to deal very cavalierly indeed with the moral presuppositions on which their support for such transformations is based. Thus we find the ethic of human self-realisation, a doctrine of what is proper or fitting for man, the alleged demands of enlightened self-interest and utilitarianism all floating about in loose, unsupported formulations – as though these conceptions had no history of discussion and criticism in moral philosophy.

There is, I think, a reason for all this. The type of views examined in this chapter attempt to avoid the problems of moral philosophy by appealing to what are allegedly common human demands, rejected only by the pathological. In doing so, the writers in question reduce ethics to politics (make it a matter of 'common consent', or counting heads) and import into ethical discussion the techniques characteristic of the political agitator. The moral philosopher is concerned with distinctions and with logical difficulties – for him, one exception to an allegedly universal rule is as fatal as ten thousand exceptions. His language is designed for precision, for bringing out the exact basis of disagreement; the politician's language tends to obscure issues in order to elicit consent. Marxist moral philosophy or ethical discussion, especially in recent years, has tended to vague proclamations of welfare and satisfaction and self-realisation of the individual as goals that all rational people pursue. In doing so, it has had more in common with election speeches than with moral philosophy or scientific enquiry. Just as the post-war enthusiasm for 'welfare' tended (on the theoretical side) to obscure all real problems and conflicts, to merge all sciences into one science and to gloss over the distinctions between policies and between men, so the Marxian appeal to what men really want, to human satisfaction and self-realisation, depends on the constant use of vague and morally loaded terms in an attempt to suggest agreement where there is in fact disagreement, unanimity where there is conflict. (This, incidentally, is why the utilitarianism of Marxists is normally negative utilitarianism – it seems even to them more plausible to say that all men want to remove suffering than to say that they pursue 'happiness'.) The philosopher's concern with examining in detail such terms as 'happiness', 'satisfaction', 'suffering' and 'interest' is entirely absent from Marxist writing.

One sociological point is worth adding. The illusion of a common interest, the notion that men all basically pursue the same thing, is most plausible at times of crisis, war, revolution, etc., when large sections of society feel that they face a fundamental, wide-ranging threat or impediment which must be removed before they can engage in or further any of their varied pursuits. It loses its plausibility in times of stability, when men resume a wider range of activities. We shall see in the next chapter how the recognition of moral complexity, and of the difficulty of moral philosophy, develops among Soviet philosophers precisely as Soviet society moves from crude war-time conditions to comparative stability and complexity, to the recognition that there is more than one interest in society, that planning can never be total and that human longings and aims conflict, both internally in the one person and as between one person and another. Co-operation and division are equally parts of human and of social life.

VI. ETHICS IN SOVIET PHILOSOPHY

Soviet Marxism–Leninism and its philosophy of dialectical materialism occupy a special, controversial, place in the history and theory of Marxian and Marxist thought. Officially, the Communist Party of the Soviet Union has seen itself as standing in true apostolic succession to Marx and Engels. It has devoted much effort to sponsoring and controlling (as a task of fundamental *political* importance) the propagation of a Marxist–Leninist philosophy, grounded in the classics of Marxism, allegedly representing a coherent and systematic Marxist view of the world. Soviet Marxism has become a pervasive official ideology of the Soviet State, taught in schools and universities as the only truly 'scientific' world outlook, deviation from which is at best an error and at worst a counter-revolutionary act. Sympathisers have claimed that the Soviet Union is the only country in which, for fifty years, a vast collective effort has gone into the study, systematisation and popularisation of Marxist thought; the results, therefore, should be viewed as those of a devoted and coherent school of Marxists, bringing many informed minds and a wealth of theoretical and practical experience to bear on each problem of Marxist philosophy. To most non-Communists, however, including social democratic Marxists, the realities of Soviet life and the theoretical constructions of Soviet philosophers have seemed a vicious and vulgar caricature of Marxist thought. The Russian Bolsheviks after 1917, they would say, transformed Marxism into a dogmatic theology meant to justify one-party rule and to establish ideological control over a backward peasant society. This theology was organised around 'sacred texts' (the works of Marx, Engels, Lenin and for a period Stalin) and an ecclesiastical authority that may not be challenged (the Communist Party of the Soviet Union); it recognised official teachers (the approved Party ideologists) and provoked or invented innumerable heresies sought out and persecuted as such. Not only did all this falsify the whole spirit of Marx's life and work, not only was it premised on the un-Marxian notion of a dictatorship *over* the proletariat in place of a dictatorship *of* the proletariat, but in making Marxist thought totally subservient to the day-to-day practical requirements and internecine power struggles of the Soviet régime it simply killed genuine critical Marxist thought and substituted philistine dogma and pseudo-philosophy for criticism and rationality.

Certainly, Soviet philosophy as an allegedly authoritative guide to Marxian thought has to be approached with great suspicion. The conditions of pervasive censorship, long coupled with the vicious use of political terror and political denunciation, successfully destroyed any public manifestation of independence or integrity on the part of Soviet philosophers as a body; we know that for many years they wrote and taught as they were ordered to write and teach. Even in the comparatively relaxed condition after Stalin, we still cannot be satisfied that the books published by Soviet philosophers in the Soviet Union today accurately reflect what they themselves believe. The Soviet philosopher suffers from the internal censorship set up by his own sense of prudence and the external censorship made ubiquitous by a police State, not to speak of the more general effects of the deliberate politicalisation and popularisation of philosophical thought.[24] Further, as Dr Z. A. Jordan has recently attempted to show in detail in his book *The Evolution of Dialectical Materialism* (London, 1967), the systematisation of Marxism popularised under the name of 'dialectical materialism' does not stem directly from Marx himself. It deviates from his attitudes in quite fundamental respects, it has gone through periods of evolution in which basic assumptions have been reinterpreted to produce substantial shifts in position. The creators of 'dialectical materialism' were Engels, Plekhanov, Lenin, Deborin, Stalin and the ideological commissions of the C.P.S.U., whose attitudes, concerns and ability were often very far removed from those of Marx himself, and, in various respects, from each other's.

Nevertheless, the consideration of Soviet Marxism–Leninism

and its view (or rather its successive views) on ethics has a certain point. A vulgarisation *can* help to illuminate a doctrine, both by bringing out more sharply its initial lacunae and inconsistencies, and by reminding us of the practical consequences to which it can lead. Dr Israel Getzler, in his biographical study of the Menshevik leader Martov (*Martov*, Melbourne U.P., 1967), shows us the moral disgust that Martov and other Menshevik leaders felt when faced, especially between 1903 and 1918, by Lenin's unscrupulous tactics and lack of nicety in moral matters (the scandal of the Schmidt inheritance and Lenin's connection with counterfeiting and bank robberies to augment Party funds are the best known instances). They felt, very deeply, that the Party of the Revolution must itself set a moral example – but, as Dr Getzler shows, they had the greatest difficulty in arguing this, in putting up an ethical counter-position, *from within Marxism*, while being still unwilling to go outside it. It is, indeed, the shifts in Communist attitudes to morality that we shall find especially instructive, while noting – as I shall argue below – that Communist thinkers have made no contribution to resolving the *problems* that Marxist pronouncements on ethics create.

Soviet Marxism–Leninism is an ideology. 'Generally speaking', as Professor Kichitaro Katsuda has recently put it,[25] 'a political ideology consists of three elements – first, a goal, a future image, or an ideal which it puts forth as the aim of the political movement or political power; secondly, an analysis and judgment of the given political situations on which policies and programmes of the political power or movement should be founded; and thirdly, a philosophy or myth to justify the formation of the party or political power.' Soviet Marxism–Leninism was able to draw from classical Marxism in quite a direct way two of the components needed – the utopian vision of the future Communist society which was the ultimate justification of the whole struggle and the Marxist analysis and critique of the class society showing that the 'old world' was both doomed and unworthy of preservation. On the ethical side, the utopian vision took up the ethic of the spontaneously co-operative, free and unalienated man, while the critique of bourgeois civilisation placed special emphasis on the 'materialist' critique of morality, on the 'exposure' of moral codes as serving class interests. The third element – the philosophy or myth justifying the Party's seizure of power and the Party dictatorship – was provided by the specifically Leninist component in Bolshevism, the elevation of the Communist Party and its cadre of professional revolutionaries as the mouthpiece of history and the representatives of 'consciousness'. It was this element which provided, on the ethical side, the notoriously end-directed ethic of Leninism – the good is that which promotes the power of the Party and hence the coming or consolidation of the Revolution; it is that which is 'on the side of history'. In the historical development of Bolshevism, as of political Marxism more generally, we shall find a historically conditioned tendency to emphasise, at various times, one element of this triad at the expense of others, coupled, however, with an attempt to keep all the options open and so to prevent the system from tearing apart in an obvious way. We shall first examine here the morality, or moral pronouncements, associated with each of these elements and then consider the way in which Soviet philosophers, as part of the recent revival of moral philosophy, have attempted to build them into a coherent philosophical ethic.

The utopian element in Russian Marxism reached its peak, as one might have expected, in the period just preceding and just following the Revolution itself. It drew, quite heavily, on religious messianic and nihilist traditions – the Revolution was to be a bloody act of purification, a total destruction of the Old World and the inauguration of a radically new society and a radically new set of human relationships. This is the theme of Alexander Blok's famous poem, 'The Twelve', where the true Christ is seen emerging from the destruction, rapine and profanity of Revolution. It was, it should be said, always stronger among 'free intellectuals' sympathetic to the Revolution than among Communists who had subjected themselves to the discipline of the Leninist Communist Party and were already concerned to impose a similar discipline on the whole society. Thus those whom Professor G. L. Kline has called the Nietzschean Russian Marxists[26] – Vol'ski, Lunacharsky, Bogdanov and Bazarov – writing

at the beginning of the twentieth century held out the vision of
the fully human, self-determined man in whom the conflict of
individual and society has been completely overcome, and whose
life is devoted to the creative mastery of things and the creative
expression of human capacities. Lunacharsky and Vol'ski, as
Professor Kline has reminded us, saw the free, creative *individual*
as the basis of the new morality: the bourgeoisie had freed the
individual in the hour of Revolution only to enslave him in the
hour of triumph, the proletariat would command the individual
in the hour of Revolution only to free him in the hour of triumph.
Bogdanov and Bazarov, on the other hand, put primary emphasis
on the collective, but as a spontaneous fusion of individuals, as
an ecstatic religious commune in which 'our tiny being disappears,
is fused with the infinite'. While there was some attempt to link
this morality with the proletariat, it was with the proletariat as the
most suffering and revolutionary class, as the class that would
destroy the old world of property and individualism, and thereby
purify man and society. To all the Nietzscheans, morality in the
truly Communist society would be a spontaneous, artistic expression of human nature – external norms and obligations would
disappear.

All this, however, stood on the very edge of Marxist thought in
Russia and did not long survive the realities of the New Society.
Bogdanov, Bazarov and Vol'ski fell into disfavour from the
moment of the Revolution; Lunacharsky, who served as the first
People's Commissar for Culture, followed them the moment
Bolshevik orthodoxy became more rigid. Those who were
genuinely concerned with ethics among Russian revolutionaries
invariably went outside Marxism – the group we have mentioned
to Nietzsche, another group (Berdyaev, Struve and Bulgakov
during their 'Marxist' phase) to Kant. Within Marxism there was
all too little to build on. The true intellectual guardians of Marxist
orthodoxy in Russia – G. V. Plekhanov, L. I. Akselrod (-Orto-
doks) and A. M. Deborin – characteristically took little interest in
ethics and ethical theory. What little they did say on the subject
was an eclectic mixture of Marx, Engels, Spinoza and Kautsky.
Lenin, the ultimately successful guardian, was, as Professor Kline

has put it,[27] 'a pure Machiavellian in the technical sense of the term: he systematically subordinated questions of individual and social morality to the tactical problem of the acquisition and maintenance of power. "Our morality", he declared in 1920, "is wholly subordinated to the interests of the class struggle of the proletariat." ' These words were echoed by Trotsky, Zalkind and the few other Party men who devoted any attention to ethics at that time. Nevertheless, certain aspects of the truly human ethic foreseen by Marx and in a less thoroughgoing way by Engels did become part of the utopian component even of official Marxist–Leninist ideology. The abolition of private property, exploitation and class conflict, it was argued, would produce a society in which the social and the individual interest came to coincide – the worker, by the conditions of his life in the factory and through his involvement in revolutionary struggle, was already the bearer of a new morality of co-operation, mutual help and dedication to a common cause. When all mankind became workers, when the very memory of private property and class distinctions had ceased to exist, the State, the police force, the bourgeois family, crime and self-seeking would wither away. So would external moral rules and sanctions. Disputes, as Lenin had said, would be settled on the spot, among comrades, the individual and the collective would be one. In the transitional period, however, all the emphasis was first on the Party and then on the collective. The educational theories of A. S. Makarenko, the conduct of Soviet schools and of the Communist Party cells, and Party propaganda generally all stressed the subordination of the individual to the demands of the group, his duty to submit to its criticism and to identify himself with its will. At the theoretical level, the precise nature of the group will and its relation to the wills of the individuals composing it were never examined; at the practical level, the group became the vehicle for the transmission of Party requirements and Party demands, handed down from above.

In the period between 1920 and 1936 – a period of the consolidation of Soviet power, and after 1928 of the attempt to impose a harsh labour discipline and harsh material sacrifices on a reluctant population – both the truly human ethic of freedom and

the utilitarian ethic of individual satisfaction were increasingly
relegated to the utopian future, while Leninist Machiavellianism
and the priority of the collective formed the content of the
'socialist' morality of the present. This was the period in which
Trotsky, in connection with terrorism and the civil war, denounced the 'Kantian-clerical', vegetarian-Quaker chatter about
the 'sanctity of human life', in which M. I. Kalinin (then and
later a sort of moral sage for the peasant and the worker) wrote:
'Our morality consists in this: all that which helps to strengthen
the working class, its might in battle and the course of socialist
construction, all that, without question, is obligatory for the
Komsomol and the member of the Communist Party, all that he
must do, all that is his moral duty.'[28] In the socialist society,
Makarenko wrote:

there should be no isolated individual, either protruding in the shape
of a pimple or ground into dust on the roadway, but a member of a
socialist collective. . . . The individual personality assumes a new
position in the educational process – it is not the object of educational
influence, but its carrier. It becomes its subject, but it becomes its
subject only by expressing the interests of the entire collective.[29]

The positive content of socialist morality was thus turned into a
form of labour discipline – emphasis on the 'duty' to work, the
'moral' value of toil, obedience to the collective, devotion to the
Soviet Union, socialism and the working class, hatred for its
enemies, readiness to give up one's self for economic upbuilding
or the victory of socialism. Thus the first, utopian component
of Marxist ideology was gradually reinterpreted to become a
theoretical base for the third, Leninist component of the ideology
– it became a morality of dedicated obedience and social conformity, a vehicle for Party power and Party control.

Neither have Soviet writers made any significant theoretical
contribution to the materialist critique of moralities, initially
linked with the second, critical element in Marxist–Leninist
ideology. Soviet criticism and analysis of bourgeois society has
been notable mainly for its crudity, vulgarity and frequent intellectual dishonesty: fifty years of Soviet philosophy have
produced nothing that can be regarded as an interesting economic

or social interpretation of a philosophical thinker or of a philosophical school of thought worthy to rank beside Francis Cornford's *From Religion to Philosophy* or E. B. Pashukanis's attempt to link civil law with the assumptions requisite for the operation of a market. The relationship between moral philosophy and the class structure of a society, though constantly proclaimed by Soviet philosophers, has not been brought out in any interesting or illuminating way. On the whole, Soviet philosophers have gone little further than linking discrete moral attitudes with class prejudices: Aristotle's contempt for slaves and women, Locke's concern with property and – at a somewhat more general level – the concern with hierarchy in 'feudal' philosophy and the growth of individualism and the assertion of individual rights as the bourgeois market begins to take over. The latter, of course, are sound points, but the Soviet periodisation of philosophy into slave-owning, feudal and bourgeois eras has tended to simplify and vulgarise their application. At the same time, the concern with periodisation and linking everything to a specific class-outlook has tended to obscure the genuine logical concerns of moral philosophers; it has led to the conflation of questions of form and content, of moral philosophy with moral attitudes. The very strong insistence on organising the whole history of philosophy around the allegedly fundamental dispute between materialism and idealism (between those who treat matter as primary and those who treat consciousness as primary) has proved particularly unilluminating in the history of ethics, where disputes and difficulties have cut right across this issue – if it was, indeed, ever an important issue in any branch of philosophy. The dispute on the relationship of 'ought' and 'is', for instance, which Soviet philosophers handle particularly badly, and the whole problem of establishing moral *obligation* are not connected with the question at issue between 'materialism' (realism, or naturalism?) and idealism. Soviet philosophers have thus far not got to grips with the real problems in the history of moral philosophy and have not contributed significantly to the understanding of this history. On the internal side, in relation to Soviet morality, the materialist critique of ethics was for a period used primarily to make moral and ethical questions subsidiary to the fulfilment of the Five-Year Plans and the tasks of socialist construction. It thus became a further prop for the end-directed ethic of the Leninist Party. It was through economic achievements and economic sacrifice that the truly human morality would ultimately be achieved, the argument ran; therefore, in the meantime, moral judgments have no independent force or significance.

In 1936, with the proclamation of the Stalin Constitution and the announcement that Soviet society had entered upon socialism, the doctrine of the primacy of the economic gave way to a new emphasis on stability and the moral and legal foundations of a socialist society. Normative law and normative morality were no longer seen as hang-overs from a capitalist past or as transitional measures in a period of struggle and construction – they were given a creative role in building the society of the future. (Dialectical materialism was reinterpreted accordingly.) Steps were taken to strengthen the family and respect for law as lasting social phenomena; increasing emphasis was put on the relatively independent force and role of morality as a set of norms for socialist living in a socialist society. The terrible purges and the Second World War limited the impact of this development for a period, but did not halt it. From 1946 onward, an increasing emphasis on Marxist ethics and Communist morality came to be felt; in 1951, a conference of Soviet and Czech philosophers agreed that the teaching of Marxist ethics was inadequate and confused and that specialist courses should be created. From that time onward, there has been a steady growth of both low-level moral exhortation and somewhat higher-level philosophical discussion in ethics. The number of articles and books, at both levels, has grown enormously. Quantitatively, at least, there is no longer an ethical lacuna in Soviet Marxism; if anything there is an unusually high degree of moralism for a modern society. (Soviet child-rearing manuals *advocate* the temporary, ostentatious withdrawal of love, refusal to 'play speaks', putting on of a sullen expression, etc., to show the offending child that it has wounded its parents in being 'selfish' – i.e. disobedient.)

The main theme that has come out of all this moral and

moralising activity, then, is the taking up of a frankly normative stand. In the last fifteen years – especially since the Twenty-Second Congress of the Communist Party of the Soviet Union in 1961 adopted 'the moral code of the builder of Communism' – the Marxist exposure of all normative morality as mere ideology or class interest disappeared from Soviet writing. A great deal of emphasis is now placed on such familiar normative ethical concepts of 'bourgeois' morality as conscience, duty, etc. The normative bindingness of Socialist morality as the truly human morality is constantly proclaimed. Its content, as listed in the new programme of the Communist Party, is devotion to the Communist cause, love of the socialist motherland and the other socialist countries, conscientious labour for the good of society, concern for the preservation and growth of public wealth (i.e. state property), a high sense of public duty and intolerance of actions harmful to the public interest, collectivism and comradely mutual assistance, humane relations between and mutual respect for individuals, honesty and truthfulness, moral purity, modesty and unpretentiousness in social and private life, mutual respect in the family and an uncompromising attitude to injustice, parasitism, dishonesty, careerism and money-grubbing, etc., etc.

'In the years of the cult of personality', the new Soviet *History of Philosophy* now says,[30] 'the inhuman, amoral character of a series of actions by Stalin and those closely associated with him – the infringement of legality, the repressive measures directed against honest people and even whole nationalities, the separation from the needs of the toilers – inflicted serious harm on the Communist education of the toilers. All this retarded the scientific working out of ethical problems.' Certainly, in reaction against the harsh inhumanity of the Stalin régime, there is now a strong tendency to emphasise certain moral values as having intrinsic worth – such values as honesty, sincerity, family love, truthfulness, etc. This has resulted in a growing interest, on the part of less servile Soviet philosophers, in the philosophy of values, in a desire to see ethics, like aesthetics, grounded on a set of categories and distinctions comparatively independent of politics. The result is that the present official systematisation of Marxist ethics, in trying to reflect various trends in the Soviet Union, is beginning to vacillate between a makeshift and eclectic view and a reactionary attempt (expressed by such 'philosophers' as Mitin, Fedoseyev and Shishkin) to maintain the older dogmatism in slightly less offensive form.

The formal position, as set out in the growing number of textbooks on Marxist–Leninist ethics designed for university use, runs something like this: Morality is the totality of norms governing the attitudes of men to one another and to society. These norms arise in consequence of social needs, and vary with fundamental changes in social relationships. In societies divided into classes, the social interest confronts the individual as an external, hostile force, in conflict with his individual interest. Further, the alleged representatives of the social interest – the ruling classes – put forward as the social interest what are in fact sectional interests, class interests, which call forth competing assertions of *their* class interests from the exploited. We thus have, in class societies, competing moralities. The moralities of the exploited classes, however, as the moralities of the overwhelming majority of mankind, contain some elements of a general, social interest which has been common to all periods. There is also moral value in the morality of classes that are or were 'progressive' in their time. In Communist-led societies, where private ownership and the class structure dependent on it have been abolished, the social interest, however, has become the conscious interest of the whole people. The individual and the social interest therefore here coalesce and true (unideological) morality becomes possible. Conscience and duty are the individual's subjective internalisation of the social interest, his recognition of his interdependence with his fellow-men. Under socialism, they provide man with moral norms that society sets before him, distinguished from legal norms only by the absence of physical sanctions.

These norms have so far not been discussed in Soviet philosophy at any level approaching logical, philosophical respectability. The precise nature and foundation of the social interest have not been examined and its relation to individual interests is consistently obscured. (The fact that the social interest both does and does not coincide with the individual interest is treated as an example of 'dialectical unity', which is to restate and not to solve the problem.) The social interest and the demand of the collective are not reduced to a summation of individual interests – yet the well-being of man is constantly presented as the fundamental norm of Communist morality. Here a passage from the Soviet philosopher S. Utkin may be cited as representative of the level of analysis:

It is part of every man's character to have an internal striving to be better, morally purer, spiritually richer. And this is the command of his conscience, which represents the dictates, first of all, of his closest social surroundings, of the feeling of responsibility before the collective in which he lives and works, before those nearest and dearest to him whose authority and opinion are the highest unwritten law for him.[31]

This running together, without serious examination and without any real supporting argument, of a particular individual's aspirations, of the 'needs' of society and the dictates of the social environment, and of the demands of other individuals, is completely characteristic of the Soviet discussion of morality in the socialist society.

At the same time, mainly as a result of certain political pronouncements by N. S. Khrushchev and the Twenty-First Congress of the C.P.S.U., there is now some emphasis on the universally human moral values of earlier ages, the so-called 'simple norms' of morality and justice, which were distorted in the society of exploitation, or not genuinely applied, but nevertheless even there recognised as having moral value. On the basis of these norms, Soviet philosophers are attempting to build up a system of *categories* of morality – such as justice, good, honour, conscience, duty and happiness, to take the categories nominated by L. A. Arkhangel'ski in his book *The Categories of Marxist Ethics* (Moscow, 1963). These they see as independent in form, if not in content, of the specific economic base of a given society. This, of course, comes extremely close to an axiology and there is, understandably enough, a revival of interest in the Soviet Union in the work of Nikolai Hartmann. The striking thing in all this is the disintegration of any coherent or distinctive Marxian view in ethics and the attempt to come back into some sort of main stream of normative ethical thought. Thus the Leningrad philosopher, V. P. Tugarinov, in his book *On the Values of Life and Culture* (Leningrad, 1960) turns his attention to such traditional values as truth, good and beauty and tries to go beyond the conception of duty (too strongly emphasised in Soviet ethics, he complains) to a conception of objective values, grounded in human nature itself (see especially p. 125). 'Good', he writes in terms all too reminiscent of 'bourgeois' philosophy, 'is benefit for people, for society, brought about *consciously*, with the aim of bringing about benefit' (Tugarinov's italics, p. 124). Truth, beauty and education are good because people are so constituted as to pursue them and to derive pleasure from them.

In a very recent article, the now somewhat discredited doyen of Soviet Party philosophers, Academician M. V. Mitin, writes: [32]

Either Marxism as a whole and Marxist philosophy in particular will retain all of their critical revolutionary substance, their inner ideological purity and *wholeness*, and will develop according to the teaching of Marx, Engels and Lenin, or they will take the path of eclecticism and . . . dissolve in a profusion of bourgeois and petty-bourgeois doctrines, superficially taking something from scientific communism but being in principle deeply hostile to it.

In forty years of philosophical activity, Mitin and his colleagues failed completely to work out a respectable coherent Marxist position in ethics, or even to address themselves to the real problems of the subject. In so far as Soviet philosophers are beginning to do genuine moral philosophy today (and they have yet to make any real or independent contribution to it), they are taking 'the path of eclecticism'.

VII. CONCLUSION

The difficulty that men – and moral philosophers – have encountered in trying 'to give ethics a foundation' stems primarily from the mixture of description and advocacy characteristic of moral claims. Emphasis on the prescriptive or advocative functions of moral statements constantly threatens to turn them into arbitrary commands; emphasis on their descriptive content invites disagreement and robs them of their normative force. Moral philosophers, despite Hume, have thus been tempted, consciously or unconsciously, to conflate the descriptive and prescriptive by using such key but unexamined moral concepts as 'value', 'pleasure', 'human nature', etc. The great progress made in moral philosophy in the last fifty years has not led to any convincing solution of its basic problems, but it has enabled us to see much more clearly how these problems arise. Moral philosophy, in this century, has passed through a vital stage of the clarification of issues, of the careful examination of the structure of moral language and the function of moral terms. Karl Marx lived and wrote before this important development took place; virtually all of his disciples have been unable to profit by it. At a time when competent philosophers have come carefully to distinguish the advocative or normative element in moral claims and disputes from the empirical, descriptive element, Marxists still insist on treating morality or moralities as undifferentiated wholes, running together their content, function and origin, devoting no attention to the character of moral arguments or moral justification, refusing to study the logic of moral disputes.

The failure to pay serious attention to questions of logic and to linguistic precision is the main reason why it is impossible to speak of a serious Marxist contribution to ethical philosophy. Soviet philosophers, for instance, attack sharply what they call the 'positivist' erection of a dichotomy between 'ought' and 'is'. But their argument against separating the prescriptive and the descriptive invariably. misses the point. It is perfectly true that demands are themselves facts, historical empirical occurrences, and that any 'ought-claim' will be grounded in such an empirical demand or principle. But the point is what function such demands or commands or principles perform in argument, whether they can be deduced from 'neutral' descriptions containing no demands or requirements, whether they can be 'refuted' or only opposed, disobeyed or ignored. In their attempt to ground morality in demands or requirements that everyone accepts (a very traditional move), Marxists, if anything, exceed the imprecision of traditional philosophers – the requirements of 'human nature' (sometimes real, sometimes ideal), social requirements, the requirements of art and culture as productive activities and the requirement of history are all run together without serious examination. This imprecision, I would argue, is necessary for anyone seeking to establish norms as though they were prescribed by the nature of society, or man, or human life. But the same imprecision arises on the critical side, in the materialist exposure of moralities. Even when Marxists treat moralities as not binding, as sets of sectional demands, they are unclear – to others and to themselves – precisely what sort of demands are in question, where they originate and what they seek.

In the field of ethics, then, Marx himself may be regarded as a social critic rather than as a moral philosopher. His argument, it is true, was directed primarily against authoritarian moralities seeking to bind man in the name of alleged moral 'laws' and his attention was devoted primarily to the lack of correspondence between social reality and alleged moral ideals. His own moral ideal – free, conscious and spontaneous co-operation between individuals – he took for granted; his concern was with removing those social conditions which, he believed, stood in the way of its realisation. His followers have on the whole maintained the habit of confusing problems of moral philosophy with problems of social reform. They claim as a virtue, instead of recognising as a theoretical defect, that they devote their attention to conditions that stand in the way of human happiness instead of asking precisely what 'happiness' means.

All this is not to say that Marx has made no contribution whatever to the discussion of ethics in modern philosophy. It was he who pointed the way to a sociology of morals, to the recognition of moral codes and moral principles as social products, formed in specific social contexts, derived from human activities and human and social demands. He has thus greatly increased our sophistication in talking about morals and he has enabled others – sociologists, anthropologists and psychologists – to increase it still further. But the problem in ethics has been the relevance of empirical information to ethical systems and moral claims, to the problems of moral philosophy. Until the logical analysis we have seen in the past fifty years was accomplished, this question could not be seriously considered. There is still sufficient disagreement among moral philosophers to make the very subject-matter of ethics a matter of dispute. But in so far as the points at issue are being narrowed down, and grasped more clearly, the philosophy of morals can once more be brought into conjunction with the sociology and psychology of morals. Moral philosophers might now recognise that there are empirical problems still outstanding, the relevance of which can now be discussed more fruitfully. The logic of moral discourse has had adequate examination, for the time being at least. Perhaps we should turn to some of the problems Marx left unsolved and that his followers have not tried to consider – what is the precise social or human empirical content of various moralities; if moralists have not been making mere empty noises, or random demands, what *have* they been talking about, what *sort* of demands do they make, *what* have they considered morally relevant and *why*? If ethics is concerned with the conditions of co-operation, what *are* the possible types of co-operation, how do their conditions vary? Are 'rules' connected with people, or with activities – is ethics concerned with individuals or ways of life? It is in these areas that a sensitivity to history and to social questions, such as Marx had, is invaluable to the moral philosopher.

NOTES

1. D. Riazanov *et al.* (eds.), *Marx–Engels Gesamtausgabe* (Berlin–Moscow, 1927 f.) section 1, vol. 5, p. 227.
2. The sharp division between Marx and Engels which needs to be made when dealing with their theoretical work is now increasingly accepted in serious scholarly work, but still seems to occasion surprise and resentment in some circles. Suffice it here to recall the words written by Joseph Schumpeter when he found himself making the same division: 'I observe that the few comments on Engels that are contained in this sketch ["Marx as an Economist"] are of a derogatory nature. This is unfortunate and not due to any intention to belittle the merits of that eminent man. I do think, however, that it should be frankly admitted that intellectually and especially as a theorist he stood far below Marx. We cannot even be sure that he always got the latter's meaning. His interpretations must therefore be used with care.' - Joseph A. Schumpeter, *Capitalism, Socialism and Democracy* (4th edn, London, 1959) p. 39.
3. See, for instance, the famous passage in Marx's Preface to the first edition of *Capital*, vol. 1, where Marx insists that the capitalist and the landowner, though portrayed in a far from rosy light in his work, are considered only as personifications of economic categories, as carriers of class relationships and class interests. The individual, Marx adds, cannot be made responsible for conditions of which he is the creature. In general terms, Marx's view here and elsewhere implies that systems, not people, are the objects of moral judgment.
4. Eugene Kamenka, *The Ethical Foundations of Marxism* (London, New York, 1962) p. vii.
5. Karl Popper, *The Open Society and Its Enemies* (London, 1957) vol. II, p. 199.
6. Herbert Marcuse, *Eros and Civilization* (London, 1956) pp. 109–10.
7. The revolutionary implications of the Kantian philosophy have been least appreciated in England, where interest in Kant has centred on the logical and epistemological concerns of the *Critique of Pure Reason* as attempts to overcome the discrete atomism of Humean empiricism and where the discussion of Kant's moral philosophy has concentrated on the concepts of duty and inclination. At the personal level, Englishmen have seen Kant as a model of Protestant decorum.

Only recently, through the work of such Continentally trained historians of philosophy as Ernst Cassirer, has the radical impact of Kant's thought been appreciated.

8. For an attempt to document this development, see Eugene Kamenka, *The Ethical Foundations of Marxism*, esp. pp. 17–86.

9. Ludwig Feuerbach, *The Essence of Christianity*, trans. by Marian Evans (New York, 1957) p. 270.

10. A. M. Deborin, *Ludwig Feuerbach* (Moscow, 1923) p. 360. This, the final sentence of the book, was dropped from the 1929 reprint; less than two years later, Deborin was condemned, in part, for failing to emphasise sufficiently the creative leap between Marx and Feuerbach.

11. Robert C. Tucker, *Philosophy and Myth in Karl Marx* (Cambridge U.P., 1961).

12. Maximilien Rubel, 'Le concept de démocratie chez Marx', in *Contrat Social*, vol. VI, No. 4.

13. Karl Marx, 'On the Jewish Question', in *Marx–Engels Gesamtausgabe*, sec. I, vol. I, sub-vol. i, p. 603, or in Karl Marx, *Early Writings*, trans. and ed. by T. B. Bottomore (London, 1963) p. 37.

14. Karl Marx, *Economico-Philosophical Manuscripts* in *Marx–Engels Gesamtausgabe*, sec. I, vol. 3, pp. 111–12, in *Early Writings*, p. 153; Karl Marx, *Grundrisse der Kritik der politischen Ökonomie* (Berlin, 1953) p. 505.

15. Adam Schaff, *A Philosophy of Man* (New York, 1963) p. 84.

16. For a detailed discussion of Engels's account of truth, see John Anderson, 'Marxist Philosophy', in *Australasian Journal of Psychology and Philosophy* (1935), pp. 24 ff., esp. pp. 26–32.

17. Eugene Kamenka, 'Marxism and the History of Philosophy', in John Passmore (ed.) *The Historiography of the History of Philosophy* (Supplement 5 to *History and Theory*, The Hague, 1965) pp. 83–104, esp. pp. 87–8; and Eugene Kamenka, *The Ethical Foundations of Marxism*, pp. 134–42.

18. I. N. Lushchitski *et al.* (eds.) *Osnovy marksistsko–leninskoi etiki* (*Foundations of Marxist–Leninist Ethics*) (Minsk, 1965) p. 17.

19. Adam Schaff, *A Philosophy of Man*, pp. 132–3.

20. Howard Selsam, *Ethics and Progress* (New York, 1965) p. 13.

21. Op. cit. p. 10.

22. Donald Clark Hodges, 'Marx's Ethics and Ethical Theory', in Ralph Miliband and John Saville (eds.) *The Socialist Register 1964* (London, 1964) pp. 227–41.

23. Op. cit. p. 238.

24. For a description of the conditions under which Soviet philosophers have worked, and of the resultant cynicism and dishonesty, see Eugene Kamenka, 'Soviet Philosophy – 1917–1967' in A. Simirenko (ed.) *Social Thought in the Soviet Union* (Chicago, 1969), pp. 77–110, and

Eugene Kamenka, 'Philosophers in Moscow' in *Survey – Journal of Soviet and East European Studies* (1967), no. 62, pp. 15–24.

25. Kichitaro Katsuda, 'Dilemmas of the Soviet Totalitarian System', in *Review – A Journal for the Study of Communism and Communist Countries* (Tokyo, 1965) no. 6, pp. 1–2.

26. See G. L. Kline, 'Changing Attitudes Toward the Individual', in C. E. Black (ed.) *The Transformation of Russian Society* (Cambridge, Mass. 1960) pp. 606–25, and G. L. Kline, 'Theoretische Ethik im russischen Frühmarxismus', in *Forschungen zur osteuropäischen Geschichte* (1963) vol. 9, pp. 269–79.

27. G. L. Kline, 'Soviet Morality, Current' in V. Ferm (ed.) *The Encyclopedia of Morals* (New York, 1956) at p. 570. The point that the ethic of Plekhanov and his disciples is an eclectic mixture of Marx, Engels, Spinoza and Kautsky has also been emphasised by Kline.

28. Cited from M. I. Kalinin, *O kommunisticheskom vospitanii* (*On Communist Education*) (Moscow, 1958) p. 93. The frequency with which Kalinin is cited in Soviet writing on the 1920s today does not reflect his importance at the time, but only the fact that he is one of the few Old Bolsheviks who have not become un-persons through association with the disgraced, i.e. Trotsky, Bukharin and, finally, Stalin.

29. Cited from A. S. Makarenko, *Sochineniya* (*Works*) 7 vols. (Moscow, 1950–2) vol. 5, p. 333; vol. 2, p. 403.

30. M. A. Dynnik *et al.* (eds.) *Istoriya filosofii* (*History of Philosophy*), 6 vols. (Moscow, 1957–65) vol. VI, book 1, p. 478.

31. S. Utkin, *Ocherki po marksistsko–leninskoi etike* (*Notes on Marxist–Leninist Ethics*) (Moscow, 1962) p. 300.

32. M. V. Mitin, 'Razvitie dialekticheskogo materializma v posleoktyabrskuyu epokhu' ('The Development of Dialectical Materialism in the Post-October Epoch') in *Voprosy filosofii* (1968), No. 1, p. 23.

BIBLIOGRAPHY

(Books are listed only once, under the heading to which they are primarily relevant, but often contain material bearing on other sections. Foreign language works, with the exception of Dr Rubel's invaluable anthology, have been excluded.)

GENERAL BACKGROUND

Berlin, I., *Karl Marx – His Life and Environment* (3rd edn, New York, 1963).

Burns, E. (ed.) *A Handbook of Marxism* (New York, 1935).

Kamenka, E., *Karl Marx* (London, Macmillan – forthcoming).

Lichtheim, G., *Marxism: An Historical and Critical Study* (London, New York, 1961).

Marx, K., *Pages choisies pour une éthique socialiste*, ed. M. Rubel (Paris, 1948).

Meyer, A. G., *Marxism: The Unity of Theory and Practice* (Ann Arbor, 1963).

Nicolaievsky, B., and Maenchen-Helfen, O., *Karl Marx: Man and Fighter* (London, [1936]).

Ulam, A. B., *The Unfinished Revolution* (New York, 1960).

CHAPTERS II AND III

Bell, D., *The End of Ideology*, esp. ch. 15 (rev. edn, London, New York, 1962).

Dupré, L., *The Philosophical Foundations of Marxism* (New York, 1966).

Fromm, E. (ed.) *Socialist Humanism* (New York, 1965, 1966; London, 1967).

Kamenka, E., *The Ethical Foundations of Marxism* (London, New York, 1962).

Marx, K., *Early Writings*, ed. T. B. Bottomore (London, 1963).

Tucker, R., *Philosophy and Myth in Karl Marx* (Cambridge, 1961).

CHAPTERS IV AND V

Acton, H. B., *The Illusion of the Epoch*, Part II (London, 1955; Boston, 1957).

Engels, F., *Herr Eugen Dühring's Revolution in Science (Anti-Dühring)* (New York, 1939).

—— *Ludwig Feuerbach and the Outcome of Classical German Philosophy* (numerous edns).

Kautsky, K., *Ethics and the Materialist Conception of History* (Chicago, 1918).

Marx, K., and Engels, F., *The German Ideology*, Parts I and III, ed. R. Pascal (London, 1939).

—— —— *The Communist Manifesto* (numerous edns).

Selsam, H., *Socialism and Ethics* (New York, 1949).

—— and Martel, H., *Reader in Marxist Philosophy*, Parts V and VII (New York, 1963).

—— *Ethics and Progress* (New York, 1965).

Venable, V., *Human Nature: The Marxian View* (London, 1946).

CHAPTER VI

Contributions in the journal *Studies in Soviet Thought* (Fribourg 1961–) esp. by Richard T. De George.

Marcuse, H., *Soviet Marxism – A Critical Analysis* (London, 1958; with new preface, New York, 1961).

Programme of the Communist Party of the Soviet Union (New York, 1961).

Translations of Soviet philosophical articles in the journal *Soviet Studies in Philosophy* (New York, 1962–).

Wetter, G. A., *Dialectical Materialism: A Historical and Systematic Survey of Philosophy in the Soviet Union* (London, 1958).

—— *Soviet Ideology Today* (New York, 1966).

5

EXISTENTIALIST ETHICS

MARY WARNOCK

I. INTRODUCTION

Anyone writing about Existentialism ought perhaps to begin by trying to define what is being discussed. Yet one may well feel apologetic for attempting yet another definition of this particular term, since the books on the subject are innumerable, and there is not one of them that does not start with an attempt at a new definition. This is understandable, for there are grave difficulties in the way of reaching a satisfactory account of the matter. In the body of philosophical writing which could reasonably be called Existentialist, there is a whole number of contrary tendencies, and trying to reduce these to order is apt to lead to no more than an historical account of the whole Existentialist trend in philosophy, starting with Socrates. On the other hand, if one tries to extract the salient point of Existentialism by concentrating on the official statement of its central concept, namely the belief that *existence precedes essence*, then this does not advance one very far. For the belief itself is not readily intelligible, and in any case it has little point except in the context of the complete system of Sartre's philosophy. But Sartre cannot be thought to have been the only Existentialist, even though he was the most systematic. (I write of him in the past since, as we shall see, he is not an Existentialist any more.) Other short definitions seem to suffer the same fate. Either they do not make sense, or they apply to only part of the field. I shall, therefore, abandon the attempt to define Existentialism.

Nevertheless, one must not exaggerate the complexities of the subject. There is, without doubt, such a phenomenon as Existentialist philosophy, and a group of Existentialist philosophers, and it is to the members of this group that I shall now turn. If one has to be content with the discovery of no more than a family resemblance between the members, one may reflect that the same would probably have to content one if the subject were Empiricism, Rationalism, or Idealism. As to the question who is to be included in the group, this too presents difficulties, but, for the present purpose, not important difficulties. For my aim is to try to state what is the *general* ethical standpoint of Existentialism, and with what *common* presuppositions Existentialist philosophers must approach the construction of a moral philosophy; and this can be done without settling the question of the exact boundaries of Existentialism itself. There are some agreed, central, Existentialist writers, and it is enough, for the present purpose, to concentrate attention on some of these. I shall in fact consider only three. First, I shall discuss briefly the work of Søren Kierkegaard (1813–55), who actually invented the term 'Existentialism', and is in many ways properly regarded as the father of the movement. Next will come Martin Heidegger (1889–), particularly his book *Sein und Zeit*, translated as *Being and Time* (London, 1962). Finally, I shall consider at some length the pre-war work of Jean-Paul Sartre (1905–), concentrating mainly on his long book *L'Être et le Néant*, first published in Paris in 1943, and translated into English, as *Being and Nothingness*, by Hazel Barnes (London, 1957).

There is one more general warning which should be given. In the philosophers who are about to be discussed there is no sharp or clear distinction between ethics and the rest of philosophy. They sought, all of them, to get us to see the world in a new light, and if they succeeded, this would no doubt affect, to some extent, the way we behaved, and the way we thought about our own behaviour and that of others, as much as it would affect how we thought about other things. Thus it is sometimes possible to deduce an ethical theory, or something like it, from their philosophy, for it may be possible to say, in their persons, 'This is how you ought to see human conduct'. But, in general, this is all that can be done. All I can hope is that, in the following exposition, the *kind* of ethical outlook that is implicit in Existentialism will emerge. But it must be clearly stated at the outset that what emerges is for the most part something less than a complete ethical theory or system. Nor is it just an accidental feature of the writers in question that in none of them is there to be found a coherent or systematic moral philosophy. To construct such a system would perhaps have been impossible, in the sense that it would have been contrary to the general intention of their work.

The most systematic Existentialist, as I have already said, is J.-P. Sartre, but even he had no properly ethical theory. All the same, most of the present essay is concerned with Sartre, and this perhaps requires some explanation. The first justification is that he is plainly the most influential living philosopher who has ever been willing to be called an Existentialist. (Heidegger, whom I shall consider very briefly, is not willing to be so described. Moreover, except in his own country, his influence has mostly been through the writings of Sartre.) Secondly, there is in Sartre an extraordinary combination of influences at work, and this extreme receptivity to the thought of other philosophers is itself a characteristic of Existentialism. Everything is grist to their mill. Everything is taken over and 'interiorised', in Sartre's word, that is to say, made personal. Thirdly, Sartre has given up Existentialism; and this fact is not irrelevant. For, as I hope to show, it was impossible for him to produce a coherent ethical theory within the confines of Existentialism; and it was partly for this reason, though doubtless also for other more political reasons, that he finally gave up Existentialism for Marxism. By discussing the development of Sartre's thought, then, we may hope to throw some light on the common presuppositions and the necessary limitations of Existentialist thought, in so far as it refers to ethics.

II. KIERKEGAARD

Let us now turn to Søren Kierkegaard. There are in his writings certain ideas which in one form or another recur in all Existentialist writers, and which are crucial in determining the nature of Existentialist ethics, though these ideas are later developed in ways which would be surprising to Kierkegaard himself, and would certainly have been rejected by him. Most obviously, the development of Sartrean Existentialism, its conversion to Marxism, and its final extinction, would have been repulsive to Kierkegaard. But, all the same, there are seeds of even this development in his own work.

What, then, are the features of his work, and indeed of his life, which make it reasonable to think of him as the first Existentialist writer? He was, as a child, deeply affected by the religious gloom and guilt of his father. As a young man he believed himself to have thrown off this influence entirely and to have escaped what seemed like the intolerable chains which had, quite unnecessarily, been imposed on him in his childhood. For a time he devoted himself to observing and enjoying the world, without any commitment either to a faith or to a set of moral principles. In 1836 he underwent a conversion to morality; and two years later he was converted again, this time to Christianity. Each of the stages he went through, as he looked back on them afterwards, seemed, to various degrees, stages of illusion. His freedom after his childhood was illusory (a stage which he called the 'Aesthetic'); his conversion to morality committed him to belief in a kind of universal law absent from the Aesthetic. This was a higher stage, as he later saw it, but could not be the final stage in his development, because it was based on the illusion of 'humanism', or the failure to recognise the existence of the *transcendental* as an element in human life. The conversion to religion was the removal of this illusion, and it was now possible for him to choose to adopt the standpoint of faith.

These stages in his own development came to seem to Kierkegaard to be general stages in the development of human beings, who have the possibility of living at any of the stages permanently, or of moving from the lower to the higher. Each move to a higher stage must be something which the individual himself decides, for himself, to make. One cannot simply be told 'Adopt the standpoint of faith', nor could arguments, for instance the argument that one would be happier if one did, be sufficient to bring about the conversion. To be converted is to see for oneself that a certain belief or set of beliefs which one had previously held was false or inadequate. The new belief must be accepted, not merely as an intellectually preferable belief, nor merely as a belief based on satisfactory evidence, but as something which was true *for* the person who accepted it — that is as a truth by which he himself would be prepared to live, a truth, perhaps, which he loved.

It is from this feature of his work that it is possible to derive all that is most important and most characteristic in Existentialism, and in Existentialist ethics in particular. Kierkegaard wrote in order to free people from illusion. Now it might be argued that this is a somewhat trivial claim if properly examined, though it sounds grand enough. For, the argument would go, anyone who believes that what he says is true, and who, moreover, believes that he is the first to see this truth, or that other people have made mistakes — any such person writes in order to free his readers from illusion. If one even writes down the true proposition that today is Thursday, and does this in order to inform, then one does it also to free people from the possible illusion that today is Wednesday or Friday. To argue in this way would be to miss the peculiar point in the concept of illusion as employed by Kierkegaard; but it would also, I think typify a kind of response to Existentialist writing which is common and understandable enough.

To take the second point about response first: I should be inclined to regard it almost as a touchstone or criterion of an

author's being classifiable as an Existentialist, that a reader may
get impatient and accuse him of gross exaggeration and pretentiousness; that the reader may be inclined to deflate him and
'boil down' what he seems to be saying to some true but absolutely platitudinous remark. Thus, the impatient reader who is
told that we face our freedom in anguish may say, 'All this amounts
to is that often we are hard pressed to decide what to do'. So,
faced with a claim that Kierkegaard wrote to free us from illusion,
this same sceptic says, 'Well, so does the bank manager who
writes to tell me I have an overdraft'. But in this case the word
'illusion' is the important one. It must be emphasised that an
illusion is not a mere false belief, and that to replace illusion by
true belief is to replace it by something, as I have already suggested, which is more than just the acceptance of an objectively
true proposition. For to see something previously believed *as*
illusion is to see it as to be detested; and to accept something as
true is to accept it as illuminating to oneself *personally*. So, to
live in a state of illusion is to live in a state in which one suffers
from some total misconception, and to be freed from this condition is to see one's whole life in a totally new way. Kierkegaard
would regard it as useless merely academically to put people right.
He aimed to change them and set them on a different path.

The worst illusion, because the most persistent and most liable
to dominate people's thought, and indeed to be welcomed by
them, was, in his view, *objectivity*. We have lost the capacity for
subjectivity and it is, he says, the task of philosophy to find this
capacity for us. Objectivity may be characterised in various ways.
It shows itself in the tendency to accept rules governing both
behaviour and thought. Thus, any subject-matter which is bound
by rules of evidence, or which can be properly taught in the class
room, is in the grip of objectivity. History is objective if it is
thought of as something in which the true can be definitely, once
and for all, sifted out from the false, or if some absolute standard
of what counts as good evidence or a conclusive argument is
adopted. Morality is objective as soon as it is encapsulated in
rules or principles which can be handed on from master to pupil
or from father to son. The ethical phase of human development,

as of Kierkegaard's own development, as we have seen, was characterised by the finding and observing of universal rules of conduct, held to be equally valid for everybody, and such that, in principle, they could have been written down.

He defines the objective tendency as that which 'proposes to make everyone an observer, and in its maximum to transform him into so objective an observer that he become almost a ghost, scarcely to be distinguished from the tremendous spirit of the historical past' and he says '. . . the ethical is, *becoming an observer*!* That the individual must become an observer is the *ethical* answer to the problem of life . . .'.[1] To become an observer is to treat life as either history or as natural science. The historical standpoint raises the question 'What is my role in history?' or 'How will I look to future observers?' The scientific standpoint forces us perpetually to raise the question: 'By what natural law is human behaviour, including my own, determined?' Briefly, then, the objective is the rule-governed. It is the *myth* of objective truth which Kierkegaard above all wanted to explode. Hence was derived his hostility to science; for his *Concluding Unscientific Postscript* is in fact not so much unscientific as anti-scientific. But the sphere in which the myth of objectivity seemed to Kierkegaard not only dominating but also disastrous was religion — in particular, Christianity. For, though he returned to Christianity, it was not to the Christianity of his father. '. . . an objective acceptance of Christianity' he writes '(*sit venia verbo*) is paganism or thoughtlessness.' And '. . . Christianity protests against every form of objectivity; it desires that the subject should be infinitely concerned about himself. It is subjectivity that Christianity is concerned with, and it is only in subjectivity that its truth exists, if it exists at all; objectively, Christianity has absolutely no existence. If its truth happens to be only in a single subject, it exists in him alone; and there is greater Christian joy in heaven over this one individual than over universal history and the System . . .'[2]

It is the task of philosophy to convert people to the subjective. But subjectivity is extraordinarily difficult to achieve, for it is

* Present writer's italics.

apparently futile to strive to be what one already is, namely, an individual human being; and the tendency of all human beings is to fall into the trap of identifying themselves with something else, with some party or sect; or else, intellectually, to become impersonal, and to think of contributing to scientific knowledge absolutely. For the question of *whose* knowledge or *whose* truth it is becomes absurd, directly any newly-discovered proposition is added to the corpus of scientific knowledge in general. Therefore the individual may get lost, either in the acceptance of the dogma of a party or a creed, or in the acceptance of this body of scientific knowledge to which he may make contributions.

Subjective knowledge is different from objective knowledge in two ways. First, it cannot simply be passed on from one person to the next, nor added to by different researchers. There could be no such thing as the corpus of subjective knowledge. Secondly, what is known subjectively necessarily has the nature of a paradox, and must therefore require faith before it is known. Now faith is more like a sentiment than a thought, and everything that Kierkegaard says of subjective knowledge is appropriate rather to the emotions than to the intellect. Indeed he says: '. . . Christianity wishes to intensify passion to the highest pitch; but passion is subjectivity, and does not exist objectively.'

The absolute contrast between objective and subjective knowledge is brought out in the following passage: 'When the question of truth is raised in an objective manner, reflection is directed objectively to the truth, as an object to which the knower is related. Reflection is not focussed on the relationship, however, but upon the question whether it is the truth to which the knower is related. If only the object to which he is related is the truth, the subject is accounted to be in the truth. When the question of truth is raised subjectively, reflection is directed subjectively to the nature of the individual's relationship; if only the mode of this relationship is in the truth, the individual is in the truth even if he should happen to be thus related to what is not true.' And: 'When subjectivity, inwardness, is the truth, the truth becomes objectively a paradox; and the fact that the truth is objectively a paradox shows in its turn that subjectivity is the truth. For the objective situation (of entertaining a paradoxical thought) is repellent; and the expression for the objective repulsion constitutes the tension and the measure of the corresponding inwardness. The paradoxical character of the truth is its objective uncertainty; this uncertainty is the expression for the passionate inwardness and this passion is precisely the truth. . . . The eternal and essential truth, the truth which has an essential relationship to an existing individual because it pertains essentially to existence . . . is a paradox. But the eternal essential truth is by no means in itself a paradox; but it *becomes** paradoxical by virtue of its relationship to an existing individual.'[3]

The typical example of this tension between the objective uncertainty and the inward truth is that of the Socratic profession of ignorance, the claim to know nothing except that one knows nothing. The inwardness of Socrates was his whole life and method of philosophical enquiry, his asking of questions and shattering of accepted presuppositions and pretensions to knowledge. Objectively, the result of the Socratic enquiry was always to produce confusion and bewilderment. But, subjectively, it was the true method. So, analogously, in the true Christian, faith is the truth which is contrasted with the objective absurdity of his life. Socratic ignorance is the precursor of the *absurd*, and the Socratic life of seeking subjective truth is the precursor of the life of faith.

In these passages which I have quoted we have, it seems to me, the salient features of all subsequent Existentialist thought. This does not mean that all Existentialists deliberately derived all or any part of their thought from that of Kierkegaard; but rather that he first manifested the tendencies which are the mark of Existentialism, whoever practises it. First, there is the serious endeavour to remove from people the illusions by which they live — the illusions of objective moral law or objective scientific truth. There is such law and there is such truth, but both are essentially trivial and pointless, Secondly, the alternative to the illusion is the recognition that each person, in his own individual existence, must receive and understand a purely personal and

* Present writer's italics.

subjective truth. This truth cannot be stated in propositions which could be handed on to another person. Just as the individual has his own passions and his own life to live, so he has his own truth.

Most characteristically, then, Existentialism will undermine the distinction between thinking and feeling, between the rational and the sentimental. And, equally characteristically, it will preach a kind of doctrine which cannot be just accepted or rejected intellectually, but will essentially influence a person's life if he accepts it. So it is clear from considering this first example of Existentialist thought, i e. the removal of illusion, that it would be absurd to expect a disunction between ethics and epistemology, between moral philosophy and the rest of philosophy. If there is any Existentialist ethics, it is to be extracted from this total view of the world, in which each man makes his own choice of the truth for himself. What we have here is not a system, for to create a system of philosophy was, in Kierkegaard's view, the very way to render philosophy pointless, something which could be thoughtlessly or merely academically read, and accepted or rejected as a whole. Each man must, we are told, *find* the truth in inwardness for himself. To objectify is to render truth trivial. For instance, to objectify religion leads to a watering-down of the central paradox. In the case of Christianity it leads to the attempt to rationalise and make easily acceptable the central paradox of the Incarnation.

Existentialism of this kind may be happily married to religion. And there have been other religious, or at least theistic, Existentialist thinkers, all of whom, to a greater or less extent, attempted descriptions of the personal and individual nature of the inward process which should lead a man to a true view of God and the universe. For example, I should at least mention the work of Gabriel Marcel, who was himself strongly influenced by Martin Büber in holding that the true essence or meaning of existence could be distilled in encounters between two persons, whether both human persons, or one human and one divine. It is easy to see how such a theory, since it explicitly seeks for a significance in the universe at large and finds it distilled in human life, might have a bearing on ethics, though not directly. For both how a man thinks he should behave, and how he thinks he should describe and analyse human behaviour as a whole, could be determined by a general view of the world in which human relationship of a personal kind was the highest value. In such a theory the essentially personal and individual nature of human experience is emphasised, even though this experience is thought to be *of* something other than mere human feelings and sensations, namely, *of* the transcendental. A man may freely choose to move to a stage of existence in which he can recognise and experience the transcendental in his own life; or, if he does not make the choice, his whole life may be given up to the illusion of the public, the agreed, the polite, and the scientific.

I want now to go on to suggest that, though this kind of belief is characteristically Existentialist, yet the foundation of such thought on a faith in God or the transcendental is by no means necessary to Existentialist philosophy; that the characteristic features of Existentialism are indeed intensified and made sharper if isolated in a purely human context. Once again I can hope to show this only by taking a single example, that of Heidegger.

III. HEIDEGGER

In the work of Martin Heidegger one can see the same features which emerged in Kierkegaard as characteristic of Existentialist thought. But it must be said that in more ways than one it is anomalous and perhaps unfair to class Heidegger as an Existentialist thinker at all. For one thing, as I have said already, he repudiates the description himself, and this ought to carry some weight; for another thing, there is one respect in which he comes at the opposite end of the philosophical scale from Kierkegaard. For he is above all an old-fashioned Hegelian system-builder, who aims to present the complete truth about the universe in absolute terms; and moreover his actual style of writing is pretentious, highflown, and dependent on technical jargon to an extent that would have disgusted Kierkegaard, the most hostile of all men to the pompous and self-important. Finally, although much of his description of human life seems, as we shall see, to be motivated by a Kierkegaardian desire to free his readers from illusion, and to explain how they may lead their lives in the truth, yet he himself denies any such motive, and claims that his terms of description are absolutely neutral and non-evaluative. I shall return to this later. For the moment it must be enough to say that on this point it seems impossible to take Heidegger at his word.

Despite these doubts, then, let us turn to Heidegger, or rather to those limited parts of his thought which have some relevance to the subject-matter of ethics. I shall not concern myself with the much-debated question whether Heidegger is really an atheist or not; I wish to concentrate on that part of his philosophy which is concerned with human beings and their existence in the world, and here, at least, there is no sign of theism to be found. It is here, too, that we can see a very natural development of Existentialist thought, for with the removal of any question of finding a relationship with God, or living according to some divine purpose, the scope of human freedom, the burdensomeness of choosing how to live, and of finding a system of values, is vastly increased. Heidegger tells us that there are two possible modes of existence, the 'authentic' and the 'inauthentic'. It is these terms which he claims, unplausibly, are entirely without evaluative connotation; they are, he says, simply descriptive of two ways of living. But if so, then he should have found some better words to describe them. And in fact the whole tenor of his thought, in so far as it is intelligible at all, is to present the inauthentic as something from which one can be helped by philosophy to escape. What, then, is this distinction? How does Heidegger make use of it?

Many of the ideas in Heidegger's description of human reality we shall look at again when they occur in the writings of Sartre; in Heidegger they are, in every case, more obscure, and it seems to me more ambiguous. I shall content myself here with the briefest possible summary.

Heidegger's main concern in *Sein und Zeit* (*Existence and Being*) is the problem of 'Being' in general. It is far from clear what this problem is, but at any rate the approach to its solution is said to be through the consideration of the nature of man, who stands in a peculiar relation to Being as a whole, because of his unique ability to raise questions about it. Man is the only being in the world who is capable of considering the nature of Being as a whole, and is therefore in a unique way exposed to it. Man is defined as 'potential existence'. This is to say that man is always *transcending* what he is at any given moment; he is always stretching towards the future and aiming at something which he is not yet. Furthermore, man is not a being in isolation. His existence is 'existence-in-the-world', and so he is conditioned, in every mode of his thought and action, not only by the material situation in which he finds himself but also, crucially, by other people in the world. Being bound up with other people is an essential mode of the existence of each of us. The being of man is 'being with' ('*mitsein*'). All individual or private concerns and standpoints exist only against the background of ways of thinking and looking common to men as members of a social group. The group is mankind at large, and is referred to as the 'One'. It is from the existence of the One as a necessary part of man's being that the distinction between authentic and inauthentic existence is derived. To accept one's role as a kind of generalised man, as *totally* part of the group, to be content with this, is to live inauthentically. It is possible, on the other hand, to seek to realise one's possibilities as an individual, alone, and as if one were isolated and independent. This is authentic existence. The way to achieve it is to treat one's life as a progress towards death, the only event, as Heidegger thinks, in which we are genuinely, each one of us, alone.

Sartre's exposition of Heidegger, in *Being and Nothingness*, is useful in helping us to understand the kind of failure involved in inauthenticity, and the kind of awakening which thinking about oneself in a new and philosophical way is intended to produce. He says: 'When I am in the inauthentic mode of the "they" the world offers me a sort of impersonal reflection of my possibilities, in the form of instruments and complexes of instruments which belong to "everybody", and which belong to me in so far as I am everybody: ready-made clothes, public transport, parks, gardens, common land, shelters made for *anyone* who needs them, and so on. . . . The inauthentic state, which is my ordinary state in so far as I have not realised my conversion to authenticity, reveals to me my "being with", not as the relation of one unique personality with another, not as the mutual connexion of "irreplaceable beings", but as a total interchangeability of the terms of the relation. I am not opposed to the other, for I am not "me"; instead, we have the social unity of the "they". . . . Authenticity and individuality have to be earned: I shall be my own authenticity only if, under the influence of the call of conscience, I launch out towards death, with resolution and decision, as towards my own particular possibility. At this moment I reveal myself to myself in authenticity, and I raise others along with myself towards the authentic.'[4]

There are several things to be noticed about the concept of authenticity as expounded. First of all, one may think that one has no choice but to launch oneself towards death, in any case.

After all, Heidegger is not advocating choosing death in a literal sense. Authenticity does not demand suicide. And if launching oneself towards death means living in the knowledge that one will die, then we all of us necessarily do this anyway. Further, it may be urged, it is a well-known absurdity to treat death as an event in one's life, still more as an event to be looked forward to as revealing oneself in some way. The whole elaborate apparatus of technical terms seems to do no more than remind us very obscurely that, for each of us, our life is our own, and we live only once.

I think there is justice in these remarks. We have noticed already that one common effect of the truly Existentialist writer is to provoke in his readers the exasperated desire to rewrite what he says in plain language, and to show that it doesn't after all amount to more than a platitude. If this is indeed a distinguishing mark of the Existentialist, then no one is so unambiguously an Existentialist as Heidegger. But a little more than the platitude that we are all mortal can be extracted from his philosophy.

For next, we may notice that the *call of conscience* leads us to question our own position in the ordinary pattern of social life. If we are to be what we are capable of being, we must not accept the given social situation, nor the ordinary ways of life involved in it, as the only or inevitable way. We must think of ourselves in a new relation to our background. Secondly, this new way of regarding ourselves amounts to treating ourselves as isolated, unique and free (and incidentally, though not much is made of this, we shall recognise that other people too are unique and free). This does not seem to entail, for Heidegger, any particular aims or goals, nor does it determine anything which would normally be called a morality. But the authentic life is the life, rather, in which, *whatever* we do, we are prepared to take full responsibility for it. We shall never be content to say 'It's what everyone does' or 'Society demands it'. Even if both these things are true, this will no longer constitute our *reason* for doing the things in question. Thus, presumably, if, even in the authentic state, I decide to take my children to the park, I decide to do so because this is something which I truly want to do, as a purposeful activity and as a fulfilment of some unique possibility of my own. I do not do it because I can't think of anything else to do with them, or because every one else does it. It seems impossible to make *precise* sense of the idea that my choices are all regarded, in the authentic state, as choices leading to my own private death; but perhaps the important imprecise point is that my choices are seen to be genuinely my own, and that I make them, knowing that I am free. I will never learn to see my deliberate actions in this way unless I contemplate the fact that there are some things, particularly dying, which happen to me individually and must be accepted and faced as happening to *me*.

What this amounts to more than anything, it seems to me, is a moral *tone of voice* of a recognisable kind. Existentialism largely consists in this tone. We have heard it in Kierkegaard, in a different context, and shall hear it again in Sartre. The suggestion is always that there is, if we will only face it, a deeper significance in what we do than we are ordinarily, in our unreflective state, prepared to allow. If we undergo the process of being freed from illusion, of being weaned from the ordinarily accepted categories and ways of judging things, then we see everything, and particularly our own life and actions, as meaning something, falling into place in a significant whole. It is for this reason that Existentialist writers characteristically have no separate ethical systems, but regard ethics as a part of a whole metaphysical or ontological scheme. For the deeper significance of our actions can emerge only if there is a wider whole for them to fit into.

Thus the whole plan of *Sein und Zeit*, incomplete though it is, is designed to put the existence of man in the context of the existence of everything, so that man can be seen to have a certain nature, in contrast with the modes in which everything else exists. This is metaphysical ethics, as practised, for instance, by Spinoza. But the upshot, in Heidegger's case, is perhaps the opposite of Spinozistic. We are supposed to see ourselves as really freer and more independent of the world than we imagined in our unregenerate state. And the conversion to authenticity can come about only if we are prepared to take ourselves enormously seriously, and devote ourselves to the cultivation of the subjective point of view. For most philosophers, especially empiricists, *subjectivity*, the fact that we see with our own eyes, feel our own pains, think our own thoughts, tends to constitute a problem. They have to account for the existence of a common and public world built out of these subjective and private elements. For Heidegger it is the opposite way round. We start with the common and public, and have to work our way towards the private and subjective. Only so will we become what we are capable of becoming, free responsible human beings.

Turning to Jean-Paul Sartre, we are now in a position to trace
those features of Existentialist thought which have appeared first
in Kierkegaard and then, in a vast incoherent form, in Heidegger.
In *Being and Nothingness*, Sartre's first large-scale philosophical
work, we can see these features clearly, and make out their bearing
on ethical philosophy. For Sartre, though not a particularly
rigorous thinker, is at least a thoroughgoing one; and he has a
gift for making memorable ideas which, though perhaps not
original, become completely his own under his hand. It is for
this reason that it has seemed convenient and perfectly proper
to treat *Being and Nothingness* as the main source-book for Existentialist ethics. In this work, above all, we will catch the Existentialist tone.

Subjectivity, then, and *freedom* are the two main themes which
we shall trace in *Being and Nothingness*. In his treatment of both
themes the influence of Heidegger upon Sartre is very strong.
I shall not, on the whole, attempt exact ascriptions of each thought
or each item of philosophical terminology to an original. Not only
would this be tedious but it would in a way also be misleading;
for, as I have already said, Sartre makes ideas his own in a most
idiosyncratic way.

SUBJECTIVITY

Sartre wrote: 'One cannot adopt the standpoint of the whole.'
It is essential to his theory of the place of man in the universe
(for *Being and Nothingness* attempts to expound nothing less than
this) that any description of the world must be a description of
the world as seen by somebody. Sartre takes over the Cartesian
cogito ergo sum and uses it for his own purposes: he argues that
our awareness of the world is always accompanied by a kind of

vestigial awareness of ourselves, and that therefore consciousness of any kind is essentially a personal matter. I am conscious of the world *and* of myself — which amounts, together, to *my* world; you are conscious of the world and yourself — *your* world. The fundamental distinction upon which the whole structure of *Being and Nothingness* is based is the distinction between Beings-in-themselves and Beings-for-themselves, or conscious and self-conscious creatures. The 'Upsurge of Consciousness', which Sartre is prepared to mention as some far-distant historical occurrence, is by far the most important event that has ever happened in the universe. Beings-in-themselves, ordinary things, are essentially what they are. Rules can be given which govern their behaviour. This behaviour is invariable, and can in principle be predicted. In the case of *artefacts*, rules can be given laying down, with absolute accuracy, how they are to be made. General laws are relevant to Beings-in-themselves and can in principle be framed so as to exhaust their possibilities. None of this is true of Beings-for-themselves. These, *conscious beings*, are without essential natures.

Sartre is not here making a simple point about the uniqueness and idiosyncracy of human as opposed to other beings. The matter is rather more complicated. For he is not interested only in the common nature or essence of man, but even of *objects*, such as trees or ink-wells. Indeed, even when talking about material objects, he is sometimes almost obsessively concerned with the unique individuality of each. In *La Nausée*, for instance, Sartre's only philosophical novel, we have a long and powerful description of how the significance of the individual being of things was revealed to Roquentin, as he gazed fascinated at a tree-stump in the park.

This concentration on what it is to be a tree-stump or an ink-well or a glass, though put like that may sound absurd, has its historical origin in the *epoche* which the German phenomenologists, Brentano, Meinong, and Husserl, demanded. They required that a philosopher should concentrate on the content of his consciousness, including his objects of perception, in themselves, as they appeared to him, when he had laid aside all the normal presuppositions, expectations, and labels with which, in our non-philosophical moments, we are equipped. The influence of Husserl is particularly strong on Sartre in all his early writings, and it is perhaps the mixture of phenomenology with the sources of Existentialism we have already looked at which makes Sartre's own version of Existentialism so much the most rewarding to philosophers. But this is by the way. In Sartre's hands the doctrines of phenomenology amount to this, that we must try to think of things without their names and their ordinary descriptions, but in their essence as they actually appear to us. And we shall find that, although the things we observe may, as it were, overflow the verbal containers we put them in, though they may, to a certain extent, escape through the net of our concepts and our language, yet, up to a point, they are amenable to being labelled, they do abide by the rules which we make for them, in the form of scientific laws, they do have shared essences, even though each thing is also an individual.

This is so simply because material objects are without *aspirations*. They cannot try, or hope, or wish, or long to be other than they are. And it is for this reason that they are said to be what they are *completely*. They are solid (*massif*). Consciousness, on the other hand, consists in the power to be aware not only how things *are*, but how they are *not*. The possibility of conceiving a situation negatively, either as *not* what it was, or as *not* what one would like, or as *not* what one could make it, is of the utmost importance in Sartre's account of human consciousness, and thus of the human position in the world as a whole. Consciousness is said to be a gap or space between the conscious being and the world. I think it is possible to see what Sartre means by this. By thinking about something, or barely being aware of it, one distinguishes between this something and one's self. As we have seen, he thinks that in perceiving something, if one is fully conscious of the object, one is also at least minimally conscious of oneself, though this self-consciousness may be more or less acute or reflective. This self-awareness in perception entails the drawing of a distinction between the observer and the object of observation, and to draw such a distinction is thought of as separating the observer and the thing observed by a space. This space, or gap, which is created by putting the world at a distance from oneself, is the essential characteristic consciousness, and is sometimes referred to by Sartre as an emptiness or nothingness within the observer himself.

It is through the existence of this emptiness, separating a person from the world of things about him, that the possibility arises of thinking or acting as one chooses. There is necessarily, in a conscious being, an area of free play, as it were, between himself and the world. The emptiness within him has to be filled, and is filled by whatever he plans to do, or to think, or to be. Consciousness, Sartre says, knowingly places itself at a distance from its objects, and the gap between itself and its objects is identical with the power to confirm or deny what it chooses. Freedom and consciousness thus turns out to be the very same thing. They are both identified with the power to consider things either as they are or as they are not, to imagine situations which are different from the actual situations obtaining in the world; and therefore to form plans to change what there is.

It is impossible to exaggerate the importance of the power to conceive negatively in Sartre's systematic account of the world. There is no bridging the gulf between conscious beings and unconscious beings. They are divided by this vast difference, the difference between being able and not being able to conceive of *what is not the case*. Though Sartre does not examine this aspect of his thesis in detail, it would be plausible to maintain that the difference he is insisting on is really that between language-users and non-language-users. For the possibility of description, in language, does depend on the realisation that each item of experience should be described so and *not otherwise*; that is, if an object is black, it follows that it is not-white, that 'not-white' is an alternative, though vaguer, description of it. To be able to describe, notoriously, one must be able to describe truly *or falsely*. There would in fact be something to be said for making Sartre's distinction in this way, partly because he is himself very much interested in the fact that we freely choose the descriptions, and even the basic categories, under which we classify our world;

partly because animals could, in this scheme, be separated from men, without thereby having to be classified as unconscious beings. Sartre is prepared, I believe, to classify animals as unconscious; but this makes one suspect uneasily that his notion of consciousness must be a bit different from the normal use. However, this is not a problem that should detain us here.

The fundamental relation, then, between conscious beings and the world is derived by Sartre from the power of negation. Thinking of how things are *not* is the indispensable preliminary to describing them, categorising them, seeing them as desirable or hateful, and therefore to trying to change them. We can sum up this fundamental relation under the technical term 'projection'. Human projects upon the world include perception of it, knowing it, feeling things about it, making plans to change it, and intervening in its course. We have seen, furthermore, that this power of negation, which marks off the conscious from the unconscious items in the world, is connected by very strong links with freedom, and indeed can be identified with freedom. Freedom can be identified, that is, with the ability to see things as possibly other than they are, or with human imagination. I shall have more to say about freedom itself in the next section. But for the moment let us notice that this connection between freedom and negation makes it inevitable that, in *Being and Nothingness*, Sartre should concentrate so strongly in the individual. This is only to say that in this part of his philosophical writing, he provides metaphysical backing of the most general possible kind for his Existentialist concern with the world and free action seen from the point of view of one man. For in describing human consciousness, and placing it in its metaphysical context in the world, he is necessarily concerned with human action.

It is impossible to act without a motive, to act, that is, as opposed to merely letting something happen to one. To have a motive is to conceive a project for the future, which in turn entails, as we have seen, the power to conceive the future negatively, as filled with situations and states of affairs not yet in being. Consciousness, that is to say, is necessarily consciousness of the world from the point of view of a potential *agent*. My acts are necessarily my own, if I am free; and I cannot be properly conscious of the world, or know or say anything about it at all, without thereby being prepared to act on the world. There is no such thing as bare consciousness unconnected with action. A state of affairs cannot in itself be a motive for action; only the awareness of a state of affairs as something to be changed can be. For instance, if I am very cold, it might be thought that the cold was my motive for getting up and putting more coal on the fire. But the cold itself cannot, according to Sartre, lead me to *act* at all. It can merely lead to a passive experiencing of it, or acceptance of it. What constitutes my motive for getting up for the coal, is my apprehension of the cold *as something to be overcome*, as something intolerable, which need not persist into the imagined future. I regard it, in Sartre's jargon, as *dépassable*. He gives many illustrations from history to show the difference between being truly aware of one's situation as unbearable and as something which could be changed, and being merely passively half-aware of it, enduring it without the belief that it is only a stage, from which one could move on to a better stage. The possibility of revolution depends, in this early doctrine, entirely upon the possibility of the individual worker being able to envisage a future for himself personally which does not resemble his past, and therefore being able freely to choose or project a change. So, free action stems from the gap which constitutes consciousness and which separates a man from the world in which he is, enabling him to imagine and envisage what is not the case.

The concept of 'projection' is, as we have seen, of extremely wide extension. Perceiving, knowing, feeling, planning, and acting are all embraced in it. There is therefore, for Sartre, no radical distinction to be drawn between all these things. This grouping together of things usually thought of as distinct has important consequences for ethical theory. For one thing, Sartre's concept of feeling or of the emotions, which is manifestly relevant to ethics, is determined by his treatment of emotions as 'on all fours' with other kinds of 'projects' upon the world. It is worth examining this treatment, however briefly, since it is impossible to understand the nature of Sartre's subjectivist approach to ethical theory without fully understanding this relation of 'projection', especially as it applies to the emotions. (In this part of his theory, once again, he is strongly influenced by Husserl and phenomenology.)

Roughly speaking, his thesis is that emotions, like other states of consciousness, are intensional, that is, they are directed upon an object. They are also modes of apprehension. That is to say, if I am angry, I am angry *about* something, and it is this that is meant by the intensionality of the emotion; my anger is my *way* of being aware of what I am angry about. But not only so: my being aware of the object of my anger in this particular way is a part of my purposes. When I behave angrily, I mean something, I have an end in view. Emotions in general all mean something. They are purposive in the same sort of way as words are. We aim always, according to Sartre, to reduce our world to order, to manage it for our own ends, to control it for our particular purposes. But sometimes the world is recalcitrant, and will not be managed as we should like. It is then that we have recourse to emotional responses, when other responses and other modes of apprehension break down or are ineffective.

He illustrates this by the case of a girl who goes to see her doctor, rationally intending to make some confession to him which she does not really want to make. She *therefore*, according to Sartre, breaks down in tears, in order that it shall be impossible for her to speak. When we have recourse to emotion we are pretending to ourselves that we can get what we want by a kind of magic. We lapse into an infantile view of the world in which things happen which we know rationally cannot happen. The girl at the doctor's knows that she cannot really make it impossible for herself to speak by crying; but she is pretending that this can happen.

All our perceptions of the world, as we have seen, relate to our own purposes. We see the world essentially as a place to do things in. But sometimes things are too disagreeable or too difficult to be managed. The world is seen as making impossible demands on us. When this happens we cannot face taking ordinary scientifically accredited steps to achieve our ends, not can we bear to admit that we cannot achieve them. And so it is that we pretend we can get what we want by non-scientific means. The power to lapse into the magical way of apprehending things is connected by Sartre with the power of imagination, and is one of the great powers that conscious beings have, all of them derived from the negating power of consciousness. This magical mode of apprehension *is* emotion. Sartre says: 'Emotion is a transformation of the world. When the paths before us become too difficult, or when we cannot see our way, we no longer put up with so exacting a world. All ways are barred, and yet we must act. So then we try to change the world; that is, to live it as though the relation between things were not governed by deterministic processes, but by magic.'[5] We *try to change the world*: there is, thus, no essential difference between feeling and acting. Feeling, or the experience of emotions, is, in Sartre's view, a kind of futile and frustrated action. He illustrates this first by the somewhat frivolous example of a man who sees some grapes which he wants, but finds he cannot reach them. So he pretends to himself that they were too sour anyway, and so feels disgust at the thought of eating them. He cannot turn them into sour grapes by chemistry, but he changes them to sour grapes by magic so that he can feel positive relief at not having to eat them. Sartre admits that this little drama played out under the vine does not amount to much. But, he says, let the situation become one of life or death, and there we have emotion. If we are terrified, we cannot get rid of the object of our fear by rational or scientific means, so in extreme cases we may even faint, to blot out the terrifying world, or we may try to eliminate it by running away. Sometimes, when we are in a generally emotional condition, we may see the world as already magical, and then we see everything in the world with an emotional colour. For instance, if we are happy, we may feel that everything is within our power, and this is a magical, not a true, power. Again, if we are frightened suddenly, then we may fear things which scientifically speaking could do us no harm (such as a spider, or the expression of someone's face) because we have relapsed from believing in ordinary cause and effect into a primitive condition of believing in magic. For the time being the world, which in fact remains the same for everyone else, is transformed for the individual into something different, and it is for his own purposes that he so transforms it. Though we may feel as if we are *overcome* by emotion and that it has nothing to do with what we want or plan, this is an illusion, according to Sartre, from which we would do well to free ourselves. What we feel depends on what we personally plan to do. Indeed, it is a part of our general design upon the world. If we changed our plan, and with it our way of looking at the world, we would change our feelings too. We cannot explain emotion, or fit it into the general picture of the world, without explaining how the particular individual who experiences the emotion sees his world.

The theory of the emotions illustrates the main theme of *Being and Nothingness*. Whatever mode of consciousness we consider, it will be explicable only if it is viewed as a project for an individual, the plan or purpose of a particular human being. And thus it is that the difference between knowing, doing, and feeling is ironed out. But it must be said that there is a great objection to accepting any such view, and this objection is felt as strongly in reading Sartre as in reading Kierkegaard or Heidegger. It is in fact repugnant not only to common sense but to all rationality, to refuse to distinguish between knowing and doing. The difference is in fact ineradicable. Knowledge is, in an important sense, impersonal. If something is true, then it can be known, no matter by whom. My knowledge, if properly so called, can be thought of as literally identical with your knowledge. Whereas of my actions I, and I alone, am the author. Choice, we might admit, must be the choice of one person alone; but knowledge, if it deserves the name, must in principle be sharable.

The consequence of the grouping of all human projects together in this way is, then, to concentrate attention primarily on the individual and his personal assessment of and dealings with the world. And this general point of view necessarily determines what kind of ethical system could be derived from Sartre's philosophy. It will not surprise us to learn that Sartre thought each one of us had to devise his *own* morality, and make his *own* choices without the help of rules or principles. We shall return again and again to this point.

It must be noticed, however, that in spite of this concentration on the individual, Sartre rejected any kind of solipsism as nonsensical. For part of the self-awareness which each of us has, along with our awareness of the world, is derived from our awareness of others. Not only could we not be aware of the world without being aware of other people in it, but in an important way we could not be aware of ourselves. Other people bring us into real existence, or rather, they complete the existence we have. Being-for-others is another and essential aspect of the existence of every Being-for-itself. For instance, it is other people who make us see how what we are doing is to be described. They make us think of possible categories for our actions, and so we ascribe these actions to ourselves and feel pride or shame in them. Other people, as it were, attach labels to us; they say we are stupid, clever, dishonest, cautious, and so on; and in the light of these labels we live our lives. We are propped up on all sides by the view which other people have of us; sometimes it is a help and sometimes a hindrance, but without it we should not be fully aware of ourselves in the world.

Sartre gives an example of a man who, out of jealousy or malice, listens at a keyhole. He supposes himself to be unobserved, and he is completely absorbed in what he hears. In a sense he is only just aware of *himself* at all. He is nothing except what he does. But then he hears footsteps behind him and he realises that someone is watching him. At this moment, Sartre says, he comes into existence again as a person distinct from his actions. He is someone who is doing deliberately something of which he is ashamed. It is essential that he should relate his action to himself as a person in order to feel shame; and this possibility was brought about for him just at the moment when he heard the footsteps.

Besides cases like this, in which awareness of the look of the other is constitutive of our knowledge of ourselves, there are other ways in which the existence of other people modifies our description of our own act, or at least seems to render it dubious and incomplete. For there is a constant possibility of conflict between our own view of ourselves and other people's view of us. It would often be a matter of extreme complexity, and would perhaps require a novelist or a playwright, to work out the details of this kind of conflict in a given case. But that there might here be a profitable subject for investigation by moral philosophers is obviously true.

Here, it seems, is an area, one of many, in which Existentialist moral philosophy is richer and more subtle, at least potentially, than other systems of ethics, which tend to assume one uniform objective standpoint. The realisation that other people regard one, let us say, as predictably unpunctual, whereas from one's own point of view each instance of unpunctuality is just a matter of chance, just bad luck, and nothing to do with one's character (there is no reason to think one will not be in time on the next occasion), the realisation that for others, perhaps, one's promises are worthless, and one's resolutions unreal, is shocking and unacceptable. It inevitably raises questions about what is the *proper* description of one's conduct. In any account of ethics, particularly an account which includes discussion of the concept of character, or of virtues and vices, it would be an over-simplification if the possibility of this double vision of one and the same situation were left out. In short, the part which other people's view of us plays in our lives is something in which Existentialist philosophers are right to interest themselves.

Consciousness of being looked at by other people, of being an object of attention or of assessment for them, is a fundamental part of our awareness of the world and of ourselves, and therefore solipsism is a theory which it is in fact impossible to adopt, and contradictory to formulate. We feel the presence of others, Sartre says, and it touches us to the heart. We could no more deny it than we could deny our own existence. I shall return later to the question which naturally follows from this, namely, 'What is our relationship with other people in the world', or 'What ought it to be?' For the moment it is enough to suggest that the existence of others is structurally a part of our world, on the Existentialist view, and that *their view of us* will have to be taken into account in moral theory, as well as our view of them.

FREEDOM

We have seen that according to Sartre's theory consciousness and freedom are in essence the same. If we are conscious beings, in his sense, then we are also free. We fill our lives by freely choosing not only what to *do*, but also what to feel and think, what to believe, and how to describe things. We may choose to see things as frightening or beautiful, disgusting or attractive, and from this kind of choice springs our character, our attitudes, and our way of life. Each one of us, naturally, has to make these choices for himself. As his consciousness is his alone, so are his choices. We must now consider what are the consequences for the possibility of ethical theory of this vast, unbounded freedom. Sartre says: 'Our point of departure is in fact the subjectivity of the individual, and this for strictly philosophical reasons . . . because we want a doctrine based on the truth.'[6] This truth is the truth revealed by the *cogito* of Descartes' 'I think'. The *cogito* reveals to us both that we are conscious, and that we can think of the world as waiting to be changed by us. We discover in it our own emptiness; we find that we are nothing but what we do and think. A man is nothing but his life, and he can fill his life as he chooses. There are two principal relations in which a man manifests his freedom to choose. The first is his relation with himself, in which he may choose to cast himself in a certain role in life; the second is his relations with other people.

BAD FAITH

The first important truth about a man's freedom is that it is unbearable. Seriously to face the world, as Sartre thinks that we should, knowing that everything is open to us, that we may do or be anything that we choose, is something which most of us would find hard to put up with; for what has been removed from us is the comfort of excuses. We are no longer, if Sartre is right, in a position to say 'I couldn't help' doing this or that. We may no longer even say 'I can't help feeling' this or that. We *can* help it, and if we do anything or become anything it is fundamentally not because we have to, but because we want to. This is a harsh thought, and in the face of it we suffer anguish. It is the agony of knowing that everything is up to us. There is no one on whom to shuffle off responsibility. Sartre identifies this anguish with what Kierkegaard described as the 'anguish of Abraham'. When Abraham hears the voice of the angel telling him to sacrifice his son Isaac, he obeys; but he may realise afterwards that it was in fact his choice to *take* the voice to be a genuine message from God. There could never be any proof that it was genuine. Therefore, believing that the voice was the voice of the angel was his own act, and thus sacrificing his son in obedience to it was his own act too. No one but he was responsible.

However, most of us do not experience this anguish, at any rate not all the time. This is because we cannot bear to; and we devise ways of escaping it, by concealing our freedom from ourselves. The most common way that we do this is by lapsing into 'Bad Faith'. Bad Faith consists in pretending that we are not free, that we are somehow determined, that we cannot help doing what we do, or having the role that we have. A description of the various kinds of pretences that we adopt, and an account of the origin of our ability so to pretend, occupies a large part of *Being and Nothingness*. As we should expect, the very possibility of Bad Faith derives from the nature of human consciousness, and therefore it is shown that if one were not in fact free one could not adopt the pretence that one was not. For Bad Faith, like the rest of our conscious apprehension of the world, depends on the power to stand back and distinguish ourselves from our surroundings. To be able to pretend means to be able to see things as otherwise than they are. I cannot pretend to be a bear unless I know that I am not a bear and yet deliberately adopt behaviour which I conceive to be suitable for bears. It is, of course, possible to pretend to be oneself, or oneself in a certain aspect. This is, once again, to stand back and see oneself in a certain role and then play the role as hard as one can. Very small children are capable of this: they may start by saying to their mother, 'You be the little girl and I'll be the mother'. But then they often move on to say, 'Now you be the mother, and I'll be the little girl', and they then go through, as it were at one remove, and rather quickly, all the things they usually do, such as having lunch and going to bed. In this situation they are *seeing themselves as* 'the little girl', instead of just being such. Playing at being what one in fact is can become a way of seeming to oneself to be determined, to have no choice but to do whatever 'little girls' *do*.

This deliberate filling of a role, so that one may seem to oneself to have no choices left — one's actions to be totally determined by the role — this is one of the two typical kinds of Bad Faith. Sartre illustrates it by the brilliant description of the waiter in the café.[7] All his movements and gestures are a little overdone, Sartre says. His behaviour seems ritualistic, like part of a game. The game he is playing is the game of 'being a waiter'. All tradesmen, all public figures have an expected, ritualistic manner; they have their own peculiar 'dance'. The outside world expects them to behave in this way, and indeed is worried if they move outside the proper steps and turns. 'A grocer who dreams is offensive to the buyer, because such a grocer is not wholly a grocer.' To be *wholly* whatever it is, a waiter, a grocer, a judge, is the aim, too, of the man himself who is acting the part. All conscious beings, beings-for-themselves, are without essence, as we have seen. They have to choose their life, and so choose what they are. Beings-in-themselves, on the other hand, are *massif*. They are wholly and unambiguously, for ever, what they are. Conscious beings long for this safe, solid condition. The hollowness which afflicts them is the same as their freedom, and it is burdensome. So the aim of Bad Faith is to bring a man as near as possible to the condition of a thing, an object, to be simply summed up in a word, a *pure* waiter through and through, who has no more choice of how to behave than a robot-waiter has. From within, Sartre says, the waiter sees himself as a person with duties, rights, conditions of employment, and so on. But to see oneself as this is to stand back and see something abstract: '. . . it is precisely this person *who I have to be* . . . and who I am not. . . . I am separated from him as the object from the subject, separated *by nothing*, but this nothing isolates me from him. I cannot be he,

I can only play at *being* him. . . . What I attempt to realise is a being-in-itself of the café waiter.'[7] To make this attempt is to conceal from myself that it is in fact I, and I alone, who confer value and urgency on the things which I say I *must* do, which I say are *part of the job*, which I feel *bound* to do. I get up at five, I get the coffee ready, saying that I have to; but in fact I *need* not. I could choose to stay in bed late, and be sacked. I could fail to prepare coffee, or pour it down the neck of the first customer. That I do not do these things is not because I cannot or must not. It is because I do not *choose* to. The realisation that it is I who confer values and who make rules for myself is like the realisation of Abraham that it was *he* who decided that he must obey the voice. In playing out his role, the waiter is seeking to avoid the anguish of Abraham.

Another mode of Bad Faith is that in which we may pretend that we are thing-like in the sense of being just a body, just another object in the world, which we can observe having things happen to it which are in a way nothing to do with us. The same detachment from ourselves, the treating of ourselves as an object of observation, is characteristic of this kind of Bad Faith as well. Once again Sartre illustrates this in a marvellous little story of a girl who is taken out by a man, and who, in order to preserve the particular excitement of the occasion, and to put off the realisation that there are decisions to be made, pretends not to notice his intentions, and who finally gets involved in intellectual conversation and leaves her hand to be taken by him, as if it were nothing to do with her.[8] The hand just rests in his, inert and thing-like. If she had removed it or deliberately left it where it was, she would in either case have faced the facts and made a definite decision. But by simply not taking responsibility for her hand and what is happening to it, she has evaded the need to decide, for the time being. This is Bad Faith.

In considering these examples — and they could be endlessly multiplied — we may feel inclined to raise the question of the relevance of Bad Faith to morality. Admittedly we can recognise the kind of self-deception and posing involved in Bad Faith, but is it so very bad? Has the waiter done anything *wrong* in playing

his part as he does, even if at times he has slightly over-played it?
The worst we could say of him, it seems, is that he is a bit absurd;
or that he has an air of unreality about him. In answer to this, I
think that Sartre would say the waiter was wrong — not *harmful*
perhaps, but wrong. And here we may see emerging an absolutely
essential feature of Existentialist ethics. Pretence, pretentiousness,
wilful ignorance, blind adherence to convention, all these are
wrong, because they are obstacles to free choice. This view is
common to Kierkegaard and Sartre and, less clearly, to Heidegger
(can he really be hostile to pretentiousness?) and to all Existentialists. It is a view of extraordinary severity. Sartre would doubtless agree that often good, in the sense of good results, might
derive from someone's seeing himself as some character, and
acting the part well. Good might come from a judge, a soldier,
a policeman, indeed from any tradesman or professional man,
successfully sustaining the role of a devoted and conscientious
member of his trade or profession. And nearly always, as he says,
there is a public demand that this should happen. But the good
that might come from it would be entirely irrelevant to the moral
worth of the man.

I do not mean I suggest that either Kierkegaard or Sartre
would use such explicitly Kantian a term as 'moral worth' to
express this thought. But I think there is something Kantian in
the particular ruthlessness of judgment which is involved. Kant
was prepared to admire or to like a virtuous disposition in a man,
which produced agreeable or useful results. But he did not think
that this kind of good was in any way relevant to the *moral* goodness or *moral worth* of a man. Goodness of the moral kind was to
be had only in choosing to act in accordance with the categorical
moral imperative. For Sartre, of course, there was no categorical
moral imperative. So far from thinking that choosing according
to rules of absolute duty would give moral worth to a man, he
thought it nothing but Bad Faith to pretend that there were such
rules. In this way his conclusion might seem to be the very opposite of Kant's. But the important point of resemblance is simply
this, that for both of them, unless a decision to do something is
a free choice, made in the knowledge and conviction that it is a

free choice, then it is absolutely impossible that it should have any moral value.

The difference between them lies in what counts for each as free choice. Rational decision in accordance with the principle of the categorical imperative, the great rule which rational agents impose upon themselves, for no other end than that it is rational — this is the only free decision, according to Kant. For only reason is free. Man in his non-rational aspects is just another object in the world, as animals and trees, though living, are just objects, and subject to deterministic laws of nature. Thus, acting according to inclination or instinct or habit is not free voluntary action at all. It is just letting things happen. There is one and only one way to break out of the deterministic pattern of events, and that is by following another law than the law of nature, namely, the autonomous law of reason. The form which this law of reason took, for Kant, was that we should act only on such a principle as we could rationally envisage as universal. That is, whatever we choose for ourselves must be what we would also choose for others. It is impossible *rationally* to choose to make an exception for oneself. Now we shall see in a moment that there was a time when Sartre toyed with an almost purely Kantian account of what constituted free choice. But no such Kantian adherence to the law of reason, whatever this may be, is actually implied in the concept of Bad Faith itself, nor in the injunction to avoid it. Indeed, in *Being and Nothingness*, there is considerable lack of clarity about what a perfectly and genuinely free choice would be. We have the uneasy feeling that whatever choice we make there must come a time when we might say: 'Very well, I *must* do this', but that if we went on to give reasons why it must be done, we should be told that it *need not* be done, and we should be accused of Bad Faith. It looks as if there is never any possible proof that we are not guilty of Bad Faith.

What will be admitted as the real limit to our freedom? Surely there must be some things that we *cannot* do, and some circumstances where quite genuinely, and without self-deception, we can say 'I had no choice'? It sometimes looks as if Sartre would never in any circumstances allow the excuse 'I couldn't do anything except . . .'. If Bad Faith is so absolutely universal and ubiquitous as he sometimes suggests, then not only do we feel that it cannot be so very wrong but it also ceases to be of much interest as a moral category. To point to the universal human predicament is not enough, as the foundation for ethics.

But, for what it is worth, I do not think that the category of Bad Faith is a wholly useless or uninteresting category. It is just that, as we have seen earlier, Existentialism of every kind is prone to exaggeration. Not only Sartre, but Kierkegaard, Heidegger, Büber, and others are liable to have a fruitful and illuminating central idea and overwork it. Sartre, for instance, is in danger of rendering futile both the concept of choice and that of freedom itself by supposing them applicable everywhere. But if we avoid exaggeration, then we may see that there are indeed kinds of characters in describing which no concept is more useful than that of Bad Faith; and that in the case of such people a full moral description, including an assessment of their moral responsibility for their actions, could not be given without recourse to such a concept.

The kind of character I have in mind is that of whom it would be impossible to answer simply whether they were sincere or insincere, whether their professions of enthusiasm or interest, for example, were genuine or derived from some picture of themselves which, for the time being, they were making real. Sometimes it may be very important to come to a conclusion on this kind of question. Can we rely on consistency in their views, or not? Is another picture of themselves likely to be superimposed on the existing one, to bring with it a whole lot of new tastes and interests, or not? There is a whole range of human judgments, not only of reliability or otherwise, but of niceness and nastiness, trustworthiness, and so on, which depend on the question, 'Does he mean what he says?' But even if the answer to this is yes, there may still be further questions: 'Why does he hold this view? Will he always hold it? Can we imagine his holding a different one?' Sometimes, in the case of a person about whom this question of sincerity seems urgently in need of an answer, it would be going too far to say of him that he was positively insincere. But it would be right to say that he acted often, or usually, in Bad Faith. He may, let us say, see himself at different times in different roles. And the role of the moment will determine his behaviour, dictate his views, regulate how much money he spends, control his attitude to sex, social class, sport, everything.

It does not matter whether the role is that of a professional man of some sort, or, more insidiously, that of a member of some admired social group. It may be that living in a certain part of London, for instance, may make a man think of himself as a certain kind of person. And then, though he will not consciously alter his tastes and habits, yet some kinds of behaviour, some kinds of furniture or books or modes of speech, may come to seem impossible, and some kinds of expenditure, for instance on food and drink or a particular kind of holiday, may seem absolutely necessary. This is Bad Faith. It is not vicious; and it is not insincere. The man who suddenly becomes interested in a fashionable subject, or who finds that all his friends have titles, does indeed become interested, does truly like the people with the titles. It is just that he does so, perhaps, because he has decided to adopt the role of that kind of person — a modern intellectual, a well-connected man. The trouble with Bad Faith is that it leads to a gulf between a man's way of looking at himself and other people's way of looking at him, a gulf which we have noticed before. The intellectual of fashionable tastes will think of himself as having this genuine interest. To others he will seem to be jumping onto some profitable band-wagon. The man whose friends are dukes will seem to himself to like the dukes despite their titles. To others he will seem a snob. And the wider the gulf is between our view of ourselves and other people's view of us, the more we are in danger of losing our identity. If for others I am just a snob, all my actions and tastes predictable, then even to myself my allegedly free choice of friends is likely to begin to look a bit unreal. The man who has a part and slightly overplays it, like Sartre's waiter, has an air of unreality and staginess about him. In contrast with this, the alternative, actually to form projects and to put them into practice freely, knowing that one is free, and clear-sightedly to do what one wants in each situation, seems both admirable and attractive.

So far, then, the man who is excessively guilty of Bad Faith has emerged as an unadmirable and unattractive man, living a life of fantasy, acting out the role of the businessman, the good fellow, the scholar, whatever it may be. But there is also a use of Bad Faith which has an even closer bearing on morals. One of the manifestations of Bad Faith to which Sartre constantly calls attention is the habit we may fall into of thinking of our lives as a path along which duties lie in wait for us, waiting to be fulfilled. We may tend to think that some things are required of us, and that if we do these we shall have done all we can or need do; that if we go about armed with a list of duties, and keep our eyes open for reasonable chances to fulfil them, then we shall be leading satisfactory moral lives. This habit, which is very natural, is reinforced by the teaching of moral philosophers who try to show either that there are some absolute duties, in the fulfilling of which, for their own sake, moral worth consists; or that no moral act can ever be performed which is not performed in the belief that such an act in such a situation would *always* be the proper thing to do, for everyone. The doctrine that such an attitude to morality is Bad Faith has an enormous significance for ethics. For it suggests that, instead of coming to situations armed with lists or sets of principles, some one of which has got to be put into practice, we must think of each situation afresh, and try to see what, stock descriptions, duties and principles apart, ought to be done for the best. If we are faced with a situation in which we have to make a moral decision, on this view, we must really decide *for ourselves*, what to do remembering that we *could* decide anything, and not seeking to evade responsibility by sheltering under the rules, the principles, what one *must* do in such a case. It is possible that our decision may be the same in outcome as what we would have decided with the help of a handbook of duties and forbidden acts. But sometimes it may not. And whichever way it is, our decision will have the merit of having been reached after thought about what exactly the situation is, and what the case in question really involves. Knowing what we are up to in deciding to do this or to do that, seeing clearly who we are and what exactly we are doing, this is the ideal which is approachable through the avoidance of Bad Faith.

OTHER PEOPLE

It is now time to return to what is perhaps the most important question of all, namely how, in Sartre's view, we should take account of other people in our moral life. For ethics must be defined as the theory of how people should live *together*. Moreover, as we have seen, for Sartre the existence of others is, metaphysically speaking, a constitutive part of the life of each one, and thus *a fortiori* must be part of his moral life. Also, it would be generally agreed that the desires and wishes of others, their interests and their liberty, constitute a limit to the morally desirable exercise of our own freedom to satisfy *our* desires. This moral platitude, which, though platitudinous, is the very foundation of morality, must have particular importance for the Existentialists, who preach the doctrine of absolute and total human freedom. For them, if freedom and its exercise are the highest good, the problem of the distribution of freedom, the reconciling of my freedom with yours, must, one might argue, present the greatest problem of all. Their systems of ethics should consist largely in its solution.

But here we come upon a paradox. For though it seems obvious that some solution to this problem must be the beginning of any ethical theory for the Existentialists, in fact they are curiously silent on the subject. Or, if it is not fair to say that they are silent, perhaps we should say that they are inconclusive. It is here that the influence of Hegel perhaps makes itself most, and most unhappily, felt. We have seen already that Heidegger's ethical theory was primarily designed to show the supreme value of Authentic life; and this meant the Authentic facing of death by each man. Other people come into this picture of life only as part of the scenery, part of that human situation which each one of us has voluntarily to accept. There is a sort of heroism in this attitude, but very little humanity. Hegel regarded the reconciling of diverse human interests as mainly a matter for law; at a metaphysical level he regarded human relations as necessarily consisting in conflict. In Heidegger too there is the same failure on, as Sartre would say, the best philosophical grounds, to take other people's interests seriously. And in *Being and Nothingness* this failure seems to me to lead in the end to the collapse of any attempt at a satisfactory ethical theory. But before I attempt to show how this comes about, we should first look at an approach to the solution of the problem which Sartre at one time tried, and which, though he afterwards repudiated it, nevertheless gained a good deal of publicity. I am referring to the essay entitled *Existentialism and Humanism* which was published in 1946.[6] This essay has been translated several times into English, and when English readers were first becoming interested in the writings of Sartre this was one of the first things they read. Furthermore, A. J. Ayer, and several other philosophers, referred to it as containing a clear statement of Sartre's ethical position. However, it seems that Sartre himself regretted its publication. The specifically ethical views in it are different from any that could be derived from *Being and Nothingness*, and at one point, as we shall see, they were later directly contradicted by Sartre himself. So, though it is necessary to look at the essay for the sake of historical completeness, and perhaps to see it as containing a possible doctrine for an Existentialist thinker to hold, yet it would be misleading to treat it as properly the theory of Sartre himself.

The main burden of this essay is that, contrary to popular opinion, existentialism is a basically optimistic philosophy. For, Sartre says, it encourages men to action by teaching them that their destiny is in their own hands, and that there is no possibility of living except by acting. There is no despair, he suggests, in a theory according to which we have to decide for ourselves how to live, and we create ourselves, become whatever we are, by making decisions. So far there is nothing here which could not have come from *Being and Nothingness*. But the peculiarity of the essay becomes immediately apparent. For Sartre argues that in saying that a man is totally responsible for his own life, we are committed to saying that he has a responsibility for other people too. This argument takes a rather dubious form. It goes more or less as follows: If a man chooses anything, he chooses it *because he thinks it good*. Nothing can be good for us without being good for everyone; therefore what I choose, I am choosing for everyone. Another form of the same argument is that in choosing my life I am choosing a certain image of man, such as I think man ought to be. Therefore I am engaging the whole of mankind in my choice by saying to them all 'this is how you ought to be'. A choice, Sartre says, is the assertion of a value; and a value is necessarily universal. Subjectivity, from which Existentialism starts, entails only that each man chooses himself; but this necessarily means that he is choosing everyone else as well. At the end of the essay this argument becomes more explicit, and more explicitly Kantian. Sartre has defined Bad Faith, and characterised it as an attempt to escape from freedom. It is the use of a fake determinism as an excuse. 'The Spirit of Seriousness' is the name of a particular kind of Bad Faith, namely, that which tries to take refuge behind a supposedly absolute moral law, or scheme of ultimate values. Moralists are frequently guilty of this seriousness. Existentialism would avoid this; but it would also avoid another insidious kind of Bad Faith. For since my choice for myself involves a choice for others, Sartre argues that it is always appropriate to raise the question, 'What would happen if everyone did as you are doing?' If anyone answers this by saying 'but everyone won't', then he too is guilty of Bad Faith, for in fact he knows quite well, or could know if he chose, that choosing for himself *is* choosing for everyone.

Now at the end of the essay, Sartre seeks to show that *what* we choose, both for ourselves and others, must necessarily be freedom, if we are to choose in good faith. For freedom to make choices is part of the definition of man; and making choices, as he has already argued, entails asserting values; so all values, the very possibility of there being any values, depends on freedom. Therefore, as a matter of logic, we must value most highly that freedom which is the foundation of the possibility of value. There are various doubtful steps in this argument, on which I shall not comment. But the further corollary of it is that in choosing freedom for myself I must choose it for others; and thus that men, unless they take refuge in Bad Faith, must admit that they are committed to the freedom of others. Now this is a doctrine which is in many ways very attractive. The trouble is that it seems to be based on an ambiguity in the concept of universality. It may well be true that in explicitly judging something to be good we mean, as part of the judgment, that it is generally good, or good in any situation similar to that in which we are making the judgment.

It is part of the general condition for the use of language of any kind at all that we should assume a consistent use, within limits, for any element of the language. If this is to be called 'universalising', well and good, but there is nothing peculiar to the use of *value* words in this phenomenon. Quite different from this absolutely ubiquitous universalising would be the conscious adopting of a principle as a guide of universal application. Such an act of adoption would take, for instance, the verbal form 'It is a matter of principle that no one should . . .' or 'One ought always to . . .'. It seems perfectly obvious that we are not adopting such a principle every time we make a decision to act. We may be just acting for the best, as it seems to us, in a particular situation, and there might be no principle involved to which we should wish to commit ourselves, let alone one to which we should want to commit everyone in the world. It may be (though this is a doubtful step in itself) that in deciding what to do we think 'It would be best to do such and such' or even 'Such and such would be good' and it may be, further, that according to the conditions of the use of language already mentioned, if we did say 'such and such is good' we should have to be prepared to say that any exactly similar circumstances would also be described by us as good. But this by no means amounts to treating the course of action that we have this time chosen as something demanded by a universal principle. The mere universalisability of language is not strong enough to carry the weight of making us responsible in all our choices for legislating for the whole of humanity.

Sartre explicitly compares his doctrine with that of Kant, but criticises Kant for supposing that one could construct a morality purely formally and by appeal to universal principles. He was right, Sartre says, to assert that freedom wills itself and wills the freedom of others, but wrong to think that one formula, the categorical imperative, could define the scope of morality. It may well be true that Kant's theory is unduly schematic and formal. But at least Kant recognised, austerely, that a morally good decision must be explicitly subjected to the test of universalisation. The question must be asked: 'Is it rationally possible to envisage a world in which the principle I am about to act on is a universal law?' This question actually entails taking the ends, the goals, and the free voluntary actions of other people into account in making one's own decisions. And an alternative formulation of the categorical imperative is that one should do nothing which would mean treating another free human being merely as a means to one's own ends. Whether these two formulations are deducible from one another, or equivalent, as Kant seems to hold, need not concern us. The essential point is that, concrete or not, Kant's moral theory is firmly based on the law that, since the only ultimate good is the good free will, the free wills of others must never be overruled for some private and individual end. And he further held that if everyone had regard to this law, human ends would somehow fit with one another, and prove ultimately compatible with each other, in a 'Kingdom of Ends'.

That there is much which is incoherent or unclear about Kant's theory will not be denied. But it does contain a serious attempt to deal with the problem, which, as I have suggested already, seems to be at the heart of morality, namely, how one is to reconcile the free choices of one person with those of another equally free agent. Sartre, on the other hand, in the essay we are considering, merely *says* that in choosing freedom for myself I am choosing it for others, but does nothing to show how to avoid my freedom's clashing with that of others, or how to reconcile conflicting free choices. Moreover, as we have seen, he tries to show that there is a kind of logical necessity in my choosing freedom for myself and that this further logically entails my choosing it for others, since whatever I choose for myself I also choose for others. Neither of these logical points is enough to serve as the founda-

tion of an ethical theory. Sartre contrasts the concrete and practical nature of his theory with the abstractions of Kant's. But in
practice my choice of freedom for myself may often entail a
lessening of freedom for others, and in this situation we can take
no comfort from a reflection on the nature of language, or the
need for consistency of use in such words as 'good' or 'free'.
The fact is that neither in this essay, nor elsewhere, does Sartre
give any convincing argument to show that we do, or indeed
should, universalise our choices in any serious sense; nor does he
show how it comes about that a choice of freedom for one, in
any concrete situation, entails a choice of freedom for all. Moreover, in the *Critique of Dialectical Reason*[9] he explicitly denies that
it makes sense to speak of treating humanity, or other human
beings, as ends in themselves. Perhaps, too, it is worth noticing
that, in the context of this particular essay, freedom means political and social freedom, so that a kind of liberal programme of
increasing freedom for everyone might be derived from the
doctrine outlined here, a Utilitarian programme of actual social
and political reforms, such as would have pleased Mill.

But in two important respects such a doctrine cannot but be
regarded as incompatible with the rest of Sartre's philosophy.
First, any belief that there is in the world some absolutely valuable end, something which it must always be right to aim at, even
other people's social or political emancipation, is precisely an
example of the spirit of seriousness which, according to the doctrines of *Being and Nothingness*, vitiates the work of almost all
moral philosophers, and is a kind of Bad Faith. Secondly, to
suppose that we can, let alone that we must, take the mild humani-
tarian and altruistic view of other people suggested in the essay
is completely in contradiction with the doctrines of *Being and
Nothingness* concerning our inevitable relations with other people.
If Sartre had claimed, in the essay, to have changed his mind, then
we should have to accept these incompatibilities. But he made no
such claim. On the contrary, he purported to be explaining his
previous writings for the general public, and disabusing them
of misconceptions about Existentialism in general. Unfortunately
the doctrines of the essay are not, and cannot be thought to be,

an exposition of the doctrines of *Being and Nothingness*; and since
they are stated nowhere else, and were never defended by Sartre
and indeed were repudiated by him, regretfully it seems that we
must leave them. *Existentialism and Humanism* cannot be taken as a
statement of Existentialist ethical theory in general, nor as a
statement of Sartre's view in particular.

We must therefore turn back to *Being and Nothingness* to find
out what answer he gave there to the fundamental ethical questions: 'How ought I to treat other people', and 'What is it which
should be valued above everything else?' The answer to the
second question is not different from that given in *Existentialism
and Humanism*, but the consequences derived from it are far more
depressing. Freedom is still the highest value, but each one of us
alone has to try to face his freedom in his own choices, recognising that he is hemmed in on all sides by temptations to deny it,
and attempts to deprive him of it. It is from this fact above all
that the answer to our first question is to be derived, for there
can be no doubt that in *Being and Nothingness* other people are the
enemy, 'the original scandal of our existence'. We are committed
to endless hostility, and our own freedom must often be won at
the expense of sacrificing the will of another, who seeks to en-
snare us. Let us look briefly at the picture of human relations in
general presented by Sartre.

We have seen how, in *Being and Nothingness*, he describes the
human situation in terms of hopes, plans, wishes, and aspirations.
Consciousness, of its nature, is committed to some kind of *attempt
upon* the world. Part of this attempt is to possess and control the
world, to render it manageable and predictable. In the case of
material objects, Beings-in-themselves, since they have fixed
essences and are subject to discoverable laws, this attempt to
organise and control the world is not entirely hopeless. But even
here Sartre represents us as partially frustrated, of necessity. Even
material objects have their own manner of existing which can
seem recalcitrant and hostile. We may experience nausea when we
survey what seems like the teeming, thick, viscous 'stickiness' of
the world. Sartre thinks that such substances as treacle and honey
are natural symbols of what we most hate in the world of things;

they represent the 'anti-value'. For, instead of being tidy and manageable, such that we can pick them up, manipulate them and define their boundaries, they are glutinous and spreading, neither liquid nor solid, possessing us by their stickiness, which clings to our fingers if we try to shake it off. We are naturally committed to feeling horror at this aspect of the world.

But if the world of things sometimes oppresses us with its refusal to conform to our categories and obey our control, the world of people is far more distressing. Other people are them-selves free, and can therefore, by numerous deliberate means, escape our attempts to predict or control them. Our first effort, therefore, in our dealings with others, is to treat them as things, for, if they were things, if they lost their free power to act, we should at least be able to exercise a reasonable degree of control over them. We therefore label them as if they, like things, had unchanging essences. We say 'He is an Etonian', 'He is a stock-broker'; or we describe their characters, as though this was to describe essential essence of them. We say they are kind, lazy, vain, and so on, and attempt to predict their actions according to these descriptions. And so, once we have fixed them with a word, we treat them like other things, arguing about their probable behaviour by inductive methods. We tend to leave out of account the fact that they make plans and projects, frame intentions and form resolutions of their own. It is thus the *freedom* of other people which is an outrage to us, and we try to overcome it by pretending it does not exist. We have seen already how the fact that other people treat us in this way impinges on us, and deter-mines our consciousness of ourselves, in a world surrounded by others. The concrete relations between one person and another which follow from these basic facts about our existence in the world are described by Sartre in chapter three of the third part of *Being and Nothingness*. He says: 'While I attempt to free myself from the hold of the Other, the Other is trying to free himself from mine; while I seek to enslave the Other, the Other seeks to en-slave me. We are by no means dealing with unilateral relations with an object-in-itself, but with reciprocal and moving rela-tions. . . . descriptions of concrete behaviour must therefore be envisaged within the perspective of *conflict*. Conflict is the original meaning of being-for-others.[10] Here there is clearly a reflection of Hegel's notorious doctrine of master and slave. Hegel had held that our self-consciousness was real only in so far as it recognised an echo and a reflection of itself in the existence of another; but that out of this fact sprang an inevitable opposition between myself and the other. For I aim to have as an integral cause of my self-consciousness a being who is only this and nothing else, who exists for nothing else but for my ends. Thus I struggle ceaselessly to reduce the other to the status of a slave. It seems fair, therefore, to describe Sartre's doctrine of our relationship with other people as Hegelian.

But one can go further; the Hegelian conflict in which we are locked is essentially hopeless. For what I want to get hold of is the other's freedom. It is of no use to me to possess him if he is not still a free human being when he is mine. If I killed him I would in a way possess him, but since he would no longer be free this would not satisfy me. He would have escaped me in the end, by dying. On the other hand, if he is still free, then he necessarily escapes me. I cannot control what he thinks, or plans to do. A free conscious being cannot be possessed. It is this which ensures that there can be no such thing, for instance, as a wholly satisfactory love affair. For though we want to turn the person we love into a thing we can control, with no freedom, yet we also want to be freely loved by this person. It would not satisfy us if the person we loved *had* to love us, if love were, for instance, the result of a potion. It has to be his choice to love us. Yet it is just his ability to choose which is a threat to us and which we want to destroy. Sartre thinks that in love there are just three patterns of behaviour which are possible, and that we shall inevitably adopt one or the other, but all are unsatisfactory. We may lapse into indifference; we may turn to masochism, which is to aim to become a thing ourselves, to be used and controlled by the other; or we may become sadists, which means trying to possess the other by violence. There is nothing possible except one of the three; and conflict is the inevitable basis of the relation. It is from the inevitability of the conflict that Sartre derives the consequence, plainly stated in the *Critique of Dialectical Reason*, that we can in no way adopt other people as ends in themselves. We cannot suppose that Sartre gave up the whole of his view of our relation with others when he wrote the essay *Existentialism and Humanism*. We must therefore regard the suggested ethical philosophy contained in that essay as an aberration.

What, then, are the possibilities for ethics? First we must notice an unresolved contradiction in *Being and Nothingness*, which Sartre does not pay enough attention to. How can we reconcile the belief that we are absolutely free to choose whatever life we want, to be what we want, with the belief that in our dealings with others we are committed entirely to an unending conflict from which there is no escape? It seems that these two beliefs cannot be wholly reconciled, and that this constitutes at least part of the difficulty with which Sartre is faced in constructing any ethical theory at all. If ethics, as we have supposed, is concerned with the fitting together of the interests and choices of one person with those of another, there is no way into the subject at all if our aim is *necessarily* to dominate the other person and subordinate his freedom to our own.

There is, moreover, another equally powerful objection to the construction of an ethical theory, which we have already noticed. We are debarred, on pain of Bad Faith, from asserting that anything is absolutely valuable. The particular kind of Bad Faith involved here is the 'Spirit of Seriousness'. The belief that some things are good in themselves, and the belief that some things are always good because their consequences are, absolutely, desirable are both equally expressions of this spirit. Both naturalism, in the form of the belief that happiness or pleasure is what, as a matter of fact, everybody values; and non-naturalism, in the form of a belief in an absolute and transcendent system of values, must equally be abandoned. Of a morality based on such beliefs, Sartre says: 'It has obscured all its goals in order to free itself from anguish. Man pursues being blindly by hiding from himself the free project which is this pursuit. He makes himself such that he is *waited for* by all the tasks placed along his way. Objects are mute demands, and he is nothing in himself but the passive obedience to these demands.'[11] Any theoretical morality appears to lead to the one thing which is hostile to morality's very existence, namely, passive obedience.

We may ask then what task is left for the moral philosopher. He may, presumably, without harm, devote himself to analysing the language of morals. For example, it is possible to state, analytically, that men assign values to whatever they please; and such an analysis of ethical propositions would be a philosophical exercise, it is true. But to offer such an analysis is both to take a short way with ethics, and to run the risk of seeming to trivialise the subject. Sartre would hardly be content with the brief few pages allotted to ethics by Ayer in *Language, Truth and Logic*. Whatever his final views about ethics might be, we would not expect them to be identical with the jaunty simplifications of the logical positivists.

We may summarise Sartre's position at the end of *Being and Nothingness* as follows: First of all men are free: 'For human reality, to be is to choose oneself.' Choosing oneself entails assigning values to things, and this we do simply by regarding some goals as worth pursuing, others not. To evaluate something, to say that it is good or worth pursuing, is not to describe it; it is to set it up as something to be aimed at. But to say of something that it is to be aimed at is to say that it is ideal, and ideals are, by definition, unattainable. That the good or the perfect is unattainable seems to Sartre self-evidently true. For anything attainable would not be such that we would seek it as an end. It is because of the impossibility of attaining what is morally valuable that, according to Sartre, moral philosophers have been in the habit of saying both that the property of goodness existed unconditionally, and also that it did not exist at all. Arguments about God's existence, he thinks, also spring from this fact. For every human being, as we have seen, forms the project of becoming somehow complete, *massif*, entirely, through and through, what he is not. But if he ever did become something in itself, with the completeness and solidity he desires, he would thereby lose the essentially human characteristic, constitutive of his consciousness, of being empty and without essence. So 'God' is the name given to that impossible conjunction of properties which we should all most like to have, the conjunction of consciousness with *massif* being, such as only Beings-in-themselves possess. 'Every human reality is a passion in that it projects losing itself . . . to constitute the In-Itself which escapes contingency . . . the *Ens causa sui*, which religions call God. Thus the passion of man is the reverse of that of Christ, for man loses himself as man in order that God may be born. But the idea of God is contradictory and we lose ourselves in vain. Man is a useless passion.'[12]

But despite being blocked on all sides, by the need to avoid Bad Faith on the one hand, and by the necessity of human conflict on the other, Sartre holds that some kind of morality must necessarily exist. He says: 'Value is everywhere and nowhere. . . . It is simply lived as the concrete meaning of that lack which makes my present being. Thus reflective consciousness can properly be called moral consciousness, since it cannot arise without at the same time disclosing values.' In choosing for ourselves, as we have seen, we are 'disclosing values', since we choose what we think worth choosing, by definition. So, since men are free, and must choose if they live at all, they are necessarily moral beings. Accepting values from another rather than knowingly and deliberately adopting one's own values in choice, indeed, accepting any general rules for behaviour, must be Bad Faith. The moralist's advice seems to be simply to avoid Bad Faith; for since we are free, we ought to realise that we are, and not evade our freedom. But such a morality, it must be said, is entirely negative. It has no positive content, so far. All we know is that morality consists in the attempt to isolate oneself, to escape the influence of one's environment, and heroically to take full responsibility for what it is that one does. There is something of a familiar and not unattractive ethos here. Anything is better than making excuses, or trying to duck out of responsibility; the only obligation is to face one's situation, no matter what it is. Moral man is sincere man; immorality is phoniness. At the very end of *Being and Nothingness*, there is a hint of how such a moral theory might be given some content. For Sartre says that once the moral agent has realised that he is himself the source of all values 'his freedom will become conscious of itself and reveal itself in anguish, as the unique source of values, and the emptiness by which the world exists'. The possibility of acting must be realised in the context of a concrete situation, where the agent is surrounded by actual other people. The moral question for each man is, then, to what extent he can escape from the bonds of his particular situation, and how much responsibility he will take for creating, act by act, the world in which he lives. Sartre promises to discuss these questions in another book written, he says 'on an ethical level'. But such a book was never written, as we shall see.

A further hint is contained in a footnote to a passage we have already noted. In the discussion of human relations, Sartre has concluded that in all relationships one is bound to fall into either masochism or sadism. To this conclusion, he adds the following note: 'These considerations do not exclude the possibility of an ethics of deliverance and salvation. But this can be achieved only after a radical conversion which we cannot discuss here.'[13] The radical conversion must be a change of plan, it must give rise to a new way for each human being to project himself upon the world and to choose his own life. It must give him a new vision of his possible life with other human beings, and one which does not necessarily end in frustration. For we have seen that, though in the essay *Existentialism and Humanism* Sartre was anxious to rebut the charge of the critics of Existentialism that it was a philosophy of despair, yet from the end of *Being and Nothingness* there is nothing offered to a clear-sighted and honest man except an endlessly frustrated attempt to break out of the deterministic circle of the only fundamental attitudes to other people which are possible for him. However much he is said to be free to choose himself and his life, what he chooses, in so far as it affects others, will always be either sadism, masochism, or indifference. Individual freedom comes to look like nothing but freedom either to face the disagreeable facts of one's situation, or to cover them up by the evasions of Bad Faith. Morality consists in choosing the former, the heroic, course.

In fact we know that the radical conversion came and was the conversion to Marxism which is set out in the *Critique of Dialectical*

Reason. The struggle between one human being and another, which in *Being and Nothingness* arose from a psychological necessity derived from the nature of consciousness itself, has become, in the *Critique*, an impersonal Hobbesian struggle of all against all, caused, not by psychological but by economic necessity. It is *scarcity* which brings about the conflict, and scarcity, though it is part of the only world we know, is a contingent feature of the world, and we can conceive that one day it might be eliminated. If it were eliminated, then human relations would change. It is therefore now possible to work towards the removal of scarcity from the world, as a goal. The society in which the struggle is unchecked is called the *collective*, and the condition of its members is the condition of *seriality*. In this condition, people are scarcely human, for each is just a generalised man — bound by his needs and by the desire to get more for himself; and any man is, in this aspect, interchangeable with any other. In such a society the only motive is greed, and men are mere units. There is no community of interests, and no one has any particular role. The way out of the serial society is in the formation of the *group*. The essential feature of the group is that there should be an absolute identity of will between the members. The situation in which the group characteristically emerges is that of revolution, where two or more people become one person, since they have an absolutely common project, to overthrow a regime which has been seen to be intolerable to each of them. What one person wills is literally identical with what the other wills. After the revolution, it is the aim of humanity to avoid relapsing, in any part of political or social life, into the chaotic and deterministic condition of seriality.

Even from this crude summary, it will be seen how very far from Existentialism Sartre's radial conversion has taken him. Indeed, in *The Problem of Method*,[14] which prefaces the *Critique*, he explicitly states that there can, in the present age, be no philosophy that is not Marxist. Marxism is, for the time being, the dominant philosophy. Existentialism is a minor ideology, which must be seen as making a contribution to thought, within a Marxist framework. The contribution which it can make is to render Marxism concrete. He complains that Marxism has become a kind of dry dogmatic orthodoxy, with its conclusions derived automatically from certain unexamined and accepted premises. Existentialism could 'interiorise' Marxism, by displaying, in their concrete and actually experienced forms, the various elements in the Marxist account of the world. It could describe, from the inside, the Group, the Revolution, the Labour of man, the actual *praxis*, or action, in which men intervene in the world of things. Sartre here seems to envisage the peculiar virtues of Existentialism being brought to bear on Marxist theory, to give it new life, the concentration, that is on *what it is like* for the individual to be in the world he is in, how he will feel in choosing to support the Revolution, how this decision will come to him, as an individual. Unfortunately, there is very little of this humanising influence to be seen in the *Critique*. But, more important, even if Sartre had fulfilled his promise to 'interiorise' Marxism, this would still have been the end of Existentialism as a kind of philosophy. For the role assigned to Existentialism is at best a minor and essentially a *literary* role. The task of interiorising is quite distinct from any kind of theory-building. It is the decoration, perhaps, which is put on, after the house is built. The rendering of the Marxist choice concrete, the presentation of the *vérité vécue* of the revolutionary spirit — all this could be done better by a novelist or playwright or film-maker than by a philosopher. If an Existentialist undertook such a task, he might very well have a moral *purpose*, but that is very different from having a moral philosophy of his own. At least for Sartre, there can be no doubt that, just as the individual of *Being and Nothingness* has been swallowed up in the Group of the *Critique*, so Existentialism itself has been swallowed up in Marxism.

V. CONCLUSION

It is time now to see what general conclusions can be drawn from our consideration of Kierkegaard, Heidegger, and Sartre. There can be no doubt that all three of them were deeply interested in ethical questions, that is, in trying to provide a theoretical and not merely a practical answer to the question 'How ought people to live?' And this preoccupation with ethics, the treating of all philosophy as ultimately leading up to an answer to the ethical question, may be fairly taken to be a common characteristic of all Existentialist thinkers. For an Existentialist, what philosophical beliefs you hold determines the actual way in which you live your life. And, as we saw at the beginning, the aim of philosophy for an Existentialist, is not to provide a pure, disinterested statement of truth, but to free people from their illusions. Thus, not only do ethical questions emerge in Existentialist philosophy as the most important questions to which all others are merely preliminary but, going along with this, the whole aim of a philosopher must have a moral purpose.

So much could be agreed. But at this stage difficulties begin to appear. For we have seen that the great illusion from which people are to be freed is the illusion of determinism. The blindness which these philosophers aim to cure is a man's blindness to his own freedom. *That man is a free agent* is the fundamental doctrine of Existentialism. But the existence of freedom is not a *doctrine* to be questioned; it is taken to be a natural *fact*, which, if we are not corrupted by fear or prejudice, we can simply experience as true in our own lives. It is no more sensible to deny man's freedom than to deny that he is capable of distinguishing colours, or of counting. That a man is free means that he is free to choose what to do. Choice consists in his looking at his situation, and seeing how he personally is going to intervene in it. I cannot choose for you, because if you act on my decision, then thereby it becomes your decision. Just as it is impossible, logically, that I should walk your steps, or feel your pain, or, in the same way as you do, raise your eyebrows, so it is impossible that I should make your decision. If you say you were acting only in accordance with my will, this is an evasion. In fact, if you would only acknowledge it, the decision was, of necessity, yours. Ethics must therefore be concerned with individuals, and how they make their choices. It is thus that the insistence upon human freedom leads directly to the other great concern of Existentialist thought, namely, subjectivity. Choices must be made by each man for himself. So they must be described as what each *individual* plans as he looks out at the world from his own personal angle. He cannot be told by anyone else what is to be valued highly and what is not, nor, therefore, what is to be done and what is not. We ascribe values to things ourselves, whether we mean to or not. If I choose to pursue a certain course of action, then in so doing I *am* evaluating. Systems of rules are of their nature impersonal. To live according to such a system is to fail to face the facts of individual freedom and responsibility. Pretending to be able to teach others how to behave is like the sophists' pretence, which Socrates was concerned to expose, the pretence that the *truth* could be taught. If we adhere to customary or code-like moral systems we are as much deluded as the people who paid the sophists money to tell them philosophical truths. To free someone from illusions, then, one must make him realise his total isolation. He is wholly responsible for creating his own world, in living the way he does.

It is easy to see how this kind of view may degenerate into absurdity. It may well develop into a view of life in which absolutely everything that a man does is to be interpreted as a sign of some real decision or real evaluation he has made, so that, for example, the particular manner in which he leans up against the bar may be taken to express his whole world-picture; his deciding to shave or to grow a beard is as essential a choice of himself, as is his decision to join the army or the police force. If choosing freely for oneself is the highest value, the free choice to wear red socks is as valuable as the free choice to murder one's father or sacrifice oneself for one's friend. Such a belief is ridiculous. It tends, moreover, to show itself in a kind of vague wordless acceptance of *everything* as deeply significant. What is so significant about his standing hour after hour leaning against the bar? The answer is that he is thereby choosing what to be; he is living out his choice to be a man who stands hour after hour leaning against the bar. As long as he knows what he is doing, then his choice is morally unexceptionable, indeed is morally commendable. The tendency of Existentialist thought to provoke in the reader the desire to deflate the whole thing is most manifest at this point. What the Existentialists are maintaining, we feel inclined to say, is that people sometimes have to decide what to do, and that they are capable of doing so. At a commonsense level, we never doubted this for a moment. At a philosophical level the problems raised by saying that man is free are enormous, and have occupied philosophers for centuries. But about these problems the Existentialists have almost nothing to say. For they simply believe that it is self-evident that men are free, and that we learn this fact directly from experience. So the doctrine of freedom seems obvious at one level and unsatisfactory at another, and, as we have suggested before, exaggerated at either level.

We are *not* in fact free to choose absolutely anything. To accept, for example, the categories under which we normally describe the world is *not* a free voluntary decision. We learn these categories as we learn to talk, and to see the world otherwise would be in many cases impossible. It seems to me that there are further features of our life which are not a matter of choice. For instance, we do not choose to prefer pleasure to pain. Despite Sartre's arguments, we may well deny that we at any rate always choose what to feel, or how to react emotionally to the world. In all these ways the extreme subjectivism and the extreme libertarianism of the existentialists seem equally unacceptable.

Besides leading to absurdity, the kind of view we have been considering has serious consequences for ethics. If ethics is concerned with the manner in which men, as rational creatures, think about their own behaviour, and attempt to solve their problems and adapt themselves to one another in society, then it must be possible to formulate certain general rules either about what people do in fact think, or about what they do in fact hold valuable. From here it is only a short step to regarding some types of action as generally to be avoided, others as generally to be pursued; or to holding some types of motives as generally to be preferred to others. But such reliance, at whatever level of discourse, upon general rules or principles is taken by Existentialism to be a denial of freedom. The only general law of ethics must be to avoid general laws. Just as, for Kierkegaard, religion became degenerate, indeed ceased to be religion at all, as soon as it was institutionalised, so morality for any Existentialist ceases to be morality the moment it is encapsulated in principles of conduct. There is value in both these positions. To insist that religion is a private matter, that merely observing certain forms has nothing to do with it, has always been the religious reformer's role. And doubtless in the same way, there is value in issuing a warning against the rigid and unimaginative view that we must always do our duty, and we have only to think a little to find out what our duty is. That there is just one right thing which is waiting to be done in each situation is moral formalism, and might lead to the view that having satisfied the formal requirements, there is nothing else that can be demanded of a man. To 'interiorise' morals, to render them both concrete and personal in contrast to such formalism is something which is well worth doing. And this is what Existentialist moralists have done. But without *some* element of objectivity, without *any* criterion for preferring one scheme of values to another, except the criterion of what looks most attractive to oneself, there cannot in fact be any morality at all, and moral theory must consist only in the assertion that there is no morality. Kierkegaard may be thought to have rejected all that is normally meant by religion in trying to purge religion of its bogus elements. In the same way one may suspect that morality itself has disappeared, and with it the possibility of moral theory, in the efforts of those who wish to clear out the worthless, the insincere and the non-genuine from the theories of moral philosophers. It cannot be doubted that the existence of Existentialist philosophy has had a profound effect both on the writing of moral philosophy, in making it more concrete and realistic, and on morality itself as actually practised. But it is far more doubtful whether it can be claimed that there is any *direct* contribution to philosophy which should be described as Existentialist ethics. For the demands of philosophy, exactness, objectivity, and the attempt to say what is true, are the very demands which Existentialism is committed, on principle, to rejecting. Perhaps we must conclude that Existentialism, as a way of thinking, is more naturally suited to express itself in novels, plays, films, and other unargued statements of how the world is. We have seen some of the characteristic features of these expressions. It seems that to be attracted by Existentialism is to be attracted by a mood. When it comes to serious thought, one may find, as Sartre did, that it is necessary to cast off the mood and start again.

NOTES

1. *Kierkegaard's Concluding Unscientific Postscript*, translated from the Danish by D. F. Swenson, with Introduction and Notes by W. Lowrie (Princeton University Press and O.U.P., 1941), pp. 118, 119.

2. Op. cit., pp. 116, 117.

3. Op. cit., pp. 178, 183.

4. [L'Être et le Néant] *Being and Nothingness: An Essay on Phenomenological Ontology*, translated by Hazel E. Barnes (Methuen, 1957), p. 246.

5. [Esquisse d'une théorie des émotions] *Sketch for a Theory of the Emotions*, translated by P. Mairet (Methuen, 1962), p. 31.

6. [L'Existentialisme est un humanisme] *Existentialism and Humanism*, translated by P. Mairet (Methuen, 1948), p. 64.

7. *Being and Nothingness*, pp. 59, 60.

8. Op. cit., p. 55.

9. *Critique de la Raison dialectique* (Gallimard: Paris, 1960).

10. *Being and Nothingness*, p. 364.

11. Op. cit., p. 626.

12. Op. cit., p. 615.

13. Op. cit., p. 412 n.

14. [Question de Méthode] *The Problem of Method*, translated by Hazel E. Barnes (New York, 1964).

BIBLIOGRAPHY

I. SELECTION OF STANDARD TEXTS IN TRANSLATION

Buber, Martin. *I and Thou* (Edinburgh, 1937).
  Between Man and Man (London, 1947).
Heidegger, Martin. *Existence and Being* (London, 1949).
  Being and Time (London, 1962).
Kierkegaard, Søren. *Concluding Unscientific Postscript* (Princeton and O.U.P., 1941).
  Philosophical Fragments (Princeton and O.U.P., 1941).
Sartre, Jean-Paul. *Existentialism and Humanism* (London, 1948).
  Being and Nothingness (London, 1957).
  Nausea (London, 1962).
  Sketch for a Theory of the Emotions (London 1962).

II. STUDIES IN EXISTENTIALIST THOUGHT

Lowrie, W. *A Short Life of Kierkegaard* (London, 1943).
Jeanson, F. *Le Problème Moral et la Pensée de Sartre* (Paris, 1947).
Murdoch, I. *Sartre, Romantic Rationalist* (Cambridge, 1953).
Copleston, F. C. *Contemporary Philosophy* (London, 1956).
Roubiczek, P. *Existentialism, For and Against* (Cambridge, 1964).
Warnock, Mary. *The Philosophy of Sartre* (London, 1965).
Manser, A. *Sartre* (London, 1966).

6

CONTEMPORARY MORAL PHILOSOPHY

G. J. WARNOCK

I. INTRODUCTION

The aim of this essay is to provide a compendious survey of moral philosophy in English since about the beginning of the present century. Fortunately, the tale that thus falls to be told is not in outline excessively complex, and can be seen as a quite intelligible sequence of distinguishable episodes. The major stages on the road are three in number. There is, first, Intuitionism, to be considered here as represented by G. E. Moore (*Principia Ethica*, 1903), H. A. Prichard (*Moral Obligation*, published posthumously in 1949), and W. D. Ross (*The Right and the Good*, 1930, and *Foundations of Ethics*, 1939). Second, in somewhat violent reaction to the undoubted shortcomings of that style of ethics, we have Emotivism; and here the chief spokesman is C. L. Stevenson (*Ethics and Language*, 1944). And third, as an amendment of and an advance from Emotivism, we shall consider what may be called, and often is called, Prescriptivism, whose most lucid, persuasive, and original exponent is R. M. Hare (*The Language of Morals*, 1952, and *Freedom and Reason*, 1963). Other authors and other works, of course, will be mentioned in their places; but the main plot is determined by these three doctrines and their leading advocates.

It will be found that my critical discussions of the major doctrines to be surveyed are (I fear) somewhat uniformly hostile; and I have brought in, in the later pages of my essay, perhaps more controversial matter than would ordinarily be looked for in a mainly expository review. But I would defend this, if I had to, as lying in the nature of the case. For the case is, I believe, that the successive orthodoxies of moral philosophy in English in the present century have been, notwithstanding the often admirable acumen of their authors, remarkably barren. Certain questions about the nature and the basis of moral judgment which have been regarded, at least in the past, as centrally important have not only not been examined in recent theories; those theories have seemed deliberately to hold that, on those questions, there is nothing whatever that can usefully be said. There seems to have occurred an extraordinary narrowing of the field; moral philosophy has been made to look, if not simple, yet bald and jejune and, in its fruits, unrewarding. But the subject is not necessarily, I believe, so lifeless as it has been made to look; and if room is to be made for future infusions of new life, it seems essential that recent inhibiting orthodoxies should now be somewhat roughly — not, I hope, rudely — handled.

It is possible, and may be helpful, to sketch out in advance one short version of the way in which things seem to me to have gone wrong. Intuitionism, to begin with, emptied moral theory of all content by making the whole topic undiscussably *sui generis*. Fundamental moral terms were said simply to be indefinable, and fundamental moral judgments to be simply, transparently and not further explicably, self-evident. Moral truths were, it seemed, such that nothing could possibly be said about what they meant, what their grounds were, or even why they mattered at all. Now this, we may say, understandably provoked the emotivist to look quite elsewhere in search of something to be said. In effect he abandoned altogether the idea — the apparently barren idea — that moral utterances should be regarded as genuine judgments having (or even not having) statable meanings and discoverable grounds, and turned instead to the quite new topic of such utterances' *effects*. But thus, though for new reasons, the emotivist like his predecessor had nothing to say on what moral judgments are, or say, or mean; he was interested only, and somewhat crudely, in what they are *for*. Prescriptivism next contributed a meritorious distinction. We should consider, it was urged, not what is sought to be achieved *by* issuing a moral utterance, but rather what is actually done *in* issuing it — not what effect is aimed at, but what 'speech-act' is performed. This was all to the good. But this enquiry, it will be observed, still stopped short of considering what such utterances actually say, what they mean, what sort of grounds can be urged for or against them. And thus there remains out of view, or at least at the margin of attention,

all that is of distinctively moral interest. For neither the 'per-
locutionary' acts studied by the emotivist, nor the 'illocutionary'
acts on to which prescriptivism fastens, are in any way distinctive
of or peculiar to moral discourse.[1] The 'locutions' of moral discourse have a better claim to be distinctive of it; but these have
yet to be rescued from the protracted neglect which seemed, indeed, merited by the ingenious vacuities of the Intuitionists, and
which was continued in their successors' preoccupation with
other things. There are other matters too which, one may hope,
will come more clearly into view, if attention can be directed at
least more nearly to the centre of the field of investigation.

That said, I would wish at once to discourage the hopes of
possible unwelcome allies. Some who have been struck by the
thinness of recent academic moral theory have laid the blame
undiscriminatingly at the door of 'linguistic philosophy', and
have seemed to adopt the notion of thickening the diet by the
means, no doubt effective in their way, of confusing all the issues.
This is, to say the least, unnecessary. It is not in the nature of
'linguistic philosophy' that it should find nothing much to say
in moral theory. That this has been so, so far as it has been so,
looks more like an aberration, and one for which the remedy
consists in getting many things clearer, not everything more
confused. This essay is much too short to do much in that way.
The most I would hope for is that it may draw attention to some
of the things that now might usefully be done. My argument, I
fear, becomes increasingly congested as it proceeds, from the
attempt, particularly in section V, to introduce large issues in a
very few words. Those paragraphs leave everything to be said,
but I hope they may be found to be, in a good sense as well as in
a bad one, provoking.

II. INTUITIONISM

(i) G. E. MOORE

Consideration of intuitionism in the moral philosophy of this century starts naturally from the work of G. E. Moore. Moore, a philosopher of most distinguished ability and very great importance in the history of the subject, was by no means at his best in the field of ethics; nevertheless his *Principia Ethica* is a good deal more interesting than most intuitionist contributions, and was in fact the most widely influential of any.

We must first ask: was Moore really an intuitionist at all? For in the preface to *Principia Ethica* he goes out of his way to 'beg it may be noticed that I am not an "Intuitionist" in the ordinary sense of the term'. The ordinary intuitionist holds, according to Moore, that moral truths of many different kinds, perhaps of all kinds, may be known to be true 'by intuition' — that is, that they are, if properly considered, simply self-evident, or just seen (though no doubt not literally *seen*) to be true. Moore disagrees with this. In his view, only a small and very special class of moral judgments consists of truths which are thus self-evident; the truth of many more must be investigated by other means, and indeed can seldom, if ever, be established with certainty. It transpires, however, that in Moore's opinion all moral judgments which do not belong to, must in the end inevitably be founded upon, that special class of moral judgments which *are* self-evident; and it is, one may think, philosophically much more significant that he should hold the fundamental truths of morals to be self-evident, than that he should hold that many propositions of morals are not. Again, while it is true that Moore does not much like, and seldom employs, the term 'intuition', he sees that those who have spoken of certain truths as being known 'by intuition' have often meant by this simply that those truths are self-evident, or are known directly, without proof or argument: and in this sense he himself undoubtedly maintains that the fundamental truths of morals are known 'by intuition', or alternatively, as he sometimes puts it, are Intuitions. He offers, certainly, no alternative expression of his own: and since he agrees so closely in substance with other Intuitionists, it is proper enough that his position should accept the name.

At the outset of his argument Moore expresses the well-justified conviction that much moral philosophy and some ordinary moral judgment have been persistently distorted and befogged by sheer confusion; and much of his book is devoted to pointing out, at times with a rather unpleasing and even arrogant self-assurance, the confusions in which other philosophers have so copiously indulged. His aim in so doing, and in setting out by contrast what he takes to be the true 'fundamental principles of ethical reasoning', is to advance the cause of correct moral judgment — to help his reader, that is, to see or to discover which moral propositions are actually true. Most of his argument, however, is directed to establishing the *nature* of moral propositions; and it is with his views on this matter, rather than on the question which such propositions are actually true, that we shall here be concerned.

Fortunately it is possible to summarise quite briefly what Moore takes to be the main, most persistent, and most damaging, confusion into which so many of his predecessors have fallen; and it is in his criticism of this that his own view can most readily be made clear. Ethics, Moore says, is concerned with, and may even be defined by its characteristic concern with, the predicate 'good' and its converse 'bad'; and though this concern may take more than one form, the central question is what the predicate 'good' means, or stands for. (It may be noted, and perhaps regretted, that the predicate 'bad' very quickly drops out of the argument.) This question what 'good' means, Moore insists, is not a verbal one; it would be beside the point, even if it were possible, to excogitate some synonymous expression conforming with the use made of the word 'good' by those who speak English. The real question is: what is the property for which 'good' stands? What is the property which any subject has, in virtue of which it would be true to say that that subject is good?

Now most moral philosophers, in Moore's view, though more or less aware that this was the question centrally at issue, have made some variant of a single blunder in seeking to answer it. They have tended, whether deliberately or inadvertently, to pick out some other property which some good things have, and simply to identify this other property with goodness; they have, in a peculiar but particularly important sense, *defined* goodness as just being, or being strictly identical with, some other property. For instance, philosophers have identified goodness with the properties of being pleasant, or highly evolved, or conducive to 'self-realisation' — widely different doctrines, no doubt, but all alike mistaken, and mistaken in the same way. For — as we read on the title-page of Moore's book — 'everything is what it is, and not another thing'; but these doctrines all allege that goodness *is* some property which, as a matter of fact, it is not.

Nor is it only, Moore holds, that those views are mistaken; any view of that kind must be mistaken in just the same way. For the predicate 'good' is, in the important sense, indefinable; goodness, that is, is a simple, unanalysable, wholly non-complex property, so that there is *nothing* — and in particular no complex of parts — with which it can be rightly identified (except itself). 'If I am asked "What is good?" my answer is that good is good, and that is the end of the matter. Or if I am asked "How is good to be defined?" my answer is that it cannot be defined, and that is all I have to say about it.'[2]

Why does Moore say this? His argument is that, if 'good' were (in his sense) definable, then it would be *analytic*, or tautologous, that certain things are good: if being good were identical with being P (where P is any adjectival expression other than 'good'), then 'What is P is good' would be analytic, true by definition, and 'What is P is not good' would be self-contradictory. But it is obvious, Moore thinks, that this is never the case. For however, he holds, any object may be described — whatever predicates (other than 'good') may be truly ascribed to it — it clearly remains a further question whether that object is good: to assert that the object so described is good is always a further assertion of substance, never a mere tautology, and to deny that it is good is, even if obviously false, never self-contradictory. If this is so, it follows that 'good' is, in Moore's sense, indefinable; and it follows from that, in his view, that goodness is a simple, unanalysable quality.

We should add that goodness is also, in Moore's view, a *non-natural* quality, and that, while he regards as grossly mistaken any view whatever which attempts a definition of goodness, he regards with peculiarly withering contempt any view which identifies goodness with 'natural' qualities and so commits what he calls 'the Naturalistic Fallacy'. About this feature of Moore's position there is, however, not much to be said: for although the naturalistic fallacy has played an important and colourful part in more recent writings, in Moore's book it amounts only to the bald assertion that the quality of goodness is *not* as other qualities are — that, in particular, its presence is not to be detected by any ordinary species of observation, experience, or investigation. How is it detected, then? Some would say: by intuition. Moore does not much like this answer, probably because he rightly feels that it is not really an answer at all, but a confession of bewilderment got up to look like an answer. However, he has no other answer to give; and so the import of the term 'non-natural' remains obscure.

Moore's views about 'right' — and about 'duty' and 'obligation', which he does not sharply distinguish from 'right' — are very different from his views about 'good'. Rightness, he thinks, *is* definable; namely, it is definable in terms of goodness. For in any situation the right course of action for any agent to adopt is, by definition, that course of action which will, as a matter of fact, produce the greatest amount of good possible in the circumstances. It is clear at once, then, that on Moore's view there is a vast difference of principle between questions about what is right, and about what is good. In the latter case there is no reasoning to be done, no evidence to be assembled, no investigation to be carried out: all we can do is attend very carefully to that about which the question 'Is it good?' is asked, mentally isolating it so far as possible from other things, and carefully discriminating its several properties one from another: then we shall simply see (though of course not literally *see*) that it has the property of goodness or, alternatively, that it has not. With the question 'Is this action right?', on the other hand, the case is very different. For to answer this question we should have to establish, first, what would in fact be the total consequences of performing this action; second, what would be the respective total consequences of all other courses of action open to the agent; and third, which of these alternative sets of total consequences embodied the most good — or more strictly, the most favourable surplus of good over bad.

It is a curious incidental reflection that this position as a whole, while highly anarchic in one way, is strongly conservative in another. Questions about what is good are firmly handed over, without any reference to reasons, experience, authority, or even thought, to the personal 'intuition' of each individual. Moore, however, partly as a result of heavily exaggerating the difficulty of determining what the consequences of our actions will be, is so pessimistic as to our chances of correctly ascertaining what is right that he recommends, in most cases, simple adherence to the prevalent conventions of one's society.[3] It may be guessed that those members of 'Bloomsbury' who have claimed, so surprisingly, to have been vastly influenced and illuminated by *Principia Ethica* were struck more forcibly by the first point than by the second.[4]

Moore's position, then, whatever its merits or demerits may be (to that question we shall turn in a moment) has at any rate the charm, such as it is, of the very starkest simplicity. All moral problems, on this view, have ultimately to do with the possession or non-possession by this or by that of just one quality, goodness. (We too may neglect here the unfortunate, much-neglected property of badness.) Since this is an absolutely simple property, distinguishable from and indeed independent of anything else, we have nothing to do but to 'intuit' its presence or absence; and in fact Moore holds, as we have seen, that to the discriminatingly intuitive eye its presence or absence is simply self-evident. Besides this there is only one kind of problem in morals, and that is the purely causal or factual problem what courses of action will pro-

duce as much good as possible — that is, are right. In view of
Moore's announced concern with 'the fundamental principles of
ethical reasoning', it is curious that his conclusion is really that
there are no such principles. For on questions about goodness
he has no place for reasoning at all, while on questions of what is
right there is purely causal or inductive enquiry into the consequences of actions, of a kind that we might engage in without
any moral interest whatever.

(ii) PRICHARD AND ROSS

Other intuitionists, among whom were conspicuous H. A.
Prichard and Sir David Ross, somewhat modified the bald simplicity of Moore's doctrine, while not fundamentally or in principle dissenting from it. (So did Moore himself, in fact, in his later
and slighter book *Ethics* [1912].) They wanted at least two in-
definables, not one, and to make 'intuition' do more work than
Moore had assigned to it.

Consider, for instance, Prichard's argument in his celebrated
paper 'Does Moral Philosophy Rest on a Mistake?'[5] He suggests
that in fact it does, for the following reason. We are, he says,
often inclined to ask — and in this inclination, indeed, is the
genesis of most moral philosophy — whether some action which
we think to be our duty, or are told is our duty, really is our duty:
or we ask of the same action, slightly differently, why we should
do it. Now many moral philosophers, Prichard rightly supposes,
have sought to offer reasons to such an enquirer as this. They
have sought to offer arguments to prove that some action which
he thinks to be his duty really is his duty, that he is not mistaken
in thinking so; also, or alternatively, they have tried to show him
what the reasons are why he should act in that way. But Prichard
now suggests, very much in the manner of Moore, that all attempts of this kind are in principle misconceived. There is no
reason why some action which is my duty is my duty, except precisely that it is my duty; similarly there is no reason, except that
it is my duty, why I ought to do it. Consequently, if one mentions
some other feature that the action may have, such as being productive of good or conducive to happiness, one is simply talking

off the point. For even if the action in question be productive of good, it is not that wherein its being my duty consists; and even if it will conduce to my own or to the general happiness, that is not why I ought to do it. If someone asks of some action, then, 'Is this action my duty?', there is nothing whatever to be done along the lines of argument; it is irrelevant to consider the results of the action in the way of good or of happiness, or to offer the enquirer grounds for acting or inducements to act in that way; one can only tell him to consider, as clearly and carefully as he can, what the action is, and he will then 'see' that the action is his duty or, alternatively, is not. In order to free ourselves from the insidious and misguided inclination to look for arguments we must realise, Prichard says, 'the self-evidence of our obligations, i.e. the immediacy of our apprehension of them. . . . Or, to put the matter generally, if we do doubt whether there is really an obligation to originate *A* in a situation *B*, the remedy lies not in any process of general thinking, but in getting face to face with a particular instance of the situation *B*, and then directly appreciating the obligation to originate *A* in that situation.'[6]

In later writings Prichard greatly elaborates upon, but does not really modify, the bleak austerity of this position. He came to think, indeed, that 'obligatoriness' is not a character of actions. For what I have an obligation to do is necessarily some action which I have not yet done — which, in that sense, does not exist; but what does not exist cannot have, and cannot possibly, in Prichard's view, even be thought to have, any characters at all. My having an obligation, therefore, must be a character of something else which does exist, and is in fact, Prichard holds, a character of me, the prospective agent. However, he still holds that there is nothing much to be said about this character; it is '*sui generis*, i.e. unique, and therefore incapable of having its nature expressed in terms of the nature of anything else' (*Moral Obligation*, 1937). Thus moral philosophy seems still to be, as he had said in 1912, 'not extensive'. It consists partly, and no doubt most lengthily, in refutation of views which seek to 'reduce' goodness or obligation to things other than themselves, and apart from that in simple recognition that those attributes are *sui generis* and immediately apprehended. There seems to be no room, on this view, even for the kind of reasoning which Moore had envisaged; for whereas Moore had held that the rightness of an action consisted in its producing the greatest possible good, Prichard holds that rightness is *sui generis* exactly as goodness is and, like goodness on Moore's view, is simply evident to the discriminatingly intuitive eye.

In the writings of W. D. Ross the intuitionist position appears as somewhat etiolated indeed, but also less fanatical. There are in particular two respects in which Ross deviates in the direction of good sense. In the first place, he is unable to swallow without qualification Prichard's doctrine of 'the self-evidence of our obligations'. Perhaps he felt that it was simply too unplausible to contend that the answer to the question, what it is our duty to do, must always be self-evident; but the consideration he chiefly dwells on is this. It is, he thinks, actions of certain *kinds* whose rightness is 'immediately apprehended' — for example, of promise-keeping, or of paying a debt. But there seems to be no kind of action of which we can say without qualification that, whenever it is open to me to perform a particular action of that kind, it is my duty to do so; for, for any two kinds of action both thus asserted to be my duty, circumstances may arise, or may at any rate be imagined, in which I could perform an action of the one kind only by omitting to perform an action of the other kind. I may be confronted with a 'conflict of duties'; and in such a case, since I *can* perform only one of those actions, it cannot be held that it is my duty to do both — nor that, as Prichard seems optimistically to have supposed, it will be immediately obvious which it is my duty to do. Hence we can hold only that actions of certain general kinds are self-evidently, are intuited as being, '*prima facie* duties' — actions, that is, which it is a duty to perform *unless* that obligation conflicts with, and is over-borne by, some other.[7]

Secondly, Ross was fully conscious of a very strange, though unstressed, implication in Moore's doctrine, and to some degree also in Prichard's. If it is insisted that goodness and rightness are simple, *sui generis*, directly intuited properties, then it must seem

that the question whether something is good or right is, purely
and simply, the question whether it possesses one or the other of
those properties; and it may seem that any consideration of its
other properties would be simply irrelevant. But this is surely unacceptable. Let us agree that the goodness of a thing is not to be
identified with any of its other properties, and that the rightness
of an action does not simply consist in its being an action of a certain describable kind: must it not be allowed nevertheless that
the goodness of a thing somehow *depends on* its possession of certain other properties, that there are other features of the action
which *make* it a right action? Goodness and rightness, then,
according to Ross, though intuitable, must be regarded as 'dependent' or 'consequential' properties; they are not, as it were,
stuck on objects or actions like postage stamps, quite indifferently
to any other features of those objects or actions, nor are other
properties quite irrelevant to goodness and rightness.

These two amendments, one may say, make some attempt to
rescue for moral discussion some kind of subject-matter. For if
all that is self-evident is that some action is my duty *prima facie*,
there is room for uncertainty and debate as to whether or not it
really is my duty *sans phrase*; and even if the goodness of something is self-evident, directly intuited, it may still be made a question on what its goodness depends. It must be confessed that
Ross's writings do not throw any light on how such questions
are to be answered; but it is all to the good that he should recognise, and even stress, that there exists at least the possibility
of asking them.

(iii) INTUITIONISM CONSIDERED

We turn now to appraisal. What — to save time by begging one
or two questions — was really wrong with Intuitionism as a
theory of morals? Not, I think, that much of what its proponents
maintained was untrue: indeed, when allowance is made for
certain eccentricities of expression, they often delineated the sur-
face of the subject with commendable accuracy. It is rather that
the theory, appraised as a contribution to philosophy, seems deliberately, almost perversely, to answer no questions, to throw

no light on any problem. One might almost say that the doctrine actually consists in a protracted denial that there is anything of the slightest interest to be said. The effect of this is worse than unhelpful: it is positively misleading.

There is, we may admit, a single grain of truth which all intuitionists grasped, and characteristically dwelt upon — the truth that moral judgments are in some important way *different* from, say, assertions of empirical fact, or commands, or aesthetic judgments, or expressions of taste. Moral judgments, they rightly insisted, cannot be identified with, 'reduced to', or analysed in terms of, any of these other things; they are *different* from these things. But their account of the differences is so jejune as to be worse than useless.

It appears to have been assumed by intuitionist philosophers that it is, in general, the business of an adjective to designate a quality, a property, or a character; or at any rate, if they would not have subscribed to this general view without qualification, they did not question that it was true of the adjectives 'good' and 'right'. Thus, from the fact that goodness was felt not to be identifiable with any ordinarily discernible property of things that are good, Moore concluded merely that 'good' must designate some *other* property; Prichard, finding that 'obligatory' did not mean the same as 'expedient', or 'desirable', or 'productive of good', inferred that 'obligatory' must stand for some *other* character. On this view what distinguishes moral judgments from other things is simply that such judgments ascribe to things *different properties*, characters which are *sui generis* to moral judgment: the difference is simply a difference of subject-matter; moral judgments attribute moral qualities, and that is all there is to it.

It might be thought, with some justice, that what is wrong with this is that, while insisting that there is a difference, it amounts in practice to a refusal to discuss what the difference is. We wish to know what moral goodness is, or what it is for an action to be obligatory, and we are not told; for the 'qualities', we are told, are indefinable. But this answer is not merely dusty, ungratifying to curiosity: it is also positively misleading in a number of respects.

There is a sense, first of all, in which it can be said to exaggerate the difference of moral judgment from other things. On Moore's showing, the fact that some item is morally good appears to be, not merely different from any other fact about it, but quite unconnected with, independent of, any other fact; for all that he says, the simple *sui generis* quality of goodness might quite well be detected as attaching to anything whatever — alighting, so to speak, inexplicably and at random upon anything, of whatever kind. For Prichard there is no reason *why* what is right is right; so, for Moore, there is no reason why what is good is good — that it *is* good is not only a distinguishable, but a totally isolated, fact about it, not just different from, but unrelated to, anything else. But if so, then it seems that morality is not only not reducible to, or identifiable with, any ordinary features of the world or of human beings; it seems to stand in absolutely no relation to any such features, and to be, in the strictest sense, entirely inexplicable. The picture presented is that of a realm of moral qualities, *sui generis* and indefinable, floating, as it were, quite free from anything else whatever, but cropping up here and there, quite contingently and for no reason, in bare conjunction with more ordinary features of the everyday world. Ross, as we have noted, was certainly aware of some deficiency here; while not denying that moral rightness and goodness were distinct 'characters' of right and good things, he asserted that these characters 'depended on' other characters, that there were features of things that somehow *made* them right, or good. But he did not do more than assert that this was so: he did not explain what this puzzling kind of dependence of some 'characters' on others might be. Though he recognised the point, he cast no light upon it.

But if the intuitionist account of the distinctness of moral judgment overstates the case in this way, it seriously understates it in others. On this account the propositions of morals differ solely, though indeed completely, from others in subject-matter; they are truths (or falsehoods) on a peculiar topic, but of a quite familiar kind. To say that daffodils are yellow is to attribute a 'character' to daffodils; to say that aesthetic enjoyment is good is to attribute a 'character' to aesthetic enjoyment. But we detect the character of daffodils by looking at them: how do we detect that other character in aesthetic enjoyment? If disputes should arise, in what way might they be resolved? If I wonder whether some moral proposition is really true, how should I investigate the question, where should I look for assurance? There are, it appears, moral facts: how, then, are moral facts established? To such questions as these the theory offers, in effect, no answer at all. For to say that moral facts are recognised 'by intuition' is in part to say, unhelpfully, that such facts are *not* recognised or established in any ordinary way, and in part to offer the optimistic (and obviously false) suggestion that there is really no room here for doubt, or argument, or disagreement at all. Presumably we are to conclude that what Prichard calls 'our moral capacities of thinking' are themselves, as moral 'characters' are, *sui generis* and indefinable — that is, in effect, that on the whole question of moral argument and moral disagreement there is nothing whatever to be said, unless perhaps that they are what they are.

Finally, we must mention that deficiency in intuitionism of which later writers, as we shall find, have been most acutely conscious. Moral predicates, it was assumed, stand for moral properties. If so, to attribute a moral predicate to some subject is simply to assert that the item referred to has some moral property — it is to state that fact, to convey that piece of information. Now we have already seen that the theory leaves it, at best, unclear how pieces of moral information are related to any other features of the world, and rather more than unclear how their truth can be established or confirmed. We must now take note that it is also left very far from clear what such pieces of information, even if recognised to be true, have to do with our conduct. Let us concede that there are, here and there in the world, some items which have the moral properties intuitionists talk about, and some which have not: why should we care? Why does the presence or absence of these properties matter? In becoming aware that some proposed course of action is, say, obligatory, I have, on this theory, added to my information, I have come to know a truth about the world. But what has this truth that I recognise to do with my behaviour? Why should I *adopt* that course of action rather than some other? The fact that the course of action is obligatory is presumably meant to be a reason for adopting it; the fact that it would, if adopted, start on a Wednesday presumably is not. But why this difference? Why is some information about the properties of things and of actions irrelevant to questions about what is to be done, while some other information apparently is not? Moral judgments, it seems, like other judgments, convey information: what is it about the information they convey which makes it important for, or even relevant to, our decisions, our choices, our advice, or our recommendations? We find, once again, that intuitionism has nothing to say here: in that theory the relevance of moral judgments to conduct appears as a bare assumption, about which, as indeed about almost everything in the subject, there is nothing to be said.

Intuitionism seems, in retrospect, so strange a phenomenon — a body of writing so acute and at the same time so totally un-illuminating — that one may wonder how to explain it, what its genesis was. The idea that there is a vast corpus of moral facts about the world — known, but we cannot say how: related to other features of the world, but we cannot explain in what way: overwhelmingly important for our conduct, but we cannot say why — what does this really astonishing idea reflect? One may be tempted to say: the absence of curiosity. And what the absence of curiosity reflects may be the absence of doubt. One seeks to explain what one feels to be in need of explanation: where everything seems obvious one may feel that there is nothing to be said. Certainly the intuitionist philosophers of the early part of this century do not strike one as men much beset by moral uncertainties; even if, as was surely the case, they were sometimes uncertain on particular questions, they had no *general* uncertainties about the status of morals; what they called 'the facts' of morality were for them simply there, simply given, in the nature of things, standing in need from the theorist of nothing but clear recognition. Their notion that moral judgment was properly to be described on the model of the very simplest assertions of fact was partly attributable, and importantly attributable, to a certain

poverty of philosophical apparatus; their general views about
'judgment' seemed to admit no alternative possibility. But it is
also important that this theoretical poverty, with the bald simplicity of doctrine which it imposed, was not felt to involve any
unacceptable consequences. Why should room be left for uncertainty, if one does not feel any? Why, unless from confusion,
should one ask for the obvious to be explained?

III. EMOTIVISM

(i) SOME EARLY VERSIONS

Ross's *Foundations of Ethics* contains what will perhaps prove to have been the last systematic exposition of pure intuitionist doctrine. When it was published in 1939 there had already begun to emerge the view, or family of views, which was shortly to succeed that doctrine in the centre of the stage. This congeries of views, which is commonly and conveniently labelled 'emotivism', certainly breaks sharply away from the intuitionist point of view; and it was thought for some years, by very many, to have brought great illumination to the study of ethics. It is, perhaps, a desirable thing in itself to change one's point of view from time to time; but it is not really clear that, in any other respect, the new point of view was much of an advance on the old one. It brought some points into prominence that had previously been much neglected; but it imported also some new confusions that had not previously been made.

The first impetus towards emotivism as an ethical theory did not in fact come from moral philosophy itself. It had been, as we have noted, an almost unconscious assumption of the intuitionists that 'moral propositions' asserted a certain kind of fact — that there were certain moral properties actually possessed by certain entities, and that (affirmative) moral judgments simply asserted of those entities that they had those properties. It seems unlikely that this general assumption was made solely for the reason that it seemed particularly well in place in the characterisation of moral judgments; on the contrary, the supposition that moral judgments were of that nature seems to have been made, at times even somewhat uneasily, as a consequence of the quite general supposition that affirmative subject-predicate judgments were *all* of that nature — they ascribed some 'property' or 'character' to that which was designated by the grammatical subject of the judgment. Rather similarly, the view that moral judgments were not of that nature was evidently first arrived at, not because on examination they appeared not in fact to be of that nature, but because it followed from a quite different and quite general philosophical doctrine that they *could* not be of that nature.

The general doctrine in question is the, by now, notorious *Grundgedanke* of the Logical Positivists, that there are just two species of significant propositions — tautologies, and empirically verifiable assertions of fact. Since, naturally and rightly, the Positivists were disinclined to swallow 'intuition' as a respectable means of verification, and since no one was disposed to maintain that moral judgments in general were either tautologous or verifiable by ordinary sense-experience, it followed that they could not be significant propositions: they could not really be, as their grammatical form might lead one to suppose, assertions in which genuine 'properties' were ascribed to things, or indeed genuine assertions of any kind at all. They must be, in their grammatical form, mere masqueraders.

What, then, were they? One rather feels that those who first encountered this problem did not greatly care; nevertheless, they were ready to hazard one or two suggestions. Carnap, for instance, observing that so-called moral judgments were often employed in seeking to direct and influence conduct, threw out the idea that they were really *commands*: 'You ought not to steal' was a misleading way of saying 'Don't steal', 'Kindness is good' of saying 'Be kind'.[8] Schlick, somewhat similarly, suggested that so-called moral judgments really formulated *rules*, and that the only real question for a 'science of ethics' was the psychological question why certain rules come to be adopted.[9] Ayer, in the very succinct sketch which he offers, in *Language, Truth, and Logic* (1936), of an ethical theory, prefers to pick out the point, surely a correct one, that moral judgments often serve to express the feelings of the speaker: it is suggested that this is essentially all that they ever do. Thus in saying, for example, that birth-control is wicked I am not really saying anything, true or false, about birth-control, but merely mentioning it and 'evincing' my disapproval, disgust, or hostility.

The objection most warmly urged at the time against this line of thinking was that it threatened to undermine the rationality of morals. One might at first sight be inclined to wonder why this should have been so; for surely it is not the case that, as between commands, or rules, or expressions of feeling, there is never anything to choose on rational grounds? Commands and rules may conflict, very much as propositions may; and some may be reasonable or justified, others may not be. And can I not defend by argument the sentiments I express, or criticise the feelings of another as misplaced or unwarranted? Nevertheless, there was genuine force in the critics' objection. For a command is justified if what it enjoins is the right thing to do: a rule is a good rule if the conduct it requires is desirable conduct: my expression of disgust is warranted if its object is actually disgusting. But such justifying clauses, of course, can function genuinely as giving *reasons* only if they do not themselves express merely further commands, or rules, or personal feelings — whereas, on the line of thinking briefly sketched above, this is *all* that such clauses could ever be construed as doing. It thus appeared that what we ordinarily think of as argument in these contexts is really no more than conflict in another guise; my 'reasons' really do nothing but repeat my original utterance, and showing that I am right is not really distinguishable from carrying my point. It might, of course, effectively have been replied that the intuitionist picture itself leaves no room for the rationality of morals; for, in that picture, moral disagreement reduces to a bare divergence of 'intuitions', to a blank disagreement about which there is nothing to be said. The intuitionist, to be sure, supposes that moral utterances have truth-values; but it is not much use to *say* that my judgment is true and yours is false, if in principle no means are to hand of showing this to be so. But this is only to say that, on this score, both parties were vulnerable.

But we may say that, in any case, the ideas thrown out by Carnap, Schlick, and Ayer were scarcely more than sighting shots, fired off rather hastily as possible preliminaries to a full-blown campaign, by philosophers whose real interests were not in moral philosophy at all. It was always obvious that at least they left a great deal more to be said; but no doubt they did not seriously aspire to completeness. The account offered by C. L. Stevenson in his very influential book *Ethics and Language* (1944), while closely akin to these earlier ventures, is more careful, more comprehensive, and immensely more elaborately presented. There are three main pillars upon which this account stands, and we must first set out what these are.

(ii) C. L. STEVENSON: BELIEFS, ATTITUDES, 'EMOTIVE MEANING'

First, a distinction is sought to be drawn between *beliefs* and *attitudes*. Consider, for instance (to take a non-moral case), a proposal to devalue the pound sterling: and let us suppose that we have two economists whose beliefs concerning this proposal are exactly the same. They are in full agreement as to what it is that is proposed, and also as to what in fact would be the economic, social, and political consequences of adopting the proposal or, alternatively, of rejecting it. It is still possible — one may think it unlikely, but it seems to be possible — that, notwithstanding this full agreement, their *attitudes* towards the proposal should differ; while agreeing exactly as to what the proposal is and would imply, one might be in favour of it, the other against. It would be conceded, no doubt, that most disagreements in attitude rest on, or are due to, disagreements in belief; when one person favours what another opposes, a full enquiry into the situation will usually bring out that they hold somewhat different beliefs as to the nature, or immediate or perhaps very remote effects or consequences, of the matter at issue. It would be conceded also that it might often be exceedingly difficult to show that disagreement in attitude did *not* thus rest on disagreement in belief; for how could one ever be sure that one had established agreement in belief on *all* matters which either party might take to be relevant, however remotely, to the point at issue? Nevertheless, it would be held that the distinction is perfectly clear in theory: disagreement in attitude is plainly *different* from disagreement in belief, hard though it may be to distinguish sharply, in actual cases, between one species of disagreement and the other. We may add that, just as there may be agreement in belief and disagreement in attitude, there may, of course, occur agreement in attitude and disagreement in belief.

Second, there is introduced the notion of 'emotive meaning' — whence the name 'emotivism'. Consider, for instance, the words 'German' and 'Boche'. There is a sense in which these words have exactly the same meaning: they are applicable to exactly the same things, for instance to the members of a certain European nation, and applicable to them, furthermore, on exactly the same basis, or in virtue of just the same facts; there would be no evidential difference between establishing that Fritz was a German and that Fritz was a Boche. Nevertheless, it is plain that the terms do differ in some way. In what way? The difference is, surely, that 'German' is what might be called a neutral expression; it signifies merely membership of a certain nation. 'Boche', on the other hand, is far from neutral. While it too signifies membership of a certain nation, its use also typically expresses the speaker's hostility to or contempt for that nation, and is liable, and often deliberately intended, to evoke similar hostility and contempt on the part of his audience. The two terms, then, are said to have the same 'descriptive meaning'; but 'Boche' has also a certain 'emotive meaning', consisting in the fact that it commonly both expresses, and is liable to arouse, certain feelings towards that to which it is applied. In general, those words are said to have emotive meaning which, besides standardly and neutrally signifying what, if anything, they do signify, also standardly express, and are liable to arouse, favourable or un-favourable feelings or attitudes towards that to which they are applied. (I say 'if anything' since, it is suggested, there are words — 'Hurrah!' for example — which have little or no descriptive meaning at all, but are *purely* emotive.) It may be added that, while any term's emotive meaning will normally be somewhat depen-dent on or connected with its descriptive meaning, it is quite possible that, if the normal attitudes or feelings of its users change, while its descriptive meaning remains more or less con-stant, its emotive meaning may dwindle or vanish, or may even be reversed. It is not very long, for instance, since the word 'democracy' commonly expressed and aroused feelings of alarm and despondency — though, indeed, it is also not entirely clear in this case either that the term has any very definite descriptive meaning, or that its descriptive meaning may not gradually have shifted as well.

Third, after these preliminaries the thesis is advanced that it is the distinctive feature of moral judgment not to convey the speaker's *beliefs*, but to evince his *attitudes*; and not to add to or alter the *beliefs* of the person addressed, but to influence his *attitudes* and hence, in all probability, his conduct. Moral discourse (in a nutshell) is primarily not informative but *influential*; it may modify beliefs incidentally, but attitudes primarily.[10] It was this point, it would be said, that the intuitionists had dimly in view when they insisted that moral predicates were not reducible to other, i.e. to purely descriptive, predicates. They were aware that in some way a moral judgment upon, say, a proposed course of action was not only not equivalent to, but was quite unlike, any mere description of the course of action proposed. They quite failed to see, however, just what the point was here. Because of their addiction to the assumed adjective–property equation, they were led to represent moral judgment merely as a peculiar kind of description, consisting in the ascription to things of peculiar, 'non-natural', *sui generis* properties. But this fudged the very point that they had dimly in view. For a queer sort of information is still, after all, information; description in terms of strange *sui generis* properties is still description. They thus failed to bring out the distinction between beliefs and attitudes, reducing attitudes in fact to a mysterious species of beliefs; and thus, still representing moral judgments as purely informative, they could make no sense at all of the essential connection between moral discourse and our attitudes, decisions, choices, and in general, behaviour. Most moral predicates, no doubt, do stand for properties. When we are told for example, that some person is generous or honest, we learn something, quite descriptively, of what sort of person he is and what he tends to do. But it is not this, the emotivist insists, that makes the judgment about him a moral one; what makes it moral is that the terms applied to him also both express and induce a *favourable attitude* towards him, both evince and arouse certain feelings towards that person. And this is not the ascription to him of an extra property; it is quite unlike the ascription of properties; it is, rather, 'emotive', 'dynamic', a question of influence.

It will be clear from this brief and somewhat simplified sketch of emotivism that this doctrine has certain undeniable and important merits. It completely does away with the perplexing intuitionist mythology of 'non-natural' *sui generis* moral properties, and indeed with 'intuition' itself. 'Emotive meaning', by contrast, points to a real phenomenon of considerable theoretical interest and practical importance. Moreover, while, as we have just mentioned, intuitionism offers no intelligible account of the relation between moral judgment and conduct, the emotivist thesis connects moral judgment with conduct in a perfectly intelligible and (within limits) clear and definite manner. Unfortunately, as we must now observe, this connection, while possessing the merit of being intelligible, clear, and definite, has the demerit also of being completely wrong, and indeed, in a certain sense, disastrously wrong.

(iii) THE ERRORS OF EMOTIVISM

It is the central thesis of emotivism that moral discourse is essentially to be characterised by reference to its purpose: as Stevenson puts it, the 'major use' of ethical judgments is 'not to indicate facts, but to *create an influence*'.[11] In any moral discourse the characteristic purpose of the speaker is to influence, not the beliefs, but the *attitudes* of his audience.

One point, I take it, will be immediately obvious — namely, that this purpose is in no way distinctive of moral discourse. It may well be the case, as Stevenson says, that ethical statements are 'social instruments' for the control, redirection, and modification of 'attitudes'; but so also are advertising posters, television commercials, political speeches, threats, 'committed' works of literature, bribes, and so on. Suppose, for example, that I wish to 'create an influence' in favour of larger families in England. It is clear that there are *many* ways in which I might try to do this — many species of 'social instruments' of which I might avail myself for the purpose in hand. I might, indeed, engage in moral exhortation, assuring the populace that they ought, that it is right, that perhaps it is positively their duty, to engage more copiously in procreation. But alternatively, or in addition, I might buy space on bill-boards or time on television, spreading abroad the image of happy, smiling parents among troops of genial, healthy infants. I might make childless adults liable to national service, and give large tax reliefs to the philoprogenitive. I might seek to make out that large families are a mark of the aristocracy, or write novels about the miseries of neglected and solitary old age. It is obvious that all these are ways of 'creating an influence', that they all have the purpose of modifying 'attitudes' and, in consequence, conduct: so that, even if it is true that moral discourse has this purpose, moral discourse is not thereby distinguished from many other things.

But now, is it true that moral discourse *has* this purpose? It is not difficult to see that the answer is: not necessarily, not always. If I set out to 'create an influence' by issuing a moral utterance, then presumably (i) I suppose that my audience does not already have the 'attitude' which my utterance is calculated to promote; also (ii) I wish my audience to have this attitude; and (iii) I think it at least possible that my issuing the utterance will tend to promote adoption of this attitude. But then I may, of course, quite well issue a moral utterance when any or all of these conditions fail. I may be conversing with someone whose 'attitude' I know to be the same as mine, whom, so to speak, I cannot *move* because he is there already. I may be concerned merely to make my own 'attitude' known to some person to whose reactions to it I am entirely indifferent or, again, who to my knowledge does not care a straw for my opinion. Moral discourse is not always so 'dynamic' as all that. A good deal of what might be called moral chat goes on in the comfortable belief that all parties to it are firmly, perhaps smugly, at one in the attitudes exposed; and though the expression of moral judgments to persons one does not care, or is not able, to influence may be thought somewhat pointless, it is not impossible, and may have some other than the usual point. Thus the alleged dynamic purpose of moral discourse is not only not distinctive of it; it may be quite absent and the discourse be not the less moral for that.

But emotivism is perhaps most seriously in error in its account of the way in which, in moral discourse, 'influence' is exerted. The aptness of moral language to the supposed dynamic ends of moral discourse is sought to be explained by reference to 'emotive meaning'. It is, it is said, because moral words have emotive (and not merely descriptive) meanings that they can play the double role of *evincing* the attitude of the speaker, and exerting *influence* upon the attitude of the addressee. They express my feelings, and will tend to arouse yours. But it is not, I think, difficult to see that this is all wrong, and importantly so.

What *are* emotive words? Why is it that a speaker or writer may be blamed, or in other cases praised, for his employment of emotive language? Emotive words are words that appeal to the feelings or (as of course the term itself suggests) to the emotions. Now this is sometimes, as for instance in certain kinds of literary work, a good thing; for here it may be the intended and entirely proper purpose to appeal to, to stir, the feelings of a reader or an audience. But of course it may often be highly undesirable. A Treasury official, for instance, summarising or commenting upon some issue of economic policy, would justly be rebuked if his minute or memorandum were couched in highly emotive terms. He will do well to avoid, even if he is tempted by, such epithets as 'scandalous', 'fatuous', 'nauseating', or 'bird-brained'. For such language is inimical to the calm and balance of bureaucratic judgment; whereas it is such as his Minister, for example, might use with propriety and effect in the very different context of his electioneering. Now it is clear enough that some moral terms are, in this sense, somewhat emotive; the feelings are quite liable to stir at such a term as 'heroic', and to stir in an opposite sense at such a term as 'blackguardly' or 'vicious'. But the pulses do not beat faster at encountering the word 'right'; there is nothing particularly stirring about 'good', or 'ought';

and if the Treasury official writes, for instance, that the financier's proposition is entirely honest, and even generous, he could scarcely be criticised for using emotive language. The fact is that expressing and appealing to the feelings is incidental to, and actually quite rare in, moral discourse, much as exerting influence is incidental to, and often quite absent from, making moral judgments. 'It would be monstrous to do that!' expresses my feelings, and may stimulate yours; but 'It would be wrong to do that' is most unlikely to do either. It expresses an opinion, not a state of emotional excitement; it gives you, perhaps, my advice against doing something, not a stimulus towards emotional revulsion from doing it. There is nothing, in short, necessarily *emotive* about moral criticism or approval; moral advice may be given in entirely dispassionate terms. Equally, of course, a piece of discourse may be highly emotive but unconcerned with morals; and one's feelings may quite well run counter to one's moral views.

It is not difficult, in the light of these criticisms, to appreciate why to many the implications of emotivism seemed peculiarly objectionable. We see that it was the characteristic feature — it was put forward, indeed, as the chief claim to originality — of emotivist doctrine to turn away from the informative content, if any, of moral discourse, and instead to locate the essence of moral discourse in its *effects*. In place of the orthodox intuitionist view that a moral judgment, like other judgments, *stated* something and was typically intended to inform, the view was advanced that a moral judgment essentially *did* something, and was typically intended to produce a certain effect. But much as the intuitionists were prevented, by their apparatus of direct 'intuition' and 'self-evident' facts, from having anything of interest to say about moral argument, so, or even more so, for quite different reasons were the emotivists. Briefly: if it is held that a certain kind of discourse is employed essentially to produce an effect, it must follow that the criterion by which such discourse is to be appraised must essentially be the criterion simply of effectiveness. If the point of some tract of discourse is, say, essentially to influence your attitude, to arouse your feelings, then that tract of discourse is good if it succeeds, or is well calculated to succeed, in doing this; it is bad, vulnerable to criticism, if it proves inefficacious, or might have been expected to do so. In logic, it is possible to make a quite clear distinction between an argument's being valid, and an argument's producing conviction; we can well say that a proof, though it convinced, contained a fallacy, or that it was a valid proof, though it happened that no one was convinced by it. The emotivist view leaves no room for an analogous distinction in ethics. Questions of belief, it is allowed, may be rationally debated; we may distinguish here between truth and falsehood, good evidence or bad, between mere prejudice and well-founded belief, belief for good reasons. But on the characteristically moral (as it was supposed) matter of attitudes, there could be no such distinctions; a moral 'argument' so-called might produce its effect or fail to do so, but there was no room for consideration, as a *further question*, as to whether it was a good argument or a bad one. In this way moral discourse emerged — notwithstanding much strenuous special pleading — as essentially in the same boat with propaganda, or advertising, or even intimidation; it was intended to influence people, to affect their feelings and behaviour, and was to be assessed not as rational, in terms of good reasons or bad reasons, but as effective or ineffective, in terms of what did or did not yield the results intended. There were many who were able to swallow this startling conclusion; but it was felt in many quarters that something must have gone very wrong.

What *had* gone wrong? Chiefly, I think, two things. First, the emotivists were understandably over-impressed by their idea of bringing in the *purpose*, or function, of moral discourse. It is true that the intuitionists had been distressingly silent on this point. Their view of moral judgments as straightforward (though in certain respects peculiar) truths and falsehoods had appeared to make a mystery of the relation of such judgments to conduct; they seemed not to have considered at all what moral discourse is *for*. But the emotivists, one might say, were inclined merely to go to the opposite extreme — to dwell, that is, so exclusively on what moral discourse is for, that they scarcely raised seriously the question what it actually is. It is a good thing, no doubt, to appreciate *that* moral discourse is quite often directed to influencing 'attitudes'; but it should have been considered more carefully *how* it does so. For the general purpose, as we have seen, is not an invariable feature of moral utterances and, more importantly, does not distinguish such utterances from many other kinds of linguistic — and for that matter non-linguistic — proceedings.

Second, so far as emotivists did consider how it is that moral discourse may influence attitudes, their account was inadequate, or indeed seriously mistaken. The trouble here arose, in large part, from a certain crudity in their notion of what 'attitudes' are. There was a constant tendency to identify attitudes with *feelings* — to identify, say, my disapproval of someone's behaviour with the disgust or revulsion which I may feel on witnessing it. But this was not merely wrong: it was disastrously wrong. For as a consequence, expressing my disapproval of someone's behaviour became identified with the widely different phenomenon of 'giving vent' to my feelings about it; and my seeking to change someone else's 'attitude' came to be represented as simply an attempt to work on his emotions. Hence the blunder of supposing that moral words as such have 'emotive meaning'; for if I am 'venting' my feelings and working on yours, must it not be the case that I am using emotive language? Thence, finally, the conclusion that moral discourse is essentially non-rational, a matter not of argument but of psychological pressure, not of reasons but of efficacious manipulation. Intuitionism had left gaps — indeed, scarcely anything except gaps — in moral philosophy; but there was a great quantity of muddle in the filling which emotivism supplied.

IV. PRESCRIPTIVISM

(i) ADVICE VERSUS INFLUENCE

The next turn taken by moral philosophy in this century can best
be introduced as — and was, I think it is true to say, in fact introduced as — an amendment to emotivism. The amendment in
question, which is principally the work of R. M. Hare, has been
extremely influential, and in certain respects is genuinely illuminating. I believe it to be by no means free from confusion;
but its virtues and deficiencies, we may hope, will prove alike
instructive.

Let us look back once again to the implicit assumption of intuitionism that moral discourse is essentially informative —
that a moral judgment typically states, or otherwise alludes to,
the ethical fact that some moral property is possessed by some
subject. It was, as we have seen, the central tenet of emotivism
that this implicit assumption is false — that, even if a moral
judgment does inform, or state some fact, this is not the essence
of the case. With this tenet of emotivism Hare emphatically
agrees. He too insists that the purveying of information, even if
the information be supposed to be of a peculiar 'non-natural'
kind, is not the essence of moral discourse, but is at most purely
incidental to it. But whereas, in rejecting the intuitionists' implicit assumption, the emotivists had concluded that the essence
of moral discourse lay in its use to 'create an influence', to *affect*
people's feelings ('attitudes') and so their behaviour, Hare contends that the essence is not influence but *guidance*.[12] In saying to
you, for example, 'You ought to repay the money' I am not,
indeed, merely stating some fact; but nor am I, primarily or
necessarily, seeking to get you to do something; I am, essentially,
telling you *what to do*. You have, as it were — so Hare puts it —
raised the question 'What shall I do?'; and I have answered that
question. Actually getting, moving, or inducing you to do what

I tell you to do is something else again. Influencing your behaviour may possibly be an effect, and is quite likely indeed, to be
the intended effect, of the answer I give you, of my issuing that
moral utterance; but it is still essential to distinguish my telling
you what to do from any effects or consequences, actual or intended, of my so telling you — what I am doing *in* saying 'You
ought to repay the money', from what I may (possibly) hope to
achieve *by* saying it.[13]

At least one great virtue of this amendment will be plain
enough; it seems at once to enable us to escape the conclusion
that moral discourse is fundamentally non-rational. The problem
of getting somebody to do something, or of influencing his feelings with that end in view, is simply the problem of employing
effective means to that end; even if in some case I should decide
that talking to a person — as an alternative, say, to frightening
him, or feeding him drugs — will influence him most effectively,
it may well not matter whether or not he understands what I say,
or whether or not what I say makes any sense. A dictum, to be
'emotively' effective, need not necessarily be understood, or even
be intelligible; it will be right — for the purpose — on the sole
condition that it works. But about guidance, clearly, quite other
questions can be raised. It is essential, here, that you should
understand what I tell you; you may ask me for my reasons, and
consider whether the reasons I give you are good or bad; my
answer to your question may be the right answer even if you do
not accept it, or wrong even though you accept it without hesi-
tation. To ask for and to give answers to practical questions is
plainly and essentially a business for rational beings, and one
that can be appraised on rational grounds. We may note the absurdity of the emotivist's notion that one who asks 'What ought
I to do?' is 'asking for influence',[14] and by contrast the perfect
naturalness of Hare's amendment: he is asking for guidance.

Moral discourse then, Hare holds, is not primarily — though
sometimes it may be incidentally — informative; but nor is it
essentially — though sometimes it may be incidentally —
'emotive'. It does not serve essentially, though it may do consequentially, to *influence* people, to get them to do things or

refrain from doing them; it is, rather, action-guiding, or, in Hare's term 'prescriptive'. Let us consider a little further what this means.

(ii) MORAL DISCOURSE AS 'PRESCRIPTIVE'

Prescriptive discourse, I think we may say quite generally (expounding Hare), is that species of discourse in which practical questions are answered — much as, one might say, informative discourse is that species of discourse which answers requests for information. If you put to me the information-seeking question 'Where do you live?', my answer ('I live in Oxford') is a specimen of informative discourse; if you put to me the practical question 'What ought I to do?', my answer will be a specimen of prescriptive discourse.

Now the simplest of all forms of prescriptive discourse, and also in a sense the basic form, is, in Hare's view, the plain imperative. The palmary case of telling someone what to do is to issue, for instance, the simple imperative 'Go away' — an utterance which may or may not have the effect of *making* its addressee go away, but at any rate *tells* him to. But in Hare's view we cannot properly say, as Carnap once did, that moral judgments just *are* grammatically disguised imperatives, for, as we shall see, moral judgments have certain essential features which simple imperatives may lack. But moral judgments, he holds, do have in common with imperatives the crucial feature that they are 'prescriptive'; and this in fact means, in Hare's view, that a moral judgment — or at any rate a genuine, typical, non-deviant moral judgment — *entails* an imperative. Just as, if a proposition p entails another proposition q, I cannot (consistently) assert or accept p and deny or reject q, so, in Hare's view, I cannot (consistently) assert or accept the moral judgment, say, 'You ought to repay the money' and deny or reject the imperative 'Repay the money'. Now to 'deny' or 'reject' an imperative, Hare holds, is simply, having received it, *not* to act on it, not to do what it says. Thus, the thesis that moral judgments are prescriptive implies that one who accepts the moral judgment that he ought to do X is logically committed to doing X; conversely, that one who does not do X is logically debarred from accepting or affirming the judgment that he ought to do X. My moral judgment that you ought to do X 'guides' your action, not in the sense that it necessarily *moves* you to do X, but in that your accepting my judgment *commits* you to doing X, and your not doing X implies your rejection of my judgment. For in saying that you ought to do it I am implicitly telling you to do it; and if you do not, you have not accepted what I said.

Moral judgments, then, are supposed to resemble imperatives in being 'prescriptive', and to be so, indeed, in virtue of an intimate logical relation to imperatives. But they have, Hare holds, a further most important feature which distinguishes them from at any rate many imperatives. I may, on a whim of the moment, tell you in particular to go away on this particular occasion, without thereby being logically committed to saying or doing anything in particular on any other occasion; the singular imperative 'Go away', issued to you here and now, does not *bind* me to taking any particular line elsewhere or elsewhen. If on another occasion, perhaps another exactly similar occasion, I happen to want you not to go away, I may issue the imperative 'Don't go' without logical impropriety. Not so, however, with moral judgments. For the moral judgment that I make in a certain situation must be founded on, made in virtue of, certain features *of* that situation; and accordingly I must, in consistency, be prepared to make the same judgment in any situation which shares those features (and does not differ in any other relevant respect). Such a judgment as 'You ought to repay the money' is, in Hare's term, universalisable; that is, if I commit myself to this judgment in your particular case, I thereby commit myself to the view that anybody — including, most importantly, myself — in the circumstances in which you now are ought to act in that way. I cannot, without logical impropriety, issue a different judgment in another case, unless I can show that other case to be different in some relevant respect. Or if I judge differently some other case which I cannot show to be relevantly different, then I am bound to correct or withdraw my original judgment. Moral judgments, in effect, cannot be, as imperatives may be, purely and completely singular; in judging this case, we implicitly judge any case of this *kind*, and cannot accordingly judge differently other cases of the *same* kind.

We have before us, then, the thesis 'that moral judgments are a kind of *prescriptive* judgments, and that they are distinguished from other judgments of this class by being *universalisable*.' [15] I shall now argue, first, that moral judgments are *not* essentially prescriptive, and second, that, if that is so, we need not claim for 'universalisability' the importance which Hare, as I think mistakenly, claims for it.

(iii) TWO VERSIONS OF 'PRESCRIPTIVISM'

I believe that there can be discerned, encapsulated in what we may call the prescriptivist thesis, at least two distinguishable doctrines which call for separate discussion. I begin with the one that seems the more obviously false.

The prescriptivist thesis is, of course, put forward as a quite general thesis about moral discourse — not only, we may note, about moral utterances in general, but even about moral words in general, which are said by Hare to have 'prescriptive meaning'. Now one way in which this thesis might be taken, and in which it has sometimes been put forward, would be this: it is the thesis that there is a certain class of words, which includes that class of words which occur characteristically in moral discourse, whose meaning is to be explained (at least in part) in terms of the performance of a particular 'speech-act', namely, prescribing. That is to say: in any discourse in which those words occur in their standard meanings, it must be the case that the speaker of that discourse is therein prescribing. He is, at any rate in part or implicitly, 'telling someone what to do'.

One might think that, as a general thesis about the occurrence in discourse of moral words, this is too obviously false ever to have been seriously believed. How could it possibly have been supposed that moral discourse, in all its almost endless diversity of forms and contexts, must consist essentially and always in the performance of any *single* speech-act? No one would think of saying this about discourse in general: but moral discourse, discourse in which moral words occur, is not much, if at all, less versatile in this respect than discourse in general; there are at any rate dozens of things which those who employ moral words may therein be doing. They may be prescribing, certainly; but also they may be advising, exhorting, imploring; commanding, condemning, deploring; resolving, confessing, undertaking; and so on, and so on. But here we may note as a possible explanatory factor the fairly obvious fact that, when Hare thinks of 'moral discourse', he thinks first of such discourse as occurring in one particular context — that, namely, in which one speaker addresses to another a moral judgment upon some course of action currently open to, and possibly to be undertaken by, that other person; in which *A* asks 'What shall I do?', and *B* answers his question. This half-conscious restriction of context was in fact already present, we may note further, in emotivism; for the context in which one typically 'creates an influence' is that in which one talks to another party with an eye to his present or future behaviour. That Hare is apt to carry over this tacit restriction is evident from his recurrent concern with imperatives,[16] which, of course, are also typically issued by one speaker to another with an eye to what that other is currently to do. Now it is certainly not grossly false to say of imperatives (though it is not quite true either) that they are tied, so to speak, to the performance of a particular speech-act. It is not very badly wrong to say, that is, that one who engages in 'imperative discourse' is therein, in virtue of what imperatives are, performing the speech-act of telling someone what to do. But if, as Hare seems to, one half-consciously restricts one's attention to the kinds of contexts in which imperatives would naturally occur, then it may seem fairly plausible to say that 'moral judgment' too consists in the performance of, is tied to, one particular speech-act, that of prescribing. This is not, indeed, a truth about moral judgment, still less about moral *words*; it might be a truth, at best, about the particular class of moral utterances which might naturally be issued in that particular kind of situation. But if the very narrow restriction of context is not noticed, the gross absurdity of the generalised thesis may not be noticed either.

The prescriptivist thesis, however, cannot yet be dismissed; for it is not merely the gross absurdity that we have just considered. Though that plainly false doctrine has certainly been propounded in its name — and even, at the price of desperate paradox, explicitly defended — the thesis is susceptible of a much less absurd interpretation. The false doctrine, in fact, has probably managed to hold the field not only because the above-mentioned half-conscious restrictions have masked its full absurdity, but also because it has not been properly distinguished from the more plausible doctrine that we have now to consider.

The more plausible doctrine, and the one that is really central in Hare's account, is that moral discourse is prescriptive in the sense that, in discourse of this kind, there obtains a quite special connection between words and deeds. Here we may glance once again at the comparison with imperatives. Suppose that I issue to you the imperative utterance 'Spare that tree'; in what would acceptance by you of my utterance consist? It seems that we must say: it would consist in your *doing* what I say, namely, sparing that tree. Generalising, we may say that imperative discourse is such that acceptance of what is said in that mode consists in appropriate *action* on the part of those to whom it is addressed: you have not accepted what I said if you do not do as I say. Now it is in this respect, Hare believes, that moral discourse is analogous, that it too is prescriptive. We need not embrace (though he sometimes does) the rather obvious falsehood that to issue a moral utterance is always to tell someone what to do; but we can and must say that any proposition in morals, whatever the speaker may be doing in issuing that proposition, is such that acceptance of it consists in acting in a certain way, either here and now, or if the appropriate circumstances should arise. Moreover (since moral judgments, unlike imperatives, are universalisable and 'apply' to the speaker himself no less than to other persons), any proposition in morals also commits the speaker to acting in a certain way; if he does not so act, then he does not mean what he says. If I remark to you that it was very

wrong of Jenkins to get so horribly drunk at his daughter's
wedding, I surely am not telling you — still less myself — not
to get horribly drunk at weddings of daughters: perhaps we have
no daughters, or our daughters are already firmly settled in the
married state, and in any case I am talking about Jenkins, not you
or me. Nevertheless, my remark is such that anyone who really
accepts it stays sober at his daughter's wedding and on occasions
of that *kind*, or at least, like you and me, would do so if so placed.
If you would not, then you do not really accept what I say: and
if I would not, then I do not sincerely mean what I say. It is not
only that, as we are told, actions speak louder than words; it is
that, in the case of prescriptive discourse, actions confirm or
refute words, in acting we 'accept' or 'reject' them. And it is, of
course, by no means obviously false that moral discourse is prescriptive in this sense; for we should all be inclined to agree that,
as Hare puts it, 'If we were to ask of a person "What are his
moral principles?" the way in which we could be most sure of a
true answer would be by studying what he *did*'.[17]

Now that there is, in moral discourse, this kind of close connection, of interdependence, between words and deeds is, at the
very least, a very plausible view. It needs, I think, to be hedged
and qualified in certain respects, some of great importance; but
let us for the moment postpone those operations. We must first
consider whether, assuming this view to be correct, it follows
that in *this* sense the prescriptivist thesis is true.

This may seem at first sight to be a very extraordinary question;
for it may seem that Hare's prescriptivist doctrine — not indeed
in its absurd, but in its other, more persuasive sense — just *is* the
doctrine that in moral discourse this interdependence of words
and deeds obtains. But this is not so. Prescriptivism has, I think,
looked persuasive to many because it has been thought simply
to be this doctrine. But it is not; for it not only asserts this interdependence, it seeks to explain it; and the explanation is far indeed from being obviously correct.

We come up here, once again, against the seductive influence of
the imperative model. It is indeed true (or true enough) to say
that to accept the imperative 'Spare that tree' just is to spare that

tree, and that accordingly we have a case here of a very intimate relation between words and deeds. The relation in this case, furthermore, is susceptible of relatively simple explanation. The deed — or non-deed perhaps — of sparing that tree is thus intimately related to the words in question in that the words *prescribe* that course of action; and it is for that reason that the course of action constitutes acceptance of what was said, and any other course of action would constitute its rejection. Now the prescriptivist thesis says (as its name implies) not only plausibly, that in moral discourse there obtains a comparably intimate relation between words and deeds, but also, much less plausibly, that that relation holds here for the *same reason*: the words prescribe, and the deeds are consonant or dissonant with the words in so far as, and because, they do or do not follow the prescription given. It is not exactly that (as on the absurd view) to issue a moral judgment is itself always actually to prescribe; it is rather that any moral judgment either is, or presupposes, or implies, or both, a prescription. As we put it at an earlier stage, it 'entails an imperative'; and it is in virtue of *that* that our relation obtains here between words and deeds, and that moral discourse can be said in general to be 'action-guiding'.

But why, we may now ask, should the relation be explained in this way? Some may have thought — some have certainly written as if they thought — that it must be explained in this way because there is no other way; the *only* way in which deeds can be consonant, or dissonant, with words is for their doing to be, or not be, what the words *prescribe*. But it is really quite obvious that this is not the only possibility; there are dozens of others. I may express a liking for the modern dance, and my behaviour may show that I do not really like it at all. I may say that I want a classless society, and my actions may betray that I really want no such thing. I may express a resolution always to be kind to children, and so act as to show that I was wholly insincere in doing so. I may say that my ideal is perfect self-mortification, and live in a way that makes clear that this is idle verbiage. I may say that I value social justice above all things, and show in practice, when it comes to the crunch, that I value many things much more.

And so on and so on. Thus, from the fact, if it be a fact, that a man's moral principles are revealed most decisively in his behaviour, it does not follow in the least that those principles have to be conceived as, or as implying, *prescriptions*. They might, so far as that point goes, equally well be conceived as expressions of taste or of approval, as avowals of wants or aims, as views about values or ideals, as resolutions, as beliefs about interests, and in many other ways too. On this score at any rate, 'Eating people is wrong' is no more closely akin to 'Don't eat people' than it is to 'I don't want people to be eaten': for in each of these cases the eating of people, or looking on complacently while people are eaten, would be in some sort of conflict with, even in a sense would contradict, what is said. Why then should we, having conceded, as we must, that moral judgments in general *are* not imperatives, still maintain that they are all in this respect *like* imperatives, that their relation to conduct is to be explained in the same way?

(iv) MORAL DISCOURSE AND CONDUCT

The fact is, as I think we are now in a position to see, that the thesis of 'prescriptivism' errs, at bottom, in attempting to answer an impossible question — a question, that is, to which *any* answer would be bound to be wrong. Imperative discourse, as we may say reasonably enough, is in some way intimately related to conduct; and here we may go on to ask: in what way, exactly? Now this is a question, as it happens, that has quite a good answer; for in virtue of what imperatives are, it is broadly true to say that one who issues an imperative, employs an imperative expression, is therein telling someone to do something, whose behaviour may accordingly conform with, or go against, what is said. Now Hare, it appears, goes on from this point to ask the same question of *moral* discourse — this is intimately related to conduct: in what way, exactly? But here we have a question without an answer; for, whereas imperative expressions form a particular grammatical class whose members (roughly) are standardly employed for one particular purpose in one particular type of situation, 'moral

expressions' are of the utmost grammatical diversity, may occur
in very widely varied types of situations, and may be employed
in doing very many quite different things. Thus, while it is reasonable to suppose that the relation of imperatives to conduct can
be characterised, broadly at any rate, in *one* way, it is entirely
unreasonable to suppose that the same can be done for 'moral
discourse'. Sometimes, certainly — namely, in that type of situation which seems always to be at the front of Hare's mind —
moral discourse will be prescriptive: the speaker will be, roughly
speaking, telling another person what to do, instructing, advising,
or 'guiding' him. But at other times not. As Nowell-Smith very
properly remarks: 'The words with which moral philosophers
have especially to do . . . play many different parts. They are
used to express tastes and preferences, to express decisions and
choices, to criticise, grade, and evaluate, to advise, admonish,
warn, persuade and dissuade, to praise, encourage and reprove,
to promulgate and draw attention to rules; and doubtless for
other purposes also.'[18] It is probably true that in all these cases
someone's conduct will be *somehow* related to, consonant or dissonant with, what the speaker says — sometimes his own conduct, sometimes that of the person he addresses, sometimes that
of specific other persons, or of people in general. But the actual
relations, quite clearly, will be widely diverse, and not to be
summed up in any *single* formula whatever.

At the end of the last section we took note of a number of
different ways in which deeds, as we put it, may be 'consonant or
dissonant' with words, otherwise than by being or not being
what the words prescribe. We can now see that it would be a
complete mistake to raise the question which of these ways is
exemplified, or even most nearly exemplified, in moral discourse.
For the fact is that they all are; and so are a great many more.
Resolutions on my own part, advice offered to another; the profession of aspirations or ideals; the expression of distaste, criticism, or commendation; reference to wants of my own, or to the
needs or aims or interests of others — *all* of these commonly
occur in 'moral discourse', just as they occur also, of course, in
discourse that is not moral. In each case there is, no doubt, some

relation to conduct, but by no means the same kind of relation in every case. We thus find in the end that our two versions of prescriptivism err, not indeed in quite the same way, but still in very similar ways. In its absurd form the doctrine seeks to incorporate into 'moral discourse', and even into the meanings of moral words, the performance of just one particular speech-act, that of *prescribing* — as if, whatever the moral discourser is saying and in whatever situation, this is the *only* thing that he can ever be doing. The other version is not so blatantly misguided as this, for it does not construe the term 'prescriptive' so narrowly as to imply that one who uses a prescriptive expression must always be, literally and strictly, prescribing; the suggestion is only that what is thus said is always related very intimately to what is done. But at this point there creeps in the very similar error of supposing that this relation is always to be explained in the same way, and explained, furthermore, on the model of actual prescription. But that moral discourse in general is related to conduct in *one* way is no more true than that one who engages in moral discourse is always doing *one* thing.

A legislator, a judge, an advocate, and a juryman may all engage in 'legal discourse'. But on the one hand they will not, of course, all therein be doing the same one thing; nor, obviously, will the things they are severally saying be related in any one way, though probably all are in some way, to human conduct. A possible 'prescriptive theory of legal discourse' — which would consist, perhaps, in taking the language of *legislation* as that in terms of which all legal talk would be sought to be explained — would share most of the merits and demerits of its analogue in ethics. It would throw practically no light on the law. I am not suggesting, of course, that there is no truth whatever in 'prescriptivism' as an ethical theory; but I do suggest that there is less truth than falsehood. The grain of truth is to be located in the very general claim that 'moral discourse' is not purely, theoretically, informative — it bears on conduct, what is done may be in conflict or in harmony with what is said. But in so far as the theory does not merely state this unexceptionable platitude, but purports to offer an explanation of it, it appears to me to be completely mistaken — and mistaken, not only in that it wrongly proposes 'prescribing' as the link between moral words and deeds, but, more seriously, in that it tacitly embodies the grossly false idea that there is some *one* way in which this linkage can usefully be described. The question how 'moral discourse' bears on conduct really needs to be separately considered for many quite different kinds of moral utterance, and for many quite different situations or contexts in which moral utterances may occur. It seems a considerable disservice to obscure this diversity beneath the appearance of a single, rather simple, monolithic doctrine.

We are left, then, with a number of questions still disconcertingly open. The intuitionist's characterisation of moral discourse we have seen to be distressingly taciturn. That moral discourse is 'emotive' is, we have further observed, not universally true nor in any case distinctive. But we now have to say, it appears, much the same about prescriptivism. For if moral discourse is in some contexts prescriptive, that is not because it is moral discourse, but because it is, in those particular contexts, discourse in which prescribing happens to be going on. How then *is* moral discourse to be, in general, distinguished? What makes it moral? What, in fact, does 'moral' mean? This is a question, far too seldom considered with the care and attention it deserves, to which we shall revert, somewhat sketchily, in later sections.

(v) ARGUMENT IN MORALS

We took note, in introducing the prescriptivist amendment to emotivism, that it had at least *prima facie* the considerable advantage of not representing moral discourse and debate as fundamentally non-rational. To guide, we observed, unlike to influence, is essentially to engage in a rational activity; advice, whether accepted or not, may be good or bad, I may have good or bad reasons for offering you the guidance I do. But now we must observe that this advantage turns out to be illusory: prescriptivism too cannot find much place for argument.

In Hare's own account of moral reasoning, very great importance is attached to the feature of moral judgment, already mentioned, which he calls 'universalisability'. It is, Hare seems to say — and, as we shall see, not without reason — solely in virtue of this feature that argument, properly so called, is possible in morals; and he is naturally disposed to make quite substantial claims as to what such argument can achieve. Now to say that any proposition in morals is 'universalisable' is, as we briefly noted earlier, to say that one who affirms or accepts that proposition is thereby committed — as a matter of logic — to a certain view of any cases of a certain kind. For me to assert that you ought not to do *X* in situation *Y* commits me, as a matter of logic, to the general 'principle' that no one should do things *like* *X* in situations *like* *Y* — 'like' meaning here 'not relevantly distinguishable from'. Generality of this sort is implicit in all moral judgment.

Now one might think at first sight that, while argument on the basis of this feature is certainly possible, yet such argument could not really achieve very much. For what, on the basis of this feature, can be argued about? What is put in issue? It is plain, I think, that what is put in issue is simply consistency. To appeal, in discussion of some moral judgment that I make, to the feature of universalisability is not to raise the question whether my judgment of the case before me is *right*, but only the question whether it is the same as, or compatible with, the judgments that I make or would make of other cases of the same kind. It is not, indeed, that this matter is unimportant. For people are indeed very commonly prone, from prejudice or bigotry or thoughtlessness, to judge differently cases which are not relevantly different — to make, for example, unjustifiable exceptions in favour of themselves or their friends, and to the detriment of foreigners, or political opponents, persons they dislike, or persons whose existence is inconvenient to them. And in such cases they may indeed be logically obliged — though not necessarily induced — to change or amend their judgments, when the requirement of consistent universalisability is forced upon their attention. Nevertheless, if it appears to you that my judgment of some particular case is morally quite wrong, you may well achieve nothing by appealing to universalisability; for all that may emerge may be that I am perfectly prepared to make the same (in your view) wrong judgment of any case of this kind. All my standards and principles may seem to you highly objectionable; but, provided that I apply them consistently in every case, they will be quite invulnerable to any argument of this pattern.

But is this point, one may wonder, too abstractly stated?[19] Is the case we envisage really, and not merely theoretically, a possible one? It is easy to say that, in theory, practically any moral judgment, however objectionable, might be consistently 'universalised', and so might stand unscathed against argument founded upon this consideration. But may it not be the case in fact that not many highly objectionable judgments actually would emerge from such scrutiny unscathed? One might think that this would probably be so for the following reason. What is really objectionable, one might think, about many objectionable moral judgments is that one who makes them does so in disregard of, or without giving proper weight to, the wants, or the needs, or the interests, of those concerned (other than himself); he ignores, let us say, or does not properly consider, the fact that the interests of other persons will be gravely damaged by the course of action which he professes morally to approve. But if so — if he is prepared seriously to hold, as a general principle, that such action to the detriment of others' interests is to be morally approved — we can point out that, in virtue of the condition of universalisability, he is committed to approving of the neglect or damage of *his own* interests if and when, as may occur, he is himself in the position of those whose interests will be damaged by the action in this case. If their interests may properly be neglected now, so, when he finds himself in their shoes, may his. But surely only the most irrational of men could want the neglect or frustration of his own interests; and if so, the requirement of universalisability may seem to impose upon any rational man the condition that, in his practical judgments, he *must* pay that regard to the interests of others which, in general, he would want to be paid to his own interests. And it is plain that this would constitute, in practice, a condition of very substantial moral significance and effect.

I think, however, that there is an important equivocation here. It is true — perhaps even necessarily true — that no rational man *wants* the frustration of what he sees as his own interests, or *likes* it when his interests are frustrated. But then what a man wants, or would like, is scarcely the point at issue here: the question is what he would morally approve or find morally objectionable; and that, of course, may not be at all the same thing. If I commend, or adopt as right, some course of action which grossly damages the interests of another, you may point out to me, correctly no doubt, that I would not like it if my own interests were damaged in that way; there is, however, no reason why I should not admit this, and yet still maintain that, if our positions were reversed, that other person would be *right* to damage my interests exactly as I now propose to damage his. The ruthless landlord, for instance, on the point of ejecting his aged, ailing, and needy tenants into the snow, may concede not only that they will greatly dislike this treatment, but that he himself would dislike it no less if he were in their place; nevertheless, he may hold, it is right that they should be ejected, and that he himself should be ejected too, if he were in similar case. That he would not like it, he says, is neither here nor there; the point is that business is business, the economic show must go on. In order, that is, consistently to defend as unobjectionable my neglect of another's interests, I do not have to go to the somewhat unbalanced length of positively wanting my own interests to be neglected, or of somehow not disliking it when they are: all that I am required to do is to concede that neglect of my own interests by others would be unobjectionable. And there is nothing particularly strained or unbalanced about this; it is, for instance, the very essence of the gospel of self-help, of untrammelled competition in the old capitalist style — a gospel which, however morally disagreeable one may find it, has been consistently adopted by very many entirely sane men, and not only by those who have been winners in the jungle war. A man cannot, in effect, by the argument from universalisability, be constrained to attach *much* weight, if any, to the interests of others; for he may be entirely ready to concede that others are not morally required to attach much weight, if any, to his own, however intensely he may dislike it when, in the competitive free-for-all, it happens that he comes out on the losing side. But if this is true, the requirement of universalisability appears, whether in theory or in practice, to set almost no limit to the practical judgments which *can* be consistently made and maintained by sane men; and if so, it does not, as a weapon of moral argument, carry much fire-power.

Why then is Hare inclined to make such large claims for this real, but limited, dialectical weapon? Because (it is not, I think, unfair to say) his doctrine does not allow for genuine argument of any other kind. If asked to give reasons for some moral view I have expressed — that is, on this view, for some 'prescription' that I have issued — I may do one or both of two things: I may adduce certain facts about the case under consideration, or some principle, or principles, of which my presently-expressed view is an instance or application. But my principles, of course, are on this view themselves 'prescriptions' of mine; and such facts as I may adduce about the present case constitute *reasons* for my expressed view of it in so far as I have adopted, i.e. 'prescribed', some principle in accordance with which that view is derivable from those facts. Thus my giving of 'reasons' for my expressed prescription consists, on this view, essentially of my referring to and relying on *further* prescriptions of my own: what are reasons for me, are, for you, not only not necessarily good reasons, but possibly not reasons at all. And thus, what we speak of as argument between two parties emerges essentially as nothing more than the articulation by each of his own position. For you to say that my view is *wrong* is to say only that your position excludes that view; for me to 'argue' that my view is *right* is to show only that my position includes it. And there is nothing else, on this view, that argument can do; for there are no 'reasons' that either party can appeal to independently of, and so genuinely in support of, his own prescriptions. In this way it must inevitably appear to Hare that *real* argument can address itself only to the question of consistency; for so long as a man prescribes consistently, then on this view he has (since he has provided himself with) all the 'reasons' that any of his particular pronouncements may require;

and if I have 'reasons' for views that differ from his, he need claim only that my reasons are not reasons for him.[20]

It is, I believe, often not really noticed how surprising (at least) Hare's view of this question is. Most of us, no doubt, would agree readily enough that in moral matters we have to make up our own minds; we ourselves must decide on, embrace, commit ourselves to our moral standpoint. Further, we are probably ready enough to agree that moral discourse seems little susceptible of demonstrative argument; we have seldom much hope, in moral controversy, of confronting an opponent with a cogent proof of our views. Now it may seem that Hare is saying no more than this; but he is saying much more. For he is saying, not only that it is for us to decide what our moral opinions are, but also that it is for us to decide what to take as grounds for or against any moral opinion. We are not only, as it were, free to decide on the evidence, but also free to decide what evidence is. I do not, it seems, decide that flogging is wrong because I *am* against cruelty; rather, I decide that flogging is wrong because I *decide to be* against cruelty. And what, if I did make that decision, would be my ground for making it? That I am opposed to the deliberate infliction of pain? No — rather that I *decide to be* opposed to it. And so on. Now there are people, I think, whose moral views do seem to be formed and defended in this way — who, as one might say, not only make up their own minds, but also make up their own evidence; who pick and choose not only on the question what is right or wrong, but also on the question what are even to be admitted as relevant considerations. But such a person, surely, is not so much a model as a menace; not an exemplar of moral reasoning, but a total abstainer from any serious concern with reason. And if this really were a general feature of the human predicament, then to find cogent arguments in morals would not merely be difficult; it would be as hopeless as trying to play a competitive game in which each competitor was making up his own rules as he went along. All this is a matter to which we shall return in due course.

V. THE CONTENT OF MORALS

(i) PRACTICE AND PRINCIPLES

We turn now to a group of questions of a very different kind, though still concerned with, or arising out of, the question how moral discourse is related to conduct. These questions may be conveniently introduced by way of further, and this time more critical, consideration of the dictum, already quoted, from which Hare's argument begins: 'If we were to ask of a person "What are his moral principles?" the way in which we could be most sure of a true answer would be by studying what he *did*.'

I mentioned before that we should all, probably, be inclined *prima facie* to agree with this dictum; actions, after all, we think, do speak louder than words. But should we not now think more carefully about *what* actions tell us? Do they necessarily tell us what are a man's moral principles? One may think, not necessarily. For there seem on reflection to be at least two ways in which what a man does may fail to disclose his moral principles. First, may it not be the case that he has *no* moral principles? And second, may it not be the case that, though he has moral principles, he does not regularly act in accordance with the principles that he has? Let us examine these possibilities (if they *are* possibilities) further: they turn out to be a good deal more complex than one might have expected.

The first possibility — that the agent may have no moral principles — must, I think, be further subdivided. First, a man may have no principles of conduct at all; and second, he may have principles, but not *moral* principles. The former case does not seem particularly controversial; for surely no one would seek to deny that a man may, in the day-to-day conduct of his life, be so changeable, volatile, whimsical, and inconsistent that he could not be said to hold — and perhaps, for what it is worth, he does not even profess — any principles at all; his conduct composes no pattern, reveals no regularities, and *a fortiori* discloses no moral principles. But the latter case is decidedly more difficult. Might it be the case that, though a man consistently showed in his behaviour his adherence to certain principles, we should want to maintain that these were not *moral* principles?

Let us here consider, first, the case of a thorough-going egoist. He acts, let us suppose, always with deliberation, always has reasons for what he does, and is regularly guided by certain general principles of conduct. He is, however, never altruistic, nor even disinterested; even those of his actions which are agreeable, helpful, or advantageous to others are performed solely because he judges it to be in his own interests to perform them; his principles are all principles of self-regarding prudence. Now Hare, I believe, is required by his prescriptivism to hold that, in that case, those *are* his moral principles; at least if he does, as of course he may, 'prescribe' universally that any person should consider and pursue solely his own interests, then he has moral principles, namely, principles of egoism. This, however, may well be thought to be highly paradoxical. Many writers indeed, among whom may be mentioned Baier and Gauthier, have held that 'the moral point of view' involves, precisely and essentially, the *abandonment* of pure prudential egoism, and a readiness to consider as justifying grounds of action the interests or 'wants', ideally of everyone, but at any rate of at least some persons other than oneself.[21] To refuse to consider anything but one's own interests, they would hold, is precisely not to engage in moral thinking at all, but to be 'amoral'. Very similarly, it is the view of Nowell-Smith that the major point of moral principles is to promote 'social harmony';[22] and this is an end which the thorough-going egoist, even if he might regard it as likely to be advantageous on occasion, would not of course regard as particularly valuable in itself. He would not mind social chaos, so long as he himself was safely above the battle.

But there are other and perhaps more interesting possibilities here. May it not be the case that a man's conduct is guided principally, or even invariably, not by consideration of the interests of people in general, or even of his own, but rather by the pursuit of some *ideal* or system of ideals? And if so, might it not be the case that such an ideal was not necessarily a moral ideal, so that, here too, we might find an instance of conduct disclosing no moral principles?[23] Consider, for instance, the somewhat Nietzschean — or, for that matter, somewhat Greek — ideal of maximal development and large-scale, stylish exercise, of human capacities: the ideal, as it were, of the eminent and excellent specimen of humankind. Is this a *moral* ideal? Clearly this is not at all an easy question to answer. We may be inclined to say that this *is* a moral ideal, on the ground perhaps that it requires of its devotee at any rate much in the way of personal behaviour that we should all regard as morally admirable, and excludes much behaviour that we should all regard as morally bad. More importantly, we may think that any criterion of excellence in human conduct, if taken seriously enough, if felt as overridingly demanding and as involving remorse and self-reproach for failure to meet its demands, deserves, for the role that it may play in the life of its devotee, the accolade of morality. But on the other side we may note that — as, often, in the case of Nietzsche himself – this sort of ideal may be felt to be deeply antagonistic to 'morality', morality appearing by comparison to be repressive, cramping, timorous, even ignoble, an attempt by the feebler, more stifled specimens of humanity to fasten shackles on those more richly endowed than themselves. We may note that even the less ferocious ideals of Aristotle lead inevitably to the condemnation of the majority for defects which it would plainly be not in their power to remedy, and that the full realisation by some of his ideal conditions seems positively to require the attendant services of many more or less defective and humanly almost negligible subordinates. By contrast, would not 'the moral point of view' insist that a man is not to be condemned for failings or deficiencies for which he is not responsible? Are not all men, as moral beings, to be thought of as equal? If so, it may well seem more natural to regard, say, Nietzsche — as, of course, he from time to time regarded himself — not as propounding an unusual system of moral principles, but rather as abandoning moral attitudes altogether and as preaching, 'beyond good and evil', an ideal of conduct and character of a quite different kind.

It seems, then, somewhat contrary to the dictum we have before us, that there are grounds on which we might well wish to hold that, even if a man's conduct does disclose his adherence to principles, it does not necessarily apprise us of his *moral* principles, since the ruling principles of his conduct may not be moral principles at all. Consider now the not unrelated question whether a man might not simply fail to act consistently on the moral principles that he has. It is one of the more controversial implications of Hare's prescriptivism that this is *prima facie* impossible: for to 'accept a prescription' *is* to do what it says, and conversely, to fail to act in accordance with a principle *is* not to accept it. It has been urged against Hare on this point that his view is over-rigorous. It may be the case that a man who never, or hardly ever, acts as some principle requires cannot be regarded as sincere in his professions of subscription to the principle. But between total non-acceptance and unvarying compliance there are many intermediate cases: a man may act in breach of a principle in many different styles or manners, and may view his lapses with many different shades of regret, self-criticism, or remorse. Surely not every voluntary fall from virtue condemns every virtuous profession as insincere?[24]

But we should note here particularly the more fundamental point that Hare's view seems also tacitly to presuppose that moral principles must *necessarily* be of overriding authority. For to act in breach of a professed moral principle would not, of course, tend to put in question the sincerity of the agent unless it were assumed that his act could not be otherwise justified — that is, that there could be no conflicting considerations for the sake of which, while perfectly sincere in his profession of the moral principle, on this occasion he thinks it best not to act as that principle requires. If, on some occasion when I might have played cricket, I do not do so, you do not decide that I am insincere in professing to like playing cricket: for it is evident that I may have weightier grounds for not engaging, on this occasion, in that activity. But is it clear that moral principles may not sometimes be in similar case? Is it not clear on the contrary that, *if* there are tenable ideals which would not appropriately be regarded as moral ideals, a man might act for the sake of his ideal, quite consciously and deliberately, in breach of some moral principle which he quite sincerely professes? To say this, after all, is to say only that a man might regard considerations of some kind as more important than considerations of morality, and hence might take himself, on occasion, to be fully justified in not doing what he sincerely recognises to be right from the moral point of view. And to maintain that this is not a genuine possibility is, by implication, to make it a necessary truth that moral considerations are weightier, more important, than considerations of any other kind. But is it clear that this is in fact a necessary truth?

(ii) WHAT DOES 'MORAL' MEAN?

The question which is in effect raised by such reflections as these is really a very fundamental one, and it has been given, it seems to me, far less attention than it deserves. When philosophers discuss moral principles, moral judgment, moral discourse generally, *what* are they discussing? What does 'moral' mean? What distinguishes a moral view from views of other kinds? I think it must be quite clear that there is no easy answer to these questions; and yet, until they are answered, it seems that moral philosophers cannot really know what they are talking about, or at any rate, perhaps no less importantly, cannot be sure whether or not they are all talking about the same thing. It is, indeed, pretty clear that, historically, they have not been. Kant, for instance, takes it for granted that the 'moral law' imposes upon all rational beings unconditional, categorical demands to do and forbear — demands that are binding without any regard to human inclinations, purposes, desires, or interests, that have nothing essentially to do with human happiness, and call only for the absolute obedience of 'the good will'; his problem is to explain how there can be demands of that kind. But for Hume, for example, this problem does not arise at all. For it does not enter his head that there *are* any demands of that kind; on the contrary, he takes it entirely for granted that moral views give direct expression to human preferences and desires, and that it is the essence of a moral system to promote the interests, the general harmony and well-being, of human communities. That being so, it is of course entirely inevitable that their accounts of 'moral discourse' should be widely divergent; for it is not really the same thing that they are seeking to give an account of.

Now it is possible, I think, to distinguish at least four types of factors each of which has been taken, either alone or in conjunction with one or more of the others, as centrally characteristic of morality. First, it has occasionally been suggested that what is really distinctive of a moral view is, to put it somewhat crudely, the way in which those who take that view feel about it.[25] There is, it is said, a special sense of being *required* to act in a certain way, not by any external pressure or sanction, but rather by one's own consciousness of the sense of wrongdoing, of the guilt and self-reproach, that non-performance would incur. It is clear that there is not nothing in this; but it is perhaps equally clear that this can hardly be, by itself, a sufficient criterion of morality. It is not merely — though of course this is true — that a person may, for one reason or another, come to attach this psychological penumbra of guilt and self-reproach to performances, or non-performances, which are as a matter of fact entirely unobjectionable; for that is to say no more than that a person's moral feelings may sometimes be irrational. It is rather that a man may himself come to recognise that his sense of guilt and self-reproach is irrational and misplaced; and in that case, while the feelings may unfortunately prove very persistent, he presumably does not take their persistence as a ground for continuing to regard the issue, whatever it may be, as a moral one. It is possible, that is, as it were to detach one's feelings from the question whether some course of conduct is morally objectionable — to have the feelings appropriate to morally objectionable behaviour, and yet genuinely not to believe that one's behaviour is morally objectionable. But if so, then the occurrence or non-occurrence of certain feelings, the presence or absence of the characteristic sense of guilt, cannot be a sufficient criterion of a moral view.

Second, it has been held — less often, perhaps, explicitly than by implication — that, for any person, his moral principles and standards are to be identified as those which are in fact dominant in the conduct of his life. This is the view which is at least implicit in Hare's prescriptivism — 'A man's moral principles, in this sense, are those which, in the end, he accepts to guide his life by.' But this, as we mentioned before, looks highly paradoxical in this unqualified form. It is true, no doubt, that there are many good people whose lives are ultimately guided by their moral principles; but, on this view, we should be obliged to say that this was true, and even necessarily true, of everybody, or at least of everybody who has any principles at all; and surely that is wrong. Surely there have been individuals, and even whole societies, of whom or of which we should want to say that moral principles did not play any large part in their lives — that, perhaps, both their ideals of conduct and their actual conduct were shaped in accordance with standards that were not *moral* standards at all. Homer, in approving the ferocity, guile, and panache of the warrior chieftain, might be said to have been employing moral standards different from our own; but he might just as well, or better, be said not to have been employing moral standards at all.

We must, I think, regard as inadequate on just the same grounds the idea that a man's moral principles are *simply* those, whatever they may be, which he 'prescribes' for everyone alike; for surely we should wish to leave open the possibility of saying that some persons, and even some societies, though perhaps they 'prescribe' universally, nevertheless do not see things from 'the moral point of view'.

Finally, then, we may turn to the idea that morality should be somehow characterised, so to speak, by its subject-matter — the idea that what makes a view a *moral* view is, not the psychological penumbra by which it is surrounded, nor its predominance in the life of its proponent, but primarily its content, what it is about, the range or type of considerations on which it is founded.[26] The detailed working out of this idea, so far as any has been done, has taken various forms. It has been suggested, in the spirit of utili-

tarianism, that rules of morality are by definition those whose
observance is at any rate believed to promote the 'greatest happiness', and whose violation is thought liable to increase the sum
of human misery. Others have argued that we should seek the
essence of morality, not in the notion of the promotion of happiness, but rather in that of the satisfaction of human needs, or of
the reconciliation and promotion of human interests. Now it is
surely hard to deny that there is very great plausibility in such
views: for must it not surely be supposed, by anyone who claims
to be propounding a moral principle, that observance of the principle he propounds would do some sort of *good*, and that breaches
of it would do some sort of *harm*? If we ask a man why he holds
the moral views that he expresses, must he not try to show, by
way of justification, that the things he commends are in some
sense or other *beneficial*, that the things he condemns are in some
sense or other *damaging*? If he were to make no attempt to explain
his position in such terms, what reason could there be for making,
or for accepting, the supposition that the views in question were
moral views?

(iii) HAS MORALITY A 'CONTENT'?

Let us now try, then, to survey our present problem from
another angle. What does 'moral' mean? How are we to identify
those principles which are moral principles, or to recognise that
species of discourse which is moral discourse? We have just
mentioned briefly — no doubt one could extend the list — four
possible 'marks' of a moral view: its psychological penumbra;
its actual importance in the individual's conduct of his life; its
'universalisability'; and its general topic — human happiness or
interests, needs, wants, or desires. Now there is an important
distinction to be found within the items on this list, and one that
would continue to be of great importance however our somewhat sketchy list might be extended. This distinction is that
between those 'marks' which do, and those which do not, assign
to moral discourse a characteristic content, or subject-matter. In
our short list, the first three items are thus distinguished from the

fourth. For a view to which a certain psychological penumbra is attached may be a view *about* anything at all; and if a 'moral' view is to be thus identified, there will be nothing that morality, *ex officio*, so to speak, is about. Similarly, a principle which is actually dominant in the conduct of a life, or one which is 'prescribed universally' for all alike, may be a principle *about* anything at all; and if moral principles are to be thus identified, again there will be nothing that morality is essentially about. Our fourth item, however, is quite different in this respect; for by this 'mark' we shall identify as a moral view a view which is, in one way or another, *about* what is good or bad for people, what they want or need, what promotes or detracts from their happiness, well-being, or satisfaction; and if a moral view is to be *thus* identified, its psychological penumbra may be seen as an open question, and likewise the question whether a man who holds it is actually guided, or demands that others should be guided, predominantly by it in the actual conduct of life. The issue is this: which questions do we take to be answerable *a priori*? Is it true *a priori* that moral views predominate in the conduct of life, and a matter for investigation with what topics, in this instance or that, such views are concerned? Or is it true *a priori* that moral views are concerned with certain topics, and a matter for enquiry what role in life (or in discourse) such views, in this instance or that, may be found to play?

In this essay I cannot hope, and do not propose to try, to answer these questions, but only to call attention to what I take to be the urgent need for their further investigation. For it will be obvious that, for the purposes of moral theory, it is of the first importance that they should be answered — on the answer that is given to these questions will depend one's whole conception of what moral philosophy is called upon to do. Is it one's task to elucidate what one might call the formal character of moral discourse, its general character as a system of 'prescriptions', or 'evaluations'? Or is one to attempt to elucidate the *content* of morals, to describe in outline and to make distinctions within the general range of phenomena to which moral concepts are applicable? But the questions I have raised are important, I believe, not only for this reason; they are important, here and now, for the additional reason that recent moral philosophers have, often tacitly, answered them quite differently, and very seldom debated the question how they should be answered. Thus one sees moral theories which are not merely quite different, but actually aiming to do, in principle, quite different things; yet the difference of principle, I think, has been seldom recognised and, for that reason, scarcely ever discussed.

My own view (if it is worth expressing a view which one does not then try seriously to examine) is that morality *has* some at least roughly specifiable content. Looking again at our sketchy list of four possible 'marks' of a moral view, a moral judgment, a moral principle, the suggestion that I would myself be inclined to hazard is that while each is doubtless *relevant* to the characterisation of 'the moral', some form or other of the fourth is likely to turn out to be by far the most centrally important. It is probably true that there is, for very many people, a characteristic way of feeling about the rights and wrongs of conduct in certain cases, a way of feeling which goes with what they take to be moral issues; but apart from the possibility, mentioned above, that such feelings may occur in cases which even the subject himself does not seriously believe to involve moral issues, would one not be inclined also to say that a special way of feeling about certain issues is consequential upon, rather than definitive of, their character as *moral* issues? Rather similarly, it would seem to me more natural to say that, for very many people, certain principles play a predominant role in their own conduct, and are applied universally in judgment of the conduct of others, *because* they are believed to be moral principles, rather than, in reverse as it were, that their being moral principles *consists in* their being treated as overriding and of general application. On the other hand, it appears at least enormously plausible to say that one who professes to be making a moral judgment *must* at least profess that what is in issue is the good or harm, well-being or otherwise, of human beings — that what he regards as morally wrong is somehow damaging, and what he regards as morally right is somehow beneficial. There is no doubt at all that, apart from its high degree of vagueness, this would not be a sufficient characterisation of moral judgment; nevertheless it does appear to me to mention a feature which, in one way or another, any intelligible theory must recognise to be of central importance.[27]

There are, I think, four grounds at any rate on which this tentative suggestion might be resisted, and in conclusion of this section and in preparation for the next, these may be briefly considered. It might be said, first, that to define the concept of morality in any such terms would be to make moral attitudes reasonable by definition.[28] Would it not preclude us from regarding as moral at all codes of conduct, perhaps very barbarous and benighted, which so far from doing any good or promoting anyone's welfare, are in fact conducive to repression and cruelty? Yet we do wish to speak of barbarous and benighted moral codes. But this objection miscarries. For it would scarcely be suggested that a code of conduct, to be a moral code, must *be* such that its observance would satisfy anyone's needs or interests, or promote anyone's welfare; it is suggested only that it must be at least *supposed* to be so. Similarly, it is no doubt true that moral doctrines are often used, and often deliberately used, simply as instruments of repression or aggression, deliberately to do harm rather than good; but even so, it seems that, if it is to be even pretended that what is enforced is moral doctrine and that it is enforced for that reason, then it must also be at least pretended that some good is likely to be done thereby, or some harm prevented. Fear, or disgust, or envy, or resentment, or a mere taste for bullying, are very frequent causes of moral condemnation; but still, to give colour to the claim to moral concern, these causes must surely be veiled in some decent pretence of beneficent intentions.

Second, there arises a question that we have already glanced at. What about 'ideals'? Is it not possible for a man's life to be dominated, his conduct and his view of others' conduct determined at many points, not by consideration of his own or of others' needs or interests, of what is good or harmful for people in *that* sense, but by some ideal picture of how life should be lived, or of what is intrinsically noble, lofty, and admirable in human capacities and character? Of course this is possible, and a most important actual determinant of human behaviour in some cases; it appears often as a concern, not for any specific advantage to be gained or good done by human activities, but rather for what one might call a certain style of activity, and for avoidance of what, while not harmful, is felt to be low, or unworthy, or disgraceful in itself. Now it has been argued by some that ideals of this type, 'pictures of life', must be included under the general concept of morality, not because they resemble more familiar moral concerns in topic or subject-matter, or are concerned with considerations of at all the same type, but simply because of the very similar role that they may play in conduct and the judgment of conduct; they bear similarly on the question 'how one should live'. It may be thought, however, as we earlier suggested, that one still can and should distinguish between those ideals that are, and those that are not, *moral* ideals. Surely it makes a great difference what kind of life devotion to an ideal would tend actually to involve, and what it proposes as grounds for respect or for condemnation. The ideals of the storm-trooper are, even confessedly, liable to be enormously destructive; those of the traditional gentleman are for the most part fairly harmless, and in some respects or in some situations may be highly advantageous. Is it not natural, and besides a perfectly defensible position, to reserve the appellation of *moral* ideals for those whose pursuit is supposed to tend actually to do good rather than harm, to make things on the whole better rather than worse, while regarding as not forming part of any 'moral point of view' such ideals as are openly destructive, or damaging, or pointless, or insane? No doubt it would be easy to think of many marginal cases; but then 'moral' is surely not, on any showing, a very exact word, or a word to be always very confidently applied or withheld.

Third, it might be urged by some that the enterprise of specifying an (even roughly) determinate content or subject-matter for morality must inevitably be vitiated by circularity. Hare has argued, for instance, against utilitarianism that the concept of happiness cannot be used to elucidate the concept of morality, if only for the reason that 'happiness' cannot be independently identified; we call a man happy not merely when we have, empirically, reason to think that his desires are adequately satisfied, but when we also approve in some degree of the desires he has.[29] Similarly, it might be urged that the notions of benefit or harm are themselves 'evaluative' notions — that they cannot be supposed to fix the content of morality for the reason that they themselves have no definite, independently specifiable content. And so for 'interests' or 'needs': a man's interests or needs cannot, surely, be the factual *grounds* of judgment, since it is a matter of judgment what his needs or his interests really are.

At this point we step, really, into a hornets' nest of problems; and once again we can here do little more than merely note that this is so. We must note first that the question crucially arises: how exactly *are* we to designate the considerations which, on this kind of view, are to be taken as fundamental to, and definitive of, moral discourse and moral judgment? Is it a question of what makes people happy? Or should we ask rather what avoids or diminishes unhappiness? Is it a matter simply of what people want, or must we bring in also the question what they really need? Should our attention be directed to human interests? And if so, does this topic coincide with, or does it not, the topic of what is of benefit to people or harms them? Obviously, not until such questions as these are first elucidated, and then answered, can we be in a position seriously to examine the question what *kind* of judgment is being proposed as fundamental to moral discourse, of what degree of certainty such judgments may be susceptible, and by what kind of investigation they would properly fall to be explored. Nevertheless, I believe it is defensible to hazard in advance the view that the charge of circularity, just mentioned, is not likely to prove effective. There are, I believe, two grounds for saying this. First, I believe that we all have, and should not let ourselves be bullied out of, the conviction that at least some questions as to what is good or bad for people, what is harmful or beneficial, are not in any serious sense matters of opinion. That it is a bad thing to be tortured or starved, humiliated or hurt, is not an opinion: it is a fact. That it is better for people to be loved and attended to, rather than hated or neglected, is again a plain fact, not a matter of opinion. We find here no doubt a very wide penumbra of indeterminacy in which judgments must be made and may diverge, in which opinions and attitudes may differ irreducibly: but who believes, except for bad theoretical reasons, that there are no facts at all? But second — and this perhaps is the sort of point which it will be felt less disreputable for a philosopher to urge — the charge of circularity will stand, *not* if the supposed fundamental content of morality proves itself to be not independent of judgment and opinion, but only if it can be shown itself to involve the exercise of *moral* judgment. Those issues in terms of which morality is to be defined, if the definition is not to be merely circular, do not have to be, without remainder, issues of absolutely neutrally determinable fact: no more is required for theoretical purposes than that they should not themselves be issues of moral judgment. And surely it is reasonable to suppose that this condition is satisfied. That a certain person, or a certain community of persons, would, if certain things were done, be in a better or worse condition, advantaged or disadvantaged, helped or harmed, may be partly or even wholly a matter of judgment; but it is, I submit, quite clear that it is not always, not wholly or necessarily, a matter of *moral* judgment. But if so there is, from the point of view of moral theory, no reason to object to the project of defining morality at least partly in such terms.

We come, then, finally to the fourth and perhaps most notorious objection of principle to the suggestion, however vaguely or tentatively phrased, that moral judgment is concerned by definition or *ex officio*, in one way or another, with human good or harm, needs, wants, interests, or happiness. Does not this suggestion involve, it will be said, 'the Naturalistic Fallacy'? Does it not offend against 'Hume's Law'?[30] For if this suggestion were accepted, it would seem that facts of certain kinds about the world — namely, facts about people's needs or interests, happiness or wants — might in principle *entail* a particular moral judgment. But this, it has been held, is manifestly wrong in principle: if anything is clear, it is that 'naturalism' is untenable. This is a matter that calls for more extended consideration.

VI. NATURALISM

In this closing section, I shall not seek to show that 'naturalism' is true; for that purpose, it is not clear enough what naturalism is supposed to be. Part of the reason for this is that there do not appear actually to be any self-confessed naturalists among moral philosophers; and the untenability of naturalism has seemed, at least until quite recently, so very evident that its critics have not thought it worth while to set out in great detail the doctrine they have so regularly rejected. Accordingly I think that the most profitable proceeding will be briefly to review some characteristic *anti*-naturalistic tenets, and to consider what follows from those, if any, which seem to be sound.

As we noted at a much earlier stage, the expression 'the naturalistic fallacy' was introduced by G. E. Moore in his *Principia Ethica*, though the idea is certainly older than that, and has commonly been supposed to originate with Hume. We need not spend time, however, on Moore's exposition of the anti-naturalist case, which has been generally recognised — by Moore himself among others — as unsatisfactory. To commit the naturalistic fallacy, according to Moore, is to make two mistakes — first, that of offering a definition of a quality which is indefinable, and second, that of offering a definition of a non-natural quality in terms of natural qualities. But these mistakes are not, in fact, necessarily connected; and it would seem that the expression 'the *naturalistic* fallacy' might appropriately be reserved to designate the second of them. Here, then, Moore is alleging, first, that 'ethical qualities' are non-natural, and second, that non-natural qualities are not definable in terms of natural ones. The trouble is that he scarcely does more than barely allege this; he does not satisfactorily explain the terms 'natural' and 'non-natural', or seek to show why qualities of the one kind are not definable in terms of those of the other kind; so that there is really nothing here for critical discussion to take hold of.

We may also dismiss with a certain briskness one more modern-looking view which has sometimes been offered as an elucidation of, or amendment to, Moore's doctrine. This is the view that 'evaluative' expressions are not definable in terms of 'descriptive' expressions. The trouble here is that there do not exist the two distinct classes of expressions ostensibly referred to. It is possible, no doubt, to distinguish evaluating from describing — for example, describing Jenkins's performance of a flute sonata, from evaluating his performance. But it is not, in general, possible to make this distinction merely on the basis of the expressions used; for it is probably true to say that any expression which occurs in the context of the evaluation of something could also occur in the context of the description of something, and vice versa — this distinction is simply not a distinction of *vocabulary*. Thus, if 'evaluative expression' means 'expression used in evaluating something', and 'descriptive expression' means 'expression used in describing something', the position will be that most, perhaps all, evaluative expressions are *also* descriptive expressions, and vice versa; so that the view mentioned above turns out to be the merest nonsense.

Criticism of this view, though, suggests a possible amendment of it. Perhaps the real point at issue — the point which, it might be suggested, was really at the back of Moore's mind — is that *evaluation* is not reducible to *description*; that there is an insurmountable difference of principle between the activities of evaluating something and describing it, between just 'stating the facts' and passing any sort of judgment upon them. There is almost certainly some good sense in which this would be true; though one must not, indeed, suppose the distinction to be a clear and sharp one in ordinary discourse.[31] In legal proceedings, for instance, comparable distinctions are formally brought out and observed with some care — the business of giving evidence, say, is clearly distinguished from that of presenting a case, and both are clearly distinguished from the business of giving judgment: at any stage there is a perfectly clear and determinate answer to the question which, if any, of these activities is then going on. But ordinary discourse is not, since it does not need to be, similarly regimented; if I am telling someone, for instance, about the career of Mussolini, it would be unrealistic to look for — to assume that there must be — a point at which description of his doings terminates, and evaluation of them begins; 'talking about' Mussolini in an ordinary conversational manner is most unlikely to be thus susceptible of decomposition into sharply distinct ingredients. However, although this distinction is not always to be found, it is probably true to say that it could always be made; the instruction 'First *describe* Mussolini's career, and then *evaluate* it' is a more or less intelligible instruction, and one has some notion of how it might be obeyed. That there is, then, a difference of some sort between evaluating and describing seems to be true, and of course is quite naturally to be expected.

I think it is clear, however, that the anti-naturalist philosopher is contending for something much more than this unambitious truism. What seems to be suggested is, not merely that description and evaluation are different, but that they are in an important sense *independent*. No description, it is said, ever *commits* us to any particular evaluation; any description might be accepted, and any evaluation rejected, without logical inconsistency. Now of most ordinary discourse this suggestion is probably false. Since, as we have just said, there are in ordinary discourse comparatively few regimented distinctions between one speech-activity and another, one might expect to find description and evaluation so inextricably intermingled as to constitute, as it were, a seamless garment; and there cannot be logically independent parts of a tract of discourse which has, in the required sense, no distinguishable parts. But perhaps this does not matter: perhaps all that the anti-naturalist thesis requires is that, though we often do not, we always *could* so 'state the facts' of any case that evaluation of that case would be a logically independent operation. It might be at least possible, for instance, to describe the career of Mussolini in such terms that, given that description, any *evaluation* of his career might be accepted or rejected without logical error.

Why is this so? The suggestion, I believe, could be formulated as follows. Evaluation of any kind, it would be said, whether of people or objects or actions or anything else, implies the acceptance of, and must be done in the light of, certain standards, rules, principles, or criteria of judgment. If, for instance, candidates are to be graded in an examination, certain features of possible performances in that examination must be accepted as *criteria* for the assignment of grades — this might be, in a very simple case, simply the number of problems solved, or right answers given. Now no one, it is suggested, is ever *logically* obliged to accept any given feature *as* a standard or criterion, or any general proposition *as* a rule or principle of judgment. While agreeing that, for example, the performance of a certain candidate does in fact have a certain feature, that it can be correctly described in that way, one may refuse to accept that feature as a criterion of merit, and so decline to *evaluate* the performance on that basis, or at all. There can be description, but no evaluation, without the adoption or recognition of standards; but if so, since one cannot be logically obliged to adopt any particular facts or features, or even any at all, *as* standards for favourable or unfavourable judgment, the specification of facts or features in a description cannot *logically* lead to any particular evaluation, or even any at all. One may concede the presence of the features specified, or admit the facts, but not adopt or recognise those features or facts as having the status of criteria, or standards, or principles, or rules.

It would no doubt be possible to object to this formulation of the anti-naturalist thesis as over-simplified and excessively schematic. The actual business of evaluation, it might be insisted, is very often both far more complicated, and also far less clear-cut, than is suggested by this simple picture of assigning definite grades by reference to definite standards. Do we always know exactly what the relevant standards, criteria, or principles are? Can we always be certain what does or does not satisfy them, or specify exactly on the basis of *what* facts or features we make the judgments we do? Again, in what sense if any is it true to say that 'stating the facts' is independent of the use or recognition of standards? I shall not, however, on this occasion object to the

G. J. WARNOCK

thesis outlined above on such grounds; for it is in any case, I believe, far less interesting and important than has often been supposed. Its importance for, in particular, moral philosophy has been thought to consist in certain of its implications; but it does not really have, as I shall try to show, those particular implications which have been thought to be important.

(ii) WHAT THE THESIS DOES AND DOES NOT IMPLY

First, I believe that the temptation has not always been resisted to dramatise the anti-naturalist thesis, as it were, by turning it round. Suppose that we agree that no one is ever logically obliged to accept any given feature as a criterion of merit; it has perhaps been tempting to see in this the further implication that absolutely anything *might* be regarded as a criterion of merit. But this is fallacious. That no one is obliged to eat any particular kind of substance as food does not imply that absolutely any kind of substance might be eaten as food. But not only is the inference fallacious; its conclusion is surely false. For to adopt some feature as a criterion of merit is to imply, in some way appropriate to the particular context, some preference for what has that feature over what does not have it; and to prefer what has that feature is, in some way appropriate to the particular context, to want, or to want there to be, what has that feature, and to want it *because* it has that feature. Now there are, perhaps, no logical limits to what a person may be said to want; and doubtless there is nothing of which it can be said that necessarily everyone wants it; but are there not limits, nevertheless, to what a person may be said *understandably* to want? What does he want it for? What appeals to him about it? In what way, should he get what he wants, does he expect to be satisfied? If we have no notion at all of answers to these questions, then someone's assertion that he wants whatever it may be is, in a clear sense, not intelligible to us; we do not understand what he says, because we do not understand *him*. How would beings from Mars, if set down, say, in London, evaluate what they found there? What would they be favourably struck by, what would they take against? Clearly one has no way of answering these questions, precisely because one knows nothing about such beings; one does not know what their needs would be, what they would want of their environment, what they would like or dislike. Thus, though in a sense one might say that absolutely any feature of their environment might be regarded by them as a criterion of merit or desirability, this is not to say that we could always *understand* its being so regarded; it is rather to concede that we have no understanding of the evaluations of hypothetical Martians. Conversely, a feature, to function as an intelligible criterion of desirability or merit, must surely be such that we could at least understand, say, someone's wanting something to have it; and it is not true that just any feature at all meets this condition. It follows further that it is not true to say, as has been said, that evaluation rests ultimately on *choice*. For we do not choose to want this or that, to prefer one thing to another; when we have choices to make, we do not in turn choose what are to be reasons for choosing. To take that line, as we suggested earlier that prescriptivism does, is to imply that in the end there *are* no reasons at all.

The 'independence' of description and evaluation, then, does not imply, nor is it the case that, just anything can function as an (intelligible) criterion of evaluation. But now, is it not even more plainly the case that not just anything can function as a criterion of *moral* evaluation? This is not the place to attempt the considerable task of determining what the limits here exactly are; but that there *are* such limits seems to me perfectly evident.[32] Could we say, perhaps, vaguely enough for present purposes, and glancing back to certain points urged in the preceding section, that the limits are set somewhere within the general area of concern with the welfare of human beings? To say this is not, indeed, to say very much; but it is not to say nothing. For it is to say, in fact, at least this: that the *relevance* of considerations as to the welfare of human beings *cannot*, in the context of moral debate, be denied. (Again, of course, we do not *choose* that this should be so; it *is* so, simply because of what 'moral' means.) It will be obvious, I imagine, that to say this does not run counter to the 'independence'-thesis. For what that thesis says is that

no one is logically obliged to accept any given feature as a criterion of merit; and if we say, as in effect we have just done, that
certain features must necessarily be accepted as criteria of *moral*
merit, we can and must go on at once to concede that no one, of
course, is obliged by logic to engage in moral judgment or
debate. That there are, as it were, necessary criteria of moral
value does not imply that anyone, let alone everyone, necessarily
evaluates things with reference to those criteria; it is only that we
must do so *if* we are prepared, as we may not be, to consider the
question 'from the moral point of view'.

What this amounts to is the proposition that the anti-naturalist
thesis as formulated above, while probably true, has really no
great importance for moral philosophy. It is a thesis, as one might
put it, about the 'general theory' of evaluation: and it says,
probably quite correctly about evaluation in general, first, that
that activity presupposes standards; and second, that there are,
so to speak, no necessary or 'built-in' standards of evaluation that
must (logically) be adopted by anyone who accepts or offers a
particular description of the world. But this, as I hope is now
plain, does not imply that there are no necessary standards of
moral evaluation; for it may be the case, as I am tentatively
suggesting it is, that certain standards — that is, the *relevance*
at least of a certain particular range of considerations — though
they do not have to be accepted at all, must be accepted *if* the
claim to be evaluating *morally* is to be seriously made. Thus I
suggest that we may concede to the anti-naturalist the (from the
point of view of moral philosophy) uninteresting point that
evaluation in general is, in the sense explained, independent of
description, and then proceed to the interesting business of in-
vestigating moral evaluation in particular — enquiring, that is,
what it is to appraise things 'from the moral point of view', and
what in particular that range of considerations is whose relevance is implicit in the adoption of that point of view. If to be a
'naturalist' is to maintain that certain kinds of facts or features
are necessarily relevant criteria of moral evaluation, then I would
surmise that 'naturalism' is true. If the anti-naturalist then maintains that there are no critieria of evaluation which anyone is

logically obliged to accept, then I believe that 'anti-naturalism' is also true. But one should doubtless conclude that, on this showing, the terminology of 'naturalism' and 'anti-naturalism' is somewhat infelicitous, since the two expressions designate views which are perfectly compatible with one another. One might say that it is proper to be a naturalist in *ethics*, an anti-naturalist in what we have called the 'general theory' of evaluation: but it would probably be preferable simply to retire both expressions from further philosophical employment, and to investigate the actual position without benefit of labels.

(iii) A FINAL NOTE ABOUT MORAL ARGUMENTS

It will probably be objected against the position we have now tentatively reached — that, notwithstanding the general 'anti-naturalist' doctrine, there are certain kinds of facts or features which are necessarily criteria of *moral* evaluation — that this implies that moral arguments might in principle be demonstrative, logically cogent. The position we have reached does, I think, have this implication; but I see no reason why we should be alarmed by that. For one thing, it seems clear that really demonstrative reasoning in morals is certain to be in fact exceedingly rare. There seem to be at least five reasons why this must be so. First, while the (necessarily relevant) notion of 'the welfare' of human beings surely has, as one might put it, a perfectly clear and determinate core or centre, no one would wish to deny that it has also an extensive penumbral fringe of vagueness and indeterminacy; there is room for much diversity of opinion as to what *constitutes* 'the welfare' of human beings, not indeed at all points, but still at many points. Second, in considering, say, the moral rights and wrongs of a proposed course of action, it is often necessary to 'weigh' short-term good or harm against long-term harm or good; and such metaphorical 'weighing', though of course not impossible, is not susceptible of great exactness. Third, there will usually be need for similarly inexact 'weighing' of good or harm to some individuals against harm or good to others; and fourth, it will often be necessary to strike a metaphorical 'balance' between the good *and* harm that would accrue to single individuals. And if we add, fifth, the fairly obvious fact that the information relevant to solution of a moral problem — conspicuously, information about the future course of events — will very often not be obtainable with any high degree of certainty, then we shall see how extremely uncommon it must be, in fact, for moral reasoning to lead *indisputably* to just one particular conclusion. One could argue conclusively that some course of action would be, say, morally wrong if one could show that that course of action would lead *quite certainly* to certain consequences, which would constitute *indisputably* some serious harm to some innocent person or persons, and that there would accrue *quite certainly* no good to anyone which could *possibly* be held to outweigh those harmful consequences. It is not that there are no cases which satisfy these conditions; it could be shown, for instance, with this sort of conclusiveness that it would be morally wrong for me to induce in my children addiction to heroin. But, of course, when *all* the relevant considerations point *indisputably* one way, it is unlikely to occur to anyone that the argument is worth stating; the question, in fact, is scarcely likely ever to be raised. Nevertheless, that such an argument, if stated, could be really demonstrative, seems to me clear; and anyone who, if such an argument is put to him, denies that the conclusion follows — who holds, while conceding the facts, that, for instance, it would *not* be morally wrong for me to induce in my children addiction to heroin — shows either that he has not really followed the argument, or that he does not know what 'morally wrong' means. It is perfectly consistent with this to admit, as of course one must, that *serious* moral disagreements — arising, that is, on matters about which some people actually do disagree — are exceedingly unlikely to be capable of being conclusively resolved, to the satisfaction of all parties, by any argument whatever.

Some may still feel that the idea that moral arguments can in principle be demonstrative must be resisted, on the ground that one cannot after all make people morally virtuous by argument. But this is a mere confusion. For even the best of argu-

ments, of course, is not 'cogent' in the way that, say, a policeman may be; it cannot prevent people from behaving badly, or
make them behave well; but that is not to say that it may not be
a demonstrative argument. For even though some moral argument be entirely demonstrative, no one has to accept its conclusion as a basis for action. One may, obviously, simply neglect
the conclusion, and proceed to act without reference to moral
considerations. One may not care, or one may think other things
to be of greater importance. Even if I show you conclusively
that your course of action is morally wrong, and even if you
clearly see and admit that to be so, you may still be entirely *unmoved* by the argument I give you.

What then, one may ask, is the value of argument in moral
matters? If, even in those rare cases in which the argument is
conclusive and the conclusion accepted without any question,
the wrong thing may nevertheless be *done*, why is it worth deploying moral argument at all? But of course the answer to this
question is very obvious. It is that those considerations to which,
as I have suggested, moral reasoning necessarily appeals are considerations by which, as a matter of brute fact, most people are
not entirely unmoved. Those considerations of good or harm
to people which, I have suggested vaguely enough, figure
analytically in setting moral standards and moral principles,
and which provide accordingly the basis for the pros and cons of
moral argument, are matters which most people in some degree
do actually care about. (They do not *choose* to do so; they *do*.)
Certainly not many people are nice enough to be *very* much concerned about these matters; nor intelligent enough to be concerned about them intelligently; nor rational enough to be actually motivated by intelligent concern. Nevertheless, if it were not
the case that there existed a certain range of considerations, having to do in general with the welfare of human beings, about
which most people cared very much some of the time, and cared
to some extent much of the time, then not only would moral
argument, however conclusive, be pointless and ineffective;
moral discourse would simply not occur. That there is, as we all
know there is, a very widespread, though of course not complete,

consensus as to what is desirable and undesirable in human affairs is a condition of the existence of a common moral vocabulary; and just the same condition gives us a reason for supposing that moral judgment and moral discussion are not pointless, because not always ineffective, activities. That moral argument is not more effective than we find it to be is probably attributable to the cross that all arguments have to bear: an argument offers reasons to people, and people are not always reasonable.

VII. PROSPECT

These closing pages, no doubt, would be properly the place for a conclusion; but I think it will be clear to anyone who has read so far that no conclusion has been reached but rather, as I would hope, a starting-point for new enquiries. I will try, therefore, briefly to recapitulate my discontents about the way things have been going in recent ethical theory, and to suggest what the chief questions are that seem to me to be outstanding.

First of all, I would insist that we must start from the recognition that there is something peculiarly puzzling and problematic, peculiarly *arguable*, about the whole phenomenon of morals. Not everyone, naturally, feels this, but even if one does not feel it the record shows it to be so. So much is unclear; so many different views have been taken — and not only, of course, about what is morally right or wrong, but about *what it is to be* morally right or wrong. How are moral problems to be distinguished from those that are not moral? How, when one meets a moral issue, does one recognise it as such? How important, among the various and conflicting considerations which bear from time to time on the conduct of human lives, is the place that moral considerations have, or should have? And why? Have there been, or could there be, quite ordinary people who had no moral views at all, to whom morality meant nothing? What is the ground, or are the grounds, on which rests the consciousness of moral distinctions? How do we, how should we, how far can we sensibly hope to, resolve or diminish moral disagreements by discussion and argument? What goes wrong, what is the penalty, if moral rules are neglected or broken? All these are quite certainly matters on which there are and have been, not only among philosophers, widely diverse opinions, and shifting, confused opinions: there is no set of answers which has any claim to be *obviously* correct.

And this is why 'intuitionism' is completely unhelpful. For all these questions, on that view, are pronounced undiscussable: we are told that there is something to be 'seen', but nothing to be said: it is all too obvious for words. But this is not true, and it seems extraordinary that it should ever have been believed.

'Emotivism' is not really very helpful either. This doctrine has hold, indeed, of one very broad truth — the truth, not wildly exciting but still sometimes neglected, that the institution and apparatus of morality have a practical point; what the whole thing is *for* is the promotion of certain kinds of conduct and states of affairs, and the diminution of the incidence of others. But the doctrine not only fails completely to distinguish the ways in which, in morals, this point is pursued from other ways; more damagingly, it positively mis-assimilates those ways to those of such purely manipulative procedures as propaganda, emotional bullying, brain-washing, and the hard sell. We ask how moral discourse is different; we are told that it is not.

The case of 'prescriptivism' is more complex and more interesting. There is retained in this body of doctrine the truth that the institution of morality has a practical point, and there is added the further truth that, in morals, this point is not pursued merely by the exertion of causally efficacious influences. Morality is for rational beings, treated *as* rational. But that moral discourse is a form of 'prescriptive' discourse is a thesis which, while seductively truistic in one sense, is fatally impoverishing in another. In so far as the thesis is that moral discourse is in some way essentially (and not just causally) related to conduct, it is a completely impregnable platitude; but in so far as it attempts a serious assimilation of all moral judgments to imperatives, it seems to leave us once more with practically nothing to discuss. There is nothing to be discovered, but only choices to be made; no reasoning can possibly be conclusive, for choices may differ; the scope of morality cannot be determined, for we cannot set limits to the choices that a man might make. The importance of morality is not a genuine question, since what predominantly guides a man's decisions *is* morality for him. There is nothing either right or wrong but choosing makes it so. What seems objectionable is not so much that these implications are false (although, as a matter of fact, I think they are); it is rather that they seem to sidetrack all serious discussion. The innocent-looking thesis that moral discourse is 'prescriptive' discourse seems, almost miraculously, to bring in its train a string of dusty answers to large and complicated questions which, while saying almost nothing, seem to leave nothing further to be said. Perhaps we do not know that this is wrong; but it is more important that, at present, we certainly do not know that it is right.

What is to be done, then? One thing that, in my view, is of the first importance is that we should begin more nearly at the beginning than is commonly done, and determine how we propose that the subject-matter is to be identified. When we talk about 'morals' we do *not* all know what we mean; what moral problems, moral principles, moral judgments are is *not* a matter so clear that it can be passed over as a simple datum. We must discover when we would say, and when we would not, that an issue is a moral issue, and why: and if, as is more than likely, disagreements should come to light even at this stage, we could at least discriminate and investigate what reasonably tenable alternative positions there may be. This surely would not be, as some philosophers have implied, a boringly 'verbal' investigation of the word 'moral'; for if we do not investigate the sense and scope of this word, how do we know what the phenomena are which moral theory is to deal with? To be uninterested in the *word* is to be uninterested in the subject — in what it is that distinguishes this particular subject from others. It may be the case that this subject is *not* distinguished in any sharp way from others that concern the appraisal of character and conduct; but if that is so, at least we shall do well to appreciate that, and why, it is so. Distinctions do not have to be sharp to be worth taking note of.

Investigation of the sense and scope of 'moral' is desirable not only because it seems prudent that, in moral theory, we should decide what we are talking about. It is also possible that such investigation should show what the basis is for making moral distinctions — that is, what class or range of considerations, identifying an issue as a moral issue, are consequentially relevant to moral assesssment of it. This *might* not be so, since it is in principle possible that the sense of 'moral' should be found to leave its range of application completely indeterminate. But that seems to me unlikely: and *if* we can properly attach the word to any even roughly determinate range of phenomena, then many further questions will come up for consideration. If we know on what basis, with an eye to what, moral distinctions are made, we can usefully consider, for example, why some would hold — and also, doubtless, why others would deny — that such distinctions are of unique importance, and uniquely authoritative in issues of practical judgment; this question, an answer to which seems usually to be assumed, would become susceptible of serious examination. And then — if we know what the basis of distinction is here, and what 'weight' attaches, and why, to the distinctions made — we may be able usefully to consider what the prospects are for the fruitfulness of moral discussion. We can consider how far disputants could, and how far they could not, properly differ in what they take to be relevant to matters at issue; how far they could, and how far they could not, properly differ in their 'weighing' of those factors they take to be relevant. This matter needs to be discussed in substance, not in form; for there is nothing formally peculiar in, or distinctive of, argument in morals; if there are special features here, as quite probably there are, I would suppose them to be founded in what argument in morals is *about*. If such arguments are, as philosophers seem usually to conclude, liable to be peculiarly indecisive, this is not because of any formal deficiencies or oddities, but because the subject-matter is some-how recalcitrant to exact, 'objective', appraisal. When we know what the subject-matter is, we shall be better placed to see why, and how far, this is the case.

It is perhaps rather late to apologise for overstating my case; but I am not quite unconscious, here and there, of having done so. In suggesting as I have done that much recent moral theory has been misguided in its aims and unrewarding in its results, I have not put in the qualifications, points on the other side, which strict justice would require but limitations of space do not allow. Of course, from recent and contemporary moral philosophers there is much to be learned and much profit to be derived. Nevertheless, this is a subject in which there is still almost everything to be done.

NOTES

1. The terminology here is J. L. Austin's, and is explained in his *How to Do Things with Words* (1962), pp. 94 ff. Briefly and roughly, the distinction Austin has in mind is that between *what is done by* saying something, e.g. getting a person to go away, and *what is done in* saying something, e.g. ordering him to go away. *What is said*, of course, is distinguishable from both of these.

2. *Principia Ethica* (1903), p. 6.

3. *Principia Ethica*, p. 162.

4. See, for example, J. M. Keynes, 'My Early Beliefs', in *Two Memoirs* (1949); and Leonard Woolf, *Sowing* (1961).

5. *Mind*, 1912; reprinted in *Moral Obligation* (1949), pp. 1–17.

6. *Moral Obligation*, pp. 16–17.

7. See, for example, *The Right and the Good* (1930), chap. ii, and *Foundations of Ethics* (1939), pp. 83–84.

8. R. Carnap, *Philosophy and Logical Syntax* (1935), p. 24.

9. M. Schlick, *Problems of Ethics* (1939), particularly chap. i.

10. For an excellent short account of Stevenson's view, see his 'The Emotive Meaning of Ethical Terms', *Mind*, 1937: reprinted in *Logical Positivism*, ed. Ayer (1959).

11. *Logical Positivism*, p. 269.

12. On this point see Hare's admirable paper in the symposium 'The Freedom of the Will', *Proceedings of the Aristotelian Society*, Supplementary volume xxv, 1951.

13. On this distinction, see Austin, *How to Do Things With Words*, particularly Lecture x.

14. Stevenson, in *Logical Positivism*, p. 280.

15. *Freedom and Reason* (1963), p. 4.

16. 'The study of imperatives is by far the best introduction to ethics.' *The Language of Morals* (1952), p. 2.

17. *The Language of Morals*, p. 1.

18. P. H. Nowell-Smith, *Ethics* (1954), p. 98.

19. On this point see particularly *Freedom and Reason*, part ii.

20. Cf. Philippa Foot's very able article 'Moral Arguments', *Mind*, 1958.

21. K. Baier, *The Moral Point of View* (1958), and D. P. Gauthier, *Practical Reasoning* (1963).

22. *Ethics* (1954), p. 229.

23. See *Freedom and Reason*, particularly chap. 8; and P. F. Strawson, 'Social Morality and Individual Ideal', *Philosophy*, 1961. There are relevant observations also in Stuart Hampshire's *Thought and Action* (1959), particularly pp. 249 ff.

24. See P. L. Gardiner, 'On assenting to a moral principle', *Proceedings of the Aristotelian Society*, 1954–5.

25. I take some view of this nature to be implied by J. Bennett in his critical discussion (*Mind*, 1965) of Gauthier's *Practical Reasoning*.

26. This is a view, of course, which has never lacked defenders. Among recent writers I think one might assign Nowell-Smith, Toulmin, Baier, Gauthier, and (most clearly) Mrs. Foot to this camp — not that they all say the same thing, but that they see the same *kind* of thing as needing to be said.

27. It might be objected that, in suggesting that a concern with human benefit or harm is essential to anything deserving the name of a moral view, one is illicitly incorporating some kind of utilitarian 'humanism' into the very definition of morality. Would not this suggestion be indignantly repudiated by, for instance, the religious believer, for whom the foundation of morality is the Word of God? But I am inclined to think that such an objection would be unsound. For I suspect that religious views differ from 'humanist' views, not by denying the essential moral relevance of human benefit or harm, but rather by incorporating very different beliefs as to what really is good or bad for human beings. The religious believer finds in a supernatural order a whole extra dimension of pre-eminently important gains and losses, benefits and harm; his difference with the non-believer is not on the question whether these are of moral significance, but simply on the question whether they are real or chimerical. He might also wish to expand what might be called the moral population to include moral beings supposed not to be human; but to this, if there are such beings, no one surely will object.

28. See H. L. A. Hart, *The Concept of Law* (1961), p. 177.

29. *Freedom and Reason*, pp. 125–9.

30. 'Hume's Law ("No 'ought' from an 'is' "), to which I have repeatedly declared my adherence.' Hare, *Freedom and Reason*, p. 108.

31. Cf. Toulmin and Baier, 'On Describing', *Mind*, 1952.

32. The case has been excellently discussed by Philippa Foot, in 'Moral Beliefs', *Proceedings of the Aristotelian Society*, 1958–9.

BIBLIOGRAPHY

(Arranged in order of publication, except where more than one book has been listed for a single author.)

Moore, G. E., *Principia Ethica* (Cambridge University Press, 1903).

Ross, W. D., *The Right and the Good* (Oxford: Clarendon Press, 1930).

Foundations of Ethics (Oxford: Clarendon Press, 1939).

Ayer, A. J., *Language, Truth, and Logic* (Gollancz, 1936).

Stevenson, C. L., *Ethics and Language* (Yale University Press, 1944).

Prichard, H. A., *Moral Obligation* (Oxford: Clarendon Press, 1949).

Prior, A. N., *Logic and the Basis of Ethics* (Oxford: Clarendon Press, 1949).

Toulmin, S. E., *An Examination of the Place of Reason in Ethics* (Cambridge University Press, 1950).

Broad, C. D., *Ethics and the History of Philosophy* (Routledge & Kegan Paul, 1952).

Hare, R. M., *The Language of Morals* (Oxford: Clarendon Press, 1952).

Freedom and Reason (Oxford: Clarendon Press, 1963).

Nowell-Smith, P. H., *Ethics* (Penguin Books, 1954; Blackwell (hard-cover), 1957).

Baier, K., *The Moral Point of View* (Cornell University Press, 1958).

Montefiore, A. C., *A Modern Introduction to Moral Philosophy* (Routledge & Kegan Paul, 1958).

Hampshire, S., *Thought and Action* (Chatto & Windus, 1959).

Warnock, M., *Ethics since 1900* (Home University Library, 1960).

Hart, H. L. A., *The Concept of Law* (Oxford: Clarendon Press, 1961).

Austin, J. L., *How to Do Things with Words* (Oxford: Clarendon Press, 1962).

Edel, A., *Method in Ethical Theory* (Routledge & Kegan Paul, 1963).

Gauthier, D. P., *Practical Reasoning* (Oxford: Clarendon Press, 1963).

Warnock, G. J., *The Object of Morality* (London, 1971).

Richards, D. A. J., *A Theory of Reasons for Action* (Oxford, 1971).

Rawls, J., *A Theory of Justice* (Oxford, 1972).

A useful collection of readings is W. S. Sellars and J. Hospers (eds.), *Readings in Ethical Theory* (Appleton-Century-Crofts, 1952).

NOTES ON CONTRIBUTORS

J. N. FINDLAY is University Professor of Philosophy at Boston University. He is Clark Professor Emeritus of Moral Philosophy and Metaphysics in Yale University. For many years he was Professor of Philosophy at King's College in the University of London; he is a Gifford Lecturer and a Fellow of the British Academy. His publications include *Axiological Ethics* (paperback 1970) and books on Meinong, Hegel, the theory of mind, the theory of value and other topics. His latest work is *Plato: The Written and Unwritten Doctrines* (1974).

ANTONY FLEW is Professor of Philosophy in the University of Reading. His publications include *Evolutionary Ethics* (paperback 1967), *A New Approach to Psychical Research* (1953), *Hume's Philosophy of Belief* (1961), *God and Philosophy* (1966), *An Introduction to Western Philosophy* (1971) and *Crime or Disease?* (1973); and he is the editor of *Essays in Conceptual Analysis* (1956) and *Body, Mind and Death* (1964), and *Malthus on Population* (1971).

EUGENE KAMENKA is Professorial Fellow and head of the History of Ideas Unit, Australian National University, Canberra, and Visiting Professor of Jurisprudence (1973, 1974), University of Sydney. His publications include *Marxism and Ethics* (paperback 1969), *The Ethical Foundations of Marxism* (1962, 2nd edn 1972), *The Philosophy of Ludwig Feuerbach* (1970), *Paradigm for Revolution? – The Paris Commune* (1971), and *Nationalism* (1973); and he is the editor of *World in Revolution?* (1970). He has in preparation studies of Marx as a political philosopher and of Freudianism and ethics.

ANTHONY QUINTON is a Fellow of New College, Oxford. His publications include *Utilitarian Ethics* (paperback 1973) and *The Nature of Things* (1973); and he is the editor of *Political Philosophy* (1967).

G. J. WARNOCK is Principal of Hertford College, Oxford. His publications include *Contemporary Moral Philosophy* (paperback 1967), *English Philosophy since 1900* (2nd edn 1969) and *The Object of Morality* (1971).

MARY WARNOCK is Talbot Research Fellow, Lady Margaret Hall, Oxford. Her publications include *Existentialist Ethics* (paperback 1967).